TAKEDOWN!

Grizzly focused all his attention on the doorway, getting himself together. Luke could feel the energy developing in Grizzly's massive frame. Six feet two inches of federal muscle was about to collide with the door of room 9B of the Harbor Light Hotel. Grizzly held up his left hand and spread his fingers.

Five.

Luke looked at the luminous dial of his watch. Walt and Rico were in position. If they weren't, Rico would have clicked twice on the shortwave radio.

Four.

Grizzly's face was bright red, the way it always got before a kick-in. His fingers were rock steady. He folded another one.

Three.

Luke took in a deep belly-breath through his nose and blew it out slowly through his open lips.

Two.

What if it isn't *him*?

Screw that. It's him.

One.

Grizzly gave Luke a final look. Then he tensed and exploded off the wall—the whole frame of the door burst inward. Before it hit the floor, Luke was racing in—a woman was screaming—and Luke heard his own voice, deep but hoarse, saying *"Federal officers—freeze—federal officers!"*

"Relentless and gripping . . . Stroud is back in his territory of true-life heroes and villains."
—*Kirkus Reviews*

"Gets into the soul of the U.S. Marshals Service."
—*Sun-Sentinel,* Fort Lauderdale

"The fact that it's
on
—*T*

DEADLY FORCE

IN THE STREETS WITH THE U.S. MARSHALS

CARSTEN STROUD

Bantam Books
New York • Toronto • London • Sydney • Auckland

This edition contains the complete text
of the original hardcover edition.
NOT ONE WORD HAS BEEN OMITTED.

Deadly Force
A Bantam Book

PUBLISHING HISTORY

Bantam hardcover edition published September 1996
Bantam paperback edition / October 1997

ISBN 0-553-57544-9

Published simultaneously in the United States and Canada

PRINTED IN THE UNITED STATES OF AMERICA
OPM   10 9 8 7 6 5 4 3 2 1

Dedicated to

Linda Mair
Beverly Lewis
Lauren Field
Barney Karpfinger
and
Irwyn Applebaum

AUTHOR'S NOTE

While the law-enforcement tactics and conflicts depicted here are real and most of *Deadly Force* is based on my first-hand observation, I have changed almost every name and altered nearly every location to protect people who trusted me with their truth and experiences. As well, and due to a request from the Justice Department in the wake of the Oklahoma City bombing, additional details that might identify federal officers or their families have been altered, and the takedown locations changed to the extent necessary to safeguard the security of federal operations and personnel. I regret this but sadly concede the necessity. I realize this may be troubling to many journalists and readers. It troubles me as well, yet I see no other way to accomplish my goal, which is to illustrate very disturbing trends in federal law enforcement, without damning the messengers.

This book is clearly not conventional journalism, but it is truth as I chose to tell it, in the voices I heard, in the only way I felt was right. If it has power, this was the gift of the men and women in law enforcement who trusted me. Its sins, and they are legion, are mine alone. And, as ever, I wish to express my respect, gratitude, and affection for my editor at Bantam, Beverly Lewis, without whose moral and professional guidance over the past twelve years, my work would be sadly diminished, and my life very different.

Carsten Stroud
Thunder Beach, 1996

Bought a second-hand Nova
from a Cuban Chinese,
dyed his hair in the bathroom of a Texaco.
With a pawn shop radio
at quarter past four
he left Waukegan at the slamming of the door
he left Waukegan at the slamming of the door

"Gun Street Girl," Tom Waits
Rain Dogs, 1985

DETROIT, MICHIGAN
September 1991

CASE FILE

SUTTER, Delbert Arthur FPS #S4357228K
Caucasian male. DOB: June 17, 1948
Hair: light brown. Eyes: green
Marks or Scars: Vertical scar left eyebrow and left
cheek to lipline.
Tattoo upper right biceps of a crucifix wrapped in
thorns.
Teardrop tattoo between thumb and index finger
of right hand.
Height: Six feet two inches
Weight: 195 pounds
Also known as: Lucas Shawn; Boyd Whitman

Notations/characteristics: Above-average IQ
Rated on Minnesota Multiphasic as dissociative sociopath.
Rated on DSM III Psychopathy Scale as functional psychopath.
Considerations: Presumed armed and dangerous

Wanted by:
Maryland Department of Corrections: Escape and felony
assault of corrections officers.
FBI National Task Force: Armed robbery; possession of stolen
goods; possession of restricted weapons; kidnapping, rape,
multiple felony assaults.
Will resist arrest. Negotiation outcome probability negative.

CONTACT: United States Marshals Communication Center
1-800-336-0102

By the middle of September he had changed his name three times and was in a new place every night. Today he was in room 338 of a Motel 6 off Interstate 94 in Paw Paw, Michigan, hip deep in a world of self-inflicted shit.

In Ypsilanti he bought a 1983 Toyota pickup from a crippled pawnbroker he knew from Joppatowne, paid for it with the cash he still had from that Denny's thing, plus he threw in the Joppatowne bull's Browning nine-mill. Yes, it was risky, but it was even riskier to run around, boost a new ride every forty-eight hours, because that sort of thing would ring a bell in every federal office in Michigan. Better to try to have a legit ride, even if it meant that this legless Joppatowne buddy could shop him if he wanted to; Delbert didn't think he'd want to, because he knew Delbert was hard-core and never forgot a fink. Can't run far in a wheelchair, can you?

He put Idaho plates on the Toyota, and he was using an Idaho state DL that the seller swore was clean until May at least, although the seller was dead, so what was

Delbert going to do if it was dirty? Dig the guy up and ask for his money back?

Insurance for the Toyota could be faked, and anyway there was no way he was going into the DMV, sit there for six hours staring into the video surveillance, waiting for some black bitch with a faceful of bad attitude to tell him, come back later, Mister Peckerwood. Anyway, God help the Michigan state trooper who stopped him and asked for his papers. Aside from the Thunderbolt hand-zapper in his back pocket and the can of Bear-Back pepper spray in the visor, Delbert always had a Taurus nine-mill tucked up under his crotch while he was driving. Let some harness bull stick his head in the window, Delbert would blow it off his shoulders, right there by the side of the interstate. Thinking about that made him grit his teeth, which was a big mistake.

A mistake because his head felt like a basketball filled with broken glass. Because his jaw hurt. And his teeth hurt. His bones hurt too, but he was getting used to that. Every morning he'd rinse his mouth out with hydrogen peroxide and spit blood into the sink. It would run down the porcelain sideways in a pink flood with ribbons of dark brown, and Delbert would think about the Pick 'N Pay, stand there watching the water run down the drain, and see that bitch-stupid chink clerk dive down, and then his wife, she pops up behind him like a NO SALE sign in a cash register, and she has that ugly little SIG-Sauer in her hand—a SIG, for chrissake; whatever happened to those cheesy little Llamas everybody packed back in the eighties?—and her broad Korean face pale as Sheetrock, her eyes narrow, no fear, full of ugly intentions, then POP POP POP. That wasn't the first time somebody had shot at Delbert Sutter, but it was sure as hell the first time somebody had *hit* him.

Actually getting *hit* was a new experience for him, and

for a while back there it had shaken him a little, made him wonder if maybe he was losing a step or two, should maybe get into something else. Also he thought about the kind of picture it must have made on the videocamera up on the wall behind the clerk's desk. He could imagine the feds sitting around, running it one frame at a time, drinking coffee and eating grilled cheese sandwiches in some puke-green and babyshit-yellow federal office, laughing like hell every time that goddamn chink broad comes in from the storeroom with that SIG in her hand, starts popping away at Delbert, Delbert standing there with his ass in neutral, yelping like a pup, head ducking, not even firing back, just hopping around there like a mope while a chink storekeep stitches him up right in his face. It was weird too, seeing the tiny black hole of the muzzle fill up with fire, and smelling the muzzle blast in his face. It smelled like burned cotton. Delbert had been on the other end of that sort of thing many times, and this was absolutely the first time he'd ever thought about what it was like for the shootee.

It was an embarrassing thing to think about, and Delbert tried not to think about it, but right now, staring at the mirror, it was hard to avoid the subject. Armed robbery was what he did, it was his main thing. Some kidnapping now and then, and whatever looked good at the time, car parts, extortion, running whores, but mainly his job skill was gunpoint robbery—pay or pop—and in all the years he'd been doing it, big complicated jobs like the Wal-Mart in Grand Island or the Key Bank in La Crosse, or little in-and-outs like all those rest area jobs on I-70, not once did he get shot. Not once. Knifed now and then, one time in the back of his left knee, on account of a belly full of applejack and a careless way with a prison punk, which was kind of trick for the punk, considering his position at the time, although Delbert made it the punk's last evening as an air breather. Gouged once in the left eye, but you had to expect stuff like that, kind of associates Delbert had to work with. But shot? Not once thank you. He had been proud of that.

Then the Pick 'N Pay thing, which should have been a gimme, make it up as you go, who knew? Now here he is in a Motel 6 in Paw Paw with a hole in his face and a mouthful of broken teeth. He turned his face right and left in the dead-blue light from the overhead fluorescent.

His left cheek was blown out like a pork belly, the eye swollen half-shut, red and yellow streaks in the white around his iris. The shank scar from Junior Beltrano in Deer Lodge looked like a gravel road. He tried his jaw again and felt the grinding where the stumps of his molars butted up against the bone spur. Moving it like that would have put him on his back in a heartbeat if it weren't for the Demerol. Demerol. Proof of the existence of God.

Now your mood management, that was a big part of the job. Delbert had read *The Compendium of Pharmaceutical Supplies* from cover to cover in the library at Deer Lodge. Also *The St. John's Ambulance Handbook*. Man in his line of work, you couldn't count on Blue Cross. Heal thyself. Have the right drug for the right situation. Valium or Quaaludes for waiting. Cocaine for a job, in and out all bright-eyed and blood-rushing. MDMA and chinabone horse for sex—him, not her—and when things go to shit, Demerol or Percocet with a chaser of Jim Beam. Vitamins too, lots of C's, and your multiples, keep those free radicals under control. A man don't have his health, he's got nothing.

He still had fifty caps of Demerol, along with some DMT and some ampicillin, and some bellergal for his ulcer. He had taken them from the pharmacy next to a drop-in clinic in Ypsilanti—just walked in and scooped them up while the nurses bumped into each other and

slammed off the walls trying to get the hell out of there—
and it was a good thing he had them, because they were
all that stood between him and some very serious pain.
Very serious. Very.

He spit out some blood one more time, wiped his face
carefully, and peeled off the bandage to look at the entrance wound. He figured the SIG was a .32 because if it
was anything with more weight, he'd be laid out on a tin
table in a room full of cadavers with the top of his skull
on a sidetray, his belly wide open from his chin to his
pecker, a bunch of federal marshals standing around grinning down at his dumb dead face, butting their smokes
out in his eye sockets.

Three rounds out and one good hit. Pretty nice shooting for a chink grocer. Bitch had her shit together okay.
The round had punched through the flesh just under his
left cheekbone, skidded around the upper jawbone, and
hammered itself into bits of lead on the big back molars
in his lower jaw. It hurt like hell even under the Demerol,
but it probably wouldn't kill him. The thing was to lay up
for a while, stop moving around so much, drop out of
sight, keep popping megadoses of vitamin C and ampicillin.

With the bandage on, he just looked like a guy who
had lost a fight. The broad here at the Motel 6 had blinked
at him, but he'd given her all of his lost-puppy bullshit,
come on real brave and quiet, called her ma'am around a
mouthful of cotton batten, and shuffled some cash across
the desk at her. She'd looked at his Idaho ID—he'd used
a laser copier to fake in his own photo and then laminated
it—then scribbled his name down: Brian Pinnock, 17780
Blue Lakes Road, Twin Falls, Idaho. She took a hundred
in advance and wished him a happy stay.

He put some more action on her, she smiled up at him
and he felt some movement in Monster for the first time

since the Pick 'N Pay. It came to him that maybe he should do her. She had a tight little body under the Motel 6 jacket, was maybe nineteen, but he could break her in good, get her up to his room, grease her up with some of his Demerol and Jim Beam, show her some real moves. It would take his mind off things.

What he was thinking must have been bubbling up somewhere in his swollen black and yellow face, because she suddenly looked down and away, and Delbert felt a thin streak of anger, like a red wire in his brain. Jesus, you stringy little scrag. You have no idea who you are looking at. This is Delbert Sutter in the fucking flesh; if you knew where I'd been and what I'd done with fifty-seven little veal calves just like you, you'd be on your knees in front of me right now, tugging at my zipper with shaky hands, big fat tears running down your scraggy little cheeks.

But the bitch never looked at him again, so he just grinned down at the top of her honey-blond head, picked up his duffel, and came up here to room 338 to figure out what to do about this world of shit he was in. He wiped his face and shut off the water, flushed the toilet, and turned off the light. He blew out a breath and smelled rot in it.

Delbert went back out into the room and lay down on the bed with the TV remote in his hand. He turned on the set and hunted around for some local news. Paw Paw was a good way out of Detroit, west of Kalamazoo, almost all the way across the thumb toward the Indiana state line, but there had been a lot of heat statewide over the Pick 'N Pay because of the video and the publicity.

They had made a big deal out of the clerk shooting the bad old robber, called her a hero, and they had put his face and name out all over the Northeast. It was a good bet that every trooper and county cop in Indiana, Ohio, and Michigan was driving around with a color shot of Delbert Sutter a.k.a. Boyd Whitman a.k.a. Lucas Shawn stuck in his clipboard. Not that Delbert looked much like his picture right now. He grinned at that, winced, and thought to himself, well hell, it's an ill wind, as his mother used to say. The bitch.

Anyway it wasn't the county mounties and state troopers who worried him. He had taken that kind of sucker on lots of times, and they couldn't shoot for shit, half of them were babyfaced high-schoolers who wet themselves as soon as the pieces came out. Ticket-punchers and chicken-coopers with no sand, and balls the size of Chiclets. No, what was worrying Delbert was the goddamn *federales*. The Marshals.

Delbert had busted out of Joppatowne by drinking six ounces of powdered coal dust mixed with urine, a very old inmate scam that turned your face gray and made your heart race. That always panicked the prison medics, who rotated out of Joppatowne monthly and never left notes on that kind of stunt. So the inmate was always sent up to Susquehanna Medical in a piece-of-shit biscuit-box Corrections van that had to be about a thousand years old.

As usual, the bored-brainless Joppatowne bulls had him in cord-cuff restraints and army handcuffs, the kind with the hinges, not the chain that you could break if you twisted it just right. But Delbert had swallowed a condom with a machine-made cuff key—prison built—inside it, and he figured he could use the sharpened edge of the key to saw through the cord-cuff restraint, which was ballistic nylon, hard as hell to break but easy to slice. More important, Delbert was ready. He had gone over every move lying there in the kitchen grease–hot air–stale sweat prison stink in the middle of the neverending prison night, worked out every possible angle, using creative visualization, getting himself a positive attitude.

On the thruway ramp he bent over and puked the key up by sticking his finger down his throat—had nothing else down there but six slices of white bread, so the hard part was being quiet. It was funny, he thought; every prisoner transport, they stripped you down, looked up your butt, and down your gut, but they never X-rayed you. Maybe now they would. Too late for these dumb bastards here.

Anyway, once he had the cuffs off, and the restraints, he used what was left of the cord-cuff belt to garrote the shotgun bull through the vent window while the other bull smacked the transport van into a bridge-support trying to get his piece out. By the time everything stopped bouncing around, Delbert clubbed the driver six times with his own Monadnock billy club and stayed around long enough to spend a few minutes with the shotgun bull, who was alive at the start and barely human at the end. That was risky, but you don't get a chance like that every day, and man does not live by bread alone.

The shotgun bull had gray serge pants without a stripe, and his blue shirt fit okay under a blue wool sweater that Delbert had worn, he'd said, "to keep the chills off," so all that Delbert had to do was step over the boulevard wall and get into the underbrush, change clothes, and start walking. That part was easy. And dodging the local nimrods and plain gray wrappers, you could do that in a trance. But there was another factor out there, the X factor as Delbert liked to think of it. You had your X factor in every job, and the X factor in the Joppatowne break was its being a federal holding cell.

A break from federal holding cells brought out not only the Maryland Fugitive Pursuit Unit but also the FBI and the U.S. Marshals Service. Every state had a takedown unit, but the training at state level varied insanely, and they hardly ever talked to each other. The staff was changing over all the time, and sometimes they even worked the takedown unit only part time, so it wasn't a professional thing with them. And they all hated the FBI, who anyway were too busy trying to get the CIA to share the glamorous stuff.

But the U.S. Marshals? Hard-core. Some of them, if they weren't cops, they'd have been great bandits. All they lived for was to bust bad guys. Paid like shit but funded like crazy. A bunch of suburban white guys who pumped iron for fun and spent their weekends at the rifle range or running takedown scenarios in between PTA meetings and tailgate parties. They talked to everybody, and they worked all over the country, and with them it was never a part-time thing. With the Marshals, the takedown thing, that was *all* they did, and they got real good at it and had no shortage of databases and manpower. What they were, when you came right down to it, they were bounty-hunters who had a reputation for no-knock-bang-bang-here's-the-warrant-oops-you're-already-dead take-downs, and that made Delbert nervous.

With that in mind, Delbert got up off the bed and walked over to the window. It was a slider, not sealed. Sealed windows were a bad idea. He had taken an outside room off the ground, but not so far off that he couldn't drop to his wheels if he had to. He pulled the drapes back and looked down at the roof of the Toyota about twelve feet below him. Then he looked around at the other cars.

It was late in the day, and the lot was filling up with family sedans and salesman specials. No Michigan Power vans, no vans with tinted windows, no road-graders doing anything but grading roads, everything normal, just a regular afternoon in Paw Paw, home of the working stiff and Mrs. Stiff in her bleached-out electrocuted do, and all the little Stiffs in their cheap-ass Wal-Mart togs. If the take-down guys were out there, they were very, very good.

Delbert stepped back from the windows, and suddenly the room got close and hot. Something with too many legs crawled up his spine. Furry things chewed at him from inside his gut. He swayed a bit, and the room went red. He knew this feeling. It was that old lockdown feeling.

He pulled on his black loafers and strapped his ankle holster onto his right ankle. He put his .38 Chief in the ankle holster. He pulled his blue sweater on over a white T, tugged on very new jeans, and put on a heavy sheepskin car coat that he had found lying in the back of a parked car in a Fred Myer car lot outside Battle Creek. He shoved his Taurus into the back of his jeans and tightened the belt to hold it in place. Delbert was losing weight, the SIG-Sauer diet; take a round in the mug and give up solid food for three months. It always worked. He popped two Demerols and a cap of ampicillin. It was time for a drive around, see if he could score here in Paw Paw, also see if he had grown a tail during the morning.

Paw Paw had a winery where they made whatever passed for wine in western Michigan, and farther on down the line there was the usual main street with a Key Bank and a First National and a Buick dealership, lots of red-brick houses under old shade trees bent crazy from the Michigan winters, up to their flanks in ragweed and bunch grass. He stopped across from the Buick dealership, in front of a rat's-ass little bar called Fred's. He backed in and sat there for a while, watching the block and the passing cars through the heavily tinted windows of the pickup. Nothing. Nobody gunning him sidelong from a parked van. Nobody *not* gunning him in that undercover-cop sort of way. Shoppers and their brats. Losers in their shit-box sedans, pussy-whipped hubbies staring straight ahead as the missus read him his rights at the top of her lungs. Brain-dead grunge-rockers cruising the drag in a rusted-out Camaro, staring out the windows with dead eyes and slack mouths, Pearl Jam sticker on the rear window. Pearl Jam? What kind of name was that? Those kids get into the lockup, they'd see more pearl jam than they could handle.

He looked back up the street at the Key Bank, had a moment of fond recollection, then over at the First National. Only two ways out of town, a river blocking him on the left, and the interstate to channel him into. Tricky. Some finesse required.

It could be done, though. That was why Delbert was so successful. He always had that positive attitude. The winner's edge. A man was nothing without self-esteem. Confidence. The key was liking yourself. Forgive yourself for your mistakes. Acknowledge your successes. Delbert did a lot of that. Plus the creative visualization.

Maybe the First National? Too exposed. The Buick dealership? What would they have? They'd have shit. What was he gonna do with car parts and petty cash? A jewelry store? They'd have cameras and zircon reindeer. Come on now, Delbert. Be open to the possibilities. Free that creative spirit. . . .

Maybe Fred's here. Yeah, Fred's. It was a wage-slave bar in a working-stiff town. Any Friday, they'd rake in a couple of grand from the townies. This was what? A Thursday. Lay over one more night, check out of the Motel 6, then come back on a side road, light this place up after midnight tomorrow. Collect two G's. Pass Go. Put Paw Paw in his rearview mirror. Let's us have a little look-see. Make some calculations.

He climbed out of the Toyota, and the wet wind kicked him right in the teeth. Winded, staggering, he climbed up the wooden stairs to Fred's and went inside, where he drank cheap Milwaukee draft for five and a half hours by the Muriel cigar clock on the wall over the door to the kitchen. Nobody but the barkeep spoke to him, and everybody knew each other. Delbert made a big impression, but no one told him that.

At midnight Delbert was back at the Motel 6 feeling little of anything. He parked the Toyota in the lot, which was nearly full now, crammed up with rusted-out foreign shit-boxes, Audis and Hondas mainly, too few Chevettes and Horizons. Damn foreign cars, and this is Michigan, for chrissake! He remembered a bumper sticker he'd read, somewhere in Wyoming or Montana: HUNGRY? OUT OF WORK? EAT YOUR IMPORT. That was the trouble with this country. The work ethic was dead. There was no patriotism. It was all ME ME ME. Yuppie larva. Buttwad nigra gangbangers. Immigrant trash. The country was going downhill fast.

Delbert came in through the lobby looking for Debbie or Kimmie or Tammy or whatever the hell her name was, maybe give her another chance at the Delbert Sutter Experience, but there was some nigger dozer-dyke he'd never seen before sitting behind the counter with her fat black face buried in a copy of *People* magazine with a picture of Jeffrey Dahmer on the cover. That made Delbert grin; old Jeffrey there, he was about as tough as rice pudding. Back at Deer Lodge, the D-Block Basket Boys would have made him the blue plate special every Friday night. With a side of flies.

He took the stairs to the third floor, and by the time he reached it, he was feeling his teeth again and was thinking about the Demerol, which was in his duffel bag. It was damn hot, and he peeled off his sheepskin coat. Fever, maybe? Get more C's into you, son. He walked along the hall toward room 338. Christ, this place is silent. No television sets playing in the rooms, no voices behind the doors. They made these places out of balsa wood and cardboard, held them together with duct tape, but here

we are, a full house in Paw Paw, and no noise any . . . shit.
Oh shit.

Delbert was now racing up the hall toward the back
stairs, had his Taurus out, thumbing down the safety, feet
booming on the cheap wooden floor, every footfall a red
thunderbolt of pure pain, his brain racing—the dozer-
dyke with the *People* magazine, the silence in the halls, all
the sideways looks at Fred's place, no Tammy or Debbie
or whatever the hell her—but *where?*—someone was
shouting—a hard voice, definitely federal—and Delbert
picked up speed, now there were footsteps close behind
him, heavy and coming fast, and Delbert turned to light
up this asshole, the Taurus a stainless-steel blur in the
lower arc of his vision, seeing the man in the hall, crouch-
ing now, a blue-white cloud of flame in front of him—a
series of huge *slams* wrapped in thunder.

The floor hit Delbert Sutter very hard in what was left
of his back—he saw the Taurus flying over his head like a
big silver bird—and he thought, well, Delbert, you putz,
you really shoulda—

They let the customers back into the Motel 6 by one
o'clock in the morning. The citizens were in a party mood.
Zenia had bought KFC chicken for everyone. A medevac
chopper from Battle Creek was airborne now, carrying
what was left of Delbert Sutter. Most of his chest was a
wind tunnel. You could hand somebody a Coke through
the hole, like they did once in South Bend. Triple tap.
Center of the visible mass, just the way they taught you
at the range. Watching Sutter's chest, Luke Zitto knew
there was no Kevlar, or he'd have put the rounds into his
skull instead.

The local fuzz was everywhere, huffing and puffing
about jurisdiction and probable cause. Screw them. It was

a righteous takedown. They'd been on Sutter since early in the morning, and he hadn't seen a thing. Horgan had wanted it done outside Fred's, but Horgan was a worrier and there was no containment. Besides, they had already cleared the motel and put Zenia behind the counter. Zenia with her face buried in *People* magazine. That made Luke smile, which took a lot these days.

Well, okay then. One less furball stuck to the skin of the planet. He looked down at his hands. The left one shook a little, but the right was rock steady. His heart was still blipping, but he was in a good place.

And Delbert Sutter was history.

Fine.

Bring on our next contestant.

BOOK ONE

THE YELLOW MAN

Tito La Gaviota expended the final sixteen minutes of his short and colorful life adrift in a hormonal reverie revolving around the girl who worked in the front office of La Luna Negra Delivery and Storage, where he was a driver at the grace of Don Florida, who was a true *hombre*, a benefactor for his people, an important man in business, *el jefe duro*, who lied to Immigration for him and let him sleep on a jute-filled mattress out in the warehouse on the weekends.

This girl was called Anastasia; she was from Quito, Ecuador, and was Don Florida's sister Angela's middle daughter. Anastasia was haughty and cold and would not talk to Tito, who was Guyanese and too dark for quality like Anastasia. Such pride, in the face of the fact that her uncle Don Florida had made his money with smuggling. And in other ways, even Anastasia would find difficult to accept. Perhaps she did not know. Still, she was prideful.

Also, by Tito's rather Catholic standards, Anastasia was

bold, a teaser, because even in these New York winters she wore short plaid kilts like those schoolgirls Tito would see walking down Fifth Avenue or Madison or Lexington, watch them from the van, those blond girls like yams and mangoes and the dark-haired ones, creamy and chocolate, their breasts pushing out the soft white blouses, juggling their schoolbooks, glimmery hair swinging like bells, heads together, laughing, French-talking in sparkly girl voices that he could feel in his hip pocket, with their short plaid skirts and socks that came up to their knees, and under that maybe little white panties—not that Tito was ever going to find out.

Now Anastasia leaned forward to do something with the ribbon on her typewriter, and the skirt rode up her legs, showing a length of smooth buttery skin where the kneesocks stopped and the skirt started, the light from the ceiling fixture pouring down on her, and past the soft nut-brown sheen of her long hair Tito could see the curve of her cheek, and the soft golden down on her skin shining, her lips half-open as she cursed softly into the machine.

Tito groaned a little and held his breath, blood pumping bright blue in his neck and in his crotch, feeling a sweet incurable pain, feeling a deep incurable longing, while on his thin brown wrist the bright red Swatch watch that Don Florida's wife had given him swept the minutes from the circle of his life, and under the watch Tito's pulse was pounding as he watched Anastasia's electric body. He sighed again, looked up past her, trying to calm himself.

Beyond the desk where she worked there was the counter, and a little space for the customers, and then the big glass window wall with LA LUNA NEGRA DELIVERY AND STORAGE painted on it. She had something on the radio, a samba, Tito Puente, drums and a lot of bright Spanish brass, speed and fire, and her body was moving to the music—*ai, qué bonita*—and Tito was burning for her, leaning against the open doorway that led back into the warehouse and the loading dock, where Don Florida was supposed to be coming with the van. What would Anastasia have on under that skirt, and what would it take for Anastasia to show him?

An act of God, Tito figured, rightly—with four minutes of his life gone and eleven remaining—help from Jesus Himself, that's what it would take for Tito to see what Anastasia had under that little green plaid skirt.

He sighed, accepted that in his Indio way, and looked past Anastasia, lighting himself an Old Port from a pack he kept in his shirt pocket, flared it up, and blew the smoke out into the still air of the little office.

Across the street the concrete pillars and the green iron girders that held up the Bruckner Expressway were a black shadow with the pale winter light all around them. Tito could see cars and trucks stalled in the Friday afternoon traffic on the elevated expressway, and more trucks were lined up along Bruckner under the El, waiting for the lights to change, trucks from Gristede's or Red Ball, Sloan's, D'Agostino, Safeway, waiting for a chance to get across the railway bridges and into the big Terminal Market in Hunts Point, everything all jammed up and steaming in a tangle of cabs and cars and trucks, people hurrying along the crumbling curbs and rocky sidewalks, bending over and walking little herky-jerky steps like people do in the winter, watching the ground and feeling the sandpaper wind scour their cheeks.

Tito looked back at Anastasia, and warmth flooded his belly. She was off her chair and down under the desk, searching for a power cord, whatever, and her little butt was sticking out from under the desk, that wonderful borderline of green plaid riding up the smooth coffee-color satin of her thighs.

Tito felt his heart begin to slam in his skinny young chest, and his eyes burned from looking at Anastasia, were still burning, when he heard a step, felt somebody very close behind him, and Tito started to turn, thinking to see Don Florida, feeling a big shame, already beginning his excuses, saw instead a big yellow-faced man with dead black eyes like stones pushed into the pocked, leathery skin of his round face, and the yellow man put a hand on Tito's chest, *lifted* him, effortlessly—the strength in him was frightening—threw him—Tito flying backward, yelling now—and Anastasia shrieking, startled, banging her head on the underside of the desk—big yellow man in a black leather trench coat and a face like a gravel road— total silence from him, just his stone face set, as he stepped into Tito and kicked him very hard in the belly, catching him under the solar plexus, lifting Tito's ass a foot off the ground, Tito folding around the boot like a shrimp on a stick as all his air—*hoof*—blew out through his lips.

Tito crumpled forward, silence taking him, his breath gone and his lungs on fire, his short skinny legs churning. Anastasia was by this time screaming, hiding under the desk, pushing herself back into the recess with the wires and the wastepaper basket, her little penny loafers scuffling on the hardwood.

The yellow man reached for her, caught her by the ankle, heaved her out from under the desk, and threw her—into the air. Tito, in his private airless world, saw her flying above him in a timeless drawn-out moment of perfect observation, her shiny brown-black hair flaring, her legs flailing, soft shell-pink panties showing—Tito's act of God had arrived—and Anastasia slammed into the filing cabinet, rocked it, and slid to the ground, wide black eyes staring up at the yellow man, at the eyes in his pitted round face, which were flat and empty.

Tito saw him too, and thought *Indio*, this man is from the south, a Miskito like him—Tito had less than four minutes to live at this point—and the yellow man reached into his jacket, still in silence, pulled out—what?

A hammer?

No, Tito saw it as the man raised it up to his face, turned it in the light from the fluorescent above him, the yellow man's face set and still but now a kind of light glittering in his eyes as he turned—it was a *hatchet*, a tomahawk with a wooden shaft and a polished head that glittered with the same light that was in his eyes.

He reached down, put his huge yellow hand into Anastasia's shiny brown hair, pulled her to her knees at his feet—her scream was thin and wild, pure pain and fear—and Tito remembered the sound that rabbits make when you pull them out of the pen and gut them, that very same baby cry. The yellow man slapped Anastasia across the face with his left hand. She reeled, and he tugged her upright again.

"Shut up," he said in English, in a flat unaccented voice, no anger in it, a soft voice. He was looking down at Tito.

"Tell her to shut up, or I'll kill her."

1705 Hours
Friday, January 13, 1995
Interagency Fugitive Operations
Federal Building
Court Street
Brooklyn

Grizzly Dalton was telling Luke Zitto a long involved story that had something to do with a retired city bull named Bigbee, they called him Big Bear, and Big Bear was waiting at a traffic light up in the Bronx, waiting for the light to change, sitting in his big old navy-blue Cadillac, so he decides to light up a cigarette, he looks down to see where his pack is, and his foot slips off the brake—

Luke was leaning against the window wall of the Brooklyn muster room, his tanned face hard-planed in the light by the window, his eyes deepset, gray-green, and hooded, his thick arms folded, already in his black raid gear, a lean Italian-looking guy in his late forties, running about six one, one-eighty, a quality of stillness around him, no wasted motions. Even a little cold-blooded, reptilian, some of the guys thought.

Luke was listening to Grizzly's voice, a low throaty sort of growling voice, breath smelling slightly of tobacco and coffee, and now and then looking out past Grizzly's head to the street, downtown Brooklyn, where a dying winter light the color of lemon-butter was sifting down on the spindly bare trees along Court, making spiderweb lines on the sidewalk. Grizzly's voice climbed an octave, apparently trying to mimic the voice of the guy who was driving the car in front of Big Bear's Caddie—What's *your* major malfunction, dickhead mothersomething, like that, in a high-pitched street-black voice—and Luke gathered that Big Bear had let his old Caddie slide forward and bump this fellow's car, so, this being New York City and not Vermont, the guy leans out the window and says a whole lot of nasty things to this cop, who just takes it, nods, he's keeping his temper, you know, the guy's an obvious nutcase, right, Luke?

Luke?

Luke nodded to let Grizzly know he was hearing him, hearing the story, but he was thinking about the room, it looked more like a college lecture hall than a squad room, it was . . . antiseptic.

Cold.

Spreading out from a large framed color portrait of President Clinton and a smaller framed shot of Janet Reno, the bare brick walls of the big room were papered in street maps, in computer printouts of crime stats, in FBI, DEA, and Marshals Service Most Wanted mug shots, a collage of photos pinned every which way to the bulletin board—no *Playboy* centerfolds, no off-the-fax filthy-sick cartoons from the holdup squad or the Probation offices—the gun lockers in gray metal at the back of the room, the computers at every desk. Big NO SMOKING sign on the wall, over a copy of the new federal regulations. Man, thought Luke, still hungry for a cigarette, these guys want to live forever. Think they're all gonna die in the best of health.

And look at them, at their desks, sitting on chairs or

leaning against the walls, crowding into the room, all in shirts and ties, expensive blue suits or gray suits, most of them young and hard looking with trick haircuts and no beards, every one with his service semiauto in a Bianchi rig or a hideaway, cuffs in the small of the back, Italian loafers and suspenders, nobody smoking or even thinking about smoking—except Luke, who was *always* thinking about a cigarette, but who right now was thinking these guys all looked like combat yuppies, like a squad of combat accountants getting ready to sprint down into the street and pull people over for double-entry anomalies and failure to reconcile.

It was very different in Luke's regular offices up in the Bronx. Luke and Grizzly, Rico Groza, Walt Rich, and the rest of his U.S. Marshals Service Fugitive squad worked out of a scruffy fifties-era lime-green office in the Bronx Borough Hall at Third Avenue and Tremont. The Marshals shared the space with parole and probation officers for the Bronx borough. Although Luke and the rest of the deputy marshals assigned to warrant work and Fugitive Apprehension were federal employees, they "rented" space from the borough because most of their informants were "clients" of the city's Probation and Parole division. It made sense to work close to the city guys most likely to be acquainted with someone who knew where your federal fugitive was hiding, and who could be persuaded, by various means, to share that insight with the Marshals Service.

The Bronx squad room was your typical New York City cop facility, a mixture of Depression-era squalor and high-tech computer gear; battered gray steel desks, brown office chairs with the stuffing coming out and squeaky rollers, banks and banks of rusting metal filing cabinets, a big holding cell with pale green steel bars and a bare concrete floor, rows of overhead fluorescents that made everyone look like extras from *Night of the Living Dead*. The walls were covered with posters from the Patrolmen's Benevolent Association, Gary Larson cartoons, *Playboy* centerfolds, bulletins from the Justice Department, even a blow-up of a *Spy* magazine cover showing Hillary Rodham Clinton in chains and leather and a studded metal push-up bra.

The atmosphere was smoky, reeked of bad coffee and dirty socks and stale air, and the southern view over the tenements and cluttered grids of the South Bronx toward Randalls Island was always yellowed by the stain of years of tobacco smoke and dust, making the borough look like a photo of New York City in the Dirty Thirties. It said a lot about Luke Zitto that he felt at home up in the Bronx and less so down in Brooklyn.

Looking at all these hard-chargers and yuppie-cops from Maryland and Washington reminded him of his age, his descending career path, and his developing sense of isolation. They also reminded him that as recently as last year, he'd been stationed in D.C. himself and had been entertaining the same delusions about promotions and pay raises and a ticket to play Beltway Bungy-Bingo with the brass at the U.S. Marshals Service HQ in Arlington. Well, all is vanity, as Miss Piggy would have said, and you can take that to the bank, my son.

Anyway, go deal with it, cops *had* changed, especially at the federal level. Luke could easily pick out the city bulls from the NYPD Fugitive Apprehension Team, the FAT squad. Three guys in their forties, solid and rumpled looking, with that NYPD distance they all had, as if they were the only pros in a room full of pretenders.

Hell, maybe they were right.

Grizzly Dalton's voice changed again as his story cranked up, and Luke looked back at Grizzly again.

Now Grizzly Dalton was *not* a combat accountant; fifty-one this May, six two, close to two-twenty, he was

providing major face-space to the World's Best Handlebar
Mustache, it rode his broad red face like steer horns on a
pickup truck, and his pale blue eyes were surrounded by a
fan of wrinkles, sliced over the left temple and forehead
by a long white puckered-looking knife scar that inter-
rupted his bushy eyebrow and made his left eyelid droop
slightly. He had one suit, a dark brown number with too-
wide lapels, and three ties, all of which looked highly infectious. Grizzly had a belly like a full spinnaker and hands
like fat pink dogs. Today he was in raid gear, a black
T-shirt with U.S. MARSHAL in big yellow letters on the back,
black jeans and combat boots, a leather belt with a silver
buckle, his gold Marshals star on the belt, and his semiauto in a rip-stop tie-down on his right thigh. He looked
like Wyatt Earp—the real one, not Kevin Costner—and
knew the name and history of every U.S. Marshal who had
ever ridden the Old West.

And Grizzly walked the Bronx just like one of those
boot-leather old-timers from Abilene or Deadwood City,
with a big cheroot and a low-slung side arm. Luke liked
him. Grizzly was in top gear now, inside his favorite story
for the week.

So now the guy is right in Big Bear's face, leaning in
the window, a card-carrying certified New York City wea-
sel-butt, but Big Bear is still holding his temper, he just
looks straight ahead, waits for the light to change, no eye
contact, ignoring the guy, dum-de-dum, just watching the
light, so the black guy, get *this!* He *spits* on the windshield, says something else, you know, where Big Bear
could stick it, pivots and scampers back to his little shit-
box Toyota with the flag of Jamaica on the back, a spray
of marijuana leaves over it, and as he gets in, he flips Big
Bear a finger. Can you see it?

Luke can see it.

1710 Hours
Friday, January 13, 1995
La Luna Negra Delivery and Storage
144th and Timpson Place
The South Bronx

Tito looked into the yellow man's eyes and saw nothing there at all. It was like looking down a well with no ending. The yellow man looked back at Tito and seemed to be a dead man breathing. You could believe he was a corpse until his lips moved.

"Tell her!"

"Anastasia, *nada más—por Dios—*"

"Speak English."

"Anastasia, be still." She froze into place, her breathing ragged and rasping, tears running. Tito looked at the yellow man.

"Okay, okay . . . what do you want?"

The yellow man looked around the office, out at the street. No one had noticed anything. They all had their heads down. It was the New York way. They were like antelopes, they never made eye contact with the killers in the long grass, and when the killer took one of them, they all ran with their heads down.

Tito was only seventeen, but he knew that it was down to the three of them, that there was nothing else in the world now but Tito and Anastasia and the yellow man with a little ax in his hand.

Tito felt something coming over him now, felt a calm coming from inside, maybe his Indio well of courage. Tito would save them, save Anastasia. He would *win* her. Tito was only seventeen, and it was all he knew. He set his face and drew a breath, working for a steady voice. The yellow man watched him like a stone idol.

"Don Florida. Where is he?"

Okay. He's the bull. Be a matador. Although the yellow man spoke English like an Anglo, he pronounced Florida the Spanish way—flor-*ee*-da. He was an *hombre*, a country-man. Maybe he would respect courage.

"I will tell you if you let go of her hair."

Anastasia's eyes widened, and Tito saw something in them, gratitude and fear mixed. There was a silence while the yellow man considered Tito on the ground. The heavy samba music from Anastasia's radio stopped, and a song began, "Perfidia," a languid tango of infidelity, betrayal, and lost love.

The yellow man's fingers loosened, and he let Anastasia's hair slip through. She cried out once and fell forward, tears filling her brown eyes, and she stopped her fall with her hands, ended up on her hands and knees with her brown hair like a bell around her face, looking into Tito's eyes, saying thank you with her look.

She was still looking at Tito when the yellow man stepped forward—Tito's fleeting moment of triumph fluttered away with the thrumming of wings; his heart was beating wildly as he saw the yellow man come forward in one smooth motion, no haste, no effort, the hatchet glittering in the blue-white glow of the fluorescent. Anastasia was still looking at Tito, at Tito's face, and he saw a terrible light in her eyes—she *knew*—then the silvery flicker of the hatchet coming down. She dropped where she knelt—boneless, splayed—and the hatchet popped loose, the yellow man stepping back again, waiting for Anastasia to stop moving. It took a little while, no more than a minute or perhaps two. In situations such as this, time becomes a very subjective calculation.

Tito had no voice, and the yellow man seemed content to wait for him to find it. The song came to an end. The yellow man smiled then.

" 'Perfidia.' "

Tito looked up at him.

"I have your attention. Yes?"

"*Sí*—yes."

"How many work here?"

"Three. No. Four."

"Names?"

"Me, Tito. Don Florida."

He looked down at her body, and his eyes jerked away again.

"Her."

"And—"

"Yes. I forgot him. The new man."

"Paolo?"

Tito's look of puzzlement struck the yellow man as convincing.

"No. His name is Roderigo Gardena. He's from Tegucigalpa."

"Describe him."

"Old. Thirty-five, maybe forty. Skinny. Black hair. He acts like a businessman. Dresses in suits and ties. He's an artist."

"Have you ever seen him dressing?"

"*Sí*. He changes in the back. He doesn't like to get his suits dirty. He tries to impress Anastasia—"

Tito's voice broke. His deep brown eyes began to shine wetly.

"He has a scar on his leg"—the man pointed to his thigh—"here?"

"He dresses in the back. I don't watch him. I don't know a scar."

"Where is Don Florida?"

Tito looked at the wall clock. It was fourteen minutes after five. Fourteen minutes ago, all he had wanted in the world was to look at Anastasia. Now all he wanted was not to look at her ever again.

"He's coming with a truck."

"Alone?"

"No. Roderigo is with him."

"When?"

"They should have been here at five."

"Yes," said the yellow man. "They should have," he said, coming forward now, that thing in his hand rising, his speed so surprising and complete that Tito had time only for a short rabbit cry, time to bring his arm up to try to deflect the blow.

The little silver hatchet caught his left wrist, sliced through the bone, shattered the cheap plastic watch, drove on through and into Tito's left temple as Tito turned his head away, turned his face away from here, and saw in the blinding white flash in his head a blue-white sun on a silvery blue-green ocean and felt a hot wind on his face as he fell forward into the deep.

He was dead a minute later.

At five sixteen. Precisely.

1716 Hours
Friday, January 13, 1995
Interagency Fugitive Operations
Federal Building
Court Street
Brooklyn

And now the light goes green.

What does Big Bear do?

Luke had heard this story before, from Rico Groza, but it was a good story, and he liked the way Grizzly could tell it.

So Big Bear thinks, man, what the hell, and he floors the Caddie, absolutely *buries* the pedal, the big rig squats and roars and bulls right up the tailpipe of that shit-brindle Toyota, plows through the intersection with it, sparks flying and the guy screaming. Big Bear rams them both into a mailbox on the far side of the street.

Nobody hurt, but *damn!*

"Damn," says Luke, seeing it.

So, long story short—hah, thought Luke; not from *you*—a year later, the fullness of time, yadda-yadda-yadda, Big Bear's in court, his lawyer has him all primed with some bullshit about mechanical malfunction, momentary loss of control, pressures of life, dreadfully sorry old chap, and so Big Bear is called to the stand. The black guy's there with his lawyer—a real Fordham switchblade, one of those bone-rack black chicks with fiery eyes, you know? A cobra with PMS, in a double-breasted suit jacket and a little miniskirt—and she's got Big Bear on the stand—

The glass doors of the squad room popped open, and Rothgar Fiertag, one of the hundreds of Justice Department liaisons for combined-force fugitive operations, blew in on a cloud of papers and energy, followed by a gaggle of suits from the DA's office and the attorney general's office in Albany. Grizzly was now into his final aria.

Okay, okay, Big Bear thinks, just hold your temper, but she really gets to him, and he can feel his control going. She asks him, "And after my client had exchanged a few words with you at the lights"—*Exchanged Words?*—"what did you . . . what were you thinking, as the lights changed?" She goes quiet, fixes Big Bear with her narrowed eyes, and the courtroom is all hushed, and Big Bear looks up at the judge, a bluff old trooper named Luther Tredwell, and he fixes the judge with a look, and Big Bear says, "What was I *thinking*, Your Honor? I was thinking, bye-bye baby!"

As he bellowed out his punch line and his big booming voice rumbled around the squad room, all the youngsters looked over at them. Rothgar Fiertag gave a weary seen-it-all headshake as he strode firmly and full of grim purpose up to the podium, where he turned, his lean gray face set and hard, silvery hair brushed straight back and curling slightly over the collar of his blue pinstripe suit, his hands splayed out on a sheaf of documents.

He lowered his eyes, glanced at the papers in front of him, and looked across the room at Luke and Grizzly—shook his head again—then looked back to the roomful of waiting men. He signaled the video tech at the back of the room.

"I want to welcome all of you to this final tactical briefing today. I know some of you from Arlington. Others I see here from as far away as Los Angeles—Bart, Dylan, good to see the DEA here—and of course Sergeant Rizzo and his men from the city Fugitive Apprehension Team, and our people from Albany and the district attorney coordinating teams, and all of you from various Marshals offices around the country. This is of course a very exciting day in law enforcement. This operation will contribute greatly to the security of our state—as you know, we in the Justice Department and our associates in the United States Marshals Service—ably assisted by local and state agencies"—a gracious aristocratic nod to the NYPD grunts leaning on the rear wall—"make over sixteen thousand felony arrests each year. Some of you here took part in Operation Sunrise in 1991—I see Luke Zitto is here— hello, Luke—you'll all remember Luke Zitto from his courageous actions in the confrontation with Delbert Sutter in Michigan—and Deputy Marshal Dalton—you'll have to tell me that joke after the meeting, Deputy—"

Grizzly smiled at Fiertag and said nothing. Luke had his head down, thinking about Delbert Sutter, also thinking, *Goddammit, Fiertag, this isn't a Shriners' potluck supper here.* Fiertag had done his level best to get Grizzly a permanent posting to Puerto Rico last year, after Grizzly had single-handedly busted a Bronx crackhouse and sent four dealers to Rikers in an ambulance. Fiertag liked corporate players. Grizzly was a nightmare for Fiertag. Grizzly knew it. Grizzly worked at it.

". . . and I know, I want to take this opportunity, with all of us here together today, to say how badly we all feel about the death of Bill Degan. Many of you got to know Bill when he ran the Sunrise Op—I can see people here from the Boston office who worked with Bill personally— and I share your grief at the death of this fine man."

There was a silence as the men in the room remembered how Degan had died, shot to death in Idaho in 1992, during the takedown of an ex–Special Forces soldier named Randy Weaver. Weaver, a survivalist and suspected white supremacist, had holed up on Ruby Ridge, far up in the Idaho panhandle, and refused to comply with ATF—Bureau of Alcohol, Tobacco, and Firearms—warrants to answer weapons charges relating to possession and sale of a sawed-off shotgun. It had gone badly, so badly that there were Senate hearings proposed for the summer of 1995, at which point Luke expected the FBI and the ATF to do their usual number—lie like wild dogs and point frantically to anybody but themselves.

Fiertag let the silence run for thirty seconds exactly, timing it on his Rolex. "Well, let's get on with this. You've all been briefed, you've all got your personal assignments. This evening Deputy Zitto's team and detectives from the NYPD will be running a takedown up in the Bronx, am I right about that, Luke?"

Was he right about that? Christ, they'd been all over it for a week. Luke pretended to think it over, as if just exactly *who* they were going to chase all over hell's half-acre up in the Bronx around midnight tonight was a matter of astrological calculations.

Luke's Fugitive Pursuit team had been assigned thirty targets from Target Acquisition in Arlington. Tonight, they had a fink ready to deliver the location of one Elijah Olney, a Blood-associated gunrunner and serial rapist who specialized in home invasions and drive-by assassinations. Fiertag knew that very well. Maybe he loved to stand up there and be seen by everyone. Or maybe he was just a really gifted world-class buttwad.

"I believe we are running an op on Elijah Olney this evening, sir."

Fiertag beamed at him, as if he had just answered a

difficult question on unsprung rhythms in German expressionist poetry.

"Ah, yes. Mr. Olney. Good luck on that one, boys. Now, today I just want to run down the latest information from Target Acquisition in Arlington and show you a couple of recent surveillance tapes. Let's start with the tapes. Pete, if you would. Gentlemen, this first tape is the Newark job. It was taken last Tuesday at 1400 hours. They came in through the main doors."

Grizzly whispered something to Luke. Luke laughed once, a short sharp barking noise.

"Perhaps you want us all to wait while your capacity for undivided attention becomes fully operational, Deputy Zitto?"

Jeez. What a complete asshole.

"No, sir. Sorry, sir."

"Fine then. Shut up. Watch."

The yellow man stepped over Tito's body, leaned down, and pulled Tito's shirttail out of his pants. He wiped Tito's blood off the tomahawk, his face empty, and smelled the copper smell of Tito's blood. He was careful not to step in the blood. Once in Miami he had been stupid enough to step in the blood, and he had left a couple of clear prints from his shoes on the street outside the bar. The shoes were Bruno Magli, just like the ones O. J. Simpson never wore. He had paid a great deal of money for them, would have been a year's pay for his father back in Guyana, and yet he had had to throw them into a cistern near the ship canal at Biscayne Bay. They were the first fine shoes he had ever owned, and it made him sorry to have to throw them away. Maybe one day he would have to think about using something other than his hatchet, but he was a superstitious man.

In the unofficial wars he had fought, the hatchet had been a good friend. A gift from the Marines, it had made everything possible, even the visa to come and live in the United States whenever he wanted. And afterward he had earned a good living with it. The others, they were all addicted to the bang-bang, loved to spray rounds everywhere, see the wood chips fly. They were children. Anyone could kill like that.

His judgment was cool, his methods his own, and therefore his life belonged to him alone. The middle management in Atlanta had approved of him, and even after all the deaths in the drug trade in the mid-eighties, he had stayed busy, had kept his arrangements in place. He never worked for two bosses, never sampled the product, never trusted a *narcotraficante* no matter what was promised to him, he never crossed over during a job, and he never forgot someone who tried to hurt him. Most of all, he never worked with anyone in any government, because once a government person had you, you were a *puta*, a slave.

Better to die.

The blade clean again, he walked over to the door and looked out at the traffic. No one had seen anything. That was one of the first things he had learned, that no one paid any attention. You could do almost anything as long as you did it without all that bang-bang. No one would ever notice.

He turned the lock on the front door and flipped the CLOSED sign over. Turning around, he made certain that no one looking in the front door could see either of the dead ones behind the counter. He walked back and looked down at the boy.

There had been a lot of blood in him. It was still running, but not as fast now. The brain had shut down the heart. Usually the body would empty itself in less than a minute. The fear did that. You had to step clear or do them from the back because the blood would come out in a big spray. Or an arc, depending on the cut. If they were awake, the adrenaline would make their hearts pump like little bird wings.

The boy looked like he might have been Indio himself. Don Florida was known for bringing in countrymen. They knew how to keep their mouths closed, especially since it was Don Florida who kept them safe from the INS agents who were always roaming around in places like Hunts Point and the Bronx factories. It was possible the boy had been trying to be brave, or to show off for the girl. If there had been more time, he would have spent some time with her just to teach the boy some manners.

He reached down and pulled the girl's head back by the hair. A stringy ribbon of blood looped down from her open mouth. Her eyes were half-lidded, as if she were drugged. He caught a scent of spice and wool.

Meat, he thought, letting go. He wiped his hand on her plaid skirt, feeling the strong muscle in her thigh. He pushed the skirt up higher, exposing her pink panties. Her bottom was brown and smooth, rounded. He considered the situation, feeling a slow heat develop in his belly.

No, not with business to do.

Maybe later, if there was time.

He stepped through the door that led into the warehouse area and closed it behind him. The warehouse was about forty feet long and was filled with jute-bound crates and wooden boxes stuffed with leather crafts. It smelled of spices and rot and overripe fruit. Cane furniture was piled up along a wall. The rear loading bay was open, its slatted steel gate rolled up into a ceiling rack. There was a smaller entrance door beside the main bay gate.

The warehouse was cold and very dark. He walked over and looked up at the mechanism that controlled the sliding garage door. Manual. Whoever wanted to get in would have to ring or knock from the outside. Most likely, getting no answer, he would come in through the door and open the main gate himself. He pressed the red button at the side of the frame, and the steel door clattered and banged down through the rails. Now the darkness inside the warehouse was complete. The air was cold and damp and reeked of foreign ports and salt water. The warehouse felt like a crypt now, or a church.

The yellow man took a position behind a large crate with GUYAQUIL stenciled on the side. He waited quietly, his heart slowing and his lips going slack.

His eyes reflected nothing.

He was still.

Five Frank was an NYPD blue and white 1991 Chevy Caprice. It was being driven at this time by Sergeant Brian Crewes, a sixteen-year veteran patrol cop with a chestful of citations and ribbon bars. Crewes's nickname was, probably inevitably, Crewcut. Crewes had earned the name by staying faithful to his Marine Corps haircut for years after his discharge. At five nine and one-eighty, Crewes was not a big man by NYPD standards, and he was considered quiet and perhaps a little shy by the other members of his squad. Crewes spoke with a soft, vaguely midwestern accent, had pale gray eyes, bristly graying hair, and a large brown mustache. He was a little vain. Certainly he took more care with his uniform and personal appearance than the average New York City cop, who tended to run slightly to seed as the years went by.

Sergeant Crewes enjoyed his life, the Pittsburgh Steelers, lifting very heavy weights and putting them back down after a while, and being a New York City patrol cop.

He did not enjoy anything connected with the O. J. Simpson trial, any kind of food you could get delivered to your house, playing board games with small children, or the wit and wisdom of loudmouthed homicidal gangbangers with bonehead nicknames.

As it happened, it was the fourth item on his got-no-time-for list that was concerning him at twenty-five minutes after five on this Friday evening. Sergeant Crewes was driving southeast along Hunts Point Avenue looking for a private spot to complete a conversation that had been imprudently initiated by a seventeen-year-old gun dealer whose street name was Doctor Dred. Doctor Dred was currently under arrest and handcuffed in the back of Five Frank and had been, until his recent ill-considered action in the back seat, on a routine run up to the Spofford juvenile facility in Hunts Point to await an arraignment.

The good Doctor had been busted by the 41st Precinct gang squad on a charge of Class A Felony Attempt Murder and related felony violations under Section 265 paras 8 and 9 of the Penal Law governing firearms. He did not seem to feel a sincere regret for the bungled drive-by shooting that had wounded a forty-eight-year-old health care worker on her way home from Claremont Village and had, ultimately, landed him in the back of Five Frank this afternoon.

A powerful, thick-necked, slope-shouldered young man who weighed around two hundred pounds, Doctor Dred suffered from a severe case of bravado overload, and he had been telling Sergeant Brian Crewes what was going to happen to any fucked-up cop who ever got in his way—talking to the back of Sergeant Crewes's head, actually, since Crewes wasn't really paying attention—when he had made the grievous tactical error of deliberately coughing up something truly noxious, which he then spit upon the back of Sergeant Crewes's head through the iron grid that separated the rear seat from the driver.

Crewes had been driving southeast along Hunts Point Avenue—was actually within a couple of blocks of the Spofford facility—when Doctor Dred's spit struck the back of his neck, a soft warm wet slap, queasily solid, and slithered down into his uniform collar. Doctor Dred howled with delight, doubled over laughing, your gang-banger humor not being very complex.

Crewes brought the patrol car to a stop, wiped the spit off the back of his neck with a tissue from the pack on the seat beside him, leaned forward, picked up the radio, and called in to Central.

"Five Frank, K?"

"Five Frank?"

"Central, I have a prisoner here complaining of chest pains. Request permission for a ten-97H."

A ten-97H was NYPD radio code for permission to transport a prisoner to a hospital.

"Chest pains, Five Frank?"

Doctor Dred had managed to contain his laughter by now and was paying fairly close attention.

"Ten-four, Central. Pretty severe."

Doctor Dred's gold-toothed smile was fading faster than a snowflake's kiss.

"Yo, Dred don't need no fucking hospital."

Crewes looked up at the Doctor's face in the rearview mirror, raised one eyebrow. "Ah, ten-six, Central. Could you say that again, sir?"

Doctor Dred repeated his statement at the top of his lungs and with a number of elaborations that were picked up by Crewes's handset and heard by Central, as well as taped by the automatic call-recording system at commu-nications HQ.

"You mean you don't need *any* fucking hospital? I

mean, setting the double negatives and that genealogical stuff aside?"

"Word, peckerhead."

"You heard the man, Central?"

"Ten-four, Five Frank. Wait one."

In the silence that followed, Doctor Dred found his enjoyment of the spitting event dissipating fairly quickly. In a moment or two his laughter had trailed off to a chuckle or two and finally subsided completely.

"Roger, Five Frank. We'll make that a ten-56, K?"

"Ten-four, Central."

1730 Hours
Friday, January 13, 1995
Interagency Fugitive Operations
Federal Building
Court Street
Brooklyn

Luke had heard, and tended to believe, a rumor that Fiertag had taken voice lessons from a drama coach in SoHo, and watching the man work the head of the room up there, it was easy to see him going up the Justice ladder off in D.C. Fiertag was All-the-Way Beltway, with helium up his ass and a smile like a moray eel's accountant.

Actually, Luke had no particular problem with Fiertag, but recent experiences in Washington had left him with a sore-tooth attitude whenever he had to deal with anyone from the Justice Department. The video screen flickered and flashed. While they waited for the tape lead to finish, Fiertag let his steely gaze cover the room, fixing on an agent here and an agent there, at random but deliberate intervals, radiating a grim and steadfast purpose, Ahab about to nail a gold doubloon to the mast. Luke wanted a cigarette and had to stop himself from going for the pack in his jacket pocket. He watched Rothgar Fiertag and remembered why he had always hated schoolteachers.

The huge video screen behind Fiertag flickered and blinked a few more times, and then a black and white image appeared, a security camera image, taken from someplace high, showing a large expanse of glass and two entrance doors. People were visible in the tape, foreshortened and dwarfish in the fish-eye overhead view. They were lined up along a cordon held up by posts. The floor of the space was marble, and in the middle of it was the logo of a major state bank. A time-code flickered in the lower left-hand corner, the time running off in tenths of seconds. The motion was herky-jerky, the way it was in these bank videos, giving the film an old-time feeling, like a silent movie from the twenties. The room was now completely quiet as the agents and the city cops watched the screen, everyone caught up in that strange half-sick, half-avid experience you have when you're about to see something violent. You know it all went down last week or last year, but in that staccato black and white video, it's always here and now.

Fiertag, the actor in him winning out, couldn't help doing a voice-over.

"Okay, here's our guy. Watch the upper left corner of the screen." Like they'd miss it if he didn't point it out to them.

Traffic was faintly visible through the glass doors, blurred slightly by the stop-motion videotape. Two men in long trench coats came in through the doors, both men wearing sunglasses and fifties-style fedoras. Even in the foreshortened view of the ceiling camera, they were easily identifiable, both white men, both large-framed and beefy, one with a full black beard, the other clean shaven, with long stringy hair tied back in a ponytail that fell over his collar. Ponytail had a square case in his left hand.

Blackbeard flipped open his long tan coat and pulled a sling-mounted shotgun up, covering the customers. You could see his mouth moving, the clerks and the customers reacting, people dropping to the floor, purses scattering. Ponytail ran straight to the counter, holding a large semi-auto pistol out, vaulted the counter, grabbed a young man in shirt-sleeves and pulled him out from behind a desk. A uniformed guard stepped into the picture area from the lower left-hand portion, and the man with the shotgun made a brief sideways motion—a puff of white flared out of the muzzle—and the guard seemed to be lifted backward on a puff of smoke. He hit on his back, crumpled up into a fetal position, black ink running from his chest area. Ponytail was holding his pistol up against the shirt-sleeved man and was yelling something at the tellers. They all stepped back from their drawers, leaving them open. Blackbeard held the doors and the front of the bank. Ponytail came up to the teller line, started emptying the cash into a briefcase. On the time-code, forty-seven seconds had elapsed. Fiertag's voice was hushed, rapt.

"The silent alarm rang at the Wackenhut substation thirteen seconds into the robbery. Watch Ponytail. He leaves the last hundred-dollar bill in each tray. He takes everything but that bill. So he knows about the trip mechanism. He didn't know about the beeper in the manager's pocket. At fifty-nine seconds Wackenhut had forwarded the alarm to the Newark PD."

Ponytail moved fast, raking the cash into his case. Blackbeard was standing facing the crowd, watching Ponytail. Blackbeard's mouth was moving.

"Blackbeard was calling out the time in five-second intervals. He had a Buffalo-area accent. Ponytail had a tattoo on his left forearm, a dagger through a skull. Here comes the citizen."

A man was now visible on the street outside, reaching for the glass doors. His head was down. He seemed to be looking at something in his hand. He was carrying a deposit bag and a sheaf of papers. Blackbeard stepped back away from the door, and the man came in, stopped, and started to turn back for the door. Blackbeard raised the butt of the shotgun, stepped forward, and struck the man in the face. The man dropped, spilling the deposit bag at Blackbeard's feet. Blackbeard scooped it up and put the shotgun back on the customers.

"Newark had Unit 97 Mobile about four blocks away by now, coming in silent. Strike Force had a robbery detail in a cover car on the way as well. The citizen's still in Newark Municipal. Blackbeard broke his zygomatic arch and took out four molars. He managed a fur shop a block up the street. He made his deposit every Tuesday. Newark reports he had seven thousand in cash in the bag."

Ponytail was now at the end of the teller line. He slammed the lid on the case and scrambled back over the countertop. A woman was lying on the floor in front of him. She flinched, and Ponytail kicked her in the head as he went by. She splayed out, blood drops spattering the marble floor.

"Sweet guy," said someone from the back of the room.

"Watch this," said Fiertag.

Ponytail was backing toward Blackbeard, still holding his piece out, covering the citizens. Blackbeard had the door open, still facing the room. Ponytail began to turn, and as he did, he shoved the semiauto down into his pants behind his belt buckle. Something seemed to explode out the right knee of his trousers. Ponytail's mouth opened, a silent shriek, and he fell forward onto his knees, a black stain marking the front of his crotch.

"Holy Christ!" said someone in the dark, a rueful whisper.

"That had to hurt," said Grizzly, laughing.

Blackbeard stepped forward and snatched up the brief-case in a smooth motion, pivoted, and ran through the doors. Ponytail clutched at Blackbeard's coattail, missed, and stumbled to his feet. The semiauto clattered to the marble floor and slid about ten feet. Ponytail made a move for it, stopped, looked directly up into the video-camera lens, his face a white oval, his eyes small and round and ringed by dark skin.

"That's Pigeye Quail," said Luke.

"Correct," said Fiertag. "Hell's Angels. Weapons. Felony murder. The semi went off as he shoved it down his pants. Crime scene guys said it was arterial too."

"Dumb fuck," said Grizzly. "How's the guard?"

"Collapsed lung, nicked his liver," said Mike Rizzo, from the NYPD Fugitive Apprehension Team. "But he'll be okay. The shotgun was a Franchi with a big choke. Bird shot, basically, so it spread out a lot. We think the beard was figuring to get a lot at once, but the guard was too far back. Took a few pellets in the belly."

Pigeye Quail lurched again, turned, and stumbled through the bank doors. His shoes left a black trail on the marble. Through the bank windows he could be seen running to the left. The citizens on the floor began to get up, and the manager ran forward into the picture, lifted up the bank guard's head. Cops came in through the front doors. The videotape stopped there. The room lights came back on. Fiertag summed it up.

"In and out in one minute and seventeen seconds. A stopwatch operation. They were pros. Believe it or not, they both got away. Witnesses saw Quail stop a woman in a dark brown import right out on the street. Quail forced her over to the passenger side, got in behind the wheel, and drove away. The first patrol unit got there thirty seconds later. Nobody's seen or heard anything of the Honda since. DMV is running us a list of every brown import, and Newark PD has already gone through a bunch. All the ERs have been warned. So far, nothing."

"What about the woman?"

"No sign. Nothing from Missing Persons either."

Luke put his feet up on a desk in front of him. The DEA man who owned it looked pained, but Luke ignored him.

"Accomplice?"

Fiertag pretended to think it over. He had no idea, but he liked to be asked.

"Possible, Luke. It's possible."

Grizzly made a noise.

Luke sincerely hoped it was not what it sounded like.

Don Florida was thinking about a number of problems as he rolled the delivery van up toward the loading dock of La Luna Negra's warehouse. There was the problem of Anastasia, for one. He could see that Tito was nowhere around. Tito was probably in the front office trying to talk to Anastasia. That was one of the problems on Don Florida's mind, this thing with Tito and his niece. Tito was a good worker, but he was in no way the kind of suitor his sister was going to accept for Anastasia. They had discussed the matter that morning on the phone. Don Florida had called her as soon as Anastasia arrived in that little skirt.

Tito, Don Florida had told his sister, is only human. Anastasia is teasing him, leading him on. Of course his sister saw it differently and wanted Don Florida to fire Tito, something he did not want to do, since removing Tito from the job meant getting Tito safely out of the country and back to Guyana, a place to which Tito would be quite unwilling to return. If Tito refused to go back to Guyana, then something permanent would have to happen to Tito since he was familiar with a number of Don Florida's import items, including the Brazilian nine-millimeter semiautomatics that were one of his most profitable items and for which many local businessmen had paid many thousands of dollars. The Bureau of Alcohol, Tobacco, and Firearms would be only too happy to provide Tito with alternative housing in exchange for his testimony.

The sodium-arc streetlamp was shining on his windshield, sending filaments of dusty yellow light all over the glass, following the cracks in its wind-blasted surface. He could see the steel door of the warehouse, see through the web of light the crates lying around outside on the concrete dock. The day was almost over, and there was a lot to get done.

And there was another issue, the issue of this Gardena. Roderigo Gardena was not a countryman, had been born here in the South Bronx actually. His manner around Anastasia was insolence incarnate. He would not have been anywhere near one of Don Florida's relatives if it were not for the fact that he was well connected. Don Florida had been informed that he was going to provide employment for a man named Roderigo Gardena. The people who controlled Hunts Point for the Hispanic organizations, in particular Manny Obregon, who was the *jefe* for the area bounded by the Cross Bronx Expressway, the Bruckner, and the Harlem River, had allowed Don Florida to operate under their protection in return for whatever services they might ask of him.

Normally, Don Florida would simply do what he was asked to do, but this Roderigo Gardena—his manner toward not only Anastasia but Olga, Don Florida's wife— was intolerable. Don Florida had made some private inquiries and had discovered that Gardena was an alias, and that whatever his real name was—his source either did not know or was afraid to say—he was apparently wanted by several federal agencies for things he had done in Washington, D.C., and also for something he had done to a prison guard in New York State. Something sexual. Sheltering a man like that could only bring ruin upon Don Florida's business and his family.

Something would have to be done about him.

Exactly what, Don Florida did not know. It was a problem.

Today Roderigo was bringing the five-ton truck. It would take another hour, at least, to load the five-ton with the cane furniture. Then Roderigo and Tito would have to drive it all the way to the TraveLodge in South Ozone Park and get it there before the hotel manager had to open up the lounge for the tourists who were coming in from Kennedy. The traffic right now was hopeless, but it would clear up by seven. He looked down at his watch as he rolled the van up to the ramp at the rear of the warehouse. It was a quarter to six. He smoothed his shirt-sleeve down over the gold Rolex watch and looked at his reflection in the rearview mirror. He ran a chubby brown hand through his thinning gray hair, saw the lines on his face, the dark shadows under his eyes. Once Don Florida had been a good-looking man—the best-looking man in Ciudad Bolívar, everyone used to say. Not now.

Parking the van, he climbed out with some difficulty, stiff and tired from fighting the traffic all the way from Canarsie. He was working too hard, he thought. His heart was giving him trouble. If he went on like this, he'd die before his fiftieth birthday. He climbed up the short stair-case and hit the buzzer twice with the fat edge of his fist.

A full minute passed. He looked around at the narrow laneway, at the closed-up rear gates of the fruit store

across the lane, at the garbage piled up and spilling over
from the Dumpster. The strange fleeting warmth of the
day was gone, and now he was suddenly cold. The sweat
on his cheeks burned him like snowflakes.

"¡Tito, abre la puerta! ¿Tito? ¿Donde estas?"

Where was the boy? If he was in there romancing with
Anastasia, if he had done anything to offend—Tito would
have to go, he would have to return to Guyana or disappear, and that was that.

Another brief wait.

Angry now, Don Florida fumbled for his keys and
thrust them into the lock that opened the little rear door.
He jerked it open, let it slam against the frame, and strode
quickly through the warehouse toward the closed office
door. By now, he was cursing softly to himself. A man
stood up in his way, a thin beam of light cutting across
the man's cheek.

"Tito!"

But it was not Tito.

The man moved into the beam completely now. He
was a big man, a yellow man. He had a bad face, and
something in it frightened Don Florida.

"¿Cual es su nombre? Que—"

The yellow man came much too close. His eyes were
dead black.

"Where is Gardena?" he said.

"Who are you?"

"You know me."

Don Florida's voice had gone away. His question came
out somewhere between a whisper and a bleat.

"Where's Anastasia? Where's Tito? Who sent you?
Did Manny send you? I can talk to Manny. If there's some
way I offended—let me call him. Please? ¿Por la virgen?"

"Roderigo Gardena. He works with you?"

"Sí. Let me—"

"Where is he?"

"But *why?*"

Don Florida's practiced Spanish baritone had developed something of a squeak. The yellow man reached out a huge hand and gathered in a section of Don Florida's sweater.

"You have a bad time paying attention, Don Florida. I will have to help you with your attention problem."

The yellow man with the bad skin pulled Don Florida down the narrow aisle between the shipping crates and the stacked cane furniture that was supposed to be on its way to the TraveLodge in South Ozone Park this evening, the timely delivery of which now seemed a matter of rapidly diminishing importance to Don Florida.

When the door to the office was kicked open and the yellow man shoved Don Florida through it, stumbling, falling, his breath coming in short painful gasps, into the office room, and Don Florida saw what had become of Tito and Anastasia, all other considerations flew up into the darkening Bronx skyline. One of these vanishing considerations was the normally routine necessity of disarming the silent burglar alarm whenever he came in through the little door beside the loading gate. The electronic pad, usually visible, was concealed this afternoon behind a large wicker bedstead, part of the shipment bound for Ozone Park. As Don Florida looked down at the terrible ruin that had been Anastasia, his sister's middle daughter, as the yellow man stood above him with his deadman stare and that little hatchet in his hand, as the first question was put to Don Florida, the tiny LED on the alarm pad out in the warehouse cycled silently from blinking green, to steady amber, and finally to a bright ruby red.

Sergeant Crewes was silent as he drove the cruiser slowly past the entrance to the Spofford facility and turned left onto Barretto. The Doctor, also very quiet now, had recently discovered in himself a gift for rueful contemplation, and he watched the Spofford gates receding into the middle distance with regret and a dawning appreciation for the consequences that sometimes come upon a man for acting without thinking.

Crewes drove south on Barretto wrapped in a silence composed of pure basalt, the unit drifting over the cracked and rotting pavement, through the grid blocks of low warehouse buildings, vacant and chained lots, ruined and deserted burn-outs, fields of dead grass and junkyard debris, past fifty-gallon oil drums burning and smoldering, oily black plumes rising into the deepening winter dark and spreading out on the wind from the river as if the black Bronx night were made out of their fires, past clusters of black men and Hispanic men and white men and

Asian men standing around coffee trucks and open warehouse doors, black silhouettes against the green glow of the factory lights, past more small shops and factories and past workmen standing here and there on loading docks and by the open doors of metal shops and packing houses, smoking cigarettes, sipping beer out of brown paper bags, men who watched Five Frank slide by with blank faces and careful eyes, saw the pale crewcut cop at the wheel, and the prisoner in the back, staring at them with worried eyes.

Finally, the developing situation and the implications for his immediate future forced Doctor Dred to set aside his pretense of stoicism and break the awkward silence. Marshaling his hitherto untapped reservoirs of persuasive charm and colloquial ingenuity, he composed a careful question:

"So, where the *fuck* we going?"

No answer from the cop.

"Yo, fuckhead! You can't do this, you know. You listening? Fool?"

"Watch me."

Sheeit. Doctor Dred shook his head, rolled his eyes upward as if he were calling on whatever gods ruled the Bronx to intervene.

"This ain't *right*, man!"

Crewes slowed as they bounced over a pothole, then picked up speed again. The radio popped and crackled with casual cross-talk from cars in the next sector.

"Yo, peckerhead, what's a ten-56?"

Silence.

"I'm asking, okay? Come on, man?"

"Advise if ambulance needed," said Crewes, finally.

Barretto dead-ended on Ryawa, at the Hunts Point Sewage Treatment Works, a low-walled facility that ran for almost five blocks eastward along Ryawa. At close to six o'clock on a Friday, Ryawa was empty, most of the business of Hunts Point being concentrated in the fruit and produce centers of the Terminal Market, several blocks away across Hunts Point Avenue.

The sewage treatment plant rode a flat delta of broken concrete and scrub plain out into the East River. About a mile away across the river the low angular buildings of Rikers Island seemed to float in a permanent haze. The river was a broad expanse of hammered tin, pale and shimmering in the glimmer of lights from Queens and Rikers Island, and the sound of the city was a muted roar from across the river. Planes with bellies tinted pale orange by the runway lights floated down into La Guardia, the sound of their jets rising and falling in the damp, chilling air.

Crewes stopped the blue and white Caprice at the entrance to an inset in the brick wall of the sewage plant, an indented space about ten feet wide and fifteen feet deep, which provided access to some water mains. The cruiser made the space a closed square.

Crewes took the keys out. He slid his gun out of the holster and placed it inside the gun locker under the dashboard, slammed the door upward, and thumbed the alarm. Then he got out of the car and walked around to the right rear door.

"What the fuck *you* gonna do, asshole?" said the Doctor.

Crewes pulled the rear door open, reached in, and dragged Doctor Dred out of the rear seat by the right ear, pulled him right out of the back seat and onto the sidewalk.

The Doctor hit hard on his shoulder and squealed with rage and fright. He kicked out at the cop's left knee and missed, huffing with the effort, using his shoulder to pivot on. Crewes stepped in fast and kicked him hard in the belly, flipped him over onto his face. He put his right boot down hard on the back of the Doctor's neck, reached down, and unlocked the boy's handcuffs.

Then he stepped back a few feet while Doctor Dred lay there on his face, thinking over the latest developments.

Still not moving, still facedown in the broken sidewalk, Doctor Dred addressed the ground.

"What's *this* bullshit, asshole?"

"Get up," said Crewes.

"Get *up*?" said the Doctor, his tone a tad less antagonistic. He craned his neck around so he could look up at Sergeant Crewes. The cop was looking back down at him with a flat expressionless face, his hands down at his sides. The Doctor looked at both of his hands carefully. Then he looked at the cop's holster and saw that it was empty.

"What's this?"

"Your lucky day, Mr. Garr."

Garr was the Doctor's actual name. Clayton Garr.

"My lucky day! Fuck *you*. I get up, you air out my ass, lay off a drop tool, say, Yo man, it be self-defense."

Crewes held his hands up to show they were empty. "No. You get up. If you can get past me, you walk."

"Oh yeah? How you gonna manage that?"

"What, you want me to read you the Patrol Guide?"

"You shittin' me."

"No shit. Now either get up and get it done, or shut the fuck up and stop whining, say you're sorry, and get back into the car."

A second passed, then the Doctor got up, quickly, a fluid motion, coming up on his toes, a fast look around at the three eight-foot-high walls that surrounded him, then back at the open daylight on the far side of Sergeant Crewes and the patrol car.

A light came into his black eyes, and a ridge of muscle between his eyes bunched up. He came straight in at the cop, his hands and arms loose, not taking an angle, not signaling a tactic or a style until he was inside his range, and then he snaked out a loopy left, felt the cop block it with his own right forearm, the cop's feet spaced slightly, his body relaxed but taking the blow the way the Doctor wanted him to, leaving his belly exposed for the Doctor's sideways knee-strike, the doctor's weight on his forward left leg, raising the knee hard and fast, aiming for the cop's rib cage—which simply wasn't there when it should have been—say!—and then the Doctor's eyes burst into a fiery red pain, he felt his head snapping back so hard, he could hear the meat and sinews in his neck creaking and grinding—his vision was gone, his nose was a blossom of blue-white pain, and he felt hot wet blood all over his teeth, tasted it—and then his crotch was lifted *up*, he felt the lightness in his toes, the weight coming off his feet as the cop's boot lifted him upward—his crotch became a corona of pains so infinite and varied he was amazed that his nerves could register every one of them. The ground hit his back very hard, and his breath hoofed out of him, and the cop stepped in again as the Doctor folded up onto his side, vomiting, blood spilling out of his nose—and Sergeant Crewes kicked him very hard right in the upper belly, kicked him so hard, the boy rolled away and fetched up against the rear wall by the standpipe valve.

He lay there for a while, struggling for breath, hoping for unconsciousness, experiencing new horizons of pain in a wide range of nerve-bundles and sensory locations.

Crewes was puffing a bit as he leaned down and pulled the boy by the left ear, lifting his skull off the concrete. The Doctor blinked, spit blood, groaned once. Crewes leaned in very close and spoke directly into the boy's ear. "Can you hear me, Mr. Garr?"

A cough, then another. Finally, "Yes."

"You're in pain, Mr. Garr?"

"Fuck—yes. Yes."

"Where?"

"Sheeit . . . everywhere."

"Everywhere, Mr. Garr?"

"Yes."

"Your balls?"

"Yes—Jesus."

"Your nose there? That looks like it smarts a bit."

"Yes."

"You wanna go to the hospital, Mr. Garr? Make a full statement? Get this whole thing on the record, how a little white cop beat the ever-loving shit right outta you, no guns, no help, just flat-out pulled your panties down and paddled your wiseguy butt?"

"No . . . no, I don't."

"You wanna call your homies, get them to help your sorry ass?"

"No."

"You wanna make a complaint, Mr. Garr? You wanna bring in the ACLU?"

"No."

"No what?"

"No. I don't."

"No you don't *what*?"

"No . . . I don't . . . sir."

"And your chest, Mr. Garr? How's your chest?"

"It hurts. It hurts *bad*!"

"See?" said Sergeant Crewes, still leaning in close, smelling the boy's blood and his juices.

"See what?"

"Chest pains. I *told* you you had chest pains. You shoulda believed me, Mr. Garr."

Doctor Dred looked up at the cop's bland pale face, struggling to focus on it. "How—why you think I had chest pains—why?"

"Excess saliva."

"What?"

"Back there, when you accidentally spit on me, that's excess saliva. It sometimes indicates the early stages of angina. It was accidental, wasn't it?"

A whisper.

"What, Mr. Garr?"

"Yes," said Doctor Dred. "It was an accident."

"And you're sorry, right?"

Nothing. A groan, then some coughed-up blood.

"I didn't catch that."

"Yes. I'm sorry."

"There you go," said Sergeant Crewes, patting the Doctor's head a little too hard. "I just knew it had to be an accident."

He put the cuffs back on the boy and walked back to the patrol car. He unlocked the car, released the gun safe, and reholstered his revolver. He checked his reflection in the mirror, then picked up the radio handset.

"Five Frank, K?"

"Five Frank? You been outta the car?"

"Call of nature, Central."

"Instructional interlude, Five Frank?"

"Ten-four. I'll clear Spofford in five, K?"

"Negative, Five Frank. Secure your prisoner and answer a ten-eleven, ten-31 at unit two niner seven, Timpson Place at 144th Street. That's a ten-31, Five Frank."

Shit. Ten-eleven was a silent alarm. Ten-31 was a burglary in progress. Crewes looked down at Doctor Dred. Christ, he'd have to cord-cuff him. The mope was gonna leak all over his back seat too. God-*damn*, shows you the price of self-indulgence.

"Units to cover, Central?"

"We're looking. Four Frank is on an aided case."

"Ten-four, Central."

"Five Frank?"

"K?"

"We mark this a ten-56 now?"

"Negative, Central. Mark it ten-97R."

"Refused treatment?"

"Ten-four, Central."

"Okay, Five Frank. 144th and Timpson, K?"

"Rolling now, Central."

Crewes got out and dragged Mr. Garr back to the open door of the squad car, cuffed him again, then cord-cuffed him using a nylon restraint kit from the glove box, securing his cuffed hands behind his back and then running the long section of the cord-cuff around Garr's ankles and back up to the handcuff links. Then he tensed, grunted, lifted him bodily, and more or less launched him onto the greasy vinyl of the back seat. Doctor Dred moaned and cursed but seemed to have other issues to deal with and offered no pertinent comments at this time.

Crewes slammed the door and ran around to the driver's side. Two seconds later he was accelerating eastward along Ryawa toward Halleck. He was about three minutes away from La Luna Negra.

It was exactly 1800 hours, six o'clock in the evening of Friday, the thirteenth day of January, in the year 1995.

Across the East River the lights of Queens and La Guardia showed dimly through a chilly gathering mist that floated above the water. Beyond Queens, beyond the Throgs Neck Bridge, a dull brown night was turning black, and Long Island Sound was disappearing into a huge murmuring undefined darkness, an absolute emptiness, as if the edge of the world were only a mile offshore and grinding in closer by the minute. Now and then the muffled clanging of the marker buoys sounded faintly from out of the fog bank.

On Rikers Island the first meals were being slapped

down on plastic dishes under red-glowing heat lamps, in the brutal white light of the huge dining hall. The noise was bright, staccato, harsh, the clangor of dented stainless trays, the brass notes of voices, and the tympana of curses, the forced laughter, chairs grating on the floor, tables pushed, flatware clattering. At the Terminal Market the dock loaders worked in heavy coats, shifting crates and pallets of produce, fish, bags of rice, swinging racks of frozen beef bound for Sloan's and Gristede's and the Red Ball and a thousand little food markets in Manhattan, Queens, the Bronx, Brooklyn, and Staten Island.

The FDR Drive was an unbroken scarlet ribbon of taillights snaking north to the bridges. In midtown the bars were filling up with people, glasses glimmered in down lights, and the talk went around; greetings, jokes, affection, lies. Grand Central echoed and boomed with crowd noise and the shuffle-and-stamp of passengers. In neighborhoods like Chelsea, Turtle Bay, the Upper West Side, people shopped for dinner and wine and hurried along toward their apartments with their arms full of brown paper parcels, heads down, wrapped up, cheeks bright, breath pluming. Limousines jammed up on the Queensboro ramps, trying for La Guardia or Kennedy. Sirens howled and car horns beeped and cabbies threatened walkers with eight circles of damnation.

Beyond Battery Park, far across the bay, the dockyards along the Staten Island shoreline burned with a dirty yellow sheen, and the rosary-bead lights of the Verrazano-Narrows Bridge shimmered and wavered in the sea mist. On the far side of the narrows the ocean boomed and rolled and sighed its way out into a black infinity filled with gull cries, the curling hiss and the liquid slap of waves, the thrumming murmurs of the deep. At La Luna Negra Delivery and Storage, questions were being asked.

1800 Hours
Friday, January 13, 1995
Interagency Fugitive Operations
Federal Building
Court Street
Brooklyn

Fiertag's next surveillance video was in color, a tele-photo camera image, extremely grainy, taken from at least a hundred yards but through a superb lens. They were looking at a broad delta of low grassy islands surrounded by choppy brown water. Luke immediately recognized the low outbuildings and the runways of Floyd Bennett Field on the distant horizon, saw a chopper rising into a dishwater sky, illuminated briefly by a weak shaft of sunlight piercing the shredding gray cloud cover. This had to be Jamaica Bay, somewhere on the Big Fishkill Channel, probably, from the camera angle. When he came back from D.C. last June, Luke had spent a lot of days on the Fishkill, trolling for rubber boots, dead rats, and tin cans, pondering the caprices of federal law enforcement as they played out inside that enchanted kingdom known as the Beltway.

In the middle distance of the video image, a medium-sized Sea Ray Express cruiser was swaying gently on the tidal swells, at anchor, trailing a couple of downriggers into the marshy waters. The camera image bobbled, blurred, and darkened as the operator struggled to adjust to the changing light levels. There was a mike open because they could hear the cameraman swearing softly, and someone else off-camera making a vulgar suggestion, and then laughter.

The camera must have been image-stabilized because there was very little shake, considering the distance. The lens went black, switched to another power, zoomed wildly, then settled and refocused, and now two men were visible in the video. They seemed very close, no more than ten feet away, as if the camera were floating in the air a few yards off the stern. The image rose and fell as the boat lifted and settled into the low rolling wavelets. The men were sitting in a pair of director's chairs on the open rear deck.

One man was dark-skinned, tanned, with a carefully manicured black mustache, wearing a bright teal-blue nylon sailing jacket, bulky with insulation. A canvas sailing hat covered the top of his face, but as he spoke, he lifted his head from time to time, and you could get glimpses of his features. The other man was sitting with his back to the camera, leaning forward as if listening carefully to what the first man was saying. This man looked huge, seemed to have shoulder-length black hair, and was wearing a shiny black leather trench coat.

The boat was fair-sized, perhaps thirty-six feet, with a big Fiberglas arch carrying a radar dome and an array of antennae. There was a rumbling sound under the low mutter of background conversation, and Luke realized the sound was wind blowing over the big bowl sound-collector of a parabolic mike; it was a sound he'd spent a lot of time listening to whenever he worked surveillance. The sound rose, fell, and someone managed to get the settings right, because you could suddenly hear a static-filled and fuzzy voice, clear enough to understand.

For once, Fiertag managed to resist a tedious voice-over pointing out the blindingly obvious. The dark man with the black mustache, the one who was talking, was known to practically everyone in the room. Even in the rolling and grainy image, the agents could make out his face well enough to identify Joachim Rodolfo Mojica.

Mojica's quasi-public persona was that of a community figure and benefactor to the Hispanic communities of the Greater New York area, a man who had made a respectable fortune in real estate speculation in Puerto Rico during the boom years of the eighties, consolidated that in the early nineties with some clever interpretations of the free trade legislation regarding the term *Made in the USA*, and whose generosity, lately, extended to any Hispanic charity or community organization with a solid business plan and a firm grip on a swing vote. Mojica was also a shining example of the distance a man could cover with a little luck, a talent for polite threats, and liberal applications of bribery, blackmail, and extortion. He was suspected to have a few of the local politicians in his vest pocket, but that part of his life was, these days, of concern only to the U.S. Attorney for the Southern District, some IRS and RICO investigators, and the detectives assigned to the DOI.

The Department of Investigations was a combined-agency unit staffed by Gold Shield detectives on loan from the NYPD. Working out of an office in Lower Manhattan, the DOI specialized in corruption and bribery investigations of city officials, the Donald Manes parking violations scandal being one of their more famous operations. Luke assumed that this video, which looked recent, was being taken by NYPD technicians assigned to the DOI. The conversation was intriguingly cryptic.

MOJICA:

—which you gotta figure out for yourself, okay, because I—

LEATHERCOAT:

I know that.

MOJICA:

I know you know that. I don't mean a disrespect. But there are business considerations, and these issues have to be clear, like, they aren't gonna go away unless—

LEATHERCOAT:

I don't like this boat for this kind of thing—

MOJICA:

What if—

LEATHERCOAT:

We should do this—

MOJICA:

Don't be difficult. I know what I'm doing: I think your best, what you should be doing right now, is to listen, because no matter where we do this, there's always gonna be a risk, so all I want is for you, I mean, we don't know each other personally—look, have a drink, okay, and relax a bit. You're too—

LEATHERCOAT:

I understand how to do this kind of thing. I thank you, but I don't need to have a drink. I wanted to see you personally because I want it to be understood that if I start this thing, then I don't stop it until I hear from you. Not from someone who says he works for you. I hear from you.

MOJICA:

I'm not used to—

LEATHERCOAT:

I mean no disrespect. It's just business. It's the way to do things right. Everything is understood, so there are no—

MOJICA:

Misunderstandings. Yeah, well, that's why I agreed to this, because I don't like to be surprised either, and some-

times—you have given some people a surprise—and that's
not what I want to happen here. I got a lot of people de-
pending on me, and I have a lot of people who want to do
my business some damage. I got one guy in particular who
we both know, and this guy is a problem for me because of
where he's from—we wonder why he's still in business
after some of the things—
LEATHERCOAT:
I wonder about that too.
MOJICA:
Yeah, well, we all do. It's not the usual thing.
LEATHERCOAT:
No, it's not. That's why, you know, I'm here because this
thing, it's got to be—
MOJICA:
Personal?
LEATHERCOAT:
Between us, between the two of us, you understand?
MOJICA:
A man could take that like it was not a friendly thing, like it
was a promise, you know, and no insult but—I know you
are a respected man, but so am I, and I feel you need to
keep that in mind, you know, when you say things like it's
personal.
LEATHERCOAT:
But it is personal.

There was a long silence here while both men looked
away across the stern of the boat. Over the low rumbling
of the wind across the surveillance mike, you could hear
the sound of waves hitting the sternboards, the creaking
of the deck chairs, and the crying of a gull somewhere in
the distance. Mojica looked angry, but his silence did not
seem to bother the man in the black leather trench coat.
The sound of his leather coat creaking carried above the
noise of the wind. Everyone in the room was struggling for

a look at the man, hoping he would move, show his face to the camera.

"Do we get a good look at this asshole in the black leather?" asked one of the DEA guys, frustration and curiosity mixed in his voice.

"No. Well, not a good one," said Fiertag. "They both go inside in a minute. We get a view then, but it's brief. If any of you can make him, sing out."

"When was this tape made?" asked Luke.

"And where's the time-code, sir?" added Grizzly Dalton.

"Monday afternoon. On Jamaica Bay. The time-code was suppressed by the surveillance guys. They do that when the tape is copied. The DOI kept the original."

"Why? Doesn't the DOI trust us?" asked one of the younger Marshals at the back of the room, sarcasm heavy in his voice.

"Do we trust them?" said Grizzly.

"Nobody trusts anybody," said another DEA guy. "I frisk myself every day just to see I ain't carrying."

"We're seeing this for one reason, to help ID the man in the black leather. Mojica is a DOI thing, not our jurisdiction, okay? We're just cooperating with the city here."

There was a distant snort from one of the NYPD Fugitive Apprehension men leaning on the far wall. Fiertag ignored that.

On the videotape Mojica drank something from a tall crystal goblet and threw the rest of the liquid over the side in a gesture of anger and dismissal.

MOJICA:
Your attitude is difficult.
LEATHERCOAT:
I ask your—I have only respect, but this is the thing I do.
You have looked into—

MOJICA:
Yes. Everyone says you are well thought of. So there it is. Yeah, okay. Well, we can have something to eat. There's some steak here, and—
LEATHERCOAT:
We can eat inside?
MOJICA:
Of course. Just remember, the point—the reason for this thing is to know, not to be left wondering. My son made a decision to help out. We return a favor. My son knows what he's doing. But it is better to be careful about charity. If damage has been done, then that's the whole idea, to know. There have to be some answers and not just—you know, not a conclusion without answers. Also, my son is not to be embarrassed. That's my main thing. You get that?
LEATHERCOAT:
I understand that. That's not acceptable, I see that. I will get answers for you.
MOJICA (getting up, the sound of chairs creaking):
Yeah. Yeah, well. See that you do, okay?

As the two men stood up and turned toward the doors into the main cabin, Mojica passed around to the camera side of the man in black leather, and that man turned to face him, both men standing now, and for one brief flash, the face of the man in the black leather coat was clearly visible.

"Freeze that, Mike!" said Fiertag.

The image froze in that maddening flicker of a video still. Leathercoat's face was round and deeply marked by some kind of childhood disease, chicken pox or measles or a severe acne that had gone untreated. His lips were thick, almost feminine, but they had a hard twist to them. His eyes were deeply set, dead black. The man seemed to radiate a kind of chilliness that was obvious even from this unsteady and slightly blurred video still.

Fiertag waited for someone to identify him. The room was filled with federal investigators from all over the eastern seaboard. Surely someone had a make on him.

"We had the still enhanced by a computer, if this doesn't do it. Anybody make him?"

The tape fluttered and rolled on for another couple of seconds. The two men went inside the boat. Someone in the background of the surveillance tape said, *"Shit,"* and another voice said, *"Can you pick them up through the portholes?"* and the first voice said, *"Nah, they're tinted, and he's got the stereo on. Fuck this. I'm freezing my ass off out here!"*

The tape ended, and the room lights came back up.

There was a long silence as each of the agents ransacked his memory of faces and names, trying for a match.

"He looked Indian. Native Indian," said one of the DEA guys.

"You mean, like a Sioux, like that?" said Fiertag.

"Yeah."

"He looks like Gall," said Grizzly Dalton.

"Who's he?" said the DEA guy.

"Sioux war chief. He killed Custer. They got a picture of him in the Smithsonian in D.C. Same bad skin, same mean eyes."

"Does anyone in the NYPD have a theory?" said Luke, looking across at the FAT squad cops. "Other than he's a two-hundred-year-old Sioux war chief, I mean."

"Not a one," said Sergeant Rizzo, shaking his head. "All the DOI has is, Mojica's not happy about something, and he picks this guy up at the King's Plaza Marina, they go for a ride, they talk, and they eat. The boat comes back to the marina an hour later, but they got no more video on either of them. Tell you one thing, that guy in the black leather, he's real paranoid. Surveillance-conscious, like. The DOI tried to get a photo of him when he came off the boat, he kept his head down, got into a dark green Jeep Cherokee with windows really black, so you couldn't even see him at the wheel."

"They got a plate number, right?" said Luke.

"Oh yeah. Virginia marker. Tango Zulu Bravo one five one one. Came back as rented out on a fleet contract to Chesapeake Realty, one of Mojica's development companies. All legit. Nothing against them. No wants, no warrants. Squeaky, you know?"

"You tail him?"

Rizzo grinned, shook his head.

"Not for long, Luke. Like I said, this guy was real surveillance-conscious. The DOI had a three-car tag team on him all the way up Utica, and he blew them off somewhere in Bed Stuy. Very slick."

More silence.

Finally Grizzly Dalton said, "Well, I'll tell you one thing, Rizzo."

"Yeah, Grizz?"

"Mojica was scared shitless of him."

Coming in silent made the thing more difficult for Sergeant Crewes because he couldn't hit the siren and blow these dimwits out of his way. He had to push his cruiser through the gridlocked traffic at Hunts Point Avenue and Bruckner with only his roof lights to force the cars out of his way. He also utilized some man-to-man voice communication out his open window. In the rear Doctor Dred was moaning a little as the car bounced over the potholes on Bruckner and jolted south toward Timpson Place.

"You okay back there, son?" asked Crewes, feeling more kindly toward the boy since they'd worked out their differences.

Doctor Dred had his face buried in the vinyl and his arms and legs hogtied, so it was difficult for him to keep his head up long enough to make his response clear, but Crewes figured it was something encouraging. He counted the blocks off as he sped down the Bruckner, weaving in and out of the crawling lines of trucks and cabs and cars.

162nd.

159th.

156th.

There you go, 144th. The silent alarm was coming from a unit that was out in a kind of island, a wide stretch of warehouse blocks formed by the widening gap between Southern Boulevard and the Bruckner Expressway. Bruckner itself ran pretty much underneath the elevated expressway, a potholed and ancient roadway that hadn't seen daylight since the nineteenth century.

All the way down Crewes had been listening to Central as Central tried to drum up some cover cars for this alarm call. So far, Four Frank was still on an aided case, Five Charlie was trying to reach him from Third and 149th Street, and two other detective cars were also pushing through the rush-hour traffic to help him out. He saw the front window of La Luna Negra coming up on his right-hand side and pulled a sharp right turn. The alley that ran up behind the rows of warehouses and car repair shops was narrow and packed with Dumpsters, trucks, a Jeep, a few wandering homeless drunks, a white van, and a great deal of random garbage. The sodium-arc warehouse lamp was casting a hard yellow light on the rutted lane. There was a steel loading door, closed, and a smaller door beside the dock. The door was wide open.

Crewes killed his lights and his engine.

"Five Frank, K. I'm ten-84."

"Five Frank?"

"Ten-four. The door's open. Where's my cover?"

"Four one three and 419 are coming. Four one three, K?"

Another voice came on, the voice of Gold Shield Detective Jerome Boynton, one of the 41st Precinct plainclothes cops assigned to Robbery.

"Four one three, K. Brian, we're at St. Francis and rolling. Wait for us, K?"

"The door's open here, Jerry."

"Don't go in without cover. We'll be there in two minutes."

That open door worried Crewes. There were citizens in there, and a silent alarm that was still broadcasting to the Wackenhut station. The Patrol Guide was clear about ten-31 calls, though. You always got a cover car.

God-*damn* this traffic.

Two minutes could be somebody's lifetime in the South Bronx.

"Where are you now, Jerry?"

Crewes could hear the frustration in Boynton's voice.

*"We're trying, we're trying—*move, asshole!*"* This was apparently shouted out the window of the car.

"Come in hot, Jerry. Central, I'm ten-six now."

Boynton's voice cut in across the transmission. *"Brian, wait one. We're almost there. Don't—"*

"ETA, 413?"

"Two minutes max!"

"I'm ten-six, 413. They don't pay us to stand around with our thumbs up our—"

"Brian—"

Crewes cut him off. Two minutes was too long to wait. Inside someone could be dying right now. Crewes looked over into the back seat. Doctor Dred had his head turned to look back up at him.

"Look, kid, I'm gonna take a look-see here. I'll be right back."

The boy blinked up at him, spit a little blood. Crewes got out of the car quietly, closed the door and locked it, pocketed his keys, and turned the volume down to one on his portable radio. He could hear a call, but he wouldn't be blasting his presence all over the lot. He took out his service revolver and went up the short flight of iron stairs leading to the open door.

The interior of the warehouse was dark. His breath floated and swirled out in front of him in a puffy cloud. In the chilly and damp winter air, he now heard a police siren, rising and falling, getting louder.

Car 413 was coming in hot. But not a lot closer. The traffic was a bitch this time of day. Sergeant Crewes stepped up into the doorway and slipped in, coming in fast, not making a silhouette in the brighter rectangle of the open door, his revolver out in front, his Mag-Lite extended in his left hand. He checked his right, his left, and straight ahead, tracking the bright cone of the Mag-Lite beam with his revolver muzzle. The warehouse was piled with wooden crates, jute-wrapped bundles, cane furniture. In the narrow and intense blue-white beam of his Mag-Lite he saw a closed door at the far end of a narrow aisle in between piles and stacks of parcels.

He could hear music coming faintly from beyond the door, a Latin rhythm, something slow and dreamy, like a waltz or a tango. Strangely, he remembered the name of the song.

It was an old Glenn Miller tune.

"Perfidia."

Out in Five Frank, Doctor Dred was working very hard to get out of his cord-cuff restraints. This was not an easy thing to do, but he was highly motivated. He knew he was headed for a very long ride up to Sing-Sing for his part in the drive-by, and life in its infinite variety had presented him a chance to fast-forward through some of the uglier bits. If he could get his feet out of the cord-cuff, he could boot a side window out. He knew where he was. One of his homies had a roost less than two blocks away. If he

could get there, the man had bolt-cutters. The Doctor
would be free and clear.

The exertion was making him breathless, and something was very wrong with his nose. Also, his crotch felt
like a pair of basketballs full of hornets. Who knew the
little white motherfucker could scrap like that? The Doctor hadn't lost a fight in years. Well, he hadn't won a *fair*
one, either, but nobody fought fair in the South Bronx.
Smoke 'em and split, that was word. He had already made
some headway with the nylon band, gotten his right ankle
free, and was working the other one loose, when Doctor
Dred heard someone's boots clattering down a flight of
iron steps.

Shit. The cop? Back already?

He craned his neck up and saw a big man in a black
leather coat coming down the steps in back of the warehouse. It was fully dark by now, but he got a good enough
look at the man in the arc-light glare to be sure he wasn't
a cop.

There was a siren sounding in the middle distance.

Doctor Dred decided to take a chance. Twisting, he
slammed his right foot against the steel doorframe of the
cop car.

"Yo! Mister!"

The man in the black leather coat jerked to a stop,
came close, and looked down into the back of the patrol
car. The Doctor looked back up at him through the
smeared glass of the side window and was suddenly
chilled. In the glaring light the man looked like a dead
body walking, like something out of a horror movie, with
a pocked face and empty black holes where his eyes were
supposed to be.

The man looked up the alley, then back down at Doctor Dred in the back. Then he tried the door handle. The
Doctor could feel the strength in that single tug, a terrible

animal vitality and power that he knew he could never match, certainly not with his hands cuffed and one leg in a knot. He felt his throat go tight, and his rib cage seemed to freeze up.

The man pulled at the latch again, and the whole cruiser rocked. The door was locked. The Doctor had a very bad feeling about what was going to happen to him if that door lock gave way. This guy didn't look like mercy missions were his kind of gig. Another hard pull, and the man's face now showed emotion, a kind of fleeting feral snarl, and his breath misted the side window, and he leaned down to strain at the lock. The door groaned, metal on metal, bent slightly, the big Caprice bounced on its shocks, but the lock held.

Thank you, General Motors.

Thank you, Jesus—

The sound of the approaching siren was louder now. The man looked in through the window of the patrol car, his face only inches from the glass. Doctor Dred found himself remembering a scene from that dinosaur movie. These kids are hiding out in this big stainless-steel kitchen, and there's this *thing*, a huge lizard with yellow eyes and a set of teeth like a crocodile, and it's trying to open the door, and you see its breath puff out onto the window in the door. Now he knew how those kids felt.

And for the first time in his life, Clayton Garr, age seventeen, found himself echelons beyond bravado, and he began to pray.

He prayed for something he had never ever prayed for before. He prayed for the cops to show up.

Soon please.

He prayed very hard.

The night had come down on the South Bronx like a slow fall of black snow, bringing with it a strange, almost luminous fog. A lung-deep chill from Long Island Sound had glided in across the city blocks, spilling down from the rooftops and filling up the streets like an invisible flood. The tenements and abandoned wrecks that lined Tenbroeck Avenue seemed to float in a field of white mist, and there was a slimy yellow light around the few streetlamps still working. The street was deserted, everyone indoors or riding the downtown trains tonight, looking for entertainment or victims on the Deuce or in the Village or along Lenox and 125th Street in Harlem. There was a low rushing murmur riding on the wind, the sound of cars and trucks on the Bronx and Pelham Parkway a few blocks to the east. A thin frost was making snowflake patterns in the mist on the inside windshield of his car.

Luke puffed at his cigarette again and exhaled, watching the smoke slide and curl around the dashboard and the window, listening idly to the radio calls on the crosstown NYPD frequency. He was sitting at the wheel of the tan Caprice they'd drawn from auto pool after Fiertag's briefing. The two other guys in their four-man takedown unit, Rico Groza and Walt Rich, were in another unmarked car, a tan Ford, a few blocks away, waiting for Luke and Grizzly to pick up their fink, check him out, and get the evening's festivities under way.

Right now Grizzly was inside the snitch's flat on the third floor of a crumbling half-burned-out brownstone. Their target, Elijah Olney, was supposed to be hiding in a ratbag South Bronx hotel somewhere around Crotona Park, between Third and the Boston Road. Oddly, that was only a few blocks away from their office in the Bronx Borough Hall.

Tonight's fink-du-jour was a crack addict named Bubblegum who suffered from a number of diseases, including AIDS. He was not the type of snitch Luke liked to count on, but you took them as they came, and this was the only lead they had on Elijah Olney, fugitive gangbanger.

Luke puffed one last time on his cigarette, trying to finish it before Grizzly came back. Grizzly had a mild case of asthma, and although he would never complain, Luke knew his smoking gave Grizzly a bad time when they were cooped up in a stakeout car. Grizzly's own rancid cigars never seemed to bother him, but then, like Clinton, he didn't inhale. Luke had the windows open to air out the interior, and a cold Bronx wind was slicing through the car, burning Luke's left cheek. He had the heater on, but the wind had shifted a while ago and was now slicing in off the ocean, carrying a slow and penetrating damp chill that went right to the marrow.

Shifting in his seat, he pushed at his chest, trying to get comfortable in his Kevlar Second Chance vest. The trauma plate was in tonight, a ceramic shield that fit into a pocket in the vest, right over his heart and lungs. It gave very good protection against high-velocity Talon rounds, but it felt like a Christmas platter shoved up against his chest. It was stiff and awkward and hot. Tonight he had on the regulation black jeans and black combat boots, black raid jacket with US MARSHALS in gold on the back, and a black baseball cap with a gold star on the front.

With the vest and the trauma plate, the shoulder harness with his Taurus nine-mill—which, when loaded, weighed around four pounds—and two sets of matte black cuffs in the small of his back, two extra fifteen-round magazines hanging from the shoulder rig on his right side, a can of Mace, and a Mini-Maglite on his belt, a large Mag-Lite with four D cells on another belt hook, the portable radio on his left side, attached to the mike mounted on his shoulder, and his gold Marshals star on a leather clip next to his belt buckle, Luke was carrying around thirty-five extra pounds of combat gear.

For some of the younger guys—those yuppie-cops he'd watched today, for instance—maybe this all-black SWAT-style outfit, all the weapons and the gear, made them feel like hard-core guys. And it also saved some lives—certainly it let other cops on the call know who was a good guy and who wasn't—but in the end all this stuff just made Luke feel like a junkman's pushcart or an extra in a Stallone movie. It made him feel like a Saturday morning cartoon hero, as if he were tricked out to *look* like a cop, as if his gear weren't a uniform but wardrobe.

Luke had worked with city and state bulls and corrections officers who went in after some very dangerous criminals wearing a Harvey Woods sports coat, Sansabelt slacks, and black wingtip cordovans. True, the city Emergency Services guys wore the same kind of black raid gear, but most of the 150,000 felony arrests the NYPD filed every year were made by a couple of plainclothes precinct detectives and maybe a few harness guys for backup. Busting a bad guy used to be a fundamental element of law enforcement, something you did every day. Now it was a job for black operations, for specialists.

Luke believed, but didn't say out loud, that there was getting to be too much military influence in what used to be a simple law enforcement detail. Now every takedown was a combat scenario, complete with masked avengers and caped crusaders. The trouble with running takedowns as if they were military operations was that your training was all directed toward one moment—shooting to kill. Maybe that was something the Special Operations Group guys had to think about—although it hadn't saved Bill Degan's life at Ruby Ridge, Idaho—but for a street Marshal like Luke, it felt wrong, as if it were turning him into something he wasn't. Less of a chaser and more of a hired killer. The fact that he was good at it, probably one of the service's best, didn't make him feel any better. He worried that the younger guys coming up, guys who hadn't seen anyone die by gunfire other than in a movie, were basing their view of real death on a Hollywood illusion, and all this army gear just seemed to support the unreality of it.

Not that the guy they were looking for tonight didn't stand in desperate need of a couple of serious rounds placed right where they would do the most good. Elijah Olney was the kind of guy you wanted out of the gene pool yesterday. But once you get into a combat mindset instead of a law enforcement mindset, you set yourself up for some serious overreactions.

Like the Weaver takedown. It wasn't entirely clear to Luke that Randy Weaver's wife and Randy Weaver's fourteen-year-old kid quite added up to the threat factor of a heavyweight thug like Elijah Olney. And it was a fact that the Ruby Ridge takedown stuck in every U.S. Marshal's throat, no matter how they tried to hide it. The charges were actually pretty minor, and a lot of agents knew damn well that the ATF was trying to set Weaver up for snitch recruitment, a classic federal ploy. Weaver said no thanks and failed to show up for his trial. Once Weaver had defied a federal warrant, it was up to the U.S. Marshals Service to go in and get him.

Now, nobody was kidding themselves that these survivalists were nice guys who loved their fellow man, but the sticky fact remained that Randy Weaver's *opinions* were not *actions*. Other than showing an unhealthy interest in lethal—but legal—weaponry, possibly a subject for psychiatric inquiry but not, currently, illegal, his only actual crime had been to deliver two sawed-off shotguns to a federal fink. No one had been threatened with them, and there was never any suggestion that Weaver intended to use them in a crime of any kind.

And not a lot of people outside federal law enforcement knew that Randy Weaver had been set up by the ATF to *force* him, under threat of prosecution, to spy on white supremacist groups, in this case the Aryan Nations, for the ATF, the FBI, and the Justice Department. The ATF added the usual juice to their allegations, claiming that Weaver was growing grass on the property—a standard federal pretext—and made up a basically bullshit list of crimes he was supposed to have committed in Oregon and Washington State—bank jobs, weapons smuggling, conspiracy. The U.S. Attorney, a man named Maurice Ellsworth, took the hook and pushed the shotgun charges against Weaver. Weaver's perhaps predictable response to Ellsworth and the fink recruitment issue was to ignore the court summons and hole up in his mountaintop retreat in northern Idaho and pretend the rest of the United States wasn't there, a position in absolute concordance with everything he had ever said, promised, or written, so there

was no point in the feds saying, Hey, golly, we didn't think
he'd do *That*!

But the Justice Department, God bless it, is like a half-
starved one-eyed gutshot pit bull with a snoutful of porcu-
pine quills; it clamps down even when it hurts. Weaver
was a *target*, by billy-be-damned, and he was jolly well
coming *in* from the cold whenever his mother said so.

They laid an eighteen-month surveillance operation on
his place that quickly degenerated into an unintentional
parody of *Marat/Sade*, with Weaver as Marat, the ATF as
de Sade, and the national media playing the inmates,
while camouflage-covered radicals scuttled about in the
undergrowth muttering quotations from Thomas Jefferson and David Duke and waving AK-47s and crossbows,
and ATF agents hiding out in the tops of trees with their
rag-man sniper suits and twigs in their Tilley hats got interviewed about their potty problems by video news twin-
kies and blow-dried network animatrons in Banana
Republic flak jackets and boots from Abercrombie &
Fitch.

Luke and his takedown unit partners had watched the
whole thing on a TV in the Bronx Borough office and
groaned aloud every time another poor son of a bitch federal agent got tagged by a breathless newshound or spotted by a videocamera on his way into the brush with a roll
of toilet paper. It was just plain embarrassing.

In short order the whole operation was blown, bungled,
buggered, and bamboozled. The Ruby Ridge siege of
Randy Weaver's hideout became about as redundant as a
free lobotomy for Al D'Amato, and if there had been anyone in the Justice Department with the brain of a newt,
there'd have been an immediate standdown and an orderly withdrawal.

Instead, Ruby Ridge became a real siege, a test of wills
between an ex–Green Beret with some bizarre political

views and a federal government that just couldn't say no. In Luke's view a regular city cop would have said, hey, lay some watchers on him and pop him when he goes for some KFC. Until then, let's all go back to our day jobs. Would that they had. Bill Degan would have still been alive.

Degan, a member of the USMS Special Operations Group, the service SWAT team, had been doing perimeter surveillance—actually, at the time of the killing, they were being chased by one of Weaver's dogs, which they shot—when rifle fire from the bushes had caught Degan in the head. Fire was immediately returned, which killed Weaver's fourteen-year-old son Samuel. The resulting standoff took eleven days and cost the life of Weaver's wife, Vicki, killed by FBI sniper Lon Horiuchi as she stood in a cabin window. Horiuchi—West Point Class of 1976—attached to the FBI's Hostage Rescue Team, composed largely of ex–Marine Corps and U.S. Army personnel, maintained that he was following orders laid out in his rules of engagement.

True, except that in this case, they were operating on a nonstandard rule of engagement that advised HRT members that they "can and *should*" shoot an armed adult, whether or not their lives or the lives of others were in imminent danger, an alteration of the standard operational language that amounted, in Luke's experienced view, to an assassination order.

And Luke also knew damn well what the view was like through a sniper scope—he'd used one hundreds of times. So when he heard that FBI sniper Horiuchi, one of *nine* surrounding the cabin, had wounded Randy Weaver while Weaver was walking toward an outbuilding and, seconds later, blown off most of Vicki Weaver's face as she stood behind the partially curtained window, watching Kevin Harris try to make it back inside the cabin, it seemed to him that Horiuchi should have known exactly who he was targeting and precisely where the round would strike her—in the neck on her left side.

It was hard, perhaps, but he really didn't give too much of a damn about Weaver's family—you run with wolves, you get hunted with wolves—but the operation at Ruby Ridge also got Bill Degan killed, for, basically, *nada*. Bill Degan was ten times the man Randy Weaver would ever be, and his death was a loss to the nation that would never be balanced by any number of prosecutions against "hate" groups or firearms fanatics.

In Boise in 1993, in the final chapter of the farce, Weaver was acquitted on all charges but the failure to appear, essentially a misdemeanor, the gap between ordinary citizens and professional law enforcement got a little wider, and that was that, except for Weaver's lawsuit, which was going to cost the taxpayers of the country millions and millions of dollars.

So in the long run the ATF had tried to turn a perhaps unstable—but up until that point harmless—survivalist into a federal fink, then wildly misjudged their man and bungled it up thoroughly; the U.S. Attorneys got their shorts in a knot, bounced into each other and panicked, sent in the Special Operations Group and the FBI's maniacally gung-ho Hostage Rescue Team, who promptly turned a misdemeanor firearms beef into a war, because that's what you get when you send in the troops to make arrests.

Arrests like the October 2, 1992, DEA raid on the Malibu ranch of one Donald Scott, a millionaire weirdo who was supposed to be growing marijuana on his property. It was an early evening raid, no-knock bang-bang style, and Scott came running out of his bedroom with a .357 Magnum in his hand when he heard shouting and screaming in the living room. He found a bunch of armed men in black suits and black face masks pushing his wife around, shouting threats, waving guns, and generally laying waste to the environment. They gave Scott about a half-second to figure out these weren't thugs, they were cops, but as he hesitated, one of the L.A. cops blew his brains out the back of his head.

As for Scott's alleged marijuana farm . . . ah, well, ahem . . . ahh, unfortunately, nobody actually found any . . . ahem . . . cough cough . . . actual, real . . . ah . . . as it were . . . grass, so to speak . . . ah, anywhere on the property, the, like, locale, you know, and so . . . and it was later rumored that the whole operation was quite likely a deliberate ruse to seize his property under federal drug-related forfeiture laws. Scott had apparently refused to sell his ranch to L.A. County for some development project the city was determined to have and was therefore branded a misanthropic obstructionist dingbat and a pain in the ass, and somebody made him a target.

And, while Randy Weaver was on trial in Boise in 1993, the ATF was off stirring up another pot of nitro stew in Waco, Texas. Another buggered-up firearms beef, more unproven accusations of marijuana cultivation and child abuse, another set of faulty warrants, another unnecessary military-style assault that went belly-up—bingo, Bob's your uncle—and you have seventy-two brand new crispy critters, seventeen of them children. Once again, a civilian ATF assault with a military attitude.

Luke was painfully aware that the ATF had actually *trained* for the Waco takedown on an Army Ranger MOUT (Military Operations on Urban Terrain) facility at Fort Hood, under the auspices of Joint Task Force 6, a Defense Department program developed after a 1989 decision by Secretary of Defense Dick Cheney that designated drugs as a national security threat.

Joint Task Force 6, which has branches in U.S. Army,

Navy, Air Force, and Marine Corps bases around the nation, in Central and South America, and overseas, exists to provide military training and assistance to any civilian law enforcement group—JTF manuals refer to them as DLEAs, or Drug Law Enforcement Agencies—fighting the drug wars. Hence the frequent, almost routine allegations of marijuana use or crystal meth labs in these targeted groups, allegations that often turned out to be false information supplied by overzealous hired finks.

Troubling to Luke as well was the Justice Department rumor that there had been U.S. Army sergeants present at the Waco takedown as observers. If so, what they *observed* qualified as a balls-to-the-wall career-blasting Fucked Up Beyond All Recognition police disaster, and Luke was sure these observers had taken the first chopper back to Benning and spent the next six days with their heads down, drinking quietly and steadily in the back of the sergeant's mess.

Well, hell, this was all getting too deep for him, anyway. And Grizzly was shuffling along the sidewalk, looking like Smokey the Bear as a *Blade Runner* extra. Grizzly reached the car and got in, huffing from the cold and the run. The hell with the big picture, thought Luke. Just do your job and keep your head down.

"Was he there?" asked Luke.

"Yeah. He's gonna come down, we'll get him in the back here."

"How is he? He straight?"

"As straight as Bubblegum ever gets. He's real cool right now, so I figure he's on something like grass or Quaaludes."

"He's scared." The comment wasn't a question.

Grizzly nodded and rolled up his side window. Luke crushed the cigarette out and pitched it into the street, where it joined a pile of five other butts and a Styrofoam coffee cup from a White Castle.

"You think it's okay to leave him alone?"

"He's not gonna call anyone, Luke. We're the only friends he's got now, and anyway, there's no phone in his crib. I'm letting him cap up. He'll never get through to-night without pharmaceuticals."

Grizzly was looking down at the clipboard in his hands. There was a mug shot, full face in color, of Elijah Olney, and a copy of the federal warrant issued in November 1994. Olney's face was grim and hostile in the shot, and the L.A. County booking number in his hand was tilted to one side, held loosely, as if Elijah resented even the act of being ID'd. Luke looked over the shot.

"Ugly son of a bitch, isn't he?"

"Oh yeah. Face like a yak's elbow. They say you get the face you deserve when you're forty. He got his early. Do I have the face I deserve, Luke?"

Luke leaned over and looked closely at Grizzly's face.

"I'd say so, yeah."

"Shit. I was hoping it didn't show. I used to be a hand-some guy."

"You got over it."

"Thank you, my son."

"What'd you make out of Fiertag today?"

Grizzly looked at Luke, raising his eyebrows.

"I can't make *anything* out of Fiertag. He won't even let me cut off enough for a wallet. Why are you asking?"

"That thing with Mojica. That's nothing of ours. Mojica belongs to the DOI and the city DA. Why the hell show us a film of some guy, nobody knows who he is, even if he's dirty—"

"Trust me, my son. He's dirty. He's got Jo-Jo Mojica scared, he's *real* dirty."

"Yeah, so anyway, where's the federal connection?"

"Fiertag said he was being cooperative. Help out the DOI."

"Fiertag wouldn't help Jesus down off the cross unless he could rent him the stepladder, sell him the bandages, and get exclusive Piece-of-the-True-Cross concession rights for Italy and Spain. I know why we saw the Newark bank job—Pigeye Quail's a Marshals target—but this dog-and-pony number out on the Big Fishkill? I don't get it. Fiertag saw something in it for himself. There's some angle there, Grizz, something we're not getting told."

Grizzly was still laughing.

"I like that bit about the True Cross, Luke. You got a fresh way with blasphemy. I admire that in a guy. About being *lied* to, what else is new? We get kept in the dark so much, they oughta call us deputy mushrooms. Why worry about it? Life's too short, Luke. Anyway, here comes our guy. Leave the windows open, Luke. He's a little ripe to-night."

A slight slope-shouldered figure wrapped in an old army fatigue jacket and baggy jeans popped out of the doorway of the crumbling brownstone. The man looked up and down the empty street, saw a car parked up the block and studied it for a while, then turned and jogged a little erratically down toward their unmarked tan Chevy. Grizzly reached into the back and popped the rear door lock. The man, a black male in his late twenties with a close-cropped razor cut and a couple of missing teeth in his upper jaw, flopped inside and lay down on the rear seat. A blast of cold damp air followed him in. The smell of sweat and crack smoke and Thunderbird began to ooze over into the front seat.

Luke found himself wondering once again how it was that his life's work so often required careful mouth-breathing and gag-reflex suppression in enclosed spaces like patrol cars and interrogation cells. Did priests run into this kind of thing in the confessional?

Probably.

"Hey, Bubblegum. You know Luke, hah?"

Bubblegum's face was slack and bleary, his skin mottled and stained with dirt and bad living, but fear was still a hectic glitter in his eyes.

"You hadda bring this unit, man. Everybody knows a car like this."

"The Bentley was in the shop," said Luke. "You up for this?"

Bubblegum nodded, slapping his arms on his chest, puffing.

"Yo, man. Just roll, okay? I got people on this block looking for me."

The car pulled away fast, and Bubblegum didn't sit up until they were across Allerton and heading south toward Williamsbridge Road.

Grizzly flipped the clipboard back onto Bubblegum's lap. He stared down at it, his face knotted with concentration.

"Yeah. That's definitely him. Definitely."

"When's the last time you saw him?"

"Yesterday. He's holed up bigtime, man. Only reason he's opening his door, he needs his shit."

"What'd you deal him?" said Luke.

Bubblegum was one of Grizzly's snitches, and Luke usually let Grizzly do the talking, but there was a lot riding on this takedown. Elijah Olney was a very bad man, a Blood enforcer from Los Angeles wanted for every brand of gangbanger bullshit brutality. Like most Marshals Service targets, Elijah Olney's route from gunrunner in South-Central L.A. to federal fugitive in the South Bronx was a long one, filled with coincidences, lies, foul-ups, and consequences.

It had all started last November, on a smoky fall afternoon, with music coming from the open screen doors and kids in the schoolyard playing stickball. Along comes Elijah Olney and a sack of homies in a stolen rag-top five-liter Mustang, a boomer car fitted with bass-boosters so deep that the rap music coming from it sounded like distant thunder. The gangbanger driver kept the music going while Olney popped up in the back seat like a homicidal Howdy Doody and added his own special nine-millimeter counterpoint to the afternoon's musical selections.

Given Olney's unsteady grasp of the concept of fire control, it was hard at the outset to determine precisely *who* this asshole was shooting at, but while an entire city block went every which way, and the kids were screaming, and teenage boys in the neighborhood were scrambling for their own weapons, and a five-year-old girl in a lime-green party dress swinging on a schoolyard railing took a round in the belly, Olney kept it up, apparently enjoying the mechanical efficiency of the Uzi. At least he *looked* happy, according to a survivor, especially when he took the time to get out of the Mustang, reload, and empty his Uzi into the pleading, cowering body of a teenage girl named Delores Fryar, whose only connection with Olney was that her older brother, or maybe he was younger, or maybe it was her father . . . well anyway, *one* of the Fryars had once said something insulting about Elijah Olney's sister. Or his cousin. Maybe it was his aunt . . . well, there was no getting around it, somebody had done something unacceptable to Elijah Olney, and in the feral dynamics of South-Central, Olney felt that he'd been "dissed"— one of Luke's least-favorite words—and had decided to make a point in the only language he felt was up to the enormity of whatever the insult actually was.

Well, none of this would have come to Bronx Division Deputy U.S. Marshal Luke Zitto's attention if Elijah Olney's demonstration of civilian firepower hadn't ticked off some local brothers, largely because of a dramatically increased level of police interference in their own rackets. They arranged to have Olney ratted out to the LAPD Ramparts District gang squad, who showed up in a foul humor on Olney's doorstep early one morning to see if they could provoke him into doing something suicidal.

Elijah declined the opportunity, it being far more entertaining to watch rounds heading *out* than to observe them coming *in*, and he was arrested and booked on multiple counts of firearms possession, unlawful discharge, various attempted murders, and a charge of murder one.

Sure as the letters NRA mean no responsibility accepted, Olney lost no time in making it known through his Legal Aid lawyer that he was now able to find it in his heart to "assist" the Bureau of Alcohol, Tobacco, and Firearms in a smuggling interdiction operation based in Atlanta, news of which had lately come to him from somewhere on the cosmic plane.

Bingo.

Elijah Olney—come on down!

Olney's charges in the drive-by killings were "subsumed" in a U.S. Attorney witness agreement—making him a "client" of the Marshals Service—and he was transferred to a federal lock-up cell that the Marshals rented from the L.A. County Jail. From which Olney promptly escaped with help from a Blood member before he could be arraigned in a federal court. The delay that led to his escape was the result of an attempt by another federal agency, the FBI, to horn in on the opportunities presented by Mr. Olney's sudden attack of civic-mindedness. (Snitches are like American Express cards—everybody wants one, even if they have to steal yours, and no lawyer will leave home without one.) And so he had been scheduled for a ride across town to discuss Blood recruiting operations in Oregon and Idaho.

The trouble here was that no one thought to make sure that Elijah was under constant guard while these various negotiations played out. In the meantime, as far as L.A. County Jail officials were concerned, Olney was just another juvenile psychopath playing Let's Make a Deal with the feds. When the jail attendant—*not* a Marshal—came to get Elijah Olney for one of his interviews, Olney's gang associate, a kid named Kap Latundi, had stepped forward in his place. The bored jail guard didn't know Elijah Olney from Marion Barry, and he simply cord-cuffed Kap Latundi and took him out to the federal transport van.

At precisely that moment—almost miraculously—Kap's Legal Aid lawyer, who later denied any involvement and actually *did* state that all gangbangers looked alike to her—showed up at county jail with a bail bond, and Elijah Olney—as Kap Latundi—simply strolled out of custody arm-in-arm with his lawyer and down the front steps of the L.A. County Jail, and off they whistling went, as Tom Waits would say, into the great dark heart of the warm, narcotic American night.

Escaping from a federal lockup made his recapture a matter for the Marshals Service. Olney's name went out on the NCIC (the National Crime Information Computer system), and a special fax was distributed to the FBI, fifty state police agencies, and all ninety-four Marshals offices in the continental United States. One of these faxes found its way onto the desk of Deputy U.S. Marshal Grizzly Dalton, who read it thoroughly and filed it away in his extremely accurate memory.

Grizzly took his job seriously and was always "browsing" through his fink connections—he called it "trolling for pond scum"—and a New York City Corrections probation officer who worked a desk next to him in their Bronx squad room had mentioned to him, in passing, that one of his clients, a crack addict and small-time mugger named William Fleer—street name Bubblegum—was claiming to have sold some drugs to a "heavy hitter" who was supposed to be a Blood from Los Angeles. At the same time, the street was buzzing with rumors.

Bronx Division gang-squad cops had also gotten wind of a possible Crip gangster on the loose in the area of the 43rd Precinct, and they had—very uncharacteristically— thought to contact Grizzly later the same week. Grizzly went back through his fax collection and spotted Olney's face third down on the sheet. The description the NYPD detectives had culled from various snitches seemed to match Elijah Olney, as did the description given by William "Bubblegum" Fleer. Grizzly saw all this as reason to think Bubblegum might actually have something other than hallucinations to sell, and he had gone out on the streets last week to see what he could work out.

Bubblegum hadn't been hard to find; he was in a lockup at the 48th Precinct, busted by Bronx Vice on a crack charge. For twelve hours he'd been sitting on his butt in the 48th holding cells, shivering and throwing up and generally whining about his influential friends in the federal government. Finally one of the Bronx Vice guys got sick of cleaning up after him and called Walt Rich, a Marshal who worked with Grizzly and Luke. He called Rich because Rich used to be on the force, and the NYPD takes care of its own. (Forget the Skull and Bones or the Masons; the Virgin Mary herself couldn't get a straight answer from the NYPD, unless she could prove that her dad had walked a beat on Sapphire Street for the 106th and played the snare drum with the Shamrock Society band every March 17.)

Walt Rich was busy with another fugitive trace, and he told Grizzly about the snitch in the Four-Eight lockup.

Grizzly showed up at the 48th, scraped Bubblegum down off the ceiling, and listened to his story. Bubblegum wanted leniency on a parole violation and immunity for the crack bust, which was his official third, and he was looking at a possible life hitch in Attica.

Life in Attica for a mope like Bubblegum Fleer, who was also HIV-positive, would probably have worked out to be about eighteen months, after which his good looks would have flown and somebody would have shanked him off to Neverland just to steal his cigarettes. Bubblegum knew this very well. Ratting out a Blood fugitive was probably a move with equally fatal consequences, but it was the last move he had, other than suicide.

Bubblegum had no doubt gone through all that up in his apartment while he smoked the last of his crack and drained a quart jar of Thunderbird. Luke was still waiting for his answer about the drugs Bubblegum had delivered to Elijah Olney. Bubblegum looked up at the roof of the undercover car and pretended to ransack his memory.

"Yeah, I, ah, well, he likes Ecstasy, and he also scored some crystal."

Luke looked at Bubblegum in his rearview as he rolled the tan Caprice down side streets toward the New York Institute for the Blind.

"Meth? Crystal meth?"

Bubblegum looked uncomfortable.

"Yeah, yeah, I think—"

Grizzly turned around and snarled at Bubblegum.

"Don't *think*, man. You know what you sold him. This ain't a truth in advertising thing. Stop fucking with us."

"Okay! Jeez, chill, man. It was crank—I think."

Luke and Grizzly looked at each other. Grizzly sighed. "Oh, great. He's on PCP. That's just peachy. Can I go home now?"

"No, Grizzly. You can't. Bubblegum, you get a look inside this crib?"

"No way, man. He's too spiky for that. Cracked the lid maybe an inch and took the shit over the chain."

"You can make the guy from a slice of his face an inch wide?"

"Well, like, it was bigger than that. I mean, like it was . . ."

Grizzly shook his head and looked at Luke. Snitches.

"So, the main question, where's he at?" said Grizzly.

Bubblegum studied his reflection in the side window. The Bronx was rolling past his window, tenement blocks giving way to apartment towers and storefronts, Harlem in the horizon, the lights of midtown casting a big rose-colored glow on the underside of the cloud cover away to the south. The crosstown NYPD frequency on their radio was a low crackling whisper in the dark and silent car.

"See the respondent 3852 Broadway—

"Eat no pay, Five Boy—enjoy enjoy—

"Aided case 344 Atlantic Avenue—

"Two Eddy stand by one—

"Citywide Auto has a BOLO—

"Oh, not for long, Five Charlie—

"Anybody got a Slim Jim for Six Adam at Fordham?

"—ginia marker Tom Zebra Boy, one five one one—

"—five foot tall had on a green jacket white fur on the collar—

"We got a ten-51 a roaming gang at Webster and Tremont, Four Eddy—

"—Detective Boynton at 144th and Timpson—

"That was dispute with a firearm, South Frank—

"Ten-four, check and advise—

"Seven hundred White Plains, Four David. That's a 90Z, K?"

"Bubblegum, you still back there?"

He came out of a kind of stoned reverie. Luke didn't have to work hard to imagine what he was thinking. *Vita brevis, Tempus fugit,* Why me, oh Lord? Your basic snitch mantra.

"Harbor . . . something. But I know it when I see it. It's next to the recruiting station. They turn me down."

"Who, the Marines? I can't see why, man—Luke, I know that place. I think he means the Harbor Light. Right, Bubblegum?"

"Yeah . . . yeah, that could be it."

"If he's shucking us, I say we dump him off the High Bridge."

"Not the High Bridge again," said Luke, in a whine. "You always wanna dump them off that bridge. I get to pick the next one."

They had reached the Bronx and Pelham Parkway and were running downhill toward the Boston Road ramp. The city lights were blurred and jaundiced in the chilly mist. Cars and cabs and delivery vans were jolting and racing alongside their cruiser, and in the distance they could just make out the towers and pillars of light in Manhattan. Bubblegum was silent in the back seat, the lights of the cars playing over his face. Luke glanced at him in the rearview from time to time, just to make sure he was still alive.

"Better get on to Rico and Walt, Grizz."

Grizzly nodded, took out his cell phone, and dialed them up. They had learned not to announce a pending takedown over the radio net. Almost everybody had a scanner now. It was true that you could monitor a cell phone call, but it was a lot harder to do. They'd use a low-power two-way system when they got close to the fugitive's location.

"Walt—Grizz here—yeah, we got him. He's telling us it's maybe a flop called Harbor Light on Crotona Park North, just at Marmion there. By the recruiting office—yeah—

yeah. . . . No, we haven't. . . . I'll tell him. . . . Yeah, seems weird to me too. . . . Yeah, we're about ten minutes away. . . . Let the city know. . . . Kisses to Rico, hah? . . . Who? He's the looie at the 48th. If he's on tonight, talk to him personally. . . . What's Rico say? . . . Well, so's he. . . . Bye."

"Tell me what?" said Luke.

"Weird. City says to go ahead. If we want a cover car, we'll have to wait until tomorrow."

"That's not like the city guys. What's up?"

"They got a thing, multiple felonies, over by Hunts Point Market. They got a lot of their units tied up in a canvass."

"Yeah. That's the Four-One. They got a cop involved?"

"They wouldn't say, but if they're pulling patrol units off the streets on a Friday night in the Bronx, whoever they're looking for, they want him bad. They don't usually get that worked up for a citizen."

"Multiple dead?"

"That's what they said."

"Fuck it," said Luke. "Just another drug hit."

"Yeah," said Grizzly. "Fuck it."

Five minutes later they pulled up beside Rico Groza and Walt Rich's unmarked Ford in an alleyway that ran behind the tenement blocks along Crotona Park North. The alley was wide and strewn with wrecked cars, overflowing Dumpsters, garbage bags broken open like shattered green eggs, bottles and soda cans clattering and rolling in a sudden cold wind that ran up the lane between the tenement blocks.

Luke stopped the car beside the other unit and rolled down his window. Rico Groza's wolfish face was lit from beneath by the green glow of the dashboard lights, making his deepset dark eyes and his bony face look even more sinister. Beyond him Walt Rich's pale Irish face and short red crew cut were just visible. They were in raid gear as well. Rico grinned, and his white teeth glittered with green fire.

"Luke, Grizzly—where's our star?"

"He's in here, down on the floor."

"Troubled, is he?"

"He's sick at heart and fain wad lee doon. How you wanna do this, Rico?"

Rico Groza was, technically, the senior agent on the scene. Rico had come out of the Puerto Rico station covered in glory after a major drug-lord takedown in Honduras, a combined DEA-FBI–Marshals Service operation that had severed a number of major cocaine- and hashish-distribution pipelines around Central America and the Caribbean. He was only here now to get some street time so he could go back to D.C. and take a major promotion to Fugitive Ops in Arlington.

The fact that this major promotion was, at one time, supposed to belong to Luke wasn't an issue between them. Rico Groza was a stand-up who had testified on Luke's behalf at the informal inquiry after the D.C. operation.

"It's your show, Luke. Walt and me, we'll take perimeter, if you want. Walt's got the peeper, if you need it."

Luke looked at Grizzly, who nodded.

"Okay, we're entry, you two take perimeter. You're telling me the city cops are letting us do this alone?"

Rico grinned again, looked at his partner in the car. Walt Rich leaned forward and said, "Yeah. They got their hands full with a cartel thing up in Hunts Point. They got an officer down too. I spoke to the CO at the Four-Eight. He's got a unit on standby, but they got shit happening all over their precinct. He says do what you gotta do, but don't kill any of his civilians. And if we step on our dicks, they'll say they never heard of us."

"I figured it hadda be something like that," said Luke. "Okay, let's get this done. It's been a long day."

The Harbor Light was a six-story ramshackle beds-by-the-hour hotel that had started out back in the twenties as a fairly decent apartment block with a limestone facade and an art deco entranceway. Back in those days Crotona Park was a high-end neighborhood, and the street was a nice little uptown shopping strip. Now the six-block stretch was a collection of tenements, groceterias, bodegas, bad bars, and flophouses. People watched Luke and Grizzly stroll up the block toward the Harbor Light, nodded politely, and lost no time getting in off the stoops. Teenagers in baggy sports jackets and floppy running shoes made pig noises from a safe distance.

Luke checked for a clocker on the stoop of the Harbor Light and saw no one who looked like he was there to warn people inside. It seemed odd to him. If Elijah Olney were really in there, he'd done something to piss off even his own gang members. Usually the Bloods did more for their runners than leaving them to twist in the wind inside some South Bronx rathole. Maybe they were tired of him too.

Maybe he really *was* going to rat out a Blood operation in Georgia and they got him out of the L.A. County Jail just to whack him, but Olney had seen it coming. And maybe the only reason the Bronx Marshals had gotten wind of Elijah Olney's presence in the city was because somebody in the Blood organization wanted him dead. It was all wheels within wheels. You never knew the whole story. As far as Luke was concerned, he didn't give a damn *why* somebody had handed Elijah Olney a black spot. Olney was sewage, and whatever he got, it was much too late and a buck short.

The entrance to the Harbor Light's once-classic art deco foyer was now a single smeared glass door flanked by rust-covered steel shutters dense with sprayed-on gang symbols. Past the doorway there was a twenty-foot stretch of stained green linoleum and walls painted the color of bad meat. In the ceiling a single fifty-watt bulb inside a steel cage cast a liverish-green light down on the hallway. A worn-out flight of stairs covered in black rubber led up into a murky darkness. The hall reeked of stale smoke and Dustbane.

The night clerk who ran the place was an elderly black man with tired eyes in a drawn but still handsome face. He had a certain air of faded elegance and a Cab Calloway mustache. He looked like his better days had been pretty good. He gave his name as Chicago and spoke to Luke and Grizzly from behind a green-tinted bulletproof plastic enclosure with a sliding tray for money and room keys to be passed back and forth. Inside the enclosure there was a gray steel desk covered with cards, a battered and over-stuffed chair, a pay phone, a cooler filled with ice and cans of Old Milwaukee, and a tiny black and white television. The sudden appearance of two U.S. Marshals in black raid gear didn't seem to faze him much. He looked at the mug shot of Elijah Olney, then raised his weary eyes again. His voice was clear and his speech careful.

"Yes, officer. I think that's the man. An unpleasant young man."

"How's he registered?"

"Registered? His ID was two pictures of Ben Franklin, officer."

"He home now?"

"Boy never goes out."

"You know his room?"

"You intend to smash up the place?"

"Why?" said Grizzly, sarcastically. "You own it?"

A flicker of something passed over the old man's face, a brief recollection of pride and power.

"I used to. I've been here for a long time. This used to be a nice place."

Grizzly gave the man a big smile.

"Well, it'll be a whole lot nicer in about ten minutes. What's his room number, sir?"

Chicago reached under the counter and pulled out a crumpled plastic sheet. It was the room plan of the hotel. He pointed to a flat on the second floor. "Number 9B."

"It have a fire escape?"

"City insists."

Luke was looking at the diagram.

"You have a room plan for 9B?"

"All the rooms are the same, sir. They broke 'em all up in the sixties. It was too bad."

He showed them a drawing on the wall.

"See? One room, bed bolted to the floor by the window, toilet to the left there, sink over the toilet. One window, sash type, that lets you onto the fire escape. No closets. Every room's got a TV though. Pay phone on every other floor, only they've been stolen."

"Anybody else on that floor?"

He looked down at a sheet of yellow paper on a clipboard beside him.

"Only one guy. He's a regular, went out to sell some blood two hours ago. He'll be at the Sonic by now, drinking bourbon. It was my intention to go over there in an hour and help him in the process. If you fellows don't spoil my evening."

"What's the door made of?" asked Luke.

The old man's face got a little more tired.

"See? You're in a mood to break things up, son."

"You wanna give us a key?"

He considered them for a long moment.

"Nope," he said after a while. "Rules are rules."

"Which rules are those, sir?" said Luke.

"The ones a man can read even if he can't read. Sir."

Luke and Grizzly looked at the old man and nodded. They turned to go up the dark stairs, and the man called to them.

"One thing, officers."

Luke stopped on the second step, turned to look down. "Yeah?"

"That boy, he's got a woman in there right now."

Great.

"A hooker?" asked Grizzly.

The old man gave him a look.

"I don't believe it was Whitney Houston, officer." He pronounced her name *How*-ston. Grizzly looked up the stairs at Luke.

"I better go get the peeper from Walt. I'll be right back."

"Okay. Tell them it's 9B, tell them take the fire escape. I'll be a few steps up here."

Grizzly was back in three minutes, carrying a black nylon case.

"They know the layout. Walt says he had a shooting here in 1979."

"Why didn't he say something?"

"I don't know, Luke. If we live, I'll ask him. Let's do this, okay? I'm getting hungry. They'll be in position in five minutes."

"What'd they do with Bubblegum?"

"He's passed out in the car. Walt handcuffed him to the door. He'll be out of it for hours."

"Man," said Luke, "he'll drool all over the seat."

"It's vinyl. Let's go, can we? I'm too old for this shit."

In silence now they climbed the rest of the creaking ancient staircase into the brown-shadowed darkness above. Luke had his nine-mill out and was holding it in front of him, forearm braced, his left hand supporting his right, his Mini-Maglite strapped to his right forearm in line with his pistol, but not switched on. Showing a bright light in this kind of situation was as much a danger as it was a protection. Grizzly was following a few feet back. They took the turn in the landing quickly, and saw that someone had broken every ceiling light on the second floor. The long hallway was a black tunnel with an EXIT sign glowing just over their heads, casting a pale red glow for a few feet down the hall. The rug was sticky and the hall smelled of fried food and urine and dry rot.

They came slowly along the hall toward 9B. A line of yellow light was showing under the ragged edge of the door. Keeping a few inches off the wall, the two men positioned themselves beside the door. Music was coming from inside the flat, and they could hear a woman's voice saying something in a tone of complaint.

Luke nodded to Grizzly, who kneeled down by the door and placed the black nylon case on the floor. He opened the lid and pulled out a narrow rod covered in black plastic. He flicked a switch, and a tiny red light came on in the top of the machine inside. Grizzly pulled at the thin black rod, and a length of black wire followed it out of a coil. He flicked another switch. A tiny liquid-crystal TV screen bloomed into pale blue light on the top of the machine. The image flickered and moved a bit as Grizzly moved the black rod. It was a fiber-optic minicam with a fish-eye lens in the tip, narrow enough to slide under a door.

Luke watched the two-inch screen as Grizzly maneuvered the rod underneath the door of 9B. The screen filled up with a rat's-eye view of the interior. Grizzly could see the screen as well. He twisted the rod carefully, and the image bounced and panned around the room. The view was distorted, but they saw an expanse of bare floor, a lamp on what looked like an old crate, and a bed about fifteen feet across the room from the door. They could see a large black male lying naked on the bed, and a woman, naked as well, leaning over the man, holding him and stroking him. She was speaking softly, her voice muffled by the door, saying something about it being okay but she charged more for that. And the man's voice, also muffled, insistent and deep, demanding something the hooker found . . . unpleasant.

Grizzly twisted the rod around until they had a clear pan shot of the entire room. The layout was exactly as Chicago had described. There were only two people visible in the room, both of them on the bed. Grizzly pulled the thin black camera cable slowly out from under the door. He gave Luke a questioning look. Luke nodded. Grizzly ran his fingers delicately across the surface of the door itself, reading it. Every door had its own way. You had to know its weaknesses and strengths. Sometimes you used a ram, sometimes you blew it up with a shaped charge. Sometimes you just kicked it as hard as you could. This door was cheap particleboard, hollow in the center.

The hinges were cheap white metal. Grizzly figured they had sold the original hardwood doors back when they broke up all the rooms and turned the place into a flop-house hotel. He packed the camera away and stood up facing Luke. Time to get it done.

They had been doing this kind of thing for years, had done it as a team almost a hundred times and practiced it more than that at MOUT facilities in Quantico or down at the training center in Glynco. Grizzly had the weight, so he'd take the door. Luke had the speed, so he'd take the target. Grizzly would cover and support. Rico and Walt would block the escape and come in to mop up. If the target got his hands up and surrendered, he'd live. Most of them decided to live, especially if the Marshals came in fast enough to control the situation. Some of them went out like Delbert Sutter, but not many. It was all routine. They'd done it for years.

So why was Luke's hand shaking?

Now, as usual, his lungs were filling up with a cold fog, and he was losing sensation in random areas of his back and belly. Grizzly backed up against the far wall and faced the door of 9B. He had his favorite raid piece tonight, a Heckler & Koch MP-5K, a minisubmachine gun with a half-moon magazine holding thirty rounds of nine-milli-meter full-metal jacket.

Luke had Delbert Sutter's stainless Taurus, a kind of superstition piece for him. Out of a long-standing habit, he did a press-check on the piece, pushing the slide back slightly to confirm the presence of a round in the chamber. Fifteen in the mag and one in the chamber. He had already done this before he came up the stairs, but the action was grooved, semiconscious, perhaps even slightly magical, as if he could not be hurt as long as he did every-thing precisely the same way and in the same order as he did in every other takedown.

Grizzly focused all his attention on the doorway, getting himself together. Luke could feel the energy developing in Grizzly's massive frame. Six feet two inches and two hundred twenty pounds of federal muscle was about to collide with the door of room 9B of the Harbor Light Hotel. He knew he'd only get one chance to take it down. Miss that chance, and Olney would be spraying the whole wall with outgoing rounds. Grizzly held up his left hand and spread his fingers.

Five.

Luke looked at the luminous dial of his watch. Walt and Rico were in position. If they weren't, Rico would have clicked twice on the shortwave radio. This close in, nobody ever talked aloud or transmitted on the two-way radio. It was choreography. A dance they all knew.

Four.

Grizzly's face was bright red, the way it always got before a kick-in. His fingers were rock steady. He folded another one.

Three.

Luke took in a deep belly-breath through his nose and blew it out slowly through his open lips. Rookies always forgot to breathe. Breathing was how you maintained self-control. He relaxed his entire body for a second, pushing the tension away, slowing the adrenaline flow. If he went in with too much adrenaline, his hands would shake, throwing off his aim.

Two.

What if it isn't *him*?

If it isn't him, I won't kill him.

Fuck that.

It's him.

One.

Grizzly gave Luke a final look. He winked. Part of the

ritual. Luke felt a sudden rush of deep affection for the man.

Grizzly tensed and then—*exploded*—off the wall, a bull rush of black cloth. His face was contorted and bright red. His right boot slammed into the wooden door right next to the middle hinge-plate—the whole frame of the door burst inward—Grizzly now rebounding—clearing the door for Luke. The door itself slammed down and back, falling into the room. Before it hit the floor, Luke was racing inward—his right boot actually drove the door the last few inches of its fall. It hit with a thunderous *slam*, and a cloud of dust flew up into the air. A woman was screaming—her voice was shattering glass—Luke heard his own voice, deep but hoarse, saying *"Federal officers—freeze—federal officers!"* The man on the bed was a blur of motion—brown muscles slithered as he clutched at the naked woman. She fell backward, fell into the sights of Luke's nine-mill—Luke with his feet spread and his right arm extended, piece out and sight picture perfect. Luke saw a flash of her pale blue-veined skin—her bright-red pubic hair—breasts caught and crushed by a huge black arm, sheets piling around the two of them as the man—on his knees now—his naked body covered by the woman— lifting her up in front of him—Luke had him in his sights and was squeezing the trigger. He saw the face clearly— froze it in time—ran it—it was Elijah Olney—the make was instant and complete, and he felt his right hand closing down on the trigger even as he heard the window smashing, heard Rico's voice shouting. Elijah Olney's face was black with rage and his eyes were huge, red-rimmed— his mouth twisted in a kind of snarl of fear and anger—his eyes locked on Luke's face, and his right arm reaching under a pillow. Luke's trigger moved, and he felt the little metallic click in his palm—he had a clear shot over the woman's shoulder—Olney's right hand was still under that pillow—he was *searching* for something—*Shoot him now*—and Rico saying, *"Freeze!"* Olney's eyes flicked away from Luke, and his head moved—cleared the white naked shoulder of the girl in front of him—Luke was ten feet away—Olney's hand definitely scrabbling for something under that pillow—*Pull now*—the Taurus jumped twice in his hand—crack crack—two tiny black holes appeared in the side of Elijah Olney's cheek. Blood sprayed the wall behind his head. His head snapped around, and again his eyes locked on Luke—his hand was coming out from under the pillow. Grizzly stepped around Luke—Luke saw him moving, his MP-5K braced. Luke fired twice more—another black dot appeared in Olney's throat, and a second in his forehead—something wet and shapeless smacked against the wall behind him—he bounced against the wall—slid—the white sheets wrapped him tight as he twisted with the woman—the room was still echoing—dust motes drifted in the huge silence—a puff of breath came out of the man's lips—a little spray of red mist—and then—he simply . . . stopped . . . moving.

As if somone had hit the pause button on a video.

A profound stillness settled on the young man's body. He seemed to turn from flesh to warm stone in the space of three ragged gasps from the young white woman. They all watched it happen.

The woman's breathing was the only sound in the room. Short sharp gasping sobs. She was struggling with the dead man's arm, still pinned against his body. Blood had sprayed her right cheek and was running in little spiderweb rivulets down her breast.

Grizzly stepped over to the bed with his MP-5K extended, put out a gloved hand, and pulled the woman away. Rico stepped up to her with a gray hotel blanket and wrapped it around her. She took it and wrapped it tighter. Then she looked back at the dead man on the bed, and her face went bright scarlet. She stepped away from Rico, turned to face him, and slugged him as hard as she could on his jaw point. Rico reeled, recovered, and Grizzly stepped in between them, gathering the woman into his arms and holding her tight. She was in the white rage phase. Later, the shock would make her sleepy.

"You *assholes!*" she shrieked at them, kicking out backward at Grizzly, struggling in his arms. "You fucking *cowboys!*"

Rico's lower lip was bleeding. He raised a gloved hand, touched the lip, and looked at his fingertips. Grizzly smiled at him.

"You caught him good there, ma'am."

She twisted to look up at him.

"He deserved it."

Rico smiled at her. "Ma'am, your trick selector is outta whack. What's your name?"

She shuddered, seemed to calm herself deliberately.

"Joanna. Can I sit down? I don't feel so good."

Grizzly led her over to a chair and sat her down. Luke was looking at Elijah Olney's right arm. It was covered to the elbow by the pillow he had been lying on.

"He was reaching," said Luke.

"Yeah," said Grizzly. "I saw that. Risky shot, though."

"Yeah. It was."

Walt Rich stepped in through the shattered window and walked across the broken door toward the bed. He stood beside Grizzly and Luke and looked down at the pillow over Olney's right forearm.

"Well, somebody better lift that up," he said.

Nobody moved.

"Okay. I will." He reached down and got a handful of the pillowcase. Hesitating, he looked back over his shoulder at each one of them.

"Come on," said Grizzly. "Don't be a smart-ass."

"Okay," said Walt.

He pulled the pillow up with one rapid jerk.

There was a large stainless-steel revolver in Elijah Olney's right hand. The hammer was half-cocked, his finger still tight around the steel blade. Walt Rich reached into one of the pockets of his raid jacket and took out a Polaroid Spectra camera. He pointed it down at the dead man's right hand and snapped a shot. The flash lit the scene for a half-second, a white bloom of light that put a brief red glitter into Olney's half-open eyes. The film buzzed out, and Walt pulled it free. He handed it over to Luke. The image was still faint, a gray fog with a black shape slowly developing, a shimmer of silver light.

Rich leaned over and examined the pistol without touching it.

"It's loaded. I think it's a .357."

"That's a Dan Wesson," said Rico, still holding the young woman by the shoulders. People were gathering out in the hallway, Chicago and a couple of other older black men. The room stank of cordite and the copper reek of fresh blood.

"Yeah. Dan Wesson," said Grizzly.

"Stupid bastard," said Rico.

"That he was," said Grizzly. "He could have lived. Had to be a hard guy, didn't you, son?" There was a genuine regret in his voice. The boy was a mess now, but there was power in his muscular frame, and a kind of grim intensity surrounded him like a strange amber light. Olney had chosen to die, maybe, but it made you sad to see something that vital turned into two hundred pounds of bad meat.

"That Wesson's a nice piece," said Walt. "Zebrawood grips."

Luke slid the Taurus back into its holster and ran a hand across his chest. His right hand was vibrating, so he shoved it into his pocket.

"You okay, Luke?"

Luke shook his head, looked down at his right hand.

"No. I'm not."

"Good," said Rico Groza, watching him. "Good for you."

"Well," said Walt Rich, "somebody better call EMS."

"Yeah."

"He might be alive, right?"

"Yeah. He might."

EMS got there a short time later.

He wasn't.

0200 Hours
Saturday, January 14, 1995
U.S. Marshals Squad Room
Bronx Borough Hall
161st and Grand Concourse
The South Bronx

Detectives from the 48th Detective Area Task Force had shown up an hour after the shooting, along with a crime scene unit and a pink-skinned junior DA named Bayliss Frick.

Watching him work, Luke got the distinct impression that Frick was in a huff because he had been dragged out of a party downtown to cover the shooting board inquiry for the Bronx DA. He was still wearing his black tie and tux, and he looked half in the bag. The whole thing seemed to bore him to tears, and Luke figured he could hardly wait to get away. The two city bulls were old friends of Walt Rich's, an Asian female sergeant named Wendy Ma and a gray-bearded, overweight Gold Shield detective named Marvin Schreck.

Marvin and Wendy thought the whole thing was cut-and-dried. They walked around the scene for a while, taking shots with a cheap Kodak throwaway camera and making sick jokes about Elijah Olney's last night on earth.

The hooker, full name Joanna Gunderson, turned out to be a part-timer, a young woman who came in regularly from New Jersey to help cover the rent and to pay for her tuition at a nursing school. There were no wants or warrants against her, and she had given a statement that backed up everything the Marshals had done—with only a little coaching from Rico and Grizzly. Then a policewoman from the Four-Eight had transported her to Bronx Municipal for a medical exam and some mild sedatives. On her way out she had apologized to Rico for punching him. She gave him a business card with a little gold angel on it. Grizzly watched Rico put the card in his raid jacket and grinned at him.

Bayliss Frick had slipped on a pair of circular wire-frame glasses and read the preliminary witness statement out loud. Then he sighed theatrically and folded it into his tuxedo pocket, telling the two NYPD detectives to have a full report on his desk by noon. He marched out into the hall, glared at Chicago and his friends, and commandeered a ride with a 48th patrol unit all the way back to his party at the South Street Seaport.

Some medics from the local EMS unit had arrived and pronounced Elijah Olney dead. The M.E. showed up about a half-hour later to confirm it and to sign off for the body removal guys from the city morgue. The crime scene team fussed and fiddled and made chalk lines and strung cord to indicate the paths of all four rounds that Luke had fired into Elijah Olney.

Rico called Fiertag's number and got his voice mail. He read out a brief but accurate description of the Elijah Olney takedown and left his pager number. They all went down the front stairs of the Harbor Light, stopping on the way to apologize to the manager.

"Who's going to pay for the damage?" Chicago wanted to know.

Rico Groza gave the man a business card. "The federal government will. The city guys will finish up in a bit. They'll tape the scene and release it to you by the end of the weekend. We're sorry about the door and the window. If you get an estimate, send it to this address, and we'll see that you get a check. Is that okay?"

Chicago looked down at the card.

"U.S. Marshals, eh? Like Matt Dillon?"

"Yeah," said Rico, around his swollen lip.

"Well, I hope you're all okay?" The old man was looking at Luke, who stood apart, his face lined and slack, his body loose and boneless.

"We are, sir. Thank you for asking," said Grizzly. "Come on, Luke, let's go." He took Luke by the right arm and walked him outside and through the crowd gathered on the sidewalk, the buzzing crackle of radio transmissions. The crowd parted for the two of them, whispering, and closed up again, watching the cops and the coroner's people with blank avid faces caught in the cycling flicker of hectic blue lights.

Grizzly drove Luke back to their office to write the whole thing up while Rico and Walt Rich took Bubblegum back to his apartment. The two detectives from the 48th came along with Luke and Grizzly, partly to wrap up the inquiry and partly to share some of the single-malt scotch that Grizzly was known to keep inside a gun locker in the squadroom kitchen.

At this time of night the big squad room was deserted, the lights low, all the desks littered with report sheets and arrest files. The corrections guys were all off duty or out in the streets looking for parole violators and probationers on a spree. The greasy yellow-stained windows of the squad room gave them a long plain-of-stars view of the apartments and tenements of the South Bronx, the bulky black outline of the Bronx Museum, and the lights of midtown away in the misty distance. Rose-colored clouds were drifting over the rooftops, and the distant bridges looked like chains of fiery light. A graveyard wind was blowing through the only window that wasn't painted shut. Luke went over to sit on the ledge beside it. He needed some fresh air, or what passed for it in the Bronx. He felt sick and weak, a natural reaction but stronger than usual this time.

Marvin and Grizzly went off down the hall looking for a water cooler with something other than dead bugs in it. Sergeant Ma came over to Luke and looked down at him. Luke was sitting on the edge of the window and sipping cold coffee out of a Thermos cap. He smiled up at her.

Wendy Ma was a butternut-and-cream Asian woman with a bell of glimmering black hair and wide almond-shaped eyes. She was wearing a blue blazer and a matching blue skirt and a scarlet blouse. Despite the late hour there was a trace of scent still on her, Opium or something like that, a spicy scent. She brushed some dust and wood chips off the shoulder of his raid jacket.

"You look a little rough, Luke."

"Yeah. Well, you don't."

"No?" She rolled her head, easing a stiff neck. Luke watched her hair, saw the reflection of the yellow city lights flickering through the shiny blackness of her hair, the pale cream of her skin, a touch of pale rose on her cheeks. Suddenly he felt a powerful emotion sweep through him, and a profound sense of loneliness. His apartment on Court Street would be just the same as it had been when he walked out of it this morning, three rooms full of throwaway furniture, a desk with a computer and a scattering of disks, and his bedroom, somehow the ground zero of emptiness in his life, with the photographs of his ex-wife and her boy, a desert landscape he had taken on a trip to Zion Canyon in southern Utah about a thousand years ago, a few framed citations from various federal attorneys, and a photo of himself with Doc Hollenbeck, Doc's big black face shining with life, champagne glasses in their hands, and in the background the dark wood walls and the brass lamps of Paddy Riley's bar in Georgetown. He thought all of this through while he looked up at Wendy Ma and watched her rubbing her neck. It was a life in four seconds, and that made him even sadder.

"Wendy . . ."

She smiled at him, her face softening, her hand still on his shoulder. Luke didn't know her well, knew that she was married but separated, that her husband was in computers, had bailed out on her a year back, reasons vague. She had two departmental citations for bravery and played the piano. That was it.

Wendy's face grew solemn. They heard Grizzly and Marvin coming back up the hall, Grizzly saying something about a cop named Big Bear and this thing that had happened up on Gun Hill Road.

"You want to go, Luke?" she said.

"Yeah," said Luke. "I do."

"Sufficient unto the day is the evil thereof, Luke."

Wendy's eyes were bright, and there was a hint of violet light deep inside them. This was just a survival reaction, right? A post-trauma surge of instinct. Perhaps. It was also true that people who thought like that usually died alone in a senior citizen's flat surrounded by pictures of other dead people and only mourned by a couple of overpriced tropical fish in a bowl by the window. This is a gift, Luke. Say thank you and accept it.

"What does that mean?" he asked.

"I'll tell you later."

Luke lay awake in the breathing darkness of his Court Street apartment, listening to a CD of Tom Waits—"Jersey Girl"—and staring up at the light from the streetlamps that lay on his ceiling, at the black tracery of tree shadows moving inside the soft silvery light. A big eighteen-wheeler was grinding up through the gears on the Gowanus Expressway, a faraway booming roar that reminded Luke of the sound of the trucks on Interstate 15 back in Utah. Provo memories washed over him again, and he was comforted by the weight and reality of the woman beside him. Wendy stirred, sighed, and rolled over to touch him, put her soft hand on his chest.

"You awake?"

She groaned a little and moved again.

"I'm a little hung over, actually. Do you have any Tylenol?"

"Sure," he said, and rolled away to get it.

She put out a hand and stopped him. "In a minute. Can you do me a favor?"

"Sure." He looked down at her. Her face was hidden in the dark, but a shaft of light lay on her shoulder like a dusting of fine white sand. Her voice came out of the shadows, a soft burring sound.

"It's a little goofy."

"Name it." He reached out and ran a fingertip across her cheek. It came away wet. He rolled back into the bed and lifted the sheet up, pulling her to him, wrapping his arm around her shoulders and turning her so her face was on his chest, her body against his.

"What?" he said, anxiety in his voice. "What can I do?"

"You're doing it," she said.

He tightened his arm around her. A few minutes passed in the kind of easy silence that can sometimes blossom between two people, a shared stillness.

"I don't usually—" said Luke, after a time.

She lifted a hand, put a finger on his upper lip.

"I know. This was a bad day for both of us, I guess."

"Not the last part."

She pulled herself a little closer to him, moved her leg to rest across his belly and hips.

"You working tomorrow? Today, I mean?"

"Yeah. We're going out after a couple of bank robbers. They hit a bank in Newark on Tuesday."

"The one where the guy shot himself?"

"Yeah. Pigeye Quail."

"Good luck with him."

"Yeah. Thanks."

She buried her face in the curve of his neck and shoulder, breathed out again, a little shake in her voice. Her belly was soft and warm against his hip, her leg a comforting pressure on his stomach. He felt sleep coming over him, a slow incoming tide, a gentle weight on his eyes and his chest. Wendy's voice was muffled, her breath warm and moist on his neck.

"I saw a little girl today. She had on a little schoolgirl skirt, you know? Plaid? With kneesocks?"

"A uniform?"

"Sort of. Somebody had split her head open."

Luke closed his eyes.

"There was another kid, a boy. Hardly looked old enough for high school. He was cut up too."

"Dead?"

"Both."

"What was this? That drug thing in Hunts Point?"

"We don't know if it was drugs. It was at a storage and delivery place on Timpson. La Luna Negra. At 144th there? Down from St. Mary's Park?"

"Yeah, I know it. Isn't that a Four-One thing?"

"We're on the task force. Jerry Boynton wants it, but he's on Robbery detail, so the lieutenant sent us down to help him out. The owner of the place is missing too."

"I know Jerry. He's a good guy. I heard there was a cop down."

Wendy moved away, sat up in the bed, and fumbled on the side table for Luke's cigarettes. Luke reached over her and picked them up along with his lighter. He lit her cigarette and saw by the sudden flare the shining lines of tears on her skin.

"Brian Crewes."

"Crewcut? Looks like a Marine? Keeps himself real neat? *He's* down?"

"His skull is cracked. He's in surgery—*was* in surgery. Stupid, really. Just waltzed into the place, didn't wait for cover. He's at Bronx Municipal. Jerry waited, said he was going to be okay, but they have him sedated, and they've given him something to keep the pressure down inside his head."

"He see who did him?"

"Not yet. The doctors don't want him worked up."

"Any witnesses?"

"Jerry has a witness, but the witness won't talk."

Luke felt a short sharp surge of anger, a red flicker like a hot wire in his head. "So make him."

Wendy looked at Luke, her eyes shining and her makeup like a bruise around her eyes. "We can't. He's in the hospital too."

"Man. Who *was* this guy? Godzilla?"

She shook her head, rubbed her wrist across her eyes, and drew on the cigarette again, pulling the sheet up around her breasts. As she spoke, the smoke trailed out from her lips and coiled, snakelike, in the light from the window. Her face was troubled.

"He didn't do it. The witness was locked up in the back seat of Brian's cruiser. Brian was taking him to Spofford. It seems the guy said something smart, and Brian—"

Luke got it all in a full-bore cop gestalt. The witness got thumped out for pissing off Crewes, and now he was holding out for all he could get. Snitches. Luke was finding it harder and harder to put up with the whole ugly board game. He lay back on the bed and rested his hand on Wendy's back. Sighing, she turned and came back to him, lying across his chest, her face hidden by her hair. Luke knew what she was thinking about.

"I guess you hadda go to the autopsy?"

Wendy moaned and burrowed into his shoulder a little more.

"Oh yes. Two for the price of one. It was swell."

Luke could see it. He'd been to a few himself. The hard white lights, the steel trays, and the body laid out, splayed out, the pathologists leaning over it with green rubber gloves and bright red blood all over their aprons, the dead body opened up like a terrible gift, the light shining on the slippery surfaces, the pinks and the grays and the purples, that rotting fruit–wet stone smell that stayed with you for days.

"They come up with anything?"

She lifted her head and kissed him softly on the lips, and then again, with a developing intensity that moved him.

"I don't really want to talk about it right now. It was sick. The guy was sick. I hope somebody kills him soon. I'd kill him if I could catch him. Kill him with his own little toy. Hack his hands off, for a start. Sufficient unto the day, Luke."

"What little toy?"

"The M.E. made the weapon. It matched a homicide they caught in the Ninth last week."

"What was it?"

She put her head back down on his chest.

"A tomahawk. Can you believe it?"

She lifted her head, feeling the tremor run through his body, an electric jolt, and the change in his breathing.

"A tomahawk?" said Luke. "Like they used in Vietnam?"

She stared at him. "Yes. It was a Special Forces weapon. They had a picture of it. In a mail-order catalog. Luke? You're scaring me. Luke?"

But Luke wasn't really there. He was in Washington, D.C., leaning on the windowframe of a Georgetown flat and watching a young woman brush her hair in the window of an apartment across the yard. It was May of last year, the famous cherry blossoms had come and gone, it was Saturday night, and Luke was waiting for a call. That call had changed everything for him. Now he heard Wendy's voice, heard the tone of it, and pulled himself back. He kissed her cheek and stroked her hair.

"This means something to you, doesn't it?"

"Yes," he said, and kissed her again, breathing her in, his hands on her satin skin, her hair falling across the back of his hands like cool well water.

"Am I going to hear why?"

"Yes," he said, after a long silence.

"Good," she said, sitting up. "I need to hear it. But right now, do me a favor?"

"Yeah, of course. What?"

"Get me that Tylenol?"

BOOK TWO

FINKS

The whole thing started small, the way the real ugly things always do, on a Saturday night eight months earlier, in Washington, D.C. Luke was in his apartment, listening to the sound of cars piling up along Wisconsin, and music coming from the bars and bistros, all the college kids and tourists out for a stroll in Georgetown, baggy-pants gangbangers rubbing attitudes with college kids and hippies and D.C. bagmen. Everyone was moving up and down the long brightly lit streets, in and out of the bars and the record stores and the restaurants. The cops cruised by with their faces blank and bored, and the local gang kids gathered in doorways to work out a plan, pick out a vic, make their names on this warm spring night in America.

Luke could see several of the major Washington landmarks from the leaded-glass bay window in his front room, see them even at night, see the red lights blinking on the white pyramid crest of the Washington Monument, the jets circling it as they floated down into National Airport, choppers drifting through the airspace with their running lights burning in the night sky around the monument like sparks flickering off a torch. There was the Lincoln Memorial at the end of the Arlington Bridge, and if he leaned way out and looked to the right, he could see the tip of the Capitol dome, the golden figure of Nike or Venus or some antique babe riding it like a bareback circus rider on a huge white horse, and through the masses of trees, he could see the shimmering surfaces of tide pools and river bends dusted with starlight and moonlight. It was dreamy, unreal, slightly hallucinatory, and impossibly beautiful, with white marble tombs and cool lawns and twisted oak trees six hundred years old, grim tangles of bronze and iron statuary, and past the Capitol dome literally hundreds of massed rectangular temples receding into a deepening twilight haze under an arc of bright cold stars. Looking at all that republican tranquillity, you could almost forget the gunfire and sirens coming from the permanent street war going on down in the Southeast, where the gangbangers and drug dealers were doing all they could to push the murder rate skyward again this year.

In the U.S. Marshals Service, D.C. was a destination town, the place where you tried to end up after putting in your years in Court Security, Prisoner Transport, Warrant Enforcement, or even Missile Escort. Luke Zitto had put in his time in various combined-agency fugitive pursuit operations for the Marshals Service, in between regular daily fugitive investigations in New York State, Michigan, and Indiana.

Before that, he had six years in Prisoner Transport and seven in Witness Protection. At forty-nine, his knees were shot and his eyes were going, and he'd killed seven men in the line of duty since he left Columbus, Ohio, twenty-two years ago.

Now he was assigned full time to the USMS Arlington HQ, a move he felt was related to his performance in the last big combined-force takedown operation, called Sunrise. In particular, he was being rewarded for his successful pursuit and takedown of Delbert Sutter. This was his final career shift.

Or so he hoped.

The time had come to back off, accept a desk pretty soon, maybe even find a woman who could stand him and try for a normal life. Buy a house in Adams Morgan like Doc Hollenbeck, get himself a Weber barbecue and a stupid chef hat, an apron with a snappy saying on it. Have all his friends over, as soon as he could find some.

That was the plan anyway.

On this particular Saturday evening, Luke was pacing in his front room with a fire glimmering in the background, wondering when Doc Hollenbeck was going to call. *If* Doc was going to call. Doc was in Fugitive Operations too, another aging chaser with the Marshals Service. Doc was supposed to have something for Luke that night, a lead on an old target from Brooklyn.

The room he was pacing in was a nice room, part of a three-room apartment with a wood-burning marble fireplace, and old oak paneling that glowed like a horse's hide at sunset. Heavy beams ran across the low white stucco ceiling. The floor was oak-and-dowel boarding, maybe a hundred years old and put down by someone who knew what he was doing. It was worn and creaking, and someone had put Oriental carpets all over the place, complicated designs that looked Moorish, in tones of deep red, pale blue, and amber.

The bedroom was furnished in heavy wood pieces, possibly solid mahogany. The carpet was deep and pale green, also brand new. The bathroom was black and white marble, with an old lion's-paw tub. The kitchen was small but bright, with a microwave and a new fridge and even a dishwasher, although Luke never cooked, so there wouldn't be much to wash. Maybe a shot glass and an ashtray.

Compared to his last place, the apartment was a palace. In the civil service you could tell how you were doing by how well they set you up. By service standards, this was a prime apartment. It looked as if it might have belonged to a professor at Georgetown, although in D.C. you could never tell; every apartment had history. The last guy who lived here might have been anything from a Clinton staffer to a black ops merc waiting for a mission from the DIA. Luke was getting it subsidized by the service, until he could get a place of his own, get it furnished. He'd left most of his things back in his place on Court Street, stuff that could only be improved by an arsonist.

It was close to ten. He was leaning against the windowframe, and he tugged out a cigarette and lit it with a kitchen match. Exhaling, he saw motion in a window across the yard, half-hidden through the branches of an old oak. An overhead light came on, a fluorescent softened by a curtain made of gauze or lace. A young woman was brushing her hair, facing what was probably the mirror over the bathroom sink. She was wearing a flower-print dress. Her hair was shoulder length, blue-black and shining. The brush moved through her hair slowly, trailing a shimmer that looked like a lake seen through trees at night. Luke watched her for a while.

She was lovely, young, and completely out of his reach. She put down the brush and leaned forward to do something to her lips. Saturday night. A Saturday night date. Part of the normal world. Thirty years ago she might have been any one of the young girls in his life, classmates in Columbus, friends of the family, people in a life as remote and lost to him as this perfect young woman across the yard, half-hidden by the night, half-revealed by the chilly blue light over the bathroom mirror. In a different life she might have been dressing for him. She ran her hands down her dress, smoothing the fabric over her breasts. Luke turned away.

His pager started to thrum silently against his waist.

He plucked it off his belt and looked at the numbers on the LED panel. He walked across the room to the phone and dialed an Arlington number.

"Ops. Brewer."

"Norm, is Doc there?"

"Yeah. Just a sec—"

Luke could hear voices, chairs moving. Some jazz from the radio on the counter by the coffee machine.

"Luke?"

"Yeah. I just got your page. I thought you were home tonight."

"So did I. Where are you?"

"Georgetown."

"What, at Paddy Riley's?"

"No. Home. What's up?"

"Okay, you put it around last week, you got a special interest?"

"Yeah, I did."

"It's not on the hit list, Luke. This is just between us."

"Between you, me, and every cop in the Northeast. Has somebody got a line on him?"

"Maybe. You know a fink named—"

"Maybe we should talk about this in person. Meet me halfway."

"Don't be paranoid, Luke. This isn't WITSEC. It's just a fink. Anyway, this is a land line."

"It's a service line, isn't it? You're in Arlington, right?"

Doc's slow laugh was more like a low growl. Every time Luke heard it, he thought of Muddy Waters.

"Luke, Luke, Luke . . . you lose one fink, you turn into

Lamont Cranston. Wait till you've lost as many as I have. You get used to it. Finks are like Kleenex. They pop up, you blow 'em off and toss 'em."

"You never had to use a claw hammer to get one of your finks off a bathroom wall. Gimme ten minutes, I'll meet you at the Lincoln end of the pool."

"Okay. I'll be the guy with a red rose in his teeth."

"Funny."

"One thing. Wear a vest, okay?"

Luke was silent for a second, reacting.

"Yeah. Ten minutes."

"Ten." The line clicked dead.

Luke went into the bedroom and took off his plaid shirt. He opened the bottom drawer of the big dresser and lifted out a Kevlar vest. He strapped it on over a white T-shirt. As he did, he looked down at the ceramic trauma plate in the drawer. What was it, seventy degrees outside? The vest was heavy enough without the trauma plate. Margot always used to say he didn't need a trauma plate anyway because he was hollow inside.

Margot. She had a tongue sharp as a dental pick. And she knew just where to stick you. That last year in Provo, she got so she could literally take his breath away with the meanness of some comment. Well, here's to you, Mrs. Calabash, wherever you are. If I get popped tonight, maybe you'll hear about it, it'll give you a smile.

He buttoned up the shirt, tucked it in, and unlocked the gun vault bolted to the floor beside the dresser, another indication of the usual profession of tenants in this apartment.

Delbert Sutter's stainless-steel Taurus nine-mill was bolted to the frame, a boltlock fitted to the trigger, next to his service Colt. He had kept the Taurus, requisitioning it from Evidence after the shooting board was over. It was hard to say why. Maybe it had to do with winning the trophies of your enemy. Whatever, it was his now, and Delbert Sutter was flat on his back in a pine box, staring up forever at a perfect blackness. Bye-bye.

Next to the Taurus was a box of semiwadcutters and two spare mags. His Toshiba laptop. His cuffs in a black leather belt-case, two speedloaders for the Colt. His field radio on a charger. All his worldly possessions.

He unlocked the Taurus, slipped the Bianchi holster into his belt, pulled the slide on the Taurus, thumbed the lock, shoved in a full fifteen-round magazine. Then he flicked the lock, and the slide rammed home, scooping up a round. He set the thumb safety and shoved the weapon into his holster. He strapped the cuffs on in the small of his back, where he could reach them with either hand. Academy training.

His motions were silent and automatic, his face set and blank. He looked at himself in the mirror over the dresser, saw a tall lean man in jeans and a bulky plaid shirt, a seamed Italian face with a salt-and-pepper mustache, short black hair with gray at the temples.

Law. No mistaking him for anything else. He might as well wear a beanie with a sign that said PIG UNDERNEATH THIS HAT. He rifled through the clothes in the closet, found a pale tan windbreaker, and put it on. He looked around the bedroom, figured it was neat enough if anything terminal happened.

Then he walked out into the front room and looked at it as well, got his cigarettes and a pack of wooden matches from the ledge by the bay window. The window across the yard was dark. He stepped to the door, tugged it open, and walked out into the Georgetown evening.

There was a definite Saturday-night-in-the-spring hum in the air. Noise and lights and crowd chatter drifted up from Wisconsin, and he could see the crowds milling past under the bright lights. Above him shreds of cloud flew by on a jet stream. Past the clouds the twilight sky was turquoise and navy blue. Pinprick stars glittered like broken glass.

His service car was a dark blue 1989 Crown Victoria with heavily tinted windows. It carried Maryland plates registered to a leasing company in Chevy Chase. The leasing company was a service cutoff, although most law enforcement agencies in the region knew about it. It was designed to keep civilians from running up a database of government vehicles. So was Luke's Georgetown residence. There were criminals in town who did nothing but sit in vans outside government buildings and videotape agents and sell the IDs to local gangs. Luke was a chaser and only went into the Arlington HQ on a limited basis. His face was still unknown to most of the local hardguys, and he wanted to keep it that way as long as he could. At least until he got a desk job and could afford to ease up, lose some of that street paranoia.

The car was parked under a low yellow streetlamp at the bottom of the walk. Party noises were coming from the apartment above him, voices and music from the open windows. A pair of professors from the university lived there, two guys in their late fifties. A lifelong couple, so the landlady told him. Luke had seen them around, shopping, said hello on the steps from time to time. Tough-looking guy in marathon condition, and a puffy character with hair like cotton candy and a bright red face. Amiable. Seemed like nice guys. They thought he was somebody federal. Hell, around here, who wasn't?

Luke used his GS 11 dashboard permit to park the Ford by the curb on Henry Bacon. The Potomac was a broad ribbon of hammered tin at his back, lined with dark timber on the Virginia shore. The parkway was crowded with a Saturday night parade of Cherokees and Audis and Bimmers going everywhere but home for supper. The air was cooler down here by the river, and a soft wind rustled the new leaves in the cherry trees and oaks along the waterway.

He set the lo-jack system and the fuel cutoff, locked the car, and walked away toward the Lincoln Memorial, a massive white stone box set atop a pyramid of marble steps. He could see Doc's huge black shape halfway up the stairs. Doc lifted a hand and set it back on his thigh. Luke climbed the steps two at a time and sat down beside Doc, looking out across the Mall toward Foggy Bottom.

"Luke. You look tired."

"Maybe I am. I'm not sleeping well. I think I actually

miss New York. You've been there, right? Couple years back?"

"Yeah. I was at John Jay for that interagency course. Security of evidence. I saw you there, with that big blond babe—a real killer. What was her name?"

"Aurora. Aurora Powys."

"Pow-iss?"

"Yeah. She's a Marshal too. In Prisoner Transport."

"You still seeing her?"

"I wasn't seeing her then. She's married to a lawyer. Has a kid."

"Nothing to you, hah?"

"Let's move on, okay?"

Doc nodded, offered Luke a bite of his pizza wedge. Doc Hollenbeck had that rare blue-black color that some Africans have, like burnished bronze, and his eyes were an odd gray-green. His massive head was shaved bald, and he was running just a bit to fat, like so many middle-aged men in the law. His smile was fleeting but bright. He smelled of Old Spice and cigar smoke. Luke didn't know him well. They'd just met a few days ago, when Luke had been taken around the Fugitive Ops room at 600 Army Navy.

"How they hanging?"

"Tighter since you said to wear a vest. What have we got?"

Doc made a bit of a production out of finding, stripping, and firing up a Muriel cigar. When he had the tip glowing like a firefly, he leaned back against the step, exhaled, and grinned a wide grin at Luke.

"I meant what I said about finks, you know. I mean, it was tough what happened to your guy. But that's the business we're in, right? Shit happens. You can't take it personal. It's not like he was on the job."

Luke closed his eyes for a second and had a very vivid

flash of the last time he'd seen Bruno Folinari thoroughly alive, waving at him from across Mott Street on the Lower East Side of Manhattan, big grin for the ladies on the sidewalk, climbing into a rusted-out Seville with two guys in the front seat, Bruno's skinny body looking birdlike in a pale yellow bell-bottomed suit, gold chains around his neck, high-top black boots with zippers down the sides.

"No, Doc. You're right. It's not like he was on the job."

"Gotta roll with the punches."

"Roll with the punches. So . . . ?"

"So, I gotta fink says—"

"He listed?"

"No. I don't list my finks. I list the useless ones, but not the good ones. No point letting some rear-echelon mope screw up your connections. I always tag some finks for the computer, but they're mainly drones. You?"

"I tag a few. Depends on how much they're running. You can't push too much through cash disbursements. If your fink's gonna get into real numbers, you have to list him. They get greedier every year. You know that."

"Tell me about it. I paid out a fink last March—in cash—fifty-six thousand dollars. You know what I make, Luke?"

"You're on the grid. What, you're GS 12? Plus overtime?"

"Yeah. I make $42,800 a year. Plus a car allowance. That little shit got ten G's more than I make, just for ratting out a bunch of Russian gunrunners for the FBI."

"I know that case. Was he yours?"

"Partly. I found out we were sharing him. My part was to pay him off and get him into WITSEC."

"I hear Justice averages ninety million a year in fink payouts," said Luke.

"I heard more. Here in D.C., finks are the main game. I try to make sure a fink of mine isn't working both sides of the street, me against some FBI or DEA guy. I try to keep them to myself as long as I can. Know what I've been hearing—not from our guys but from some sources? Guys who really want to cover a fink? Sometimes they run him as a line item in somebody else's file. Some other fink, I mean. Say the company wants you to pony up for Fink One. You got your expense sheet, down there on line seven, where it says Incidentals, you deduct the max, keep it in another file, pay Fink Two with it when it gets large enough. That way there's no paper on him, and you know he's solid. You know he's not double-booked, running for someone else too."

Luke stared at Doc. "That's a damn dangerous way to run a fink. You tell your sources, they get caught at that, they'll wish they'd never been hired."

Doc nodded. "Maybe. But damn, I'm getting real sick of finks who work two, three agencies. Only you don't *know* he's got an agenda, got obligations to the FBI or whoever for some operation you know dick about. So you can't blame guys who cover theirs as long as they can. Or can you?"

"Sounds like a good way to get popped for falsification. It could look like embezzlement. How would you prove the funds went to Fink Two?"

"He signs for it, just like they all do."

"But the guy doesn't log the chit?"

"No. Not until he has to."

"Man. That's too hairy for me, Doc. Lose those chits, and your operator is under a federal investigation, and some stringer for the *Post* is stuffing a hi-fi transmitter up his dog's butt."

"You never do that in the Bronx?"

"Not like that. You always been in D.C., in Fugitive Ops?"

"No. I was in Asset Seizure, in Kansas City. Got transferred two years ago. It's not too bad, if you stay away from the top floor, don't mess with the brass, and don't play golf with the suits."

Luke nodded, lit up a cigarette, drew it in deep, and felt his pulse kicking over quietly, a tiny rumble-pop in his neck. He blew out a stream and settled forward, leaning his elbows on his knees.

"So, my guy?"

Doc came back forward, set his hands on his knees, blew out a long breath. "Okay. Rona, Paolo Coimbra. DOB one May 1961. Also known as Quarco, Q, Roderigo Gardena, a string of aliases. Albany warrant, suspicion murder, a payment dispute. Mainly a forger, supplies bogus ID to wiseguys and gangbangers. Man, he's only thirty-three!"

"Started young, up in Hunts Point."

"Yeah? Middleman for counterfeit documents—isn't this a Treasury thing?"

"They want him. So do I, and he's a federal escapee."

"Anyway, a forger. But flexible. Also into multiple serial rapes, felony assault, unlawful confinement, sexual assault female corrections officer, escape custody—we know the corrections chick, don't we?"

"We know her."

Luke closed his jaw on the sentence and held it shut, waiting for Doc to say something, to bring up her name again. Down on the Mall, a gaggle of black kids had come out of the hollow near the Vietnam Memorial and were heading toward the Lincoln Memorial. One thing sure, they weren't tourists. Bulls jackets, Hoyas caps on sideways, those stupid clown-baggy pajama pants, oversize sneakers. They looked like a pile of laundry with ten legs. Luke and Doc could hear them talking from a hundred feet away.

Doc watched the kids. "Man, I hate gangbangers. They

depress the shit outta me. This why we fought for civil rights? So black teenagers can walk around armed to the nuts and dressed up like Emmett Kelly? This a personal thing, Luke?"

"Against policy, Doc. You know that."

Doc studied Luke's face for a while, considered his beak-nosed profile and the seamed skin of his cheek, the hooded eyes as Luke stared down the steps at the gang-bangers. It was clear to both men that Luke was evading the issue, and that Doc was going to let him.

"Okay . . . let's see . . . Jeez, sodomy, that still a crime?"

"It's the way he does it."

"Ouch—well, it goes on. Man, I *love* this. In Sing-Sing he took courses in computer graphics and offset printing! Courtesy of New York State. They goddamn *trained* him, the silly bastards!"

"Cons can take karate lessons, lift weights, get a law degree. I've seen them angle for certain prisons—they like the library or the gym better. I quit trying to make sense of all that shit a long time ago. Some writer I once read said he figured the trouble with humans was we were smart enough to think up civilization but not smart enough to run it right. There you go."

"Yeah, there you go. Anyway, I guess you know his sheet."

"Right."

"So we have something, I think. I got a guy, he's from Haiti, name of Celandre Marcuse—"

"What?"

"See-lan-*dray*. It's French. He's been one of my finks for two years. I got him from a guy in Drug Enforcement, had used him up in a Haitian thing but didn't want to cut him loose. The guy has dependents now, and his only thing these last three years is professional informant."

"He a posse guy? Or a Crip, a Blood?"

"No. Those mutts don't last. They have no self-control. No manners. Say one thing on Tuesday, forget it by Wednesday. Rat you out by Friday lunch. Dead by Sunday midnight. I never take them on. This guy, we set him up in a gypsy cab—"

"A gypsy cab! On whose ticket?"

"Us—we went for it. Fugitive Ops."

"We *paid* for this guy's cab?"

"Paid for it, hell, I picked it out! I like this guy, he's a stand-up. For a fink. He keeps his word. I figure he wasn't born here, hasn't been infected with the American work ethic."

"I thought finks were like Kleenex."

Doc's smile was thin.

"They are. Don't misunderstand me here. I see to it this guy gets his cab, I see to it he keeps it. Everything he has, I gave him. His girlfriend, his walk-up on K Street. The Mickey Dee's he scarfs every Friday night. I say 'Celandre—have a heart attack,' he says, 'Which ventricle?' He belongs to me."

Down in the Mall the black kids had gathered together in a tight knot, and now and then they'd look up the stairs toward Luke and Doc. Man, no one could be *that* stupid.

"And?"

Doc took the hint.

"And last Wednesday night, maybe nine o'clock, he picks up a hooker outside the Zanzibar. That's a flop on K Street Southeast, near the navy yards. This young girl, she's a wreck. Bleeding so bad, my guy doesn't want to let her in the cab, right?"

Doc fell silent as the crowd of young black males started to work their way up the steps of the memorial, looking casual, looking like a mugging about to happen. Maybe they *were* that stupid.

"I see them," Luke said. "So what happened?"

Doc was silent for another moment, his broad black face hardening as he watched the group come up the steps, talking loud, shoving each other, but always coming up.

"Rough trick. Looked like a kind of Hispanic yuppie, clean cut, dressed okay. But a mean streak. While he's doing it, this hooker gets a look at his right leg."

"Front of his thigh? The right thigh?"

"Bingo. Burn scar, inches around, shaped like a Q."

Now the kids were less than twenty feet down the steps. Three of them took an angle on Luke and Doc, while the other two checked out the other tourists and then came up toward the two men. Luke sighed, and Doc shook his head slowly.

"Man. And on the steps of the Lincoln Memorial too."

aolo Rona, a.k.a. Roderigo Gardena, set his Glock off
to one side, not too far, tuned his scanner to the
Southeast D.C. cop frequency, and spread his papers
out on the table, fanning them out like a poker hand,
twisting the lamp around to get a good look. He dumped
out the paper bag, spilling the contents across the surface.
Latex gloves, onion paper, a cutting knife with extra
blades, rubber cutting board, tape, spray glue. A clear plastic ruler. Several sheets of Letraset in Arial, small-point
type, a variety. Even a loupe for looking at slides. The
scanner started to pop and crackle with the usual cross-
talk. He butted his cigarette and put the pack and the
matches to one side, listening to a burst of static, a whole
lot of cars trying to report at once. Then the dispatcher's
voice cut in hard.

"Okay, 294. Go for your transmission."

*"Okay—you been told. Homicide at 1369 Stevens
Road—"*

"You want units for crowd control?"

"one seven one three and 1903?"

"I copy 188 responding to that location."

"Can we have a time-code on that?"

"Twenty-two-fifty-seven hours."

"Ten-four radio."

"Captain Wiseman, you on the air?"

"Copy direct."

"We got Vernon Jones and Redrum on the way in."

Boys with guns. Todovia bang-bang.

Well, man, this was sure the neighborhood for it. Coming from the Bronx, Paolo was used to crowded blocks full of red-brick and brownstone tumbledowns, and rows and rows of stoops and doorways, every one of them filled with teens going nowhere and kids racing around screaming and yelling. But here in Southeast D.C. it was different, the threat level was higher. It had the same ratty buildings as the Bronx, bars and bodegas on every other corner, smokeshops as fronts for dealers, crackhouses three to a block, burned-out cars at the curb, cars being stripped and torched in the alleys. Every third streetlamp shot out for fun, no light bulbs in any of the halls. But back in the Bronx you knew that some people carried. If you were in business, you carried a piece. If you were just a kid, maybe you knew where you could borrow one. But here in D.C. everybody in the hood had some kind of piece. Tec Nines and Uzis, Colts, Llamas, Astras, Smith nine-mills, Berettas, even M-16s and AK 47s.

Out on K Street the clockers were hanging on the stoops, and cars were rolling up the lane, pipes burbling. They sounded like bulls in a chute, waiting for the corrida, butting and honking. A blanket of stale dead air lay on the neighborhood, heat rising up into the flats and tenements and driving the people out onto the steps. The night sky was amber and smoky.

Paolo heard voices floating in from the street, shouts, people laughing, kids bullshitting each other, that *negrito* trash talk. Deals going down, crack and blow and ice. Ritalin. Valium. Crystal meth. Like a market square in the barrio, only you couldn't get no mangoes.

And man those people liked to talk. Talk was their main thing. Talk and *las enervantes*. As if the world was safe enough, you could afford to fog your brain up with that shit. Coffee was Paolo's drug. And beer, but not too much of either. *Pisto malo*, that was his code. And *la chiva*, the heroin, you could save that for the walking dead around here.

Through the cardboard walls of the flop, Paolo could hear somebody else's television, hear Barbara Walters and Hugh Downs talking, Barbara saying "We're in touch so you be in touch," and then the newsbreak music. Under that there was some rap coming from down the hall on the other side. Loud. If they kept up that shit, he was gonna go over there, put an end to it.

He wiped a hand across his face. It came away wet and shiny, streaking the dirt on his palm. He reached for his beer and pulled at it, feeling it burn the back of his throat. His throat had been sore for over a month now, and there seemed to be something blocking it, as if some food was stuck there. It hurt now and then, but it wasn't so bad a few Darvon couldn't cover it. If he had any, which he didn't right now.

He pulled in a breath and smelled a number of things, most of them pretty bad. Stale air. Gasoline. Old pizza. Piss from the *orinal*. He needed a bath, for one thing. He was a guy, liked to keep himself clean. Not like these *marranos negros* down here.

Up in Hunts Point, people kept themselves clean, no matter how bad it got. His people had some pride. Roses in the gardens. Kids down in the street, music coming from the windows. Arboleta Arboleta. Guitars. Brown-eyed little boys, they looked like little antelopes. ¿Cómo si dice en inglés? Gazelles, like in those TV shows about Africa.

Out of the corner of his eye he saw motion. Down by the baseboard under the combination sink and toilet there was a gray shape. Paolo had spotted the hole almost as soon as he came in here, figured it for a rathole. He tried stuffing it up with tin foil, but the next day it was all shredded up, spread around, and something had been at his stuff on the bed. Looking at the size of it, Paolo figured it was too big for a mouse. This was a rat. He'd get it soon. Business first.

He looked back at the cards and licenses in front of him. Three different ATM cards—a Key Bank, a First National, and one for Maryland State. The American Express. And la prima, a Virginia driver's license—blank, complete with iron-on laminate cover. And better still, a color photo of his client, passport-sized. The guy had taken it at the photo booth by Eastern Market. Paolo had checked out the machine and agreed. The print had to be a certain kind, and not all the photo booths had the same kind of film.

He looked at the photo for a while, thinking about the man in the picture. The man's face was pocked, as if early childhood acne had plowed it up and it had healed badly. It looked like leather now, a deep brown-gold. His eyes were flat black, like shark's eyes.

His street name was Crow, like the Indian tribe. His hair was flat, blue-black, held back in a ponytail. His mouth was womanish, the lips thick. He'd been in the army, so they said. Carried a little steel hatchet like a pickax, some kind of Special Forces weapon. Came across like a stone-cold Indian killer. Street talk was that the guy was an inquisitor—he asked questions for somebody else.

One question, an answer. Crow don't like the answer, he takes out his little steel hatchet. You lose a part. Then another question.

The story was, Crow's first job had been with a crew of Guyanese coke smugglers down in Florida. Somebody had ratted them out to the DEA, and they all got wrapped up by the Coast Guard in a bayou chase. Crow had done six years in Angola, ended up running a whole block; punks, smoke, guns, favors—Crow was the cardinal. Said to have killed two men in the block, one of them during or after sex. Crow liked to hurt; it was entertainment. Looking into that face, Paolo believed everything he'd been told about the man. Paolo Rona didn't mind hurting, especially a broad, a *puta*. That was what they were for. But it wasn't his thing. Crow—pain was his thing. Somebody else's pain.

Rona wiped his hands on his jeans, pulled on a pair of latex surgical gloves, and leaned over the table. The gloves kept your fingerprints off the card. He met a guy in Ossining who had made one mistake with an INS card. He'd left a clear print of his left thumb on the back side of the card, *under* the laminate. That was all it took to put him in the yard. Paolo heard he died a year later inside the Covered Wagon in Attica.

This was going to be crude. There were better ways to do all of this; a color scanner, a really hot 486 with CorelDRAW, clip-art, and a color laser printer. Vellum or bond to print on. Do it all on a Super VGA screen. Or better yet, real offset photoengraving. None of which he had.

Using the X-Acto blade, he cut the white trim off one of his color shots of Crow, trimmed it all down to a one-inch square, then rounded the upper left-hand corner. Now and then a sweat drop would land on the tabletop, and he'd wipe his face with his sleeve. Inside the gloves his fingers felt hot and gritty with the powder they put in there, but his hands were steady, his motions precise. This was something he enjoyed, like doing artwork back in grade school. Be slow, be careful, be patient. Get an *estrella d'oro* from the DMV.

He held the shot up to the light and used the point of the X-Acto blade to split the surface coating away from the cardboard backing. Done right, he could lift a thin semitransparent film off the backing, taking the image with it. Driver's license photos taken at the DMV were very thin so there'd be no ridge when the laminate was laid on. Cops looked for a ridge around the photo. That was how they could spot a forgery. Normally, Paolo used a Polaroid shot for this kind of thing, but he didn't have the time to set up the right lighting, nor the money for a Spectra.

And Crow was careful, would never agree to be somewhere at any particular time, was always changing his plans at the last minute. Very surveillance-conscious too. Crow had delivered the shot—one shot only—and that was all he was going to do. Make it work, he said. There won't be another.

The shiny steel of the blade cut into the backing easily. Slowly, his hands steady, he worked the thin photo film off the paper.

Good.

Next he sprayed the back of the film lightly with an aerosol glue, making sure the overspray didn't settle on his papers. It smelled good, reminded him of when he was young, just a *niño* with his face in a brown paper bag, sitting out behind the *carnicería* under the Bruckner at 160th. Head full of buzz and fire. No more of that, though. It made your hands shake.

He studied the shot carefully, looking for drops and spots. Then he laid it down on the license blank, using his

X-Acto and a clear plastic ruler to line up the edges. He put onion paper over the license and rolled his fist back and forth, fixing the film to the license blank. He stripped the paper back.

Perfect.

This license was a tricky one to do. They were all tricky now, had holograms and state seals and letters that showed up only under ultraviolet light. That's why you had to get the laminate straight from the DMV. Then you had to lay in the driver's license number in red under the blue Commonwealth of Virginia lettering, and then lay in the date, the class, the expiration date, the restrictions, his DOB, all of this in four-point type. Next came the name in the lower left-hand side, in ten-point Arial, last name first, an address—he always used names right out of the phone book, and the addresses, because sometimes it helped to be able to show a phone book listing. Crow wasn't Hispanic, but he could pass for one.

Paolo was using GARCIA, Lucio, 1553 Jefferson Avenue, Richmond, Virginia. The American Express card was also in the name of Lucio Garcia. It was a forgery, using a real subscriber number, unsigned. Very expensive, but Crow wanted straight plastic. He'd been pretty clear on that. Crow had put the job out there and asked for *him* specifically. Paolo figured his rep was getting around, that he was a reliable operator. He was, too, they just didn't know *how* reliable, or for whom.

Getting all this laid down in Arial, using press-on lettering, took him over an hour and a half of silent concentrated work, with the noise growing in the streets below and the rap music thumping through the walls now, and that goddamn rat chewing away on some cockroaches over in the corner. It was in the open now, watching Paolo with one tiny black eye, its little pink paws busy, tail twitching.

The rat's eye looked like a black pearl in the yellow light from the table lamp where Paolo was working.

Finally, he was ready to lay down the laminate. He walked over to the bed and pulled out a travel iron, brought it back, and plugged it into the outlet. While it warmed, he held the laminate up to the light. The hologram was flawless, showing the commissioner's signature when the light caught it right. This had to cover part of the photo and part of the data area. Getting the laminate right was the key to everything. This was where you could screw it all up, waste hours of labor. Plus you'd have to get a new laminate, one with the hologram like this, and that would cost another two hundred and fifty dollars, even supposing the supplier could get one, or that Crow would give him another chance. The iron was warmed and ready by the time he had the laminate down and cut and positioned.

This was the moment of truth. You had to lay the onion paper down on top, and then slowly, carefully, most of all evenly, press the plastic sheet down with the iron. Keep it moving. Not too hard. Not too hot. One bubble in the plastic, one burn, one twisted letter, maybe melt the photo film, and you were screwed.

He ironed the license standing up, one hand supporting his upper body, leaning a little, moving the little travel iron back and forth and around in circular motions, counting softly to himself. This was hard work. Maybe after this he'd go get a hooker. The trouble with women, they didn't like it prison-style. It would be better to get a boy, but he didn't know any chickenhawk runs around here, and anyway the kid would probably be black. Paolo didn't like them black. When he couldn't get a woman, he liked the little gazelles with light brown skin and big round eyes like deer eyes.

. . . *Ocho* . . . *nueve* . . . *diez* . . . Go slow. Don't screw this up, *pachuco*.

The rap music clicked off, and in the sudden inrush of silence, Paolo heard the televsion set next door, the gosh-golly voice of the newsreader saying "breaking news." Bullshit, it was never breaking news. Break *this, maricón.* He leaned back away from the table and stared down at the onion sheet. Okay. Say a little prayer to the Virgin.

Holding his breath, he peeled the sheet back, like taking a bandage off a wound. Next door the televsion set was turned up louder, some chick with a high-pitched voice going on about the latest crime wave in Baltimore, a tourist hijacking near Dulles, shots fired somewhere in Woodley Park, federal agents foil an attempted mugging at the Lincoln Memorial, the Hoyas win again, stormy weather coming up from the Carolinas . . . blah blah blah . . . The sheet came away cleanly.

Underneath it was a perfect copy of a Commonwealth of Virginia driver's license in the name of Lucio Garcia. Crow's blunt face stared up at him, flat-eyed and ugly. Paolo had considered asking the man to go back, get a shot that wouldn't frighten small kids and old ladies.

What did he want, Crow smiling? Paolo didn't want to think about the kind of thing that would make a guy like Crow smile. This would do, though. This was good work.

Now, let's take care of our little friend over there.

Meanwhile, out in the street, halfway up the block, all the local people were watching a dark blue Crown Victoria pull up and park. A tiny red spark showed through the heavy tint on the front window, somebody puffing on a cigarette. The spark flared bright red, then dropped down out of sight. There was a short pause while the car gathered attention from the locals, then both doors opened up, clinching everyone's worst suspicions. Doors open, but no dome light comes on. This is not Meals on Wheels. This is the cavalry.

Two men got out, one black and huge, the other guy a wolfy-looking white dude with a mean face. They walked away down the street toward the Zanzibar Hotel. People turned and watched them pass, kept their faces blank and hostile. When the men reached the front of the hotel, they stopped for a moment, talking quietly. Then the black guy pulled open the streaky glass door and they went inside.

Up the street, a D.C. patrol car turned the corner and moved slowly down the block, coming to a stop beside the blue Crown Victoria. The street got very quiet as everybody waited for whatever was going to happen to happen.

The awareness of the sounds fading outside did not get through to Paolo Rona as quickly as it would have normally, because Paolo was busy with his little friend. It took him almost a minute to corner and kill the rat with his *filia*, his boot knife, pinning it to the wall by the corner board next to his bed. The rat twisted on the blade point and squealed up at Paolo, Paolo watching the look in its small black eyes, thinking to himself how he must look to the rat, wondering in a detached sort of way what it would be like to die like that. His scanner popped and crackled a bit, and although it had been doing that all evening, something about this call got his attention. He stepped up to the table and turned up the volume.

"—*Maryland plates, radio.*"

"*What's your twenty, 290?*"

"*Fourth and K.*"

Paolo went to the window, strained to look back up the street. There was a D.C. patrol car stopped in the middle of the street, two cops still in the car. Shit. They looked to be checking vehicle plates. But why?

"Okay, those plates come back ten-95."

"Okay, radio. Ten-four. Mark it 99."

Paolo watched as the patrol car started to move. It rolled past the entrance to the Zanzibar without stopping, reached the corner, and turned right onto Fifth. Whatever they wanted, they had it.

Paolo started to relax, and then he looked back up the street and saw the dark blue Crown Victoria. That car looked federal as hell.

Ten-95?

That meant—referred to another agency, didn't it?

Paolo stepped away from the window, scooped up his Glock, and stuffed it into the back of his pants. He snatched up the AmEx card and the Virginia DL and his scanner, started to gather up the papers and shove them into his bag. He gave the room a quick look, snatched up the can of spray glue, and pressed the button, holding it out at arm's length for a fifteen count, moving it back and forth, a billowing cloud, covering everything on the tabletop. His heart was slamming through his chest. Throat aching, a pulse in his neck thudding painfully, he watched the cloud of mist settle. Then he grabbed the matches from his cigarette case, struck one, and stepping back, lit the whole matchbook and threw it at the tabletop.

The cloud of misted glue flared into a huge ball of blue-yellow fire six feet high and as wide as the front of the room, the heat driving him backward. The tabletop burst into flames.

The front door took two huge slams from someone outside. Through the flames and the smoke Paolo saw the hinges shake, and dust fell from the doorframe. This is why you always booked a ground-floor room, man. He turned and bolted for the open window.

The doorway shattered in, plaster flying, slivers scattering, the doorjamb coming away in two pieces. A white man with a mustache stumbled into the room, ran right into the fire cloud, and recoiled. He saw Paolo at the window, saw him through the fireball.

Then the man kicked the table flying and came through the fire after Paolo, his face set and hard, his eyes wide, lit by the fire and the burning papers. He looked like a nightmare. Paolo knew him.

Paolo never looked back. He bailed right out the window, landed in a tumble on trash bags piled up outside. The radio skittered out of his hand. He looked up, saw a large black man coming down the steps, saw the gun in his hands, saw it coming up and centering, but not *yet*.

Paolo fumbled for his Glock, missed it. Doc fired once, the muzzle full of fire from Paolo's point of view, and he felt a round thud into the garbage bag beside his head. Paolo scrambled up and took off running. Behind him he heard the black man saying "Freeze! Federal officers!"

The muscles in Paolo's back tightened, but he kept running, his head up, his mouth wide open, legs a blur, people dodging and ducking out of his way, the street scene jiggling crazily, lampposts strobing by, his heart now thrumming like a bird's heart, Paolo expecting the front of his shirt to blow out any second now, his lungs to spatter the sidewalk in front of his running feet.

Fifty feet behind him and losing ground, Doc lumbered after him, huffing into his radio. "I got him out here, he's eastbound, on foot. I'm on him."

Luke felt the heat from the fire, backed off from the window, and ran back through the front entrance. He ran to the car, holstering the Taurus, cursing. A couple of black kids hooted at him as he ran by, made pig-snorting

noises. Luke reached the car, fumbling with his keys, rag-
ing now. What a fuck-up, what a totally fucked-up night.

Luke ripped the door open and flicked off the lo-jack,
started the car, cranked the wheel with one hand as he
held the radio up.

"Doc, where are you?"

Doc came back, his voice hoarse and unsteady, keeping
time with his footrace up along K Street.

"I'm losing him. He's almost to the corner of Fourth."

Now Luke had the car out and was pulling it around in
a tight U-turn, the street scene spinning crazily.

"Shoot him!"

"I can't, I got no backstop."

Paolo heard the squawk and crackle of the radio, heard
the big man's shoes slapping down on the sidewalk, saw
black faces as he passed, saw the corner—the blessed corner—coming up. *Run, chico!*

Luke hit the accelerator, saw Doc's big black figure
about a half-block up, people jumping out of his way, and
then he saw Paolo Rona in black jeans and a hot pink
T-shirt, flying—literally *flying*—away toward the intersection of Fourth and K Streets.

The big blue car squealed, jumped forward. Luke
leaned over the wheel, his eyes fixed on Paolo's pink
T-shirt, on Paolo's pumping legs. Tonight's the night, you
goddamn little fuck.

"Doc, I'm on him."

Breathless, Doc's voice came back.

"I hear you coming."

Doc swerved out into the street, ran through the
parked cars to the north side, turned, and looked at Luke
closing up. Luke hesitated, then hit the brakes.

Shit, Doc, he thought but didn't say. Doc was into the
car in a half-second, just getting his right leg in when the
jolt of the car accelerating slammed the passenger door.

"You shoulda stayed on foot!"

Doc's face was wet and shiny.

"Like hell! I wasn't gonna catch him!"

"Lose some weight!"

"Fuck you, no offense. There he goes!"

Paolo was almost to the corner. Luke had his foot to the floor. Rona made the corner, a black and pink blur, looked back for a second, his face a brown flash, his eyes widening as he saw the big blue car closing up fast, heard the roar of the engine. Doc was on the radio.

"Radio, this is Bravo Sixteen federal agents, we are eastbound on K Street at Fourth Street Southeast, Seven District. Radio?"

"Bravo Sixteen, identify your agency!"

"Deputy Marshals. We're in vehicle pursuit of a running suspect. Male Hispanic aged thirty-three, five-eleven, one hundred sixty pounds, black jeans, pink T-shirt, wanted on a federal warrant. Armed and dangerous."

"Ten-four, Bravo Sixteen. Units to support Marshals Bravo Sixteen in · pursuit eastbound K and Fourth Street?"

Paolo looked back again as they got alongside, Luke slowing the car, one hand on his door, and Paolo rounded the corner, still flying, skittered, recovered—and dashed directly in front of them, crossing the intersection northbound. Luke jerked his door open, sighted the Taurus on Paolo's right temple as the man flew past. Beyond Paolo's head he could see cars and trucks stopped at the lights, white and black faces behind windshields, directly in the line of fire. Shit!

Luke braced the door with his left hand, bellowed at Rona.

"Rona! Freeze!"

Paolo's head twitched right, his eyes wild. He knows me, thought Luke. Then Paolo was rolling over the hood of a parked car. A city bus was idling at the corner, fumes rising from the pipes, and Rona was headed right for it. The doors were open, interior lights shining down on the heads of twenty or thirty passengers. Doc saw it too.

"Luke, we're gonna make the front page."

The radio crackled back with patrol units coming on.

"Two nine oh, we're in the sector. Say again description!"

"Two oh five, we're at Fifth and—"

The radio burst into chaos as at least five different units jammed the channel, voices wild and shouting, and Radio trying to shut them up. Useless panicky half-trained assholes. Luke heard that metallic ping that his temper made when it snapped. Goddamn amateurs.

Doc held his star out the window, holding up the cars on his right, as Luke cut across the curb lane, going north after Rona on Fourth Street. He smacked his fist on the horn as a cab blocked him, the driver leaning out of the window, his black face ugly with anger, swearing at them. Luke stayed on the horn, looking past the tangle of cars. He saw Paolo reach the bus, his legs flailing, saw him get a hand on the door, something in his hand. In the white glow from the bus door, he saw it was a pistol.

Luke jammed on the brakes, jumped out of the vehicle, Doc yelling something at him, and he pounded up the street after the bus. He knocked down two young women coming out of a storefront, slammed into a man who stepped into his way, shouldered him off—

The bus was starting to move.

Twenty feet.

Luke yelled at the bus driver. "Marshals! Stop!"

Ten feet.

Now the bus was accelerating. Luke raced up alongside it, slamming his left hand on the side of the bus. It rang like a cheap tin gong. The passengers stared down at him like cows going to a slaughterhouse, dim, oblivious, doomed. An elderly woman shook her head at him, showing yellow teeth like old ivory, she was yelling something down at him. Four feet, he was keeping up, gaining on the door. If he could just reach the aluminum handbar, he could swing up, break the glass with his Taurus.

Two feet. His chest was starting to burn. His knees were going out, fire coming up the right thigh. He raised the Taurus.

Close. He was close.

He cleared the side panel, the bar was right there at his left hand, he got his fingers on it, tightened, felt his feet begin to drag as the speed of the bus caught his body, heard the huge tire whining against the bumpy blacktop, very aware of the weight and power of the machine now, of the big black tire spinning at his hip, of the road streaming by underneath him, the wind making his eyes water.

The door opened up—

Luke wrenched at the handbar, lifting himself off the pavement, feeling the ground give away—

A hand reached around the door, a face—Rona was staring down at him, his mouth wide, his eyes glittering in the streetlight.

"Hey, *Culebra!* Bite this!"

In Paolo's other hand was a huge weapon. A Glock, Luke thought, in a strange hallucinatory moment of silent concentration.

Luke pulled the Taurus up, tried to aim it forward—

Paolo's hands looked odd. Shiny and white. Rubbery. He had gloves on, surgical gloves. The bus slammed over a pavement crack. The Taurus bobbled in his right hand, his left shoulder felt like it was coming apart. Under his feet the road was a black blur. The tires roared at him. The Glock was in his face, he could even see the skin tightening under the latex as the grip hardened, see the index finger inside the matte black trigger guard, see the light in Rona's face, the gleeful intent—

Luke let go, hit the pavement rolling, tucking the Taurus up under his belly, the world spinning as lamplights and car lights and red lights and the gutter and staring faces and more lamplights and more car lights all rolled and rolled, the ground slamming his shoulder, then his back and his hip and his knee, and then he hit—*hard*.

Time passed.

He opened his eyes slowly, looked up, and saw a shiny white metal tube, bent at angles, and above the tube a black greasy cone-shaped surface. He moved his head to the left, feeling pavement under his skull, and saw a tire, low and wide and shiny black, with brand-new treads. He looked back up and realized he was looking at the transmission of a car.

He was under a car.

He lay there for an uncertain time, aware of feet gathering around the edges of his vision, of faces appearing under the car to peer at him; aware of voices and a siren growing louder, aware of a massive numbness in his left shoulder. He tensed his fingers and felt the weight of the Taurus in his hands. Pain was starting to register, along with a deep sense of embarrassment.

He was thinking about trying to move when heavy feet thudded up to the car, and he could hear Doc's voice, close to panic, full of fear, but controlled, yelling for the crowd to back off.

Knees thumped to the ground, then huge black hands appeared, followed by Doc's blue-black face, his eyes full of grim expectations. He looked at Luke, who looked back at him.

Doc's face went away. Then it came back. Then he grinned at him.

"That didn't go too well, did it, Luke?"

1200 Hours
Sunday, May 22, 1994
Eight Ball Cinema
G Street and South Carolina Avenue
Washington, D.C.

Paolo Rona spent the rest of Saturday night and most of Sunday morning in a gay porn filmhouse on South Carolina Avenue, sitting in the back row in the steaming dark of the low arch-shaped hall with his shoes up on the seatback in front of him and his face covered with a copy of *The Washington Post*. It was better than sleeping in a sewer pipe, although the only difference was the screen full of naked boys at the far end of the pipe.

The theater ran an endless loop of hard-core porn, most of it filmed in Europe fifteen, twenty years ago. All the guys in it had long scraggly hair and sideburns, wore white socks, and had needle marks all over their arms and pimples everywhere else. They were as attractive as interstate roadkill, but the clientele was strictly in-the-closet suburban white guys who came down to Seven District for cheap thrills and anonymous gropes in the latrines. Look at them, like hanging dogs—no one in here ever looked anyone else in the face. They were too busy keeping their heads down and their hands busy. If you could stand the atmosphere, it was a very good place to hide out until the D.C. cops got their usual case of Fugitive Alzheimer's; there were so many people running from the cops in D.C. that anybody not caught in the first twelve hours was pretty much home free.

He checked his watch by the glow from the aisle light. Noon. He'd been in here for almost twelve hours. Even the Marshals would have packed it in by now. Even that son of a bitch Luke Zitto. What the hell *he* was doing in D.C., Paolo had no idea.

The last time Paolo had seen Zitto was on the steps of the Bronx Borough Courthouse in 1989. Paolo was with his lawyer, Jimmy Della, dead now but alive then, before he crossed one of his clients up and got his throat opened up with a chain saw. Jimmy Della was talking about Paolo's plea bargain, and a bunch of *federales* had come down the steps heading for a big white van. Jimmy Della had gone pale, shut up, and stepped back behind a pillar, pulling Paolo with him.

Marshals, he'd said. See that one, lean guy with the big black mustache?

Paolo said, Yeah, so what?

That's Zitto. La Culebra.

The Snake? *That's* the Snake?

Sí, La Culebra, the one who took out Jugo Sarpente, the Ching-a-Ling armorer. Paolo had looked around the pillar and watched Zitto pass, marking the face. Jugo Sarpente had been a major force around the South Bronx. In 1984 he'd machine-gunned a bar up near Gun Hill Road, killed a federal officer and six other people. He was wanted nationwide for executions, neck-ties, rapes; a very bad man, an *hombre*. The story was that Zitto had found the guy through some finks, taken him down with only two other guys, a couple of Bronx detectives. Killed him flat too, so the story was told. With a twelve-gauge.

And now here Paolo was, on the make in D.C., and who the hell comes in his front door but La Culebra himself. And he was no Jugo Sarpente.

Somehow he didn't feel good about it. Not good at all. He had maybe a hundred dollars in a canvas money pouch strapped to his ankle. The Glock was shoved down into his crotch, where it was making a very uncomfortable package. And he had Crow's Virginia driver's license. So not only was Luke Zitto of the U.S. Marshals Service looking for him, but so was Crow. It was a bad situation. But it was also an opportunity. Because he was the only guy in the game who knew *all* of the players. Sitting there in the dark, running through the possibilities, Paolo Rona finally reached a decision. He gathered himself together, zipped up his jeans, readjusted the Glock, and walked out of the theater, where the noon sun struck him in the face like a blow.

The broad street was packed with cars and people, lined with low-rent shops and secondhand stores, car lots, bars, bodegas, and groceterias. The summer heat poured down from a hot flat disk of sun hanging like a pimp's medallion in a lemon-yellow sky. Paolo's head began to pound. His skin went hot, then cold. At that point a D.C. cop car went rolling by like a cruising shark, following the curb lane, two black cops in the dusty car, their caps back, faces slack, uniforms rumpled and shirts open.

He stood there outside the theater, got a grip on his pain, and watched the car go by, watching the cops, where they were looking. They missed him, never even looked his way. He saw a pushcart peddler, went over and bought a crushed-ice drink, raspberry, and drank it down, feeling the chill numb the ache in his throat. This was bad, this throat thing, and he had better do something about it, get some medicine, because there was no way he could afford to come down with the flu or anything right now. He needed to change his cover, change the way he looked, change the odds.

At a place called Simba's he picked up an army surplus fatigue jacket and a boonie-rat hat. Also some black boots and a couple of black T-shirts. Sunglasses and a sling bag to carry the Glock in. Soap and a toothbrush, a couple of pink Bic razors. A huge black woman took his cash without even looking up from her paper. He changed in one of the back rooms, stuffing his jeans and the pink T-shirt into the sling bag, covering the Glock. The Glock's mag held fifteen rounds. That was all the ammunition he had. There was a shop called Blue Star Sports at South Carolina and Thirteenth. They'd have some nine-mills under the counter for sale to their select customers, at fifty bucks a box. But they might have surveillance on them too. Well, he'd have to risk it. No ammo, and your piece is just a paperweight.

The jacket was hot as hell, and a few minutes under that noon sun had Paolo running with sweat inside it. He kept it on because half the addicts down here wore jackets just like it all the time. About the only advantage crackheads enjoyed was that the summer heat never bothered them; they were cold all year round. If Paolo wanted to pass as just another street person down here in Seven District, he'd have to put up with the heat and the sweat.

There was a row of pay phones at the corner of Thirteenth Street, across from Blue Star Sports, a low bunker of a building with iron bars across the painted windows. Out of the four pay phones, one was gone entirely, one was gutted and smashed, one was covered with spit or something worse. And one was working.

He dropped in a quarter, dialed, and leaned against the phone, looking out at the people passing by, at the traffic, and at the rooftops around the intersection. Rusted-out cabs chugging by, spouting blue smoke. A bagel cart manned by a skinny black kid who looked about nine. Delivery trucks idling at the curbs, unloading crates of food at the grocery store. Garbage and scraps of loose paper lying in heaps in the gutters. Crowds of blacks hanging out all down the block, leaning on stained and graffiti-covered walls, sitting on the stoops, walking back and forth with their hands in their pockets and their eyes taking in everything. If there was routine surveillance in place around Blue Star Sports, he couldn't see it. Chances had to be taken. The line was answered.

"Tintoreria."

A woman's voice, Indio accent, Miskito. No one he knew.

"Hey, is Joey Rag there?"

"Who are you?" She made it sound like "Whuare choo?"

"I'm looking for him. It's business."

"Juss a minoot."

There was a wait. Paolo could hear high-pitched female voices in the background, speaking an unknown language, and the steady thumping of machinery.

"Who's this?"

"Joey? This is Paolo Rona from Denver. I need to see Crow."

"He's not here. You moved last night, hey?"

"What, was it in the papers?"

"No. Crow went over, sees nothing but cops."

Christ.

"What'd he say?"

"He was disappointed."

"You can see, I mean, if Crow knows I moved, well then—"

"You got a situation?"

"Do I? Do I have a situation?"

"I'd say you got a situation."

"Jeez, Joey, here I am calling, I mean, you know the guy. Why—"

"Well, I got nothing to say about Crow. He's not here."

"I really need to—"

"Where are you?"

"Joey, I'm not—I'm in a position, you understand. I don' wanna put that out there right now, you follow?"

"So what can I do?"

"You can tell me something, man. I'm in a thing here, I gotta get—"

Three black kids had settled down along a wall right in front of him, no more than ten feet away. Sharks jackets, hats on full-lock, black and teal colors, heavy lazy-eyed black faces, and all three of them sizing him up, unblinking, chilly. Joey Rag sensed the change in Paolo's voice.

"Problem there?"

"Maybe. I absolutely gotta know where to look for Crow."

"I'm not gonna help you there. You know that, man. But I—you say where you can be, I'll see what I can do. That's all."

The three black kids looked like dogs waiting for dinner. No, wolves. Paolo turned to face the phone booth, and the muscles along his back crawled like snakes and eels. He had the sling bag in front of him, his hand fumbling for the Glock under his clothes. If he was going to have to wait somewhere to meet Crow, he'd want to do it in a wide-open place, see the man coming. He wished to hell he knew this city better. He looked up and saw a white pyramid rising over the low ragged line of the storefronts, hazy in the distance, red lights strobing.

"The monument. The big needle. How about that?"

"Yeah. When?"

You'd think Joey Rag paid by the letter. It was like talking to a machine. Paolo didn't know the guy well, had only met him once last week, when Joey Rag had driven Crow over for their first meet in Chinatown. They said he had been a worker for Barra back in Honduras, but he looked soft now. Paolo was looking for some kind of human comeback and was getting a robot. Probably there was nothing inside Joey Rag but wheels and gears and calculations. Paolo figured, if you were in bed with the guy, you could hear his generator running, it would keep you awake all night.

"It's twelve-thirty. I'll be there at three. Down the hill toward that big pond."

"The pool? Okay. I got no guarantees. Three o'clock."

The line went dead. Paolo turned around, looked at the three black guys, only now there were five, all staring at him. He leaned back and stared out at them, pulled the Glock out of the sling bag far enough for them to see what was in his hand.

There was a long pounding time where nothing happened. Then one of them smiled and got to his feet and walked away. Then they all left, walking slowly and swaying in that kind of drunken-sailor walk they had. He watched them until they were a long block away, and then he dropped another quarter into the pay phone, dialed, and waited.

The line connected. He heard a hollow click, a pause. Then a voice. "Yeah?"

"Yeah, well, ah, this is Paolo Rona."

The man's voice was calm, deep, and very cold.

"Go ahead."

"He's pissed at me, man. What do you want me to do?"

"What'd he say?"

"He wants to meet. I told him the Washington Monument."

"When?"

Paolo thought about it.

This was the tricky part.

"I told him four o'clock, man."

"What happened last night?"

"Hey, you tell *me*! That's *your* end, man."

"We'll deal with it. Stay cool. Keep your end up."

"But he wants a *meet*, man."

"So meet him."

"That's all. Just meet him? You don't get it. It's risky!"

"I'm crying. West side of the monument. Be there at four."

The line went dead.

Chilly fuck.

Paolo looked at his watch. This was going to take timing.

But it could be done.

1233 Hours
Sunday, May 22, 1994
Quality Industrial Cleaners
North Capitol Street
Washington, D.C.

Joey Rag went back down the hall past the rolling drums where the dry cleaning was spinning around, feeling the heat on the side of his cheek. He passed through the larger area where fifteen Miskito women were pushing irons over huge flat tables piled high with hospital linens.

At the back of the pressing room was a flight of iron stairs that led up to a catwalk, and the catwalk went back out over the pressroom to an office made out of Sheetrock and plate glass. You could see the whole factory from the office, as well as the street outside.

Joey Rag climbed up to the office and went inside. A man in a pale green *guayabera* and tan slacks was leaning back in an oak chair, his heavy arms folded across his chest, his smooth red leather boots up on Joey Rag's wooden desk, his head forward, his long black hair hanging down in front of his face.

As soon as Joey Rag got the door open, the man came

forward, awake, alert, and in his hand he was holding a shiny steel hatchet. Joey Rag looked at his eyes and thought they looked like painted stones, or like the eyes that you saw on lizards or dead fish.

"He's gonna be at the monument at three."

Crow smiled.

"How did he sound?"

"He wanted to know if he had a situation."

"What'd you tell him."

"I said it was cool. Not to worry."

"He nervous?"

"Yeah. He's nervous. You want something to eat? A chorizo?"

Crow stood up, tucked the hatchet into his belt, and pulled the *guayabera* down over it. When he wasn't using his hands, they hung at his sides, limp. There was no nervous motion in the man. When he moved, it was quick, no wasted time, then he went right back to stillness.

"No."

"We got time."

"No, we don't."

Crow picked up a leather satchel and stuffed his hatchet inside. Joey could see a lot of cash in there too, thousands. Whatever Crow was going to do with Paolo Rona-from-Denver or whatever his real name was, there was a lot of money involved. Joey Rag watched the man's back on the way down the stairs to the Quality Cleaners truck and began to feel that he would not want to be the one who had to ask this man for money, even if he had earned it. Especially if he had earned it.

During the night Luke had had his Margot and Jeffery dream. He was in a small town, a town in the Southwest that had to be Provo, although it seemed oddly changed. It had that wide, flat, and bleached-out look, a box of spilled bones and stones spread out over the foothills and ragged peaks of the western slopes of the Rockies. In the sky ten black crows wheeled and turned against a field of cobalt blue. The sun looked like a whirlpool of white fire. Crows circled it like scraps of burning paper. He could hear their rasping cries from a great distance. They made the same grating noise that his boots made on the concrete sidewalk. The air was clear, flat, as if it were composed of molten glass.

He was walking toward the center of the town. He could see the taller buildings, the banks, and the gates to Brigham Young. The street went up a slight grade, and off to his right a low range of barren brown hills rose to a distant line of snow-covered peaks. The heat was on his back and shoulders, burning the muscles of his back and searing his neck. He could smell the asphalt, the heat of the sun burning it, and the dust of the street. In the middle distance he could see Margot and Jeffery walking toward him on the opposite side of the boulevard, almost a mile away.

He tried to call out to them, but since the air was made of clear glass, the sound would not carry. He walked faster, feeling a sense of urgency and fear, and in a while they were closer to him, walking hand-in-hand, a young woman and a boy about ten; his wife Margot and Jeffery, her son, his stepson. Margot turned her head to watch him as she walked past him, now no more than fifty feet away from him across the boulevard.

Luke walked to the edge of his side of the street and put a foot out into the asphalt, but it was like a river, it wasn't solid, it was like a river of lava, although the surface was smooth and still. The sun had melted the street, and Luke knew that if he stepped into it, he would sink out of sight in the middle of the road, and in the morning cars and trucks would drive over the spot where he had sunk into the street. He'd hear them passing over his head and feel the rumble of their tires, but his mouth and his lungs would be full of tar. He stepped back onto the walk.

Margot waved to him, knowing he couldn't reach her, taunting him. She was wearing the dress she wore when he saw her last, a deep blue dress made out of some sort of light cotton that was like crepe paper, and her red hair glowed in the hard white sun. She'd be naked under the dress; that was her way. Jeffery walked with her but would not look at Luke or speak to him or in any way seem to know that Luke was there. Luke stood and watched them passing. They reached the corner of that block where there was an ARCO station, closed, but bright with pennants and banners that hung motionless in the still air.

Luke looked down and considered the service Colt he was holding in his right hand. It was a long shot, maybe fifty yards—but it was within his range.

The sun glimmered along the length of the barrel, and a heat haze made the foresight blurry. Margot's face was a tanned oval beyond the foresight. Her mouth was open, and she must have been saying something to him, but no words reached him through the thick glass air. He tightened his grip on the frame. He could feel the hot bar of the trigger pressing against the bone of his index finger and feel that delicate metallic sliding inside the pistol, the mathematical certainty of the surfaces, the perfection of the machinery inside the weapon, the black shroud of the hammer starting to tremble . . .

. . . Luke put the dream aside deliberately, the way a sleeper will throw off a quilt that feels suddenly suffocating. He began to struggle toward waking, reached it like a swimmer surfacing.

It took a full minute to recognize the bedroom. He was in Georgetown. It was Sunday. There was music coming from above, something classical vibrating through the ceiling, a stringed instrument like a cello or something deep. It sounded like a bumblebee, a soothing sound, rising and falling in a sweet, sad sort of way.

Luke lay there for a while, watching the ceiling, aware of the sunlight filling the bedroom, the sunlight filtering through leaves outside the window so that it looked like a pool of bright green water on the wall of his bedroom, bubbles and whirlpools of amber and green light shimmering with the wind that moved the leaves.

He could smell the coffee brewing in the kitchen and realized that even as bruised and beaten as he had felt last night, he'd still remembered to set up the coffee machine. That was typical of him. If he had come home in a rolling drunk, he'd still have carefully removed his clothes, hung up the pants in a press, put his jacket away, set trees in his shoes. Barely able to stand, he'd weave in front of the bathroom mirror while brushing every tooth and rinsing carefully with undiluted hydrogen peroxide. He'd set out his vitamins and feed the cat, if he had one.

Routine. That was what held a man together.

Margot always said that he had that kind of obsessive ritualism because his inner life was such a mess that he had to keep his outside neat just to live with himself. Margot liked to talk that way. The hell with Margot. She was history now. Unfortunately, so was Jeffery.

All of this had taken place years ago, back in Provo, Utah. Luke had been a G7-grade deputy marshal assigned to the Witness Protection Program. At that time he and Margot had been married for five years, the second marriage for Margot. She had one child when Luke met her, a boy named Jeffery. He was ten by the time they moved to Provo.

After they got assigned to Utah, Margot got involved in something Luke later found out was called the New Age movement. She was seeing some therapist who apparently convinced her that her thymus—yes, her thymus—was out of sync with the infinite, or maybe her chakra was the wrong color. Luke was a little unclear on the issue, other than that the neat thing about New Age stuff was, it was *all about you*, that Margot was the star of it all, and that saving her aura or getting Rolfed or learning to channel, whatever it was, it was certainly a hobby where the main thing was to think only about yourself.

However it came about, Margot became convinced that she was in deep psychic doo-doo, and it was during this period of searching around for a target, someone to blame for her "dysfunctionality," that she had settled on Luke, on Luke and the Marshals Service—and the Program—on what she called the "moral lockjaw" that confined and limited Luke's "self-awareness."

It was as if she had gone to night school to learn a foreign language and would now speak nothing but that language around the home. Luke's response to the change was to become even more silent, sensing that his words were a trap she set for him. No matter what he said, Margot found it "typical," every straight sentence a geode she could crack open to expose something toxic inside. Marriage to Margot had gradually turned into a prolonged moral interrogation. Luke spent most of the latter months of it simply trying to hold his temper. When he first met her, he thought, man, this poor woman, she *has* had a tough life. Later he figured it hadn't been terrible enough because the bitch had lived through it. Someone should have hunted down her inner child and beaten it to death with a rolled-up copy of *Guns and Ammo*.

Although Luke was failing badly with Margot, he believed that he had worked out a pretty good relationship with the boy. Jeffery's real father had remarried, walked away from Margot and the kid. Never looked back.

Luke had forgotten the guy's name. Neither of them had heard from the man since the separation, although Luke had used a couple of connections to find out where he was; in Washington State, some little town called Ellensburg, running a bank branch and living common-law with a nineteen-year-old girl named Shawna or Sinead or Shanelle, something like that. After Margot reinvented herself in Provo, Luke had thought about calling the guy up, out there in Ellensburg, and telling him she'd done it again, slam-dunked some poor son of a bitch's heart. Then he figured, fuck it.

But he still missed Jeffery, even after all these years. The kid had been sharp, with a good sense of humor, always taking a shot at himself, passing himself off as some kind of Woody Allen clone, a little skinny-shouldered buzzcut kid with an honest generous heart. He never complained, seemed to be happy that someone as organized as Luke had come into his mother's life to put some predictability into it. Like Luke, Jeffery loved order, liked things to happen in an orderly way. Margot loved a disaster, had a boredom threshold about an inch high. She had a phrase for it. Crisis-conditioned, she said.

Jeffery and Luke used to go out for drives, go to hardware stores and pick up things for their tract house in Provo. They built a butcher-block island for the kitchen. Put up a sunshade in the back yard. Planned trips to anywhere but Utah.

Jeffery was in a religious phase at the time, so Luke found them a local Catholic church, and they'd go together for benediction on Friday evenings or for mass early Sundays. His own Catholicism had worn away slowly and certainly over the years, corroded by the bitter wind of experience, hammered down by stony questions that religion seemed unable to answer.

Now it was little more than a slab of pitted granite with obscure words barely visible, hints and allegations about right behavior and truth in a world constructed entirely out of moral confusion. Going to church with Jeffery had been a way for Luke to see a dim shaft of the light that had once seemed so brilliant to him when he was a young altar boy in Columbus. Jeffery wasn't a showy believer, but there was a grace available to him that Luke managed to share in. That grace had become very important to Luke while they were in Provo. It was one of the many things he had lost.

Luke knew that he wasn't Jeffery's father and didn't try to be. But he loved him, and the kid loved him back. They both knew that. It had been a good time in Luke's life, in spite of the assignment itself.

Which sucked.

Witness Protection. The Program.

For Luke, the Program consisted of nursemaiding families of federal witnesses assigned to various locations around Utah and Idaho. Most people didn't stay long in Witness Protection, largely because the Marshals Service was so goddamn *bad* at it in those years, and the life lived by people in the Program was ugly.

Back in those days, the service routinely bungled new identities, failed to deliver on reasonable jobs, treated the people in the Program like infectious bacteria. A few agents used their power to extort sex and services from wives trapped in the situation. The jobs available were mainly minimum wage, working for a chain store as a stock clerk, flipping frijoles for migrant workers, pumping gas. The housing was ragtag clapboard or fifth-floor walkups, and furnishings supplied by garage sales and Salvation Army castoffs.

Not that the people in the Program necessarily deserved anything better. Keeping them alive was the principal service of Witness Protection. But the dreary low-rent hopelessness usually came as severe culture shock to the adrenaline-addicted career criminals who routinely ended up in Witness Protection.

Many of them had lived at the top of the food chain in places like Newport Beach, Lansing, West Palm Springs, Long Island, Dallas, San Diego, up to their hand-sewn collars in gold American Express cards, stock splits, weekends in the Caymans, summers in Montana, big homes up the Taconic Parkway. And they were all guys for whom a real job was, at best, a distant nightmare, men who had spent the better part of their lives in crime, liars and conmen, sleazy lawyers, corrupt bondsmen, extortionists, loan sharks, thieves. If they had ever spoken the absolute truth, it had not been intentionally. Regular work was an alien concept to these people, something for the marks and the suckers out there in Main Street America. They were none of them ready for Provo, nor would they ever be, any more than a brace of weasels could pull a plow.

So they usually put up with the Program for a year, perhaps two, rarely three, sustained by the aftereffects of adrenaline, distracted by the machinery of lengthy trials where they were the star witnesses—still Players, people of respect. But that faded fast, illusions and lies bleached out by the unrelenting sun of the American Southwest, the monotony of the straight life.

At that point the families shattered under the strain, or the guy got back into crime somehow and was ejected from the Program, or he walked on his own, usually after cleaning out the family bank account. Fear fades, but for these guys greed was eternal.

All of this was a big secret back in the early years, at least for the general public. But not for the law enforcement community.

The reputation of the U.S. Marshals Service was at rock bottom in those days. Held in general contempt, Marshals were seen as uniformed drivers for prison transport, semi-trained and dim-witted security guards who couldn't make the grade on a real police force. Their pay was among the lowest in law enforcement, which guaranteed low-quality recruits.

Luke had more or less fallen into the service after being turned down by the FBI. Something about his belief system, his cynicism, had irritated the recruiter. His knees, ruined in high school football, had kept him out of the army and away from Vietnam. It had also barred his service with the Ohio State Patrol and the Columbus Police Department. Regular civilian work was hard to find in the early seventies. Luke's father had been a trial lawyer before his stroke. The law held some magic for Luke, seemed to be a force in the world. The Marshals were looking for people. Luke was looking for . . . something to believe in.

Margot called Luke's problem "career drift," which was close enough to the truth to be hurtful. Luke drifted into the Marshals and drifted, eventually, to Provo and Witness Protection.

The year it all fell apart for Luke, he was down to two families, one in Ogden, north of Salt Lake City, and the other in Provo. Luke spent most of his time on Interstate 15, shuttling back and forth to deal with one low-grade cluster fuck after another. And these two remaining guys were typical Witness Protection inmates. Luke wasn't allowed to know their whole story, but he'd been around the law long enough to smell a fink if it backed up in his drain. He figured these guys—and their wives—had gotten tangled up in one or another of the RICO sweeps that were all the rage back in the early eighties.

Both guys were obvious accountants, something fiscal anyway. Book bouncers for one of the families or toadies for a stock manipulator. One of them had that polished silky look you could only get from sliding around in sleaze in Lower Manhattan, a sly guy with a natural lip-curl and black darting eyes. Expensive Italian loafers, scuffed and dirty, with the heels worn down. A rack suit with the pants too long, the cuffs worn at the back. An MBA, but not from Harvard. Nobody from Harvard ended up in Witness Protection. This guy had worked his way up some financier's pantleg, was always calling Luke "Lucy," and used the phrase "Hi, guy" far too much. Luke had nicknamed him Brett, figured him for a Main Chancer who had run afoul of the SEC or a Senate committee or, for all Luke knew, the CIA.

The other guy was more complicated, looked Connecticut or New Hampshire, tall and professorial with a close-cropped white beard and pale blue eyes. He managed a clipped Yankee accent, wore baggy Dockers and blue shirts, had a fishing hat covered in flies. Luke called him Conan the Librarian. He had that fake-preppie style you saw on the Upper West Side of Manhattan. He came across as soft-spoken, charming, could mix a decent martini, played golf, was unfailingly polite, presented himself as sensitive, caring, kind; sort of a human version of a golden retriever.

According to his file, he had taken a bribe roughly equal to the GNP of Belgium to cook a set of books that allowed a Maryland corporation to go public, float an offering, and eventually ruin, among hundreds of other investors, the entire pension plan of a union in Peekskill, New York. People had committed suicide. Others had died in penury. The boss had disappeared and resurfaced in the Turks and Caicos. Conan had burned the board of directors, nine senior staffers, and one SEC inspector in return for immunity and Witness Protection.

The service had gotten Conan a job at Brigham Young, where he did something clerical for them. He smoked a pipe and worked in the garden, had one wife he'd admit to, but his chief contribution to the state of Utah and the hapless people of Provo was a deeply venomous, palpably evil son named Keenan, a baggy-pants skateboard thrasher with a trick haircut and the personality of a mongoose.

Keenan was far and away the worst thing in Provo. Keenan kept Luke busy running around Provo bailing him out of various small-time break-and-enter raps, shoplifting, drinking in public, smoking dope, petty schoolyard extortions. Even an attempted rape.

All this in a state that had a beehive as its logo, a state so tight-assed and by-the-numbers that it provided almost all of the senior FBI brass and a lot of CIA button men as well. Utah, in Luke's view, was the only state in the union where joy was a prohibited substance. It was as if a toxin of dim-witted sincerity, a kind of dull earnestness, saturated the Mormons and everything they built. The state drug was definitely the Quaalude.

On the other hand, little Keenan's drug was aggression with a side of sadism and sexual assault. Luke didn't detest many things, but Keenan was definitely a candidate. Evenings he'd fantasize a call to New Jersey to blow Conan's cover and get some real heat down here; maybe they'd kill Keenan in the cross fire.

Conan and Brett were married to a couple of Wal-Mart potted plants bred for Park Slope or White Plains, stunned-looking trophy babes who spent their Utah days sitting around the pool in the back yard belting back margaritas, watching their skin shrivel in the desert heat, and planning a day trip to the mall. And their nights lying awake listening to the air conditioner rattle and their hearts pound, wondering what the hell had happened to their lives. Luke had some sympathy for the women; at least they hadn't bilked fifty thousand pensioners or helped to put a steel plant out of business somewhere in the Rust Belt. The husbands were two different brands of the same toxic waste.

Naturally, baby-sitting toxic waste wasn't a happy time for Luke. He couldn't even get too friendly with the local troopers. His boss was the U.S. Marshal for Salt Lake City, and he could only speak safely with the FBI guys stationed there. Although the Marshals in general were not respected, Luke was seen as an exception. He and Margot had been invited to a lot of barbecues and parties, but Margot always managed to get into an argument with one of the husbands, usually taking a left-wing liberal stand at the top of her lungs and generally carrying on like a dental drill.

Gradually the invitations had declined, but Luke still met some of the FBI people for drinks and commiseration. Everyone else was outside the federal loop, and since Luke had to spend a lot of time running interference for Keenan, the Provo cops and the Utah State Patrol guys had come to dislike Luke almost as much as they hated Keenan, just by association, even though they had a good idea that he was just doing his job.

Maybe they were right. Maybe some jobs ought not to be done at all. Keeping Keenan out of juvie hall was one of those jobs. As it turned out, one of Luke's *last* jobs in Utah.

It was late in November. He was driving home from Salt Lake City one stormy evening with Keenan lying in the back of his service van, cuffed, sullen, and stinking of vomit. Luke had the window wide open and was working out the precise phrasing of his latest request for a transfer, when he saw Margot fly by in the family sedan, going northbound on Interstate 15. Even in the twilight he could see that she had a guy in the car with her.

He dropped Keenan off at his house. Conan was out somewhere, and Keenan's mother was working her way through a bottle of Gallo burgundy in front of the television. Keenan went downstairs to his room without a word to her. Luke looked at Keenan's mother in her white cotton sundress, spread out on the floral print like a very expensive French pastry filled with whipped cream, but well beyond the stale date. Her eyes were bruised and heavy with drink and self-pity. She offered him a glass of wine and whatever else he wanted that wasn't being used right now.

When he got home that night, Jeffery was sitting in the darkened living room watching rap videos on MTV, entirely alone. Luke asked Jeffery where his mom was, and Jeffery was evasive, uncomfortable, wrapping himself inside a *Star Wars* quilt.

Standing in the living room surrounded by things that

meant less than nothing to him, looking down at Jeffery wrapped in guilty knowledge, it occurred to Luke that his life was spinning away from him like a blown leaf. He patted Jeffery on the shoulder and went into the kitchen, where he popped the cap on the first of several bottles of Pinto beer and sat down at the table.

He held the beer in his hands for a long time while he stared out the window, watching the lightning dance along the distant mountain peaks and hearing the rain lashing at the roof.

When the storm moved away, the darkness was perfect and complete, the bottles of Pinto were lined up in front of him on close order drill, each one a milepost in the rearview mirror of his life, and the only light in the home was the blue-white flicker of the television in the front room.

He went back out and lifted the sleeping boy off the couch and put him to bed. As he left the boy's room, Jeffery woke up and said, "I'm sorry, Luke."

"So am I. You okay?"

"Yeah. Luke . . . what's going to happen?"

The question cut into Luke in a way he found hard to understand.

"Hey, relax. Everything's gonna be fine. You get some rest now. We'll do something tomorrow, okay? Maybe play some ball?"

"Yeah, okay. That would be great. Luke . . ."

"Yeah, kid?"

"If something, if Mom . . ."

"Your mom's fine, Jeff. She's just out for a visit."

"Yeah, I meant—you're gonna be around, right? You're not gonna go away, like, on assignment or something. You'll be around, okay?"

Luke felt the tears burning at the back of his eyes, and a great consuming sadness came over him. There was no sorrow like simple domestic decay. He sat down on the side of the kid's bed, ruffled his hair, pulled the quilt up around his neck. His throat hurt, and his eyes were burning a bit. He guessed this feeling was love. Jeff's eyes were a perfect sky blue, and he looked about four years old. Luke felt a sudden powerful rush of emotion, an all-consuming thought-terminating drive to keep this kid safe, to take him outside and get in the car and just disappear with him, take him to Montana or Oregon, get a job as a security guard, go fishing with the kid, go to the sea and watch him swimming, watch him grow up straight. He didn't do anything like that. Later, he would wish that he had. But by then it was too late. He straightened the covers and smiled at him.

"Jeff, you worry too much. Everything's gonna be fine!"

But everything didn't turn out fine.

It took him another couple of weeks to work out what Margot was doing. Or rather, who Margot was doing. Not that he really wanted the answer. It was just that he was too much of a cop to leave the thing alone.

Luke would have put money on one of Margot's therapists, or a friend in her pottery class, or one of her night-course instructors at Brigham Young. Mormons were very large in the adultery field; it was their only state sport. Luke was wrong. When he found out who Margot was seeing, he knew his career with Witness Protection was over. Margot was sleeping with Conan the Librarian. It was out of his hands the next day.

The service transferred him to New York City the very next week. To disobey was to risk a federal indictment. Margot stayed in Utah until arrangements could be made to move Conan to an undisclosed location. When Conan left, his wife and Keenan stayed in Utah. But Margot went with him.

And she took Jeffery.

That was the last Luke ever heard of either of them. He tried to find out where they were a couple of times, and both times he got a letter from the chief of the WITSEC branch, telling him to cease and desist or face charges under the Witness Protection Act. And that was Luke's only and final go-round with love and fatherhood, with Witness Protection and Provo, and eventually with emotions of any kind.

Fugitive pursuits in New York State. Very clear. Locate a bad guy and take him down. Or out. It was precise, clean, and cold. Some of them got killed. Sometimes they killed one of his friends. Luke had found his war. He met Grizzly Dalton, who brought Luke into his family, helped him to feel at home, was as much of a friend to Luke as Luke could handle.

The two of them pulled takedowns all over the state, sometimes even further, in Michigan or Ohio or Pennsylvania, wherever the trail would lead. They worked out of a ramshackle old squad room in the Bronx Borough Hall. Luke had a walk-up flat on Court Street, over a fern bar. It was life, it was just fine, really. Luke had found his place in the world. He had found his true role. Speaking of which . . .

Two years back, around the time they were planning Operation Sunrise, he got a call from one of the Salt Lake City FBI guys. Keenan No Last Name had been shot dead in a roadside rest stop off I-80 near Winnemucca, Nevada. He had apparently tried to rape a woman sleeping in an RV at the rest stop.

In the Southwest almost every woman carries a weapon. This one had a SIG .380 under her pillow. She put five rounds into Keenan, spacing the shots evenly around his upper thorax and belly but, miraculously, missing his heart. Or Keenan didn't have one, always a possibility.

Keenan spent forty-nine hours dying, according to the FBI agent, who won ten bucks on Keenan's endurance in the office pool. His body remained unclaimed for the statutory sixty days and eventually ended up at a trade school for morticians in Carson City. They paid $79.80 for the corpse, not including freight. As far as Luke was concerned, they paid too much. But it was nice to know that Keenan had finally found the job he was born for.

Fertilizer.

The cello music faded away, turned into something lush and rolling, filled with violins and woodwinds. So much for nostalgia, he decided. He rolled out of the oversize bed and limped into the bathroom to check himself over.

Naked, he stood in front of the bathroom mirror. His belly was cross-hatched with road rash and scrapes. There was a large spreading bruise on his upper right shoulder. The hairs on his forearms and hands were singed off by the fire he'd run into face-first last night. The right side of his face was speckled with dried blood. He needed a shave. With his beard growing in white, and the scars, and the dried blood, he looked like a wino coming off a bender. He flexed his knees, felt the grinding. He grinned at himself in the mirror.

Years back he had seen a *60 Minutes* segment concerning the amount of time it took Dick Butkis to get out of bed each morning. It had taken Butkis over twenty minutes. Dick was so banged up and hobbled by his pro football years that he could hardly walk. His knees looked like skin bags full of washer parts. Luke's own football career had lasted about eight years, including grade school in Columbus. Luke was going to end up looking just like Dick Butkis. Luke Zitto, law enforcement professional.

Federal gladiator. Too old for the job. Too young for his pension. Too ugly to stuff and mount for the Smithsonian.

He climbed into the shower and stood there for a long time, breathing in the dense steam, letting the force of the water and the heat drive the bone-deep aches away. Then he dried himself off, checked the time by the bedside clock, sat down on the side of his bed, and stared at the phone for a good three minutes.

He picked it up and dialed a number in Yonkers. It rang long enough for Luke to think about hanging up, and then it was answered, a woman's voice, sleepy or drowsy. Or drugged.

"Hello?"

"Aurora, it's Luke."

"Luke . . . ?"

"Luke who do you think? Come on, kid."

"Luke . . . I was asleep."

Luke looked at the bedside clock. It was one o'clock in the afternoon. "Sleeping late?"

"Yes. Sleeping late. How's Washington?"

"Busy. How are things?"

"Okay. Not great."

"You get your clearance yet?"

"Not yet."

"What's Fielding saying?"

"I stopped seeing him."

"Why? I thought you liked him?"

There was a silence. Luke could hear her breathing, picture her lying on her bed in her Yonkers apartment, see the view of the Bronx and Harlem from her bedroom window. He felt a short sharp pang of loss and regret and anger.

Aurora's voice came back guarded, defiant. "Well, I stopped. It wasn't doing any good anyway."

"Honey, you have to see Fielding. He's the door-keeper."

"He's also an asshole. I've asked for someone else. A woman."

"Okay, I was just asking. You sound a little—"

"I'm fine. Really. I miss you."

"Yeah," he said, feeling guilty now. "How's Doug?"

Aurora laughed, not a musical sound. More of a low snarl.

"Oh, Doug's just peachy, Luke. Peachy. So's Payne. And the cat too. You're not a subtle guy, are you?"

"How's the law practice?"

"Mr. Powys is doing very well, thank you. He made partner. We have a great deal of money now. He's going to take Payne to Narragansett next week. They're going sports fishing. They want me to come with them."

"You should."

"I don't want to fish, Luke. I want to work."

Another silence. Luke thought about the young woman he'd seen yesterday, brushing her blue-black hair in the bathroom across the yard. Aurora was blond, with large blue eyes. Luke hoped she was staying away from bathroom windows. He took a long breath and got it said.

"Aurora, we got a line on Paolo Rona last night."

He heard her breathing stop.

"Where is he? Is he in custody?"

"Not exactly." He ran through the details with her, feeling his anger coming back, anger at Doc for missing his one clear shot at Rona, fury with himself for letting the little prick bail out that window. Aurora listened, asked a couple of basic questions, listened some more.

"What do you think he's doing in D.C.?"

"Everybody gotta be somewhere. You remember a Marshal named Doc Hollenbeck?"

"Yeah. He the one who ran that lecture at John Jay a

couple of years ago? About security of evidence? Big black guy?"

"Yeah. He was with me last night. He has a lead. I'm going over to his place today."

"Luke, can I come down there?"

"Not officially. You know that."

"I can come to visit, can't I? Doug and Payne will be away. The cat hates me anyway. I could stay with you. Would that be okay?"

"No, it wouldn't. You know I can't let you in on the project. You're on leave until you're cleared by Fielding. Or somebody in the service. I don't think they'd be too crazy about me letting you come down here looking for Paolo Rona."

"What the service thinks is at the bottom of my list right now."

"You still going to the meetings?"

She laughed, once. More of a bark, really.

"No."

"So you're not seeing Fielding and you're out of AA?"

"You always had a keen grasp of the essentials. Yes. To both."

"Aurora—"

"You're sure it was Rona? Positive?"

Luke saw the thin black shape, the pink T-shirt fluttering up K Street like a runaway kite, Doc lurching after it, saw Rona's face behind the Glock, the white rubber glove stretched over his right hand. Rona had called him something. La Culebra. The Snake. Well, he was from the Bronx. That was a name they'd laid on Luke because of his way with finks. Cold, distant. Without sympathy. Mainly he saw the slanted eyes and the heat in them, the crazy red glitter, half taillights from the cars going by, half pure hatred.

"Oh yeah. It was him."

"I'll be there Monday night. Meet me at the shuttle?"

"That's not—"

"With you or without you. You call it."

She meant it too. He wished now that he'd never called her.

"Aurora, if you come to D.C., that'll be it for your job. Fielding will burn you up and throw you away."

"I'll have a disability pension. I can get a job with the city cops."

"You won't *get* a disability pension unless you go all the way through the program. And if you don't go all the way through the program, no city bulls will take you either. You have to stay there, see it through."

Now the silence was electric, an open wire.

"Luke, I need to . . ."

"I know. I know."

"You're a real bastard, you know that?"

"Yeah. I'm a snake, actually. Look, this is hard for me too. Will you give us a week? Doc and me, we're going out again today. We'll get the little prick, save you the airfare. I promise you. I give you my word."

Silence.

Finally, she sighed, defeated, resigned. Hollow.

"Luke, you'll keep this to yourself, okay?"

"You mean, will I call Fielding?"

"Yeah. Or anyone?"

"No. I won't call Fielding."

"Or anyone?"

Damn.

"No, I won't call anyone."

Doc Hollenbeck's house was a red-brick Federal-style townhouse with white-painted shutters set on a small lot close to a low treelined bluff overlooking the valley of Rock Creek and the Woodley Park Zoo. A magnolia tree stood at parade-square attention out front, fiery pink and hot rose torches burning on a tiny front lawn as smooth and green as a billiard table. The yard was edged with low green wooden fencing, and the little driveway was covered in interlocking peach-colored stones. A wall of poplars and a few spreading willows swayed above the roofline. The magnolia had apparently dropped its blossoms recently, and Doc was out on the lawn as Luke drove up, sweeping the soft pink petals into a bushel basket. Luke parked his blue Crown Victoria behind Doc's Jeep Cherokee while Doc got to his feet with some obvious difficulty. He limped over to the drive as Luke was reaching into the back seat for the beers.

"Luke, you dago dipshit. You see the shape I'm in?"

Luke looked him over. Doc was wearing patched brown corduroys, penny loafers, no socks, and a hooded dark green sweatshirt with a raised crest embroidered in gold and red thread around a schooner. Doc's blue-black face was shiny, his grin huge and carnivorous.

"Dago dipshit?"

"Look at me, I'm a cripple!"

"You look like the Ozzie and Harriet poster boy. What does the schooner stand for? Don't tell me you're a sailor?"

Doc looked down at the crest on his sweatshirt.

"Why not?"

"Man, I can't see *you* sailing."

Doc took the beers, held them up to the streaming afternoon sunshine. "St. Pauli Girl? *Out*-standing! What? Darkies sailing? Man, what's the world coming to? Yeah, we sail. Come on in, nobody else is here yet. I got something to show you."

They headed up the walk toward the house, Doc limping still, his broad back marked with perspiration.

"Yeah, I'm early. Punctuality is the last refuge of the bored."

Doc snorted, put out a huge hand and shoved open the front door, sweeping Luke into a formal front hall. The inside of the house was dark and cool, but sunlight glimmered on polished wooden floors, shining through from a sunroom at the rear of the house. The rooms were low and painted in soft pastel tones, the furnishings heavy and comfortable looking. The sunroom was filled with flowers and white wicker furniture. Its floor was stone, some kind of pink granite. Beyond the windows of the sunroom, Luke could see more of those poplars, a rose garden, and past the rose garden a low valley lined with willows and green brush. A glimmer of silver ripple showed through the thick brush down in the valley. Rock Creek.

"Christ, Doc. This place is gorgeous."

Doc smiled, nodded, as he popped the caps off two of the St. Pauli Girls. "Glass?"

"No thanks, just in the bottle. What's this area called again?"

"Adams Morgan. A lot of Clinton's people live here. Mostly Beltway Bandits, civil service drones like me."

"Looks expensive."

"Washington's an expensive place. Adams Morgan is kind of like Forest Hills in New York. People work in Foggy Bottom, mostly they live here or in Georgetown, or across the river in Rosslyn or Arlington. There's a lot of money in D.C., but it's quiet money. The city's kind of frozen in 1955. Tell you the truth, I like it that way."

"Not the Southeast."

"No, not Seven District. You wanna sit down here or go outside?"

Luke looked around at the cool white wicker.

"Here's fine. I still can't get used to the *heat* down here. I got here, it was March, still a lot of chill. Now it's like New Orleans. Like the Delta."

Doc sat down opposite Luke. The big chair creaked under his weight. He drank from the green bottle, sighed.

"It *is* a delta. Most people don't think of it, but Washington's really part of the Old South. That's Virginia across the river. Most of the Civil War was fought less than two hundred miles from here. The first big battle, Bull Run, was fought less than twenty-five miles from here, down at Manassas. July 21, 1861. McDowell got his ticket punched. Union boys ran all the way back to the Potomac. People from Washington went down in carriages to see the South get beat, almost got trampled during the retreat. Soldiers fighting around Henry House, they'd look up, see the dome on the Congress. The Shenandoah Valley starts at Harper's Ferry, runs between the

Blue Ridge Mountains and the Shenandoahs, uphill all
the way to Lynchburg, almost. Most of the Civil War happened up that valley. You should take a drive, see some of
the places."

"You're a buff? Civil War?"

"No. But there's history all around here. That's why I
like it. I used to be down in Houston. Hated it. Glass.
Steel. Rained all the time. Texans are all loud, cranky, full
of themselves. Business guys with cell phones surgically
attached to their heads. Yuppie larvae all over the place.
Lois hated it too. Around here, it's like you're in the center
of America. You want to feel American, this is the place."

"Maybe. It's also a gangbanger's Disneyland."

"Yeah, well, while we're on the topic, I want to take
this opportunity to impress the bejesus out of you. Come
on down to my office."

Doc led them down a flight of stairs into a cool carpeted basement lined in wood paneling, covered with
family pictures and souvenirs. There was a big scruffy
plaid couch in front of a fireplace. A massive rear-projec-
tion TV with huge speakers took up another wall, next to
a long bar with a sink and another fridge. The room
smelled of cigar smoke and firewood. A striped tabby cat
the size of a beer cooler was lying on the couch. It opened
one eye and looked at Luke, yawned, showing a ridged
pink mouth and a set of fangs that his ex-wife would have
envied. This is a rec room, thought Luke. This is how regular people live. It gave him a twinge to see that even
someone in law enforcement could make a real life for
himself. It undermined all his rationalizations. Doc sat
down at a desktop computer and flicked it on.

"You remember the Letraset we found last night in
Rona's place?"

"We found?"

Doc grinned. "I'm being gracious. Lois makes me be

gracious at least twice a week. I went out, bought some of the same stuff. It's on the bar there."

Luke walked over to the long bar. Several sheets of Letraset in Arial Mixed were spread out over the top, next to sheets of blank paper and sheets with letters scribbled over them.

"You compared the sheet you found with a new sheet, figured out which letters Rona was lifting. Right?"

Doc beamed at him.

"Excellent, Luke. You should be a cop."

Luke came back to stand beside Doc. The screen blinked a couple of times and settled into a program window.

"This is an encryption program. I got it from Target Acquisition. I defined the parameters based on what we figure he was cutting."

"What do we figure he was cutting?"

"You got your Virginia DL yet?"

"No. Mine's still State of New York."

Doc flipped his own DL out onto the computer table. "See there. Those address numbers, the letters?"

"Arial?"

"Absolutely. Point size he used is strictly for the name and address. So I got the numbers. That was easy. Rona made several passes at the same five numbers in that Arial point size. Two 5's, a 1, and two 3's. Then he lifted a set without a mistake. He lifted three 2's and one zero."

The screen showed a grid pattern with these numbers entered in separate sectors.

"The program knows the template for the Virginia DL. It also recognizes the Arial point size. They're definitely address-related numbers."

"Man, how do you work this out?"

"I don't. This encryption program runs a comparison with all possible zip code numbers for Virginia. Watch."

Doc hit the enter button and sat back to let the screen run through a series of letter and number patterns. It took a few seconds.

23220 = RICHMOND VIRGINIA

"See. Outstanding."

"How does it know that?"

"Probabilities, whatever. Don't worry about that. So now we can eliminate one of the 3's—he used it up in the zip code."

"And the zero?"

"Yep, and the zero. That leaves us two 5's, a 1, and the last 3. We work that out exponentially—"

"*You* work that out exponentially."

"The machine does, anyway. And we have all these letters, but we already know that some of them got used up to make RICHMOND VA. That leaves us with—"

"Doc, I hate crosswords."

"Luke, how can I impress you if you won't stand still? I ran all this stuff through encryption and decryption and got a hundred and four possibles, combinations of names and addresses in Richmond, Virginia. Most of them were obvious garbage. The program doesn't know that NOSCRAG EERS is not your usual American name."

"Jeez, how many combinations could there be? You have twenty-six letters there, including the duplications? It would take a year to work out all the ways they could fit."

"Took about an hour. I did it when I got home this morning."

Luke looked at Doc, shaking his head. "So you have the answer already."

"Yeah, yeah—listen, Luke, you want to snag a desk job here in D.C., you gotta learn about this stuff. Okay?"

"Okay."

"Anyway, once you can give it a city, it compares all the letters in this grid with all possible street name combinations for Richmond. Once I cut out all the junk names, what I had left was this."

Doc hit a function key.

1553 JEFFERSON AVENUE

"And that left the apartment—no, there's no numbers left. All that's left is the name, right?"

"Right. Here it is."

LUCIO GARCIA

"Terrific. What about all those little letters left over?"

Doc flicked the papers with his hand. "These are all a different point size. They fit DOBs, these little details up here in the upper right-hand corner of my license. You can forget those."

"So Rona was making a Virginia driver's license? In the name of Lucio Garcia, with an address of 1553 Jefferson Avenue in Richmond?"

"Check it out. Here's a Richmond phone book."

Luke flipped through the pages, found GARCIA, and ran his finger down the list.

"Christ, there really *is* a Lucio Garcia at 1553 Jefferson."

"Your guy pulled it straight from the Richmond directory."

"Why? What if somebody checked it out?"

"That's why, Luke. The ID's even better if the guy can show it as listed in last year's phone book. Gives it credibility."

"Credibility for *what*, though? This isn't just a check scam. Why would he need that kind of depth in the ID?"

Luke stepped back and picked up his now-warm beer, pulled at it for a second.

"Doc, what we do next is put out a BOLO on that DL. Whoever Rona was making it for, he's gonna have to use it, or else why get one in the first place?"

Doc shut the machine off and stood up. "Yeah, and what do you usually have to show your DL for?"

"Bank accounts? Renting a hotel room if you don't have a card? Hospitals? Welfare?"

Doc led him back upstairs to the sunroom. The big cat followed them, snaking in and around Luke's legs as he climbed the stairs.

"Hey, Stonewall likes you."

"Stonewall's a damn big cat, Doc."

"He's a Maine coon cat. No jokes."

"What do you feed him?"

"Whatever he wants."

Doc pulled out a couple of fresh beers and sat down in the big wicker chair. "How about car rentals?"

Luke shook his head. "You can't rent a car without a credit card. They won't take cash at all. They can't ding you for tickets later if they don't have a credit card on file."

"I thought credit cards were one of Rona's things?"

"Not to use. He sells them."

"So this time he's selling a forged Virginia DL *and* a credit card. Maybe we should run this Garcia guy past NCIC and VICAP, see if he rings a bell. And the card companies. Let's see if he lost some credit cards. Also get the Richmond PD to see if he ever reported his wallet stolen. Somebody's getting a whole new life here."

Doc looked out through the sunroom windows at the poplars swaying in the afternoon breeze, their leaves silvering as the wind ruffled through them.

"Yeah, Luke. But who?"

When Paolo Rona was a little boy back on the Fordham Road, one of the games they used to play was Spider Sex. They'd get one of those big wolf spiders you could find in the vacant lots around Crotona Park, stick it into a jar with some holes punched in the lid. Drop some bugs in there to watch it eat. Paolo's friend Chulito, who later drowned in the East River, used to know where the females lived. They were always a lot bigger than the males, and their webs were like a city, stretched from one bush to another. You found them by going out early in the morning in the spring, you'd go deep into the basements or out into the parks, see the webs still covered with dew or with water from the basements, find them in the flashlight beam. The female would be right there in the middle, fat as a garden slug, with gray fur all over her, little black eyes with red lights in them, and legs as long as a Chesapeake crab.

They mated in the spring too, and the entertainment was watching the male spider try to get close enough to the female to mate with her, but not get killed and eaten in the process.

They never made it, especially when they were both stuck in a glass jar and a bunch of kids were shaking it to keep them together. The female would move—a flicker—those legs would wrap around the male, and he'd struggle, his whole body would jerk and twitch, and then his sex drive would kick in and they'd do . . . something, it was hard to tell . . . and when it was done—*bang*—he was outta there!

Or at least he'd *try*. Scrabble scrabble up the glass walls— Rona sometimes wondered if bugs understood the whole idea of glass. Well, they probably didn't waste too much time on it, because most of them were gonna be lunch for something else in about a heartbeat and a half, like that spider—like everybody on the planet, as Rona later figured out. Words to live by, anyway, and there goes that spider, kicking and twitching. Hey, it served him right for going anywhere near a broad. They were all spiders inside. Practice safe sex? Do what Paolo does, tie the *puta* up first, do her eight ways from Tuesday, then clean the place out and let her kids find her after school. *That's* safe sex!

Oh yeah, those were the golden days, back on the Fordham Road—a lot of the guys he'd grown up with got their tickets punched one way or another over the next ten years, by the cops, or Immigration, or in a turf war, or drugs, or suicide—everybody was somebody's lunch eventually.

But never him. And not today. Even Crow would think twice about chopping a man down in front of a thousand witnesses. Rona was going to get in there, get some spider sex, split with his life and five thousand dollars in cash. And Crow wouldn't be doing too much about it, because Paolo had seen to it he was gonna be pretty damn busy himself.

La vida loca, hah?

He was strolling down the long angular pathway that led to the black stone walls of the Vietnam Memorial, still wearing his fatigue jacket, still carrying his black bag with his pink T-shirt and his jeans stuffed inside on top of his Glock. His throat had settled down after he'd bought a crushed ice drink from a vendor on Constitution Avenue. It was a hot May day, a Sunday, the sun hanging up there in a dusty blue sky, and the crowds were thick in front of the black walls, people stopping here and there to look up at the names carved in the stone, kids leaving little flags on wooden sticks propped up against a certain wall, or older guys of all shapes and sizes standing back off the path, their eyes fixed on a certain part of the wall, on a particular name.

Rona watched them as he passed by, heading eastward along the pathway with the huge white tower rising above the trees way in the distance, watched the men standing there with their eyes filling up, blank stunned looks on their faces. Rona could sympathize, although he would never have been stupid enough to get trapped in a dumb war like that one, even if he'd been old enough. But it was like that when you stayed alive while somebody else died, although why you'd be *crying* about it was a mystery to him, but still, when you made it and your buddy from Fordham Road didn't, it made you think about things.

Like, better you than me, *maricón!*

He pulled in a long breath, feeling good, feeling in control finally, feeling that he had made good moves today, that he was finally going to get a real payday for his work. He passed the Vietnam Memorial and walked down a road that led to the edge of the reflecting pool. The water was rippling, clear, a dusty warm wind stirring the surface. It smelled of chlorine and hot stones. He looked up the length of it toward the big white needle at the other end, then he scanned the faces around him.

Nobody he knew. Not yet, anyway.

But he was happy about the crowds, the hundreds and hundreds of tourists milling around the wall or staring at the three bronze soldiers. And more of them walking along by the reflecting pool, climbing the steps of the Lincoln Memorial. People everywhere, and a lot of places to hide, places to lose yourself in, wooded areas, side streets, all those big white buildings running for miles up to that dome, had to be ten thousand people spread out along the huge park and the big rectangular pool.

He looked at his watch. It was a little after two. He broke into a slow trot, the black bag bouncing against his side, his jacket flopping on his shoulder. He had a half-mile to cover. Crow'd be here soon. The thing to do was to set up, locate a position, and check out the exits. He had given himself an hour to work with. The big needle had been built on the top of a big low sloping hill at the far end of the reflecting pool. A couple of service roads ran up to it on the eastern and western sides of it, and tour buses were parked all around its base. He could see them from where he was, and yet the needle itself looked like he could reach out and touch the thing. It had to be a mile high, like if it fell over, the top of it would crush him flat all the way down here.

Crow's papers were stuffed into a rip in the seam of the fatigue jacket. What he would do when he got there, he'd just set the jacket down on a chair or a bench up there by the needle, sit down beside it, lean back where he could watch people coming up toward him.

Crow'd show up—bring Joey Rag too, more than likely—and they'd be standing there, looking down at him. He'd say something, you know, cool, like he was in control, not showing any fear. Everything friendly, a business thing, right. No need to get all worked up. I mean, I'm *here*, right? So chill, *jefe*, chill. Yeah, it'd be okay.

Anyway, when you came right down to it, he had no reason to be afraid of Crow anyway. He had the thing done, good work too. He just had to be . . . cool . . . about it. Show he was somebody to respect. The main thing was not to get into any car or anything. Just sit there, keep calm, get his cash, and . . . drag things out a bit. Just long enough.

He picked up the pace. He wanted to get there before Crow showed up, and it was already two-fifteen. He was jogging along the road that ran parallel to the edge of the pool, his head on a swivel, looking at every face he passed, seeing only the dull sleepy faces of the citizens in their Sunday togs, loud colors, T-shirts, floppy sandals, sports shirts, and ball caps, everybody with those stupid fanny-pack things belted around them so they could have their hands free to slurp up ice cream cones.

There you go, he thought, jogging along toward the big white needle, that's the straight world for you; you're fat and you're stupid and you're sound asleep at the wheel. If everybody was somebody else's lunch, this place was a supermarket.

1410 Hours
Sunday, May 22, 1994
The Washington Monument
Washington, D.C.

Joey Rag butted his cigar out on the dashboard, brushed the ashes onto the floor, and leaned back into the passenger seat to watch Crow work the binoculars. He was hungry and hot. He'd even gotten tired of watching the broads go by in their summer T-shirts. Frankly, what he really wanted right now was for Paolo-from-Denver to show up, for Crow to do whatever he had to do, and then for Crow to fuck off and never come back.

They were parked on the side of the service road that ran around the base of the Washington Monument, sitting in a dark green delivery van with QUALITY INDUSTRIAL CLEANERS in big gold letters painted on the side. The road was elevated, riding the top of the long grassy hillside that led down to 17th Street. The end of the reflecting pool was on the far side of 17th. From where they were, they could see almost two hundred degrees around. They'd been there since one-thirty. They'd already done a slow cruise around the base and made certain that this guy who called himself Paolo wasn't there.

Paolo knew Crow and Joey Rag to see them, had met them last week in Chinatown, but he had never been out to the plant on North Capitol. He wouldn't recognize the van. From the little that Crow had said, Joey figured the idea was to get this Paolo into the van and take off. Whatever happened from there was up to Crow. Joey Rag didn't think it was going to be very nice to watch.

Nobody had told him anything about Crow's business with the guy. He knew the photo thing with the driver's license was just a ploy—Crow could get first-class ID from Barra's people any day of the week—so Crow was playing Paolo for some deeper reason. Crow was the company security guy. Maybe Paolo was suspected of finking, but Barra didn't know for sure yet, so they were letting him stay loose to see who he was meeting with.

Or maybe it was money.

One thing he knew, if Crow owed Paolo money, or Paolo was running a number on Crow, then Paolo was going to have to be real smart to get it done and then get back out alive.

If the guy ran true to his type, he'd show up any minute now, thinking to get in position and all set up before Crow and Joey got there. Crow had a set of Zeiss binoculars, a very fine set, and for the last forty-five minutes he'd been scanning the western end of the pool and the park lands all around, looking for Paolo.

Watching him sweep those lenses back and forth, the guy not saying anything, not feeling the need for small talk, for any courtesy, it made Joey Rag feel sorry for anybody this guy was looking for. He was like some kind of reptile, like he could sit under a rock for a year, looking like he was dead or something, and then *snap*, you were in his jaws and he was gulping you down whole.

Joey Rag was helping him out this week because the guy was somebody important to people who were in a position to tell Joey Rag what to do. Joey Rag was just a worker. A nondescript, balding and slightly overweight man in his mid-forties, he was born Miguel Jorge Ragundo in Honduras. Back there, he had been a tough street kid, had done some throat-cutting and some knee-breaking for Guillermo Barra's people. Once he'd killed a whore by stuffing her mouth with bits of cloth. It was how he got his name. Why she had to die, nobody explained to him.

After that job Barra had taken a liking to him and had contracted him out to the United States end of things to do what he had been doing now for ten years. He ran the laundry—it was a legit business and had lately been making real decent money, some of which Joey had found a way to skim—and he also ran some of the local sidelines for Guillermo Barra's friends in Atlanta.

They were a loose association of families from Central America, a kind of brotherhood-syndicate that was into a bunch of things; they loaned money to illegals for a huge vig, sometimes scamming the government for local initiative grants through front organizations like Hispanic churches, dealing some weapons from time to time, moving some coke if it was already in the country and just needed to go from one state to another, fencing, of course money movement and laundering—one of the uses of the legit business Joey ran for them—and now and then they helped out somebody from another outfit with a problem. They had a famous problem-solver who worked free-lance for them, a reliable man. He was the one who asked questions, who figured out who was lying and who was jacking the firm around. They'd loan him out from time to time.

As a favor. For a consideration.

He'd heard a lot about this problem-guy they had,

heard he was a Miskito from Guyana, did time in Angola, used to be in the army. Heard he was very good and very scary. He imagined the guy would be something special, a role model. But he'd never seen him until a week ago, when Crow turned up at the plant and said he was going to stay upstairs. He'd been here a week, and Joey had counted every second of it like it was a teardrop of blood from the eyes of the Virgin of Guadalupe.

When Crow wrapped up this thing with Paolo-from-Denver, he was supposed to go away on a job, something about a guy who was going to rat some of their people out to the DEA. Joey could hardly wait. The guy had the personality of a scorpion. Never drank, didn't go with boys—or girls. Never seemed to sleep. Never made small talk. If he found out the guy lived on flies, Joey would not be surprised.

Joey sat in the van and looked out the window at the tourist chicks and tried to stay awake in the damp heat of the afternoon. His shirt was sticking to his chest. His face was dripping. His eyes were closing. . . .

Somebody slapped the wall of the van, banged it, making it ring. Joey jumped a yard, but Crow just put the glasses down and turned to look at the uniformed D.C. cop standing beside the driver's door.

"Yes, officer?" said Crow.

"You waiting for something here, sir?"

The cop was black, hard-faced, with a huge curved mustache and a pair of mirrored aviators. His hat was set square on his head, and his shoulders were braced. His nameplate read CULLEN. His voice was cranky; he was tired of shifting tourists and gawkers out of restricted parking areas like this one. Crow's voice was calm, almost friendly.

"Yes, officer. We're supposed to meet my mother here. She's walking up from the pool there, and we didn't want to miss her."

The cop's face showed nothing. Joey Rag leaned forward and saw Crow's reflection in the cop's glasses, and his own distorted image upside down behind Crow.

"What's this truck—" He leaned back to read the letters on the side. "You guys cleaners?"

Joey Rag leaned over Crow's chest and gave the cop a business card. When the cop lowered his head to read it, Crow moved his own hand down between his legs.

Joey Rag's heart surged with fear. Jesus Mary. Not a cop. He made a supreme effort to sound casual. "Quality Industrial, Officer—ah—Cullen. We're sorry we put you out here. Ernest, let's go, okay?"

Crow turned his head to look at Joey Rag. There was a short moment of silence, and then he smiled and turned back toward the cop.

"Yes, officer, we'll get out of here. Sorry."

The cop stepped back, keeping the card with him. Crow started the van up and pulled away from the curb. Joey Rag watched the cop in the side mirror. He was writing something down in a pad.

"Man, he made us," said Joey Rag.

"No, Joey," said Crow, in a dead calm voice. "You did that. You handed him a card. And you shit yourself. You embarrass me."

"What was I gonna do?"

"What you're supposed to do."

Crow had the van up to speed and was running it down the long entrance road toward Constitution Avenue, which ran parallel to the Mall on the north side. As he came down off the monument hill, he glanced to his left out the window.

"There he is," said Crow.

Joey Rag leaned forward to look in the direction Crow indicated.

"Where?"

"There. By the popcorn seller. At the corner."

Joey Rag saw him. Paolo was standing close to a lamp-post at the corner of Constitution and 15th. He was no more than a hundred yards away, a skinny Hispanic in a black shirt and jeans, an army fatigue jacket over his shoulder, carrying a black canvas bag. His hair was cut in a floppy razor style that Joey associated with snotty school-boys and pimps who dealt coke in the cocktail bars of tourist hotels.

Crow bulled the van across the intersection and came to a stop at the curb on the far side of Constitution. A huge limestone building with a Greek roofline took up the entire block. The street was lined with oaks and chestnuts inside little wrought-iron fences. Crow twisted in his seat to watch Paolo at the intersection a block down.

"What do you want me to do?" asked Joey, now extremely nervous about having upset the man. He would make it up, he would be helpful. He was having some trouble with his breathing right now, and his throat felt tight. Looking back on it, he could not believe that he had given that cop his business card. He was losing it. He had run a legitimate business and let himself believe that he was really a straight guy now. Crow was right.

"Go get him," said Crow.

"Get him?"

"Yes. Bring him to the van."

"He won't come."

"See that he does," said Crow, his stone face blank and his eyes fixed on Joey Rag's face.

"How?"

Crow reached down between his legs, pulled out a small Llama .32 semiauto. It had once been blue but was now worn, and much of the steel showed. He handed it to Joey Rag. It was warm and sweaty from the man's crotch, and Joey did not want to hold it.

"My thing—it's not this. I do laundry. I do—"

"What you're told. Now go."

There was nothing more to say. Joey Rag was not a legit beez-neez guy, and now all of that had come back to haunt him. This was his real life, to do what men like Crow told him to do or to get killed for not doing it.

Joey opened his door and climbed down onto the sidewalk, stuffing the little gun into his jeans pocket. He walked up to the intersection of Constitution and 14th. Paolo was on his way east along Constitution Avenue, going in the direction of the Capitol dome, on the far side of the street next to the grassy slope of the monument. All of his attention was focused on the needle and the cars and people milling around the base. Joey watched him walking and tried to see if anyone was following him. Maybe this car over here, with two women in it? Maybe that man there, looking at a map? Or that guy, talking into a cell phone? He was truly afraid now and wished that he had never agreed to help with this thing. To kill a teenage *puta* in Old Town, that was one thing, and anyway he had been young and stupid. But now, this thing, he was not ready for this.

As if he had a choice.

He went forward now, timing his approach, stepping lightly in his expensive Brazilian loafers, closing in on Paolo as the man walked eastward on the far side, still looking up at the needle. All he could hope to do was to get close, get the little piece up against the man's chest, tell him what to do.

And if he wouldn't?

If he wouldn't, then Joey was going to let him go, make some kind of excuse, because he had privately determined that he wasn't going to shoot a man in plain sight on Constitution Avenue and end up in prison for the rest of his life. Crow could kill him if he wanted, but Joey had been in prison once, in Honduras, and he never wanted to go back. Even *holding* this gun was a prison thing. Firearms were illegal in D.C. No private person could own one. Everybody did, but that wasn't the kind of excuse that would get you far with a D.C. cop—Say, boss, why pick on me? Everybody's carrying!

He stepped more quickly now, taking a jaywalk angle across the wide avenue, dodging cars and taxis, setting a line that would bring him even with Paolo on the sidewalk but a little behind him. The heat was on his back, and he pushed his hand deep into the pocket of his jeans, wrapped his fingers around the Llama pistol.

Fifty feet. Forty.

Thirty.

Now he was on the sidewalk. Paolo was about ten feet ahead of him, moving at a slow jog, his attention fixed on the base of the needle. Joey Rag tried to step quietly. He pulled the Llama out of his pocket and let his right hand hang loosely at his side. He could see Paolo's hands, see the black bag on his shoulder and the army coat over that. Now he was close enough to see the close-cropped hairs on the back of his neck and the shiny stuff he used on his hair to keep it slicked back.

In his heart Joey Rag wished very deeply that he had gone into another line of work. He looked around him. There was a man walking toward them, a short white-haired man in a brown suit, reading a paper as he walked. Cars rolled past in the wide street, their tires booming and hissing on the hot pavement like ocean waves on a beach. Joey looked back behind him. Nobody was close. Nobody looked out of place, or like they were paying attention to him and what he was doing. At the edge of the park a big red-haired woman was sitting on the grass, her dress gathered up around her knees, sunglasses on, her face tilted back to let the sun shine down on it. There was a little grove of trees and a bench coming up. When they got even with the bench, then Joey would do it. Almost on the man's heels now, Joey Rag lifted his hand up, pushed the shiny little semiauto forward. Sunlight glittered along the worn-down metal of the barrel.

Ten feet . . . five feet.

Now.

D oc Hollenbeck was making a point Luke didn't want to hear, but he liked Doc, so he was trying to be patient. They were waiting for the other members of Doc's Fugitive Pursuit unit to show up and working their way through the rest of the St. Pauli Girls. Doc was winding himself up on the subject of race warfare. He grimaced, leaned forward.

"That's the thing about this town. Our new HQ? You been in the mall across the street? Can *you* afford to shop there? I can't. I can hardly afford the coffee. But there it is, a going concern too. So somebody has the money. You see all that money around, and you don't have any—"

"Doc, not from you, okay?"

"What?"

"All that Marxist crap, the downtrodden darkies, the uppity white folks. Man, I got all of that bullshit I could handle from my ex-wife."

Doc's face was a little stony. Luke held the beer bottle

up to a shaft of light coming in through the sunroom window. It was empty.

"Doc, I'm sorry. Really, I'm out of line. Let's drop this, okay? This shit always gets me down. My ex-wife was always on me about this kind of thing. She used to call me a 'minion.'"

"A what?"

"A minion. You know, a tool, a running-dog lackey, that kind of stuff."

"Charming broad. I'd like to know her. What was she, a Rottweiler?"

"No. Couldn't pass the finals. How about a beer?"

Doc groaned and leaned forward, extricated himself from the wicker chair, walked over, took Luke's empty beer out of his hand. Talking over his shoulder, he wandered into the kitchen, his voice muffled by masses of greenery and a huge vase of dried flowers sitting on the dividing bar between the kitchen and the sunroom.

"Some of the guys are coming by, but I don't think I'm up to no damn game of flag football. How are you doing?"

"You ever see a 60 Minutes thing on Dick Butkis? How he was so banged up, he couldn't get out of bed?"

Doc limped back into the room, handed Luke another St. Pauli. It was so cold, it hurt Luke's fingers.

"Hell, where are you keeping these?"

"In your ex-wife's heart. Got it back there in the kitchen. Lois uses it to freeze-dry her flowers. Yeah, I saw that show. That how you feel?"

"My body's not a temple, it's an arena. Is Lois home? You don't want to introduce her to lowlifes like me?"

Doc laughed, knowing that Luke was changing the subject, letting the issue of race warfare slide.

"Lois is out, taking a course at Georgetown. Modalities of—something. Dissent, I think. She's studying that Benning Road pool thing, that trial's on right now."

"Yeah, I heard about that. Last year?"

"June 22. The Alabama Avenue Crew, they call themselves. Two kids, one seventeen, the driver, and the shooter, get this, fourteen years old. They got an Uzi, opened up on a swimming pool full of children, full auto. Put over thirty rounds into the shallow end. Wounded six kids, all of them under twelve. Benning Road school."

"Christ, yeah, I remember that. Lois a lawyer?"

"No, she's upgrading to be a teacher. She's studying gang dynamics. You want to see gang dynamics, Luke, you drop by the courthouse and stand around in the halls, you'll see gang dynamics. They're all out there in the halls, scaring the shit out of witnesses, letting everybody know, they talk against an Alabama crew member, they're dead. They already frightened off one woman, she saw the driver. Last week somebody fired fifteen shots at her teenage daughter on the way home from school. Yesterday the woman told the prosecutors she 'can't remember' what the kid looked like."

"Why don't the guards clear them out?"

"Constitutional rights. They get through the metal detectors, there's no legal way to keep them out of the halls. American justice, Luke."

Luke held his hands up, palm out, shoulders raised, his face saying clearly although silently, see what I mean?

Doc's face hardened. "Look, all I meant about these kids is that they aren't at the *bottom* of society, they're *outside* it completely. If your only stake in life is respect, respect based on whatever you can deliver, then respect—"

"You mean fear."

"Yeah, okay, fear. Then fear is what keeps you alive, it's what gives you any power at all. So if somebody—I know you hate this word—"

"*Disses* you?" Luke said.

"Yeah, *disses* you, that's like in normal society, you're waiting on line, gonna get yourself a Raspberry Slurpy, a guy shoves his way into line in front of you, you say, hey man, and he says, so what, numb-nuts, fuck you. You have now been officially dissed, right. So what do you do? Say your girlfriend is there. What do you do?"

"Is my girlfriend a black belt in karate?"

"You know what I'm saying."

"Okay, okay," Luke said. "I guess I make a point of it, get him to understand that he's not staying there in front of me."

"How far will you go?"

"Up to him. I guess, I have to, I'll deck him."

"Over a spot in line?"

"It's more than that," Luke said.

"Yeah, you're gonna lose what?"

"My self-respect, I guess. I mean, the guy's an obvious asshole."

"And if he comes back with a piece?"

"I'll protect myself, I guess."

"Kill the guy?"

Luke could see where this was going. "Look, Doc, this guy started it, he escalated it, this is *his* thing, not mine. I'm just—"

"You're just going to kill a guy rather than let him get a Raspberry Slurpy before you do. That's what you just said."

"What you're saying, this is a once-in-a-lifetime thing. These schmucks down at the courthouse, they do this every day. I'd say that's different."

"In degree, maybe."

"No, it's not just that. These kids defile themselves, they *choose* to be assholes. Just like the guy getting in between me and my Raspberry Slurpy. *He* knows the rules, just like me. He made a choice, that's all. He *chose* to get in my face. Then he *chose* to prod me. That was *his* thing. I was just a consequence, that's all. I was a piece of cosmic machinery in that buttwad's karmic cycle, whatever. If growing up in a bad neighborhood was enough to make you a criminal, Stanley Crouch would be doing life in Attica. A lot of kids in the hood don't go that route. All those middle-class black families, we just don't *hear* about them. Look, Doc, I understand what you're trying to do here, and I appreciate it. But I'm not into accepting bullshit excuses for brainless killings. Any society that shows more creativity in making up excuses than it does in fixing things isn't going to be around very long."

Doc sat back and laughed out loud.

"Good one. I'll use it on Lois. But the little picture is, getting dissed and letting it go, for a gangbanger, that's like you start pissing blood, you look down and say, whoa, gotta cut back on the cranberry cocktail. It's a warning, and everybody knows it. In that world, you let it slide, they all close in on you, and next day, *bam*, you're a speed bump in somebody else's fast lane."

"I know that, Doc. But that doesn't mean I cut that guy any slack at all. That's not my job. Yours neither. You oughta leave their souls to God."

"You think *he* cares?"

"If *he* doesn't, why should I?"

Doc shook his head. "You're damn close to burned out, Luke. You need to be careful."

"Of what?"

"I don't know. Your light, I guess."

"My *light*?"

Doc looked at him for a while.

"Maybe we better drop this, hah?"

Luke looked at him, puzzled.

"Yeah, maybe we better."

In the difficult silence that followed, they heard voices

at the door, someone laughing, and then the bell rang. Doc got up to answer it, leaving Luke alone for a time to consider the state of the nation and his personal relation to the infinite. Say what you want, Doc was an interesting guy.

Irritating, but interesting.

Doc came back into the sunroom followed by three other men, two of them in blue sweats with the five-point star of the U.S. Marshals Service on their chests, and a third man in jeans, cowboy boots, and a white T-shirt. Luke stood up as they came down through the hallway, still laughing.

"Okay, guys, this is Luke. Luke, these are my guys. You know a couple, I think."

The man in the jeans and white T stepped forward, put his hand out.

"Luke, I'm Walt Rich. We met a couple of times at the Four-Six."

Rich was short, maybe five nine, solid across the chest and belly, with skinny slightly bowed legs and close-cropped bright carrot-red hair, a freckled Irish face, green eyes, and a badly dented nose, the bridge pushed almost flat. As soon as Luke saw him, he made the connection.

"God, yeah. You used to be Bronx Vice, didn't you? You knew Coles, those guys. We worked once on that Ching-a-Ling thing, when was it?"

Rich's smile was thin. He held his right hand up to show Luke his gold detective's ring. "It was in eighty-nine. You popped Jugo Sarpente with a twelve-gauge. I got this ring outta that project. Gold Shield. So did Darcy Coles."

"You're a deputy now?"

"Yeah. They made me an offer I couldn't refuse. A living wage."

"You made good money in New York."

"Not enough to live there. I'm out in Jersey now, and my kids don't need an armed escort to get to school."

"So you're going back?"

"Yeah. I'm taking your job, so I hear. I'm gonna work with Grizzly Dalton."

"He's a good man. A great street operator. You'll like him."

"I know him. I met him when I was in Bronx Vice. He was always coming around trying to horn in on our snitches. Guy's a bloodhound."

"I know. I worked with him until last year. How long are you here?"

"I been here a year, taking computer training. I'm going back to New York in September. They got an operation planned. Grizzly's gonna run it, along with Rico here. You gonna be in on it?"

"Not if I can help it. I'm assigned to HQ here. Got moved after the Sunrise operation."

"Yeah? Full time? I'm impressed. You'll *hate* it here."

One of the men in the blue sweats stepped up, offered his hand. Six feet or more, very slender, his skin was deeply tanned, almost mahogany in tone, with a growth of dark beard and a haggard, starved-looking face. His cheekbones stood out, and his black eyes rode far back in the skull, but his grip was strong and his skin hot and dry. His teeth were uneven, as if he'd grown up in a place without dentistry. His voice had a faint Latin accent.

"I'm Rico Groza. I heard they call you Snake, La Culebra."

Luke grinned back at him. He'd heard of the guy. Groza had worked undercover in Central America on loan to the DEA in various drug-interdiction operations. There was a department story going around—probably mythical—that Groza had spent six months in Mexico hunting the men who had tortured and murdered DEA agent Enrique Camarenas, and that when he left on the hunt, they found his ID case and his star on his desk. When he came back and picked up his ID again, there were rumors of two men missing down in Zihuatenejo and one man crippled in Ciudad Obregón.

Watching Groza at his ease in the sunshine, the sunken depths of his black eyes, Luke wondered about the man, about departmental secrets, about his own secrets.

"You brought in Zamarro last year, didn't you?"

Groza smiled.

"Not by myself. Good to meet you, Luke. Call me Rico. This ugly guy here, he's Slick Stevens. Give him your paw, Slick."

Stevens put out a hand the size of a pot roast. He was a large white man with a completely bald head, round red cheeks, and heavy brows, but his eyes were a blue so light, they were almost clear. His skin was darkly tanned, and a radius of white creases fanned out across both temples.

"Luke, good to know you."

"I saw your picture in *The Pentacle*, didn't I? You were on that sweep down here, back in 1989? Operation STOP?"

"Yep."

Doc laughed as he brought out some beers and handed them around. "Slick's a man of few words."

"Deeds, not words," said Stevens, pulling up a white stool. Luke watched him lower his weight onto it, braced for disaster. Groza looked at Doc's clothes, and then over at Luke in black slacks and a blue denim shirt. "Somethin' tells me we won't be playing football today?"

Doc groaned. "Hey, Luke and me, we kicked some serious butt last night, while you guys were sitting around playing with your—"

Walt Rich snorted. "Serious butt? I heard you stepped

on your dicks real good with that Rona buttwad. Luke ends up under a car? You learn that at Glynco, Luke?"

Doc frowned. "That was later—numb-nuts had a scanner. Who knew?"

"You shoulda," said Slick, grinning.

Walt was still laughing. "My wife calls me in, you're on the eleven o'clock news. I fell over, Slick, it was priceless. They showed a film of those kids, some D.C. cops shoving them into a transport van. The look on their faces, man."

Luke grinned, remembering. "Yeah, they came up the steps, I don't know what they were thinking."

Doc broke in. "Yo, we bad, we bad, we—whoops, we fucked—that was about it. Luke just stood up and went down into them, one of them goes for something—"

"Probably his rosary," said Walt Rich.

"Luke just stuck this huge stainless—what *is* that thing you carry, anyway."

"It's a Taurus."

Rico Groza's voice was low and raspy.

"They said you still had that guy's piece. Am I right?"

"Sutter. Yeah, I have it. Who said?"

Stevens, who had been watching the group and quietly putting away most of his beer, leaned forward. The stool groaned underneath him. Silhouetted in the slanting sunlight streaming in through the windows, his face in shadow, his voice seemed to come from a stone well.

"I said. I knew that asshole."

"Sutter? From where?"

"He did a job on a friend of mine, a Wells Fargo guard. In 1986."

Luke focused on the man now, his mind working. "Grand Island, Nebraska. The Wal-Mart?"

Stevens nodded.

"What happened?" asked Walt Rich. Stevens looked at him, then down at the beer bottle in his hands. It looked like a dark green salt-shaker, lost in those massive hands. He told the story in a flat monotone, the way people do when the story is a bad one.

"Two o'clock in the afternoon, right there in the parking lot in front of the main doors. Sunny day, just like this. A Saturday, too, kids running all over the place, an ice cream truck sitting there with families lined up for a Sno-Kone. Hundreds of people saw it happen. He must have been sitting in that brown van for a coupla hours, tinted windows, you couldn't see inside. Up comes the Wells Fargo truck. They have a pickup to make. You know Wal-Mart, that one in Grand Island, that's a money-mill. They said the take was almost two hundred thousand. Small bills."

Doc was interested. "What'd he do?"

"Lone wolf operation. He sees the truck come up, right there by the double doors. Guard in the back, driver up front. And one guy to go in there, carry out the bags. Two of them."

Rich groaned. "One in each hand?"

Stevens's massive bald head lowered once.

"And no cover. They were farm kids, a bunch of half-trained cherries. Sutter got out of the brown van. Came up behind the Fargo truck, waited until the outside man came through the doors. Then he throws a set of cuffs around the rear door handles, steps around the truck, the guys in the truck are just now tumbling to it. They said Sutter just walked up beside the guy, no words, no yessir nossir. Put a big revolver right up against the side of the man's skull, the guard said no, turned his face away from the muzzle. Sutter flew his face off. Parts of it stuck to the ice cream van, splattered the kids in the lineup. He was twenty-four, two kids. Less than twenty feet from the Wells Fargo truck, both inside guards just staring at him, totally in shock, and the guy's down on his back, blood running out like a big red lake."

Luke believed him.

"Did they get out, try to take him?"

Stevens shook his head, held up his empty beer. Doc got up and took it from him. The other men were silent, seeing the thing in the hot midwestern sun, the body shadowless, splayed, the glitter of red like taillight glass, spreading out in rivers and lakes at the feet of the children.

"No. The cuffs held the back door, and the driver froze. The inside man got a shot off through the gun port, broke a plate-glass display window. Sutter ran to his van, threw the bags in, was onto I-80 in a minute. They found the brown van two miles down the line at a rest station. Empty."

Groza wanted to know how they had identified Delbert Sutter.

"Videotape. The Wal-Mart security cameras picked up the whole thing through the glass doors. FBI made him from VICAP files."

Stevens nodded again, a single inclination of his big bald head, his face still in darkness. He lifted his beer to Luke.

Luke returned the salute, considering.

"The piece he used, it wasn't a Taurus was it?"

"No. A Colt Delta."

"Good."

Doc's phone rang, a short sharp trill. He limped off down the hall to answer it. The talk went around in a casual way; finks, chasers, warrant work, runners, the next big career criminal sweep—rumored to be set for sometime in the coming winter—cases they knew or wanted to know about, gossip about the brass down at HQ, speculation about the new director, about Janet Reno and her heavy hands on the Justice reins.

Doc came back into the room and motioned to Luke. They walked back into the kitchen together. Doc leaned against the counter, glanced out at the other men in the sunroom, and spoke in a soft voice, an official voice.

"That was Brewer in Ops."

"Yeah?"

"You know a Treasury bull named Canaday? Bolton Canaday?"

"Yeah. I know him."

"He's over at 600 Army Navy right now. Waiting for us."

"For *us*? Why?"

"He thinks he's got some news for us. He heard about our go-round last night, apparently. He knows we're after Paolo Rona. It seems Treasury agent Canaday wants to help us out."

Luke was interested but not impressed. Bolton Canaday was a bloodless career guy with the ethics of a Tanzanian stoat. If he wanted in on the Rona thing, it was for his own reasons. Treasury reasons.

"It seems they had a big takedown just now, on Constitution, just by the monument. They were rolling up a buy-and-bust. One of the guys had a piece and showed it, and they dropped him."

"Rona?"

"The face was wrong. The picture on the license was not the guy on the ground."

"But it was Rona?"

"That's what they're saying. Canaday wants to meet us at HQ and fill us in. Wanna go look? Or do I tell him to fuck off?"

Luke was going through a number of emotions, some of them hard to pin down. Doc watched him in silence.

Out in the sunroom the guys were listening to Walt Rich tell a story about a body they found up in Crotona Park, had no head, no hands, and no feet, and was also skinned. But it wasn't a murder and it wasn't suicide, and in the end it wasn't even indignity to a dead body. So what was it?

Luke knew the answer, but his mind was somewhere else. Maybe this was very good news for Aurora Powys.

"Yeah," he said, finally. "Let's go see him."

It was an indication of the rising fortunes of the United States Marshals Service that it had recently acquired a brand-new headquarters office, a huge eleven-story bronze-tinted glass cube, one of a set of four in a block-long square of federal office towers across the Arlington Memorial Bridge over the Potomac a mile down Jeff Davis Highway from the Pentagon. It was a significant step up from their former HQ in a nondescript strip-mall somewhere in Rosslyn. The director's office had a skyline view of Washington and all the capital landmarks, one of the true status indicators in the eternal game of Beltway Bungy-Bingo. The next building over, an identical bronze glass cube, was the headquarters of the DEA. The directors could wave to each other from their top-floor office suites. They probably did. Other federal agencies, including the ATF and liaison units of the DIA, the IRS, and the NSA, had suites in the other two buildings, along with hundreds of unmarked and unidentified offices whose work was, now that you ask, actually none of your damn business, thank you very much.

The whole Arlington federal area was a broad flat concentration of brand-new offices and a very expensive mall, built over what had once been a magnificent stand of old red oaks and copper beeches. All the streets were six lanes wide, separated by broad central boulevard gardens with well-tended shrubs and flowering plants. The cars on the street tended toward battleship-gray Bimmers and Volvo wagons, or Ford vans with black-tinted windows carrying grim-faced men hither and yon on apparently vital errands, or federal-blue Lincoln Town Cars with bulletproof glass and Kevlar side panels driven by solid-looking chauffeurs with surgically bypassed smile muscles, who wore single-breasted blue suits and aviator glasses and had white flex-cord earplugs stuck in their ears and who were always looking around at the rooflines and keeping one hand inside their jackets.

The main garage for the Marshals Service HQ had an unmarked driveway that led down into a multilevel underground parking area heavy with surveillance cameras and motion-detector sensors. The garage included storage areas for command trucks, satellite uplink communications vehicles, armored raid tanks, all-terrain vehicles, even some multiengine high-velocity offshore racing boats. The rooflines and lampposts were studded with security cameras, and plainclothes perimeter guards were always strolling around the walkways and parkettes between the four bronze towers. Everything about the place said SERIOUS BIGTIME FEDERAL LAW RIGHT HERE. Every time Luke drove down the parking ramp toward the steel-barred entrance gate, he felt like Jonah sliding down the whale's gullet.

He slowed the Crown Victoria to a crawl and triggered the infrared code beam in his grill. The steel grate lifted with a hydraulic whine, and the surveillance camera mounted over it swiveled and centered on the car. Somewhere inside the building the car was being run through a recognition system and the entrance time noted on a database. If it failed that clearance process, the primary gate would still lift, but the car would be trapped in between this grate and the secondary barricade about fifty feet farther in. Once inside that fifty-foot concrete hallway, there was no escape, and the hallway itself was reinforced with ferro-concrete blast deflectors that would direct the force of any suicide-bomb explosion back up the parking ramp and away from the building's substructure. Armed guards positioned in observation posts and hardened shelters would overcome and arrest anyone who tried to get through on foot. There was even a halon gas system in place to put out secondary electrical fires. And that was only the stuff Luke knew about.

Everyone realized there was a lot more to the security systems than they'd been told about, but no one was stupid enough to demonstrate any interest in the subject. The HQ was classed and graded as a level-one hard-target building, partly because of the Witness Protection admission facility it contained and partly as a response to the alarming increase in bomb threats—and bomb deliveries—against federal facilities around the country. The Marshals Service was taking the escalation in domestic terrorism very, very seriously.

There was a security station at the second gate, framed in bulletproof glass, staffed by two guards, one of them sitting in front of an array of video screens and sensor boards. Luke fished out his ID and rolled down the window as they reached it. One of the blue-uniformed guards was a young black woman, stony-faced and carrying a Hechler & Koch MP-5 machine pistol. She was wearing a Kevlar vest. Luke looked at the fire-select switch on the

MP-5 as she came forward to the car. It was set to three-round bursts. The weapon was on a shoulder sling, but the little black muzzle of the piece was aimed right at his head, and her right index finger rested along the outside of the trigger guard, a twitch away from the firing position. She leaned down and looked at Luke's ID and then took another long look at Doc's as well, matching the pictures to their faces. If she was impressed, she managed to conceal the reaction very well. "Can you pop the trunk, sir?" was all she said.

She looked about fifteen to Luke. Doc opened the glove compartment and pressed the yellow trunk release. The trunk lid popped, and she walked away to check it out. The car was sitting on a steel grid, and a surveillance camera was giving the other guard inside the station a look at the underside of the car. Luke and Doc said nothing to each other, mostly out of habit, since there were also high-sensitivity directional mikes aimed at their windshield. Doc drummed on the dashboard and sighed while the woman did a complete circuit around the car. Finally she nodded and went back to the station. The second gate rose up into a recessed slot, and Luke drove over the tire-damage spikes and into the Level One parking area. The entire floor was lit with halogen lamps in recessed ceiling fixtures covered with steel grids. It was high-noon-bright inside. Fugitive Ops had a special section on Level Three, and they rolled down the ramps and past hundreds of other federal cars and vans in marked-off sectors.

WITSEC—NO ACCESS

COURT SECURITY COORDINATOR—RESERVED

LIAISON COMMISSION—RESERVED

U.S. MARSHALS—NO ACCESS

DIRECTOR—RESERVED 24 HOURS

SPECIAL OPERATIONS

TRAINING

INTEL AND ANALYSIS—NO ACCESS

ASSET SEIZURE

FUGITIVE OPS—TARGET ACQUISITION

FUGITIVE TEAMS

Luke's slot was next to Norm Brewer's charcoal-gray Jeep Cherokee. They climbed out, and Luke set the lojack and the alarm with his hand remote as they walked away from the car. The car chirped and beeped, and Doc chuckled a bit to himself as they got to the steel door that led to the elevator banks.

"What are *you* laughing at?" said Luke, as he punched their floor number on the board. The machine rose with a silent rush of power and speed, pressing them into the carpeted floor. A surveillance camera in the upper right corner of the elevator whined once and settled on them.

"I'm just remembering what it was like in the old offices. They had a buzzer at the bottom of the stairs and a glass door with 'Marshals Service' on it in gold paint. Upstairs the place was all baby-shit yellow and puke green, you know, those two-toned walls they always painted our offices in. The guard was an old war vet named Homer Bukowitz. His piece was a Colt .45 I think he got in Roosevelt's ride up San Juan Hill. The whole place was made of plywood and ripple-glass, and the director's office was in the corner overlooking the parking lot and the ARCO station on the corner."

"Things change, I guess."

Doc chuckled again. "I guess our pay raise is in the mail then, hah?"

Luke grinned at that. "Oh yeah, any day now. I think it's coming in on the *Titanic*, isn't it?"

The elevator stopped, and the doors rolled back. They walked out into a broad entrance hall with closed office doors running down one wall. Luke walked to a door like all the others and slid his ID card through the reader slot. There was no sign on the door, no sign on any of the office doors on any floor in the building. If you didn't know the number, you didn't belong there anyway. The door buzzed and popped open.

Fugitive Ops was a large cluttered office floor filled with wood-veneer desks and dark green filing cabinets, desktop computers, gun cabinets, and work tables. Just about every flat space was piled high with computer print-outs of felony stats, Justice Department crime projections, and updated Wanted lists filed by almost every state and local police agency in the nation. The two inside walls were covered with duty rosters and assignment sheets, car vouchers and trip sheets, all the usual paperwork and housekeeping lists you'd find in any law enforcement facility.

It was a corner office, so the other two walls were tinted bronze glass and shaded with slatted blinds. The sun was still high in the sky, but the light through the glass was a brilliant amber, and black shadows from the slatted blinds gave the whole office the feel of a seaside hotel. The glass itself was treated to resist infrared surveillance, and a white-noise generator made electronic eavesdropping a technical impossibility, even with a laser surveillance system, which was designed to translate sound-wave impacts on the inside of the windows into minuscule changes in the distance reading on the laser and then back again into sound waves on the system recorder. The white-noise generators gave the whole office a muted, hushed feeling, as if an ocean were somewhere close, just beyond hearing range. It made speaking and hearing a little tricky, giving you the illusion that you had a slight hearing problem, but you got used to it.

Today was a Sunday, so there was no one in the place

but Norm Brewer, who was holding down the weekend
duty officer spot. Norm was sitting in the coffee lounge
next to the washrooms, dressed to the nines in a custom-
tailored white shirt, a striped rep tie, Italian navy-blue
slacks, and dark blue leather Italian loafers. He had on a
shoulder-rig holster with a stainless Beretta nine-mill on
his left side and a double-mag case on the right side. He
was reading a copy of the ATF Seized Property Notice that
ran regularly in most national newspapers. This one was
inside a copy of *USA Today*. Luke always got a kick out of
the ATF 800 number that ran with the notice: 1-800-ATF-
GUNS.

Norm Brewer was a crewcut kid about twenty-six years
old, built like a running back with a neck size somewhere
in the three-digit area, pecs like dinner plates, and a very
narrow waist. A squeaky-clean Methodist kid from Nebraska, Norm had spent several years in Court Security
and was one of the few younger men to make it to Fugitive Ops, a position usually reserved for men with a lot of
seniority. Since there were only thirty-four hundred Marshals in the service, the prime positions were hard to come
by, and there was a lot of hard feeling between the old
guard and the new crop of recruits fresh out of Glynco.
The D.C. courthouse was a particularly bad example of
this sort of intramural tension, and *The Washington Post*
had been carrying an ongoing feature detailing the small-
minded bitchiness of the combatants on all sides of the
struggle. Seniority struggles made a great deal of the daily
operations of the Marshals Service as tricky as a tenure
fight in a faculty lounge, except in the Marshals Service
all the contestants were armed.

Norm Brewer had made it to Fugitive Ops because his
uncle had once been a U.S. Marshal, but once Norm got
inside, it was his willingness to do *anything*, work whatever
god-awful hours no one else would accept, run whatever

miserable stake-out he was asked, and do it all with an inexhaustible cheerfulness, that kept him on the right side of the door.

Norm looked up from behind the paper as Doc and Luke came in looking for fresh coffee. It was typical of Norm Brewer that the pot was not only full but full of a really excellent blend of Colombian-Kenyan that he shopped for in Georgetown. The rich complex scent filled the small lounge.

"Mr. Zitto," he said, getting up from the battered vinyl couch and putting the paper down. "Let me pour that for you."

Luke raised a hand, grinned at the boy.

"Take a break, Norm. I can pour my own. And the name is Luke, okay? You make me feel like I should have a walker."

"You should," said Doc. "You told me so yourself. We'll get you one outta Stores, okay? Sit down, Norm, will ya? He's the cripple, not me."

"Mr. Hollenbeck. Your wife called."

"She did?" said Doc. "What'd she want?"

"She said to tell you a Mr. Marcuse called."

Doc turned and looked hard at Brewer.

"She said that?"

Brewer reacted to the look. "Well, yes. I'm sorry, sir."

"He called my house?"

"Yes, sir. Is that bad, sir?"

Luke watched the exchange. Celandre Marcuse was Doc's Haitian cab-driver fink, the one who had tipped them off about Rona's location yesterday. He had no idea what Doc's protocol was with his finks, but he was pretty sure that a call to the house was one of the major no-nos. Luke never gave a fink his home number. That's what pagers were for. If Doc was giving out his home number, Doc's style of snitch control was strictly against the rulebook. Luke sipped at his cup and waited to see how this would play out. Fink management was the slipperiest aspect of the job. An agent without his own fink network was like a hunter without a gun dog.

Doc gave Luke a meaningful glance and went out to the main office to call his wife. Norm Brewer watched him go with a worried expression on his unmarked face.

"Did I do something wrong, Mr. Zitto?"

"Not at all, Norm. Doc's a husband. They get that hunted look after a while. You're not married, are you?"

"I'm still GS 7, sir. I can hardly afford my underwear."

Luke laughed at that. Norm gave him a grin, and then slapped his forehead. He fumbled in his pocket and pulled out a slip of pink paper.

"This call came for you just now, sir."

"From the CO?" said Luke, taking the slip.

"No," said Brewer. "It's from Rothgar Fiertag."

Luke took the slip and read it. Rothgar Fiertag's role was supervisory and nonoperational, but he had to be somewhere up there in the chain of command, since the commanding officer of their fugitive team tolerated his incessant interference. His note was short and to the point:

> My office at 1720 hours.
> Canaday's with me.
> Fiertag.

Great. Somebody had tipped off Rothgar Fiertag. Probably Bolton Canaday himself. If Canaday wanted to make this an official visit, then he had an agenda that wasn't entirely selfless. *Quelle surprise,* as Aurora would say. Doc Hollenbeck came back into the room, and Luke handed him the note. Doc read it and sighed theatrically.

"Well that's just jim-dandy, Luke. Let's go see what they want."

They said good-bye to Norm Brewer and headed back out to the elevator banks. Waiting for the elevator, Luke quietly asked Doc what the problem was with Celandre Marcuse. Doc looked puzzled.

"He's not supposed to call my home unless it's an emergency. He has my pager. I called him. He was on duty last night. This morning, he was talking the night over with some of the other drivers, and one of them—guy named Raj—said he had been all over the K Street sector, including the Zanzibar."

That bothered Luke. "Why? You think Marcuse tipped him off?"

"He wouldn't do that. Raj said he was dropping off a fare at the Marine barracks and rolled by there on his way to the navy yard, says he always gets a fare at the yard, and he was going past the Zanzibar when a guy flagged him down."

"So? I still don't see why this would attract Marcuse's attention."

"Well, he sure as hell knew we were interested in the place. He's not stupid. The guy has an education, Luke."

Luke nodded. He just had an instinctive mistrust for snitches, and *active* snitches really made him nervous. Doc's face reflected some of the same feelings.

"Anyway, this fare made a big impression on this Raj guy. For one thing, he was real surveillance-conscious, kept checking the rearview, made the guy go around K Street three times."

The elevator door opened up. A couple of agents were inside, a woman who worked in Target Acquisition named Vivian Cruz and a man Luke didn't know. Doc nodded to them both and kept his mouth shut until they reached the top floor. He stopped Luke in the hall outside Fiertag's office door.

"So, three times around K Street?"

"Yeah," said Doc. "The D.C. cops were still writing up the fire in Rona's room, and when they went past that, the guy seemed very interested, and he asked Raj if he knew what was going on."

"What'd Raj say?"

"What do you think? Raj says he doesn't know. The guy makes him go around one more time, he really guns the location, like there's something there he needs. Down in Southeast, that's a scary area, all the drivers are paranoid, so this kind of behavior, it rings the guy's bells. Raj is watching him real close."

"He get a good ID?"

"Oh yeah. Told Celandre the guy was scary. Had a pocked-up face and a twisted lip, from a scar. Black eyes. Big, maybe six feet or better."

"Any accent?"

"None. Spoke regular English."

"I don't get it. What made this Raj so interested? This could be anybody. Everybody looks at cops when there's something going on. What's the big deal with this one fare?"

"How should I know? From what Raj told Celandre, I think the guy scared him, like he just seemed . . . weird. Hinky. Whatever, he made a big impression on him. The guy stood out."

"He record the fare?"

"Took him to an address up on North Capitol. Long run. On the way up, the guy starts making small talk, only this is not a small-talk guy. He starts asking Raj if he works that area a lot, what kind of fares does he get. Say tonight, did he pick up a guy who—"

Luke could see it coming.

"He asked about Paolo Rona?"

"Not by name. But Celandre pushed him a bit on it. He says it sure sounds like our guy. Age, size, markings, hair color. Said he was a friend from Guyana. Except he doesn't give Raj a name. From what he says, I think the guy was looking for Rona."

"I want to talk to this driver."

"Yeah, I—"

At that point the door to Fiertag's office opened up, and Rothgar Fiertag appeared in the doorway. He was in Sunday golfer clothes, complete with one of those silly flat hats. He was actually wearing plus fours and argyle socks. His silvery hair was curling out from under his hat, and his lean tanned features were set and disapproving.

"I heard you talking out here. I have two people from Treasury waiting. Where the hell were you?"

He stepped back out of the way as they walked into his outer office. The secretary's station was empty, and Fiertag kept up a low-level stream of complaints about their sense of timing as he ushered them through into his main office. The office draperies were drawn, and the blinds closed. The room was as dim as midnight, the only light coming from a green-shaded banker's lamp on Fiertag's desk.

Fiertag always worked in the dark, with the draperies drawn. He liked to believe that *they* had heavy surveillance on people like him. Who *they* were depended on the last op-ed column he had read in *Jane's Intelligence Review*. As they came through the doors and into the bookcase-lined office, two men rose up out of a pair of leather wing-backs and turned to face them.

Coming across Fiertag's Oriental carpet, Luke recognized the dark Celtic features of Treasury agent Bolton Canaday. Canaday was short, perhaps five eight, and theatrically skinny, with a thick head of pure white hair and black shadowing on both cheeks. His eyes were recessed and red-rimmed—he suffered from a wide range of allergies and was always sucking on an asthma inhaler—but his body was as sinewy and lean as a marathon runner's under the baggy brown suit, the blue shirt, the vaguely greasy black tie worn loosely around his corded and blue-veined neck.

Luke thought of him as a prototypical IRA whiskey priest and even entertained the amusing speculation that Canaday had some tenuous but working connection with Sinn Fein, as absurd as that would be. It was damn unlikely, but Luke held on to the thought just because it made him feel warm all over every time he had to work with the man, whose dominating credo in interagency operations was strictly predatory; he offered nothing but vague intimations while scooping up every bit of hard data he could reach, and when he left the building, it was wise to count your rings.

Canaday offered Luke his hand, shook it once, hard, and then dropped it as if Luke had something contagious. He smiled, showing a ragged picket of yellow sticks and pale tumbled tombstones in a vivid red field. Treasury had a great dental plan. Why the hell Bolton Canaday wouldn't use it was a mystery to Luke. Doc shook hands all around while Luke tried to size up the other guy.

No one he knew, but he had the look of a Justice Department lawyer, with his gray Hugo Boss pinstripe suit and black loafers, a very expensive Mara tie, and his hair swept back in that leonine, windblown look that was all over the capital like a persistent skin rash these days. The little round wire-frame glasses—probably made of plain glass—completed the perfect image of the Ivy League lawyer, and he had that tall, lazily athletic frame you saw on professional tennis gigolos and Beltway psychiatrists. In his hand he held a thin black plastic case, an IBM Think-

Pad model that Luke knew went for over nine grand retail. Laptops had replaced cell phones as the official status accessory of the Beltway desperado.

Fiertag made the introductions with the expectant air of a lab tech dropping four rats into a Cuisinart as he settled in behind his desk, seeming to grow in size as he reestablished skin contact with his official furniture.

"Deputy Zitto, Deputy Hollenbeck, I think you know Special Agent Canaday. And I'd like you to meet Reed Endicott."

Endicott shook hands firmly, establishing his Real Guy credentials so mechanically that he might have been battery-operated. It was unclear whether the smile made it to the eyes, which stayed hidden behind the lenses through a trick of the green light on Fiertag's desk.

"Mr. Endicott is with Justice. He's here purely in an advisory capacity, am I right, Mr. Endicott?"

Endicott inclined his head and offered a radiant and only slightly reptilian revelation of truly outstanding dentistry. His hair shimmered in the green glow of Fiertag's desk lamp, one black lock falling artfully—even coyly— over one chiseled brow. Two flat circles of green light appeared and disappeared in his lenses. Setting the laptop on his—well, on his lap—Endicott spoke quietly and apparently to no one in particular while he pressed buttons and flicked switches and powered up his machine.

"Thank you, Marshal Fiertag. Yes, I'm just here to advise Special Agent Canaday. This is a routine interagency consultation, but you'll understand that, while we all share the same goals, there are some operational considerations, ah, that we have to . . ."

"Consider?" said Luke.

Fiertag shot him a look. Endicott smiled.

"Yes, of course. Now I'm going to let Bolton fill you in

on today's . . . events . . . and I'll just step in if I think there's anything that needs . . ."

"Distorting?" said Luke, ignoring Fiertag's death-ray stare.

Endicott laughed once, out loud, a true Bar Harbor snort, a kind of nasal whinny that suggested amusement without confirming its source.

"They said you were droll, Luke. I see we'll have to be on our toes around here. I think we understand one another."

That was too easy. Luke let it go. They all looked at Bolton for a few seconds until he realized they were waiting for him to speak. He jerked upright in the wing-back and leaned forward, placing his elbows on his knees, folding his hands as if in prayer or, in his case, as if listening to an altar boy's confession.

"Okay. Here's the thing. We've developed information through some overseas assets that leads us to believe that a Central American cartel is shipping counterfeit U.S. currency through Atlanta. This stuff is very very good. Virtually undetectable."

Endicott's fingers were flickering lightly over his keypad. His head was down, but it was clear he was listening intently. Canaday was obviously stepping through a pasture here, and in his bare feet. Just to trip him up, Luke tossed him a grenade.

"Syrian?"

They both jumped.

What'd they think, he couldn't read?

"Gimme a break, Bolton," he said. "This isn't the CIA here. It was in the *Times* last year. Hell, the year before. The Iranians or somebody, financing a professional counterfeit ring in the Bekaa Valley. They had real U.S. mint plates of one-hundred-dollar bills, and they were using real currency paper to print out thousands and thousands of these bills. The idea was to undermine the U.S. dollar, or something along those lines. It was in the news for a few days, then *bing*, it drops off the pages and nobody is saying anything."

Bolton managed to avoid looking across at Reed Endicott. He went up a tiny notch in Luke's estimation. Canaday smiled carefully and fumbled for his asthma spray. He put it to his lips and inhaled for quite a while. When he pulled it away from his mouth, his sallow face was slightly pinker.

"Well, you're bang on about that, Luke. It was the Syrian stuff. So we had someone on the inside—a source, you understand. I can't say anyt'ing about that."

Fiertag obviously felt he hadn't been heard from often enough.

"We understand the protocols, Bolton. Please go on."

"Yes sir, t'ank you, sir. So anyway, t'ings go along, we've got some help from the Big Eye—"

Big Eye was one of the geosynchronous satellites in a permanent orbit over the Central American isthmus and the Caribbean. Access to it was controlled by the National Security Agency, but most qualified federal agencies could have it zeroed on a target sector if they gave the NSA enough lead time.

"And we don't want to roll 'em all up too fast. We have an AWACS and some National Guard choppers, we get IR shots of the hand-off in Georgetown—"

"Where's that?" asked Doc. "Not the D.C. one?"

"It's in Guyana. On the coast."

Doc nodded.

"Okay, so the route from there, it's tricky—"

"I don't think these men need to hear the entire narrative, Bolton," said Endicott. Bolton sent him a brief but malevolent look, and then canceled it with a gnomish leer.

"I go on a bit, I know. You'll understand, Luke and Doc

and me, we're all cops together. We find this stuff real interesting, don't we, boys?"

"I'm riveted," said Doc. "Couldn't move if I was goosed."

Canaday laughed again. "Well, to make a long tale short, we spend a lot of time and taxpayers' dollars rolling up these people. We made some good arrests last year. Some of those people are in our care right now, Mr. Fiertag."

Fiertag nodded in solemn and wise concurrence. He had no idea in hell who was in Witness Protection right now—Mary Magdalene? E.T.? Elvis?—but he liked the flattery.

"So where does all this lead but right here to the capital? What happened today, we had a big street operation going on. We had reason to believe that a transfer was set for someplace around the Washington Monument. Our guy was in place—"

"Your fink?" said Luke.

"I think that's obvious from the context," put in Endicott.

"Yes," said Canaday, after a short pause. "Our fink. So who should come along but someone we know—he's on the sheet as a Known Associate—and my people make him as soon as he shows up—"

"On foot?" said Doc.

"Yes . . . on Constitution Avenue, there at 17th. By the aquarium."

"And this guy is Paolo Rona?"

"Well, we didn't know that at the time. We just knew him as a buyer."

"How?" said Doc.

"How what?"

"How'd you know him as a buyer if you didn't know

who he was? You just said you didn't know it was Paolo Rona at that point."

"Gentlemen, this isn't an interrogation," said Fiertag. "This is a consultation between agencies, and it's being held for *your* benefit, Deputy Hollenbeck. Yours too, Deputy Zitto."

Luke watched Fiertag during this little speech. Dammit, he's *covering* for these guys. Canaday had gotten his act together during the distraction.

"He was, according to our source, *one* of the buyers our source had been doing business with."

Endicott looked up from his laptop.

"I think I can help you there, Bolton. Agent Canaday is trying to be discreet, of course, but I think we can speak freely here. Our source is, naturally, someone at ease in the criminal circles. He came to our attention during a Treasury buy-and-bust operation a few months ago, and since then has been most helpful in . . . assisting our inquiries, as the Brits would say. One of his sidelines consists in stolen credit cards, as well as various templates and laminates related to the production of federal documents."

"Such as driver's licenses?" asked Luke.

"And American Express cards," said Endicott, smiling at Luke. "I think you see what we mean here, when we say that, while our source is an active participant in our investigations, he nevertheless must continue to appear to be in his old life—"

"Appear?" said Luke. "He's getting a free ride, you mean."

"Would you have him suddenly stop selling stolen or forged documents, then? How to explain his sudden good fortune to his criminal associates? How to preserve his . . . access . . . to the criminal milieu? Access, for example, to a buyer who, when the arrest occurred, happened to be the object of a rather . . . inefficient . . . takedown attempt on the part of the two of you just this last evening. Or am I misinformed?" He looked at Fiertag over the tops of his wire-frames. Fiertag squirmed in his leather chair.

"Our deputies conducted a thoroughly professional arrest process last night, but these events are by nature chaotic, and it sometimes—"

Canaday was grinning hugely.

"You stepped on your dicks, boyos, don't say me different. It happens to the best of us, *Mister* Endicott. I didn't see *you* out there on K Street trying to run down our fella, now did I. Don't be tugging on Luke's chain like that, there's a good lad. Luke, they tell me, at one point, you ended up under a car or some such. Things got a bit hectic, I'd say. Had you dropped your wallet or like that?"

In spite of himself, Luke had to grin. Canaday might be a sleazeball careerist with the soul of a swamp adder, but at least he wasn't a lawyer.

Doc was smiling too.

"No, it was his contact lens. Didn't find that, did we, Luke?"

Luke shook his head. "No, no we didn't, Doc, thank you for asking."

Endicott and Fiertag seemed to resent the alteration in room dynamics. Endicott flicked a switch on his laptop, closed it softly, and folded his long delicate hands on top of it.

"Well, I think you see the picture. This Rona fellow, he was apparently trying to buy some of the counterfeit currency that our source was handling—"

"We're at the stage where what we're trying to do is get what's left out there off the street, roll up all the buyers we can, you understand?" put in Canaday, helpfully.

Endicott paused, took a breath, and went on. "As I understand it, as Agent Canaday came forward to effect the arrest, your man made some resistance."

"Resistance!" said Canaday, throwing up his hands. "He tried to blow me head off with a bloody great cannon. And I unshriven, a Catholic too." Canaday was clearly having a very good time, which made Luke uncomfortable, although he had no idea why.

"What'd he show?" asked Doc.

"Show? He showed me a Glock. He showed me the rude end of a bloody great Glock machine pistol. Leave it to the Nazis to come up with a plastic gun."

"What happened?" asked Luke.

"One of my people shot him. Shot him into a complete state of death."

"Who?"

"Who was the agent? I don't think you know her. Sherry Wolokoff. She used to be with our Miami station? Plays soccer all the time? Big-shouldered girl, with a wonderful head of bright red hair."

"I know her," said Doc. "She played shortstop last Memorial Day. She's the one?"

"Yes. Her first."

"How's she doing?"

Canaday put on a long face. "Not well. It hits them hard, the young ones. She's in the shooting board now."

"Where's it being held?" asked Luke. Canaday looked at Endicott. Endicott looked at his watch.

"Over at Treasury. As a matter of fact, we need to be there soon, Bolton. So, if that—"

"I'd like to come along," said Luke.

"Me too," said Doc.

Endicott looked at Fiertag. Fiertag put his hands out on the carved leather top of his rosewood desk, like a cardinal saying the Kyrie Eleison.

"Luke, I hardly think that's appropriate. Treasury doesn't drop in to audit our shooting inquiries, do they?"

"No sir, but we have—"

"I wonder," said Endicott, "I wonder if you have a *personal* . . . if there's an element of private vendetta here, to be perfectly . . . . ahh . . ."

"Presumptuous?" offered Luke.

Endicott bared his teeth.

"Hah, yes . . . if I may be . . . presumptuous. Luke—may I call you Luke?—I understand that this Rona fellow was responsible for an assault on a court security guard—"

"A U.S. Marshal," said Fiertag. "Her name was Aurora Powys. She's on a disability leave right now." The way he said it made it clear that the disability was not simply physical. Endicott inclined his head in Fiertag's direction.

"Yes, Aurora Powys. You worked with her at one time, didn't you? Luke?"

Arrogant little snot. Doc shifted in his chair, moving forward to the edge of it, keeping half an eye on Luke. Luke said nothing. Endicott took the point as made and stood up, gathering his laptop. Bolton Canaday sent Luke a warning look, then rose to leave. As if in an afterthought, he slapped his breast pocket and pulled out a brown manila envelope. Endicott turned to watch as Canaday walked over to Luke and handed him the envelope.

"What's this?" said Luke.

"I figured you'd be the Doubting Thomas. You get that way when you want a man real bad."

Endicott stepped close. "Bolton, I think we've given Luke here all the information we really—"

"I know you do, sir, and I thank you for your participation. But you've never actually *chased* a man, have you, sir?"

Canaday waited. Endicott fussed but subsided.

"I thought not. What we do, it's not quite like a fraternity paper chase across Boston Common, is it Luke? I thought you'd want to *see*, you know, to get . . . what do they call it now, Doc?"

"Closure?" said Doc.

"Yes," said Canaday, raising his bony hand, exposing a grimy cuff. He smelled of beer and sandalwood.

"Closure. That was the word."

Walt Rich, Rico Groza, and Slick Stevens were already at
Paddy Riley's bar on M Street when Doc and Luke
came in through the door. Rich and Stevens were sitting in their usual cubbyhole hideout by the back door of the
long, dimly lit, and slightly smoky room, playing a game of
Liar's Dice and drinking beer. Rico was standing at the battered wooden bar, presiding over the construction of a *mojito*
according to his own extremely—not to say maniacally—
precise instructions, a ceremony that the bartender, whose
name was Janet, had been subjected to many times since her
appearance behind the bar in January of that year. It was
Luke's impression that Janet was studying philosophy at the
University of Georgetown and subsidizing her income here
at Paddy Riley's. Almost six feet tall, tanned and lean, with
jet-black hair, luminous gray eyes, and a wry sideways sense
of humor, she was a magnet for male attention but was rumored to be in a long-term relationship with another woman.
That was Walt Rich's story, anyway. At the moment, she was
telling Rico a joke about the Royal Marines—perhaps to dis-

tract him—and crushing mint leaves with a little marble mortar-and-pestle set that Rico had bought for that purpose a year ago.

Paddy Riley's was one of the older bars on M Street, placed just a few streets down from the oldest building in Georgetown, the Old Stone House, which had been built in the late 1670s. Over the years most of the eighteenth-century Federal-style buildings along M Street had been replaced with grocery stores and clothing shops that catered to the mixed crowds of tourists, college kids, and drifters who mingled and collided along M Street or Wisconsin Avenue, but Paddy Riley's still retained some of that old colonial feeling. Some of the Marshals who used to eat regularly at a pricey Georgetown restaurant over on Wisconsin had started to drop by Paddy Riley's instead, and now it was a regular bar for the men of Luke's takedown unit. Doc and Luke sat down at the chipped wooden table with Walt and Slick Stevens and ordered a couple of Beck's. Slick was holding an inverted tin cup in his paws and staring down at it as if he could see through the sides if he thought hard enough. Walt Rich was leaning back in a creaky wooden rail-chair and puffing on a cigarette stuck in the corner of his mouth, watching Slick struggle with his decision.

Doc nodded at Slick and said, "What's he got?"

Walt Rich grinned around his cigarette and puffed out a blue cloud.

"What does he *have* or what does he *think* he has?"

"Either," said Luke.

Slick growled at them without lifting his head.

"The little leprechaun over there thinks that I *think* that *he* thinks that I have bought the idea that he's got two pairs to the queen, *but*, in actual *fact*, I only *want* him to think that, because—"

"We get the point," said Luke.

The game of Liar's Dice consisted of five dice, each die

marked with six playing cards from the nine to the ace. All the nines were in one suit, the tens in another, the jacks in another, the queens in another, and so on up to the five aces of spades. The idea was to put the dice under a cup, shake the cup, lift it up carefully, and look underneath, keeping the results hidden from any other player. Then you set the cup back down, pushed it across the table at the next player, looked him right in the eye, and told him with all the sincerity and guile that you could muster either the simple truth—a pair of nines—or an outrageous lie—four queens to the ace—and then you leaned back, pulled at your beer, and watched the guy try to figure out if you were lying or telling the truth.

If he believed you, he slid the cup closer and took a peek. The trick was, if you *said* you had four queens to the ace but all you *really* had was a pair of nines, the guy had to beat your *lie*, not what was actually under the cup. And so it went, back and forth, sometimes going all the way around the table until an even more outrageous lie came back to you. It was a good bar game for the Marshals because it was kind of a metaphor for their basic business, which was to listen to snitches tell them stories and then try to decide whether to believe them or to pick the snitch up and turn him upside down and say *bullshit*, which was how you called your opponent's bluff in the game of Liar's Dice, not to mention most real-life confrontations. An added attraction was that the loser had to buy the next round. Slick finally looked up from his telepathic interrogation of the tin cup. His large red face was blank, his eyes narrowed.

"Okay, I buy it."

"I told him I had a full house," said Walt, keeping his face straight. Slick raised the cup, lowered his massive bald head so he could see under the rim, and then he slammed it down again.

"Shit," was all he said.

Walt chortled quietly to himself.

Slick looked across at Doc and Luke.

"How'd it go with Canaday?"

"You're just trying to change the subject," said Walt. "Pay or play, you scumball." Slick ignored him, but he did pull out two queens—Walt had rolled a pair of queens—and set them aside, taking the last three dice and shaking them in the cup while he waited for Luke's answer.

"He gave me this," said Luke, dropping Canaday's brown manila envelope onto the table. Walt picked it up and spilled the contents out across the table as Slick hammered the cup down and then peeked underneath it.

"Jeez," was all Walt said.

Slick kept his hands on the cup and looked at the papers in front of them. The sheets were a typewritten intake report with the logo of D.C. Municipal Hospital on it. It was the ER surgeon's report on John Doe K4776/05/22/94. It described the DOA arrival of an Hispanic male, apparently in his late thirties or early forties, who had "presented" with a couple of penetration wounds in his upper body and skull, the most obviously fatal of which had penetrated the thoracic radius and appeared to be the result of a large-caliber bullet that had been fired from a distance of more than ten feet—no residual powder burns, no speckling, no star-shaped entrance wound—said bullet having traveled through the upper thorax and the right lung until it struck the number seven vertebra, at which time it seemed to have tumbled and rebounded into the aortic chamber of the heart, where it produced what the surgeon described as "severe trauma and concomitant hydrostatic shock" to the heart and the upper aorta, causing "catastrophic loss of blood and tissue damage." It was his opinion that the wound had been fatal within a few minutes.

Slick read it along with the others, then pushed the cup over to Walt Rich.

"Aces and tens to the king," he said, still reading the sheet.

"Who signed this?" asked Walt, taking the cup.

Luke studied the signature.

"Hard to say. It's the usual scrawl."

"Was there a city bull who signed?" asked Slick. "There usually is, if the takedown happens in their jurisdiction."

Luke squinted, trying to make sense out of the press of various hands and the poor quality of the copy.

"Maybe.... What's this look like?"

Walt peered at it for a while.

"Collins, maybe? A D.C. sergeant, it looks like."

"No idea, Luke."

Walt looked under the cup, said, "Damn," picked it up, and began to shake it as Rico Groza came back to the table with his *mojito*.

Some music started to play. Quite loud. Something with an insistent beat. It was the theme music to the Fox TV show *Cops*, a song called "Bad Boy," by Inner Circle. Janet turned the volume up and waved her fingertips at them as they turned around to stare at her. Rico looked at the papers, frowned, and then took a short experimental sip of the *mojito*. Satisfied, he reached out and tapped the pages.

"That's him, isn't it? The physical description?"

The question was open, but Luke answered it.

"That's their story, anyway."

"Why no full-face shot?" Slick wanted to know.

"Presumably they wanted to spare us the shock," said Doc. "According to this report, the guy would have looked like somebody'd started a fire in his face and put it out with a rubber mallet."

"Oh yeah. Delicacy. That'd be it," said Walt, his tone heavy with sarcasm.

"What'd Fiertag say?" Slick wanted to know.

"He said that the entire shooting was a matter for Treasury, that until the shooting board cleared Agent Wolokoff, the identity of the dead person was part of the evidentiary packet, and they could not afford to have that identity compromised by unintentional circulation to the media."

Walt barked out a bitter laugh.

"Unintentional circulation? What? Fiertag thinks if they give you the head shot, you're gonna sell it to *People*? EXCLUSIVE! Our *People* photog caught up with Cadaver-About-Town Paolo Rona today, seen here with his cortex splattered all over Mia Farrow's simply cunning little Donna Karan bustier at D.C.'s famous Ford Theater. Is that a Lincoln impression, Mr. Rona, or did your ego just blow up in the heat?"

They all stared at Walt Rich for a while.

"Okay, Walt . . . ," said Slick, rolling his eyes. "Doc, you were saying?"

"All he said was, Treasury wasn't ready to release a face shot yet because they didn't want to"—Luke searched for the exact phrase—" 'to alert other persons with whom Rona may have been involved.' "

"Releasing it to the press isn't the same as letting someone else in Justice see a shot of the guy's face. Last time I checked, the Marshals were still part of Justice," Slick said. "Didn't you go to the ER, see the stiff?"

"No . . ." said Doc. "Fiertag warned us off, said we had duties to attend to ourselves, that the case was Treasury's anyway, wanted us to go back to work Monday morning on Target Acquisition analysis—"

"Reading fink information sheets, collating and analyzing motor vehicle registrations, voters' lists, welfare rolls, booking reports, fingerprint verifications, VICAP bulletins, and then calling up parole officers, court clerks, county sheriffs, and prison guards all over the eastern seaboard," said Slick. "Welcome to Washington, Luke."

"Wolokoff?" said Walt, who had apparently been trying to

figure out Fiertag's position in all of this. "Did you just say Wolokoff?"

"That's what they said. Sherry Wolokoff."

"I know her," said Walt. "We used to play on the same softball team. Big-boned redhead. A while back, I offered to bear her children. Silly girl turned me down too."

"I can see that," put in Doc. "Two fish-belly-white red-heads. Your kids would be the single biggest melanin shortfall in law enforcement."

"At least you could *see* them, Doc. Unlike our sepia-hued brother here, hah, Luke? You ever notice how, when you get into a dark bar like this, put him up against the oak paneling like that, Doc just kind of *fades*? Here, Slick, gimme the camera. I'll prove it."

Doc groaned as Slick rummaged around in his equipment bag, finally retrieving a Polaroid Spectra. All the takedown teams carried one, just in case things went haywire and somebody needed a photographic record of the scene. Walt took the camera and aimed it at Doc. Doc struck a pose, and Walt pressed the button. The film buzzed out, and Walt laid it down on the tabletop to develop.

"Walt . . . Sherry Wolokoff?" prompted Luke.

"Sherry baby. Yeah, I know Sherry. She's a hell of a short-stop too. I have her number around here somewhere. I'm gonna give her a call."

Walt found his notebook and stood up, fishing for a quarter.

"Oh yeah, before I forget, Slick?"

"Yeah?"

"Three aces to the king."

Slick took the cup as Walt got up to make a phone call. Rico was still looking at the ER intake report in his hands.

"So, either the entire Treasury Department—wait a minute, what time is it? It's seven-fifteen."

Slick raised his paw. "Seven-fifteen on a Sunday, Rico."

"Right," said Rico. "Too early for the paper."

Janet brought over a round of drinks, leaning close to Slick as she set them down on the table. Slick inhaled theatrically. On her way back to the bar, Janet blew him a kiss over her shoulder, putting some deliberate feminine physics into the passage.

"What a waste," said Slick, watching her go.

Janet heard him, turned around, and did a credible Lauren Bacall sashay back to the table. She draped herself around Slick's beefy shoulders and pinched his cheek.

"You'd need a crash cart and ten cc's of epinephrine just to watch me blow-dry my hair, Mr. Stevens. You do remember *hair*, don't you?"

"Sounds like a good deal to me," said Slick. "Tuesday? Your place? I'll bring the oxygen."

Janet laughed, rubbed the top of his bald head.

"I'll bet your wife keeps this shiny just so she can see the TV in the other room while you're making love. You ever wonder why she never lets you know when she's had an orgasm?"

"I'll bite," said Slick, his huge right arm tucked around her waist.

"Because you're never in the room."

Doc bellowed at that one. Janet slipped over and sat down on his lap, sliding her arm around his neck. "Now *you*, that's another story."

Doc leered at her, pulling her in close. "Thank you, my child. Like all truly sensual women, you sense my power."

Janet laughed, patted his cheek.

"Mr. Hollenbeck, how can a woman tell if her husband is dead?"

"No idea."

"The sex is the same, but the garbage tends to pile up."

"Janet," said Slick. "You know what was long and hard on Doc?"

"Yes," she said. "I'll bet it was third grade."

She got up off Doc's lap and rubbed Slick's bald head again as she strolled back toward the bar. Halfway across the creaky wooden floor, she stopped and looked back at Slick, knowing he'd be watching her.

In a low throaty baritone drawl, she said, "Mr. Stevens, what's twelve inches and white?"

Slick stared at her for a second, reddening.

"I don't know, Janet. What *is* twelve inches and white?"

"Nothing," she drawled, walking away toward the bar, her voice carrying back through the smoky air and the muted jazz. "Absolutely nothing."

Slick, still chuckling, picked up the Polaroid shot. It had developed into a flat black screen, totally dark. He used the tip of a ball-point pen to pierce two small holes in the picture. He held the picture up to the overhead light so that two tiny glowing sparks showed in the black.

"See what I mean, guys? Walt's right! Doc just *fades*. All you can see are his eyes."

Doc took the picture out of his hands. "Next time, use the flash, smartass." He handed the camera to Luke. "Here, take a picture of Slick and me. We'll see who's the ugliest."

"Okay," said Luke, taking a series of pictures around the table, the glare of the flash vivid and blue-white, black shadows leaping up on the walls behind them. After five shots the camera shut down.

"Broken," he said, and shrugged.

"Figures," said Doc.

They were still laughing when Rico, who had been staring out the front window for a while, raised his voice to get their attention.

"So the working theory here is that either Treasury is trying to sell a couple of no-account deputy marshals like yourselves a bill of goods for reasons that have so far escaped us but that will no doubt turn out to be vital issues affecting national security—"

"Man, I *hate* that phrase," said Luke.

"*Or*—no, listen to me—or your guy Rona simply walked into something that was long overdue for the little son of a bitch, and now we can all sleep safe in our beds again. My advice, drop it here, walk away. Stop sticking your finger up somebody else's nose."

"Nice image," said Luke.

"It'll do," said Rico, his smile slipping a little. "You go on like this, the next sound you hear will be the CO shoveling gravel on your unmarked grave. My honest and heartfelt advice, Luke, is *keep off*, in big red letters."

"There be monsters?" said Luke. "Is that it?"

"That's it," said Rico.

Doc Hollenbeck was nodding.

"He's right, Luke. So far, no coverage. No television yet. Maybe tomorrow, there'll be a small story somewhere. My guess, Treasury slammed a lid on things," said Doc, leaning back and looking at Luke.

"I guess that wraps it up, hah? I mean, for you guys?"

Rico picked up his *mojito*. "It would seem to. What about it, Luke?"

Luke was quiet for a while.

Slick Stevens watched him mull it over for a few seconds, and then he said, "Bullshit."

"Bullshit?" said Rico. "The game or the story?"

"Both," said Slick, knocking the cup over, revealing the dice underneath it, just as Walt Rich came back to the table. In the bright yellow downlight from the metal shade above the table, they could all see Walt's last roll. There were no aces showing at all. Two nines, a ten, a jack, a king.

"You lied," said Slick.

"No," said Walt, sitting down. "You wound me! Well, if I did, it's contagious."

"What do you mean?" said Doc.

"I called Sherry Wolokoff at Treasury."

"Yeah?"

"She wasn't happy about talking. She says she got out of the shooting board a half-hour ago, says there was some weasel from Justice there named Reed Endicott, was a real shit to her—"

"*That's* no lie," said Doc.

"Yeah. Actually, I know Endicott from way back, when I was in Bronx Vice. Reed Pryor Endicott, outta Rutgers, I think. He used to be with Southern District, used to steal our finks all the time, liked to cite 'overriding national interests,' had a laugh like an adenoidal goat. Thinks he looks like Richard Gere. Anyway, Sherry said she'd been told not to talk about the shooting, that if I had to know anything, I should go through channels, talk to Fiertag or Canaday. She was damn nervous, for a tough broad like her."

"Well, she's just been through a killing, Walt. What'd you expect?" said Slick. "And while you're talking, this round's on you."

"I know that," said Walt. "That's not what I was talking about."

"Jeez, Walt," groaned Doc. "Get to the point!"

"Whoa. . . . A little PMS there, Doctor? What I was going to say was, if I recall it right, Luke, your guy stuck a big Glock up your left nostril last night? Am I right?"

"Yeah."

Luke could still see it, see the index finger inside that rubber glove, see the trigger tightening under it, the black hole of the muzzle an inch from his right eye.

"Okay. So Endicott was going after her about the shooting—"

"He was actually part of the board?"

"No, but he kept sticking his oar in. Sherry says Canaday finally told him to fuck off. But Endicott was bugging her, how'd she know the guy was really armed? Was she *sure* she was in mortal danger? Did she have a clear look at the weapon?"

"You gotta love him," said Rico. "A guy like that, the only incoming round he's ever gonna have to face is a forehand smash."

"Thank you for that irrelevant but, I'm sure, intriguing observation, Rico. You're deflecting my narrative. Where was I?"

"You were at a straight to the queen," said Slick, pushing the tin cup across to him.

"Sherry was defending her defense," said Doc.

"Yes, had she seen a piece? Sherry said, yeah, she did, she could see it in his hand, at first she thought it was a knife because she could see the sun shining on the steel, but then she saw it was a piece, and she told the guy to drop it, but he—she said he panicked or something—but he wouldn't drop it—so she covered the visible mass and gave him four in the chest and face."

They were all silent for a moment, picturing it, remembering their own first shootings. Walt looked at them for a minute, as if he were waiting for something to occur to them.

"Okay," said Doc. "And your point would be . . . ?"

"Jeez," said Walt, shaking his head in disappointment. "And you guys call yourselves cops. Last I looked, your basic Glock came in—"

Luke slammed the table, making the tin cup jump, bouncing the dice all over the table.

"Matte black or gray!"

Walt beamed at Luke. "And the one you had shoved up your nose last night was . . . ?"

"Black. Matte black."

"So . . . therefore?"

Rico cut in at that point. "He could have had more than one piece on him."

Walt looked disappointed.

Luke shook his head. "I almost had him at the Zanzibar. When I came through the door, he set fire to the table and went out the window in a flat dive, Rico. All he took with him was a couple of pieces of ID and that Glock."

"And when he came *out* through the window, all I saw in his hand was a Glock," put in Doc. "I don't think he had time to get another piece before this afternoon."

"And why would he?" asked Walt. "A Glock's as good a piece as you're gonna find on the street."

"*And*—and Canaday said the guy waved a Glock at him," said Luke. "A 'bloody great Glock,' is what he said."

"So?" Walt raised his hands, palms out, eyes wide and innocent.

"So . . . bullshit," said Luke.

"Exactly," said Walt, taking the cup away from Slick and shaking it up, the dice rattling around inside like a shaman's rune-stones.

"So now what?" asked Rico Groza.

Walt slapped the cup down, raised the edge carefully. Then he set it down again and pushed it across the table-top toward Luke.

"Low straight," he said.

"Yeah," said Doc. "Now what?"

"Now?" said Luke. "Now we do . . . nothing."

"That would be the sensible course," Rico said, studying Luke's face carefully. "You have no idea what's going on. You've been officially warned off. Go any further and get caught at it, and you'll be doing court security in Ultima Thule. Fiertag will see to it. Reed Endicott will rip your heart out with a claw hammer and feed it to Janet Reno. On the face of it, you have every reason to believe that Paolo Rona is either extremely dead, that Sherry Wolokoff just got the weapons confused—"

"Bullshit. You've been in shootings, Rico. You know damn well that in a firefight the gun pointed at you is the absolute center of your universe. You could count the hairs on the back of his hand. You could read the serial numbers on the trigger frame from fifty feet away."

"Perhaps, Luke. My basic point is, and I don't want you to take this wrong, okay?"

"I'll try." Luke had a good idea what was coming. Hell, the guy was right too.

"Your hook in this mess is Aurora Powys. I can see that. We all feel that way about it, and you know her. Worked with her. But what real good can you do by poking around in this thing? Either he's dead, and *nada más*, thank you Jesus, or he's not, and Treasury's got him into a project, and they'll strangle kittens to keep him covered. Tell her he's dead, give her . . ."

"Closure," said Doc. "I've been hearing that word a lot lately."

"Yeah," nodded Rico. "Closure."

"Even though I don't *know* he's dead?"

"It's *possible* he is. It makes more sense than believing that this Rona guy is . . ."

"Is what?"

"A fink for Treasury, would be my guess," said Slick Stevens.

"He's an escaped *convict*, for chrissake!" said Luke. "He goddamn *raped* a U.S. Marshal! I cannot believe that . . . even *those* assholes . . . would recruit a slime like that. He's *wanted*."

Slick nodded, waved it away.

"Maybe he's got access to something nobody else can

get. Treasury's like any other agency. Budgets are being slashed, Luke. The pie is shrinking. Either you show good stats, make the spectacular busts, get mentioned in the *Post* and the *Congressional Record,* or next year Congress has reallocated half your op costs, and most of your people are looking for work at Wackenhut or Wal-Mart."

Slick's feelings on the issue were a tad raw. He'd almost been cut last year because of a back injury he'd received playing football. The argument ran that he wasn't "cost-effective" anymore. He had to file a grievance to get the bosses to change their minds. That was the loyalty they were showing to a man who had risked his life hundreds of times for less money than they paid out to finks in one week of operations.

"Yeah," said Walt. "And now the service is a threat to all the other agencies. We've got brand-new offices. We're not HQ'd in some rat's-ass strip-mall. We've snagged all the DEA's Fugitive cases, it looks like they may clear us for a big hiring program to cover the abortion clinics, and if one more federal building gets bombed, they'll vote us into the biggest agency in D.C. They'll make an *army* out of the Marshals Service, because one of the reasons we *exist* is to protect federal property or to enforce federal laws when the states won't cooperate. Those rag-heads bombed the World Trade Center, the Branch Davidians were hoarding military weapons, the ranchers have been setting fire to BLM facilities in Wyoming and Montana—"

"BLM?" said Luke.

"Bureau of Land Management. They control grazing rights on state parks, you know, like Yellowstone? Out in the far west, the BLM guys have been harassed and threatened, had pipe bombs mailed to their wives, park rangers have been shot at. Stuff like that, that's a clear Marshals Service mandate. And how about these militia guys, all those camo-wearing numb-nuts leaping around in the deep woods in places like Idaho and Michigan and western Montana? What's the next bullshit stunt *they've* got planned? Somebody's gonna have to take those guys on. Who else but us?"

"And maybe the Feebs," said Luke.

Slick grunted at that. The FBI was generally hated around D.C., and particularly hated by other law enforcement agencies, because of its unbearable arrogance, its mammoth budget, and its chronic habits of glory-hogging, snitch-stealing, and information-hoarding. Of all the Justice agencies, the FBI was the least cooperative. There wasn't a man at the table who hadn't tried to get a little help from the FBI, only to be told "go through the proper channels" or "talk to Public Affairs" or "Are you sure you're *cleared* for that level, son?" or "I'll have to check that out with the Special Agent in Charge, so let me get back to you." Right. In thirty years.

Slick drained his beer and tossed the bottle across the room into a trash can. "Walt's right, Rico. And all of that stuff scares Treasury, scares the ATF. Sure as hell scares Freeh and the FBI. You know the game, Luke. If Treasury had to barbecue a busload of toddlers—"

"Didn't they already do that?" asked Doc.

"No, that was the ATF, and the bus was in the basement bunker at Waco, but the point's the same. If that's what they had to do to make a high-profile bust, even if it meant using a piece of slime like Paolo Rona, they'd do it in a heartbeat. This is D.C., Luke. This is ground zero here. Power is the only product. The FBI wants the DEA gone. The DIA is worried about the CIA. The NSC is dogging the CIA. The CIA chief is trying to *force* the Pentagon to put Army Intelligence and the NSA under his agency's control. Hell, even the GAO guys are carrying guns now. And it looks like the Republicans are gonna get in *big* come the fall, and if they do, mark my words, boys, they'll shake this town like a pit bull shakes a poodle, they'll shut down the FDA, the EPA, maybe the DEA and the ATF—half the Republicans owe their jobs to the NRA, and the NRA hates the ATF. God knows what else is on the block, my friends. Heads are gonna roll, sides are being taken, asses are being covered. Justice barracudas like Reed Endicott would recruit Vlad the Impaler if they thought it would get them a jump on a high-profile case. Rona's a forger. Forgery's a Treasury thing. They could have scooped him when he was in Sing-Sing."

"What? And *arranged* his escape?" Luke was trying to take all this in—these men had all been in Washington a lot longer than he had. "Why not just transfer him quietly, and then put him back outside. Keep him on a leash. That's the drill. That's how it's always done."

"No way they *arranged* for it. I agree—not even those guys. . . . Okay, maybe he contacted them *after* he busted out? He had to know that we were gonna come after him in a big way," said Slick, after some thought. "I mean, he assaulted a Marshal. If any one of us had a shot at the guy, he'd be a grease spot in fifteen seconds. Whoa. Sorry, Doc. No offense."

"None taken," said Doc. "I missed. Nobody feels lousier about that than I do." Luke put a hand on Doc's shoulder and gave him a gentle shove. Slick paused for a second, and then went on.

"Yeah, so, they'd have to pick him up with a blotter. He's a career criminal. He knows how the game is played. He's a walking corpse. He knows his only hope would be to get himself under the skirts of another agency as soon as possible."

"But then why the hell was he on *our* hit list?" said Rico. "Doc pulled him off it for Luke last week."

Doc shook his head. "He *wasn't* on it. I searched Rona

on my own. One of my finks lucked onto him, and I ran it straight through to Luke on Saturday. So if there was an RTA on him, I wouldn't have seen it anyway."

An RTA notation was a coded numerical addendum to a criminal's computer file that told any inquiring officer that contact with this criminal was a matter of interest to another agency or investigator. RTAs did not always show up on the screen, either. Sometimes they were hidden or accessible only to a senior staffer with the clearance code. But they were there, even if you didn't know it, and hitting one, even unintentionally, meant that the National Crime Information Computer, or NCIC, itself would log *your* inquiry and automatically notify the agency that had put the original RTA on the file. Since your inquiry was linked to your own personal access code—you couldn't get into the system without logging on and using your password—then the other agency would know the precise *who, when,* and *where* of your inquiry.

Over at Justice, there was a whole department, with a bank of mainframe computers, that did nothing but tag, correlate, and compile every law enforcement request logged onto NCIC, looking for hits that related to, or affected in any way, a government investigation. The mainframe was programmed to pick up key words or phrases—such as an undercover officer's false ID or a fink's street name—and alert the on-duty ops officer, who had a protocol book filled with hit requests relayed by various agencies. If the unit detected one of those trigger words, the ops officer got the beep and relayed the originating inquiry to whatever agency had filed the hit request. The NCIC was a nationwide database shared by all law enforcement agencies. It was a wonderful tool for investigating officers, but it worked very well as a clandestine monitoring device as well. It was like a pool of data. As soon as you dipped into it, you sent ripples all through the system. Sometimes you woke up things that were better left sleeping. There was no way around that.

Doc raised a hand.

"So we don't know if there was an RTA on Rona or not, because so far I don't think any of us have queried the system."

"Not everybody logs a fink with an RTA anyway," said Walt. "Hell, *anybody* in any precinct house can get that stuff."

Logging a fink's name was crazy enough, but tagging it with an RTA notice was extremely risky. True, there were access levels to the NCIC database, with the most sensitive information being routinely restricted to senior brass and intelligence guys, but those cutoffs were notoriously unreliable. Any cop with a little nerve—or a lot to hide—could find a way into the deepest recesses of the NCIC data bank. It was an indication of the throwaway status of finks that most agencies logged them anyway. After all, what was a fink but a crook who got caught? As Doc liked to say, finks are Kleenex—they pop up, you blow them and burn them. There's always another fink in the box.

It was a tar-pit world. Get close to it, and it stuck to your skin. Fight it, and you sank without a trace. Stirring around in the Treasury tar pit looking for a fink named Paolo Rona would take a very long stick. But somehow during the long evening the unit had closed up ranks around Luke and his suspicions. Blood was blood. If Luke wanted to push it, they seemed ready to help him. Within reason.

Reaching that consensus had been the subtext of everything they'd been talking about that evening. Since the decision *might* ruin them all, everybody had to be in on it. There was a long resonating silence. The bar was starting to fill up with Sunday night regulars now, and Janet had some Tony Bennett on the stereo. In the yellow glare of the overhead lamp, the faces of the men around the table were drawn, shadowed, and solemn. Slick's hands rested in the circle of light, holding the tin cup with the liar's dice. Luke watched their faces for a time, thinking that in many ways someone in law enforcement was never alone, that you always had a family of a kind. It was a warming sensation, but it was also a goad, since there was another member of the circle, not present today, who had the same claim on him and, through him, on the rest of them, and the real truth was the only honorable thing he had left to offer her.

"Look," he said. "Let's do this right. Roll me a set, Slick. If I call it, we do it, if I don't, we don't."

Doc gave him a look. "Why that way?"

"It's the only fair thing. If it's no, we walk away with our—"

"Pride?" said Walt.

"Yeah."

"Okay," said Slick, shaking the cup. The tinny rattle drew looks from the building crowd in the front room. Janet was watching them, sensing a shift in the mood. Slick slammed the cup down, looked underneath it, his eyes black shadows, the amber light glowing on his shiny pink skull. Walt puffed some cigarette smoke into the circle, where it curled and drifted and rose in the heat from the light. The rest of the bar seemed to fade into a formless black space. There was only the breathing of the men and the creaking of their wooden chairs and the drifting woodwind-and-whiskey sound of Tony Bennett singing "Boulevard of Broken Dreams." Slick raised his head, pushed the cup across the table toward Luke. Luke reached out and pulled it in, looking at Slick, waiting for his call.

"This is silly," said Doc.

"No," said Walt. "It spreads it around."

"Queens to the ace," said Slick.

"How many?"

"Three."

Luke stared down at the cup.

"Okay," he said. "I buy it." He lifted the cup off the dice. An ace, a jack, two queens, and a nine.

"You lied."

Slick sat back in his chair and gave him a wolfish grin. Luke pulled the two queens out to the side, gathered up the three remaining dice, and shook them in the cup. Then he set it down with a rattle and, without looking at the results, pushed the cup across to Slick.

"Four queens."

Slick raised his eyebrows, gave Luke a look.

"To what?"

"Doesn't matter."

Slick considered the cup. Luke was giving them all an honorable exit from the problem. Slick looked at the two queens lying on the scarred wooden surface of the table, then back at the tin cup. The two queens showing made Luke's call of four queens a little more reasonable, but still, it was a big gamble on Luke's part.

"If you lose, we're not gonna do this? *You're* not gonna do this, either? We all just walk away. You tell the woman whatever, but we leave it at that? Right?"

"Right," said Luke. "That's the deal."

Slick reached out, tensed, and lifted the cup into the air.

A nine. And a pair of queens.

"So . . . ," said Slick.

Walt pulled in a lungful of smoke, held it, and then blew it out into the cone of light. "So—Doc says he developed Rona out of a private fink and didn't go through

NCIC or any other web. What about now?" he said. "I've got a mobile VDT in my van. Let's check out Rona right now."

"Okay," said Luke. "Let's."

Walt's charcoal-gray Windstar was parked a block down on M Street. He and Luke went down past the thinning crowds and the shuttered grocery stores. The night was still and hot, the air heavy with mist and ripe with the smell of rotting fruit, fried food, fumes from the traffic. Overhead the yellow glare of the streetlamps seemed to float inside a shimmering halo of beaded light. Four black teenagers in hip-hop clothes pushed their way in between Walt and Luke, their faces as solemn as pallbearers, their eyes hooded and unseeing, as if the two white men in front of them were apparitions, as insubstantial as the mist around the streetlights.

"Glockers," said Luke, loud enough for them to hear him.

The group went on a few steps and then stopped. A kid about six feet tall, wearing a Bulls jacket and blue polka-dot do-rag, stepped out of the circle and stared at the two white men.

"Yo, peckerwood."

Luke and Walt moved a little apart. Suddenly, massively, there was blue ruin in the thickening air.

"Yeah?" said Luke, walking a few feet back toward the kids.

"What'd you call us?"

"I called you Glockers. That do-rag pinching your brain, numb-nuts?"

The kid's face went slack.

"You *dissing* me, asshole?"

Deep inside Luke a couple of stones grated across each

other, and a low soundless growl worked its way up his carotid. Now the kids had spread out slightly as well. The whole thing was profoundly stupid all around the circuit, but that was the way these things went. Luke was conscious of Walt's presence, knew precisely where he was and what he would do if it came to it. He also knew this was crazy, but dammit, all he had said was Glockers. Who owned this goddamn town anyway?

"*Dissing* you? Oh yes, I'd say so. Definitely."

The kid stared at him, his hands open. Luke was aware of the way he was wearing his Bulls jacket, alive to the possibilities inside it. Walt was watching the other kids closely.

"You *crazy*, motherfucker."

"Talk or walk, asshole," said Luke, contempt in every syllable, pushing it, facing him down. The kid looked like he was about to burst into flames. Finally he reached some sort of decision, based on whatever finely calibrated street logarithms he had worked his way through in the last nine seconds.

"You the Man, ain't you?"

"Dead right. Talk or walk, little fella. I got better things to do."

The large kid held his place for a few seconds. A strolling couple had stopped a few yards behind them, suddenly aware of the menace. Luke moved slightly to the right to get them out of his line of fire. The gang kids saw that, realized that Luke and Walt were ready to take this all the way.

Something changed. Something was said in a low dry voice, they all laughed, and turned to walk away.

Walt and Luke watched them walk for a while. The strolling couple hurried past them, keeping their faces low, avoiding eye contact.

"Can we go now, Wyatt?" said Walt.

Luke laughed at that. They relaxed and went on toward the van.

"Why'd you do that?" asked Walt, professionally intrigued. "That's an NYPD thing, face them down like that."

"Somebody has to."

They reached Walt's van. He used his remote to close down the alarm and pop the locks. The VDT was mounted on a swing-arm bolted to the dashboard. Walt flicked it on. The screen glowed bright orange, faded to black, and an amber cursor began to blink in the lower right corner.

Walt punched in his access code. The screen flickered, and then a menu list appeared.

```
INQUIRY / SEARCH / RETRIEVE / LOCATE
ENTER D-BASE CODE:

    nysiis
    holmes
    ani-ali
    catch
    ncic
    maglocen
    cpic
    internal
    vicap
```

Walt hit a function button, and NCIC activated. "What were the numbers on Rona?"

"Rona, Paolo Coimbra. DOB one May 1961."

"What'd the ER report say about the Hispanic male?" Luke was silent for a moment.

"I think he said 'late thirties or early forties.' "

"Sounds a little old. Rona was only thirty-three."

"Maybe he looks older dead."

"Yeah," said Walt, typing. "I know I do. Here we go."

The screen went blank, flickered. A few seconds passed, and then a string of amber letters and numbers threaded themselves out across the screen.

```
RONA . . . PAOLO COIMBRA FS#C229745/94
AKA QUARCO AKA Q
AKA RODERIGO GARDENA AKA MULTIPLES
FIVE FEET ELEVEN INCHES 170 POUNDS
Q-SHAPED CIRCULAR SCAR RIGHT THIGH
MULTIPLE NATIONWIDE WARRANTS
ALBANY WARRANTS FEDERAL WARRANTS
ESCAPE OSSINING WARRANT USMS
MULTIPLE SEXUAL ASSAULTS
ASSAULT FEDERAL OFFICER
SEE NOTATION B1221/5/22/94/
```

"Okay," said Walt. "There's no RTA showing, but that B1221 is an incident report filed by a local force. That'd be the D.C. cops."

"That's today's date. That's the Treasury takedown, right?"

"Right. But instead of pulling up the Treasury report, let's see if we can just pull the D.C. version."

Walt hit a couple of keys. The machine asked him for a search protocol and, again, for his access number. He entered that again, and then he hit a retrieve key on the pad. Thirty seconds passed, and then:

```
INCIDENT REPORT B1221
Units 355 and 376 respond to ten-95 at Constitution
and 17th time marker 1433 052294 shots fired. On
arrival Treasury agents at scene with one male
multiple gunshot wounds. Agent Canaday and Agent
```

Wolokoff provided warrants and informations.
Shooting self-defense crime scene detectives.
Referred to another agency. Units assigned to control
crowds and to assist in shooting assessment team.
EMS transport to DCMH subject DOA cause of death
gunshot wounds
charges resulting: none
further action: none
filing officer: DCPDSGT #448256

"Short and to the point," said Walt.

"Yeah. Got a pen?" Walt gave him one, and Luke wrote down the badge number of the reporting officer.

"That's a sergeant," said Walt.

"Yeah, and a sergeant signed the surgeon's death certificate. Collins or something like that."

"Chances are it's the same guy. Want to see what else we can get?"

"What'll you query?"

"Holmes. That's ours, not a general web."

Holmes stood for Home Office Large Major Enquiry System, a Canadian database program that was gaining some popularity in D.C. circles.

"Go for it." Walt hit a few keys and waited while the screen ran through some system alterations. Finally, the screen burst into a string of capital letters.

NAME OF DECEASED:
RONA PAOLO COIMBRA DOA DC MUNICIPAL
HOSPITAL 1500 HOURS 05/22/94 SEE TREASURY
CASE NUMBER 664-208711 FILE BACKDATE
SEQUENCE RESTRICT THIS INQUIRY HAS BEEN
LOGGED AND TAGGED THIS INQUIRY HAS BEEN
LOGGED AND TAGGED CONTACT SPECIAL
AGENT CANADAY ASAP ACCESS RESTRICTED

"Well," said Luke. "That looks real final."

"It is," said Walt. "So there *was* an RTA on him, but it's cloaked. I can try to get through to that, but this 'access restricted' means that if I ask again, I'll get shut down. Canaday has, basically, put a bugger-off sign right out front so we can't say we missed it. Fiertag must have given him access to Holmes, so that's that. Right now we look innocent enough. The computer web will let Canaday and Fiertag know we asked. As long as we don't do anything else, they probably won't either. Unless you want me to reroute the protocol architecture through an off-system server, and then we could maybe try to hot-link the database codes with a double-blind cutoff server out of Helsinki, which would disguise our originating algorithm—"

"Ease up, Walt, you're gonna make yourself sick."

"You could tell I was making that up, hah?"

"I'm not as stupid as I look," said Luke, staring at the screen. Walt turned his head to study Luke's profile by the light of the VDT screen.

"You're not, eh? Well, *that's* a relief."

"Now what?"

"Now?" said Walt, stretching. "Now, you know."

"What do I know?"

"You know that you can't use any of the service databases, or any of the national ones either. You know they mean business too. You know that if you poke around inside this thing anymore, you're gonna lose a body part. Maybe one of your favorites too."

"So let it go?"

Walt gave it some serious thought, his face saddening.

"I hate to say it, but that would be my advice, Luke. We had this kind of thing a lot in Bronx Vice. Wheels within wheels. Interagency war. We're grunts, Luke. This kind of thing will blow your career up real fast. Blow us all up, maybe. I know we rolled dice on it, but . . . Doc's the problem, really."

"Doc? Why?"

"He's close to a big promotion. Corner office. He's getting on, Luke, and he's overweight. He's one of the best I ever saw, but he's losing a step or two. That's part of the reason they moved him out of Kansas City. The heat was getting to him. Five years back, he'd never have missed a shot like he did last night. You know those little pills he's always popping?"

"No," said Luke. "I hadn't noticed."

"Maybe he's not popping them in front of you. He takes Dilantin. It's a vasodilator. He's also taking aspirin. Next February is his annual checkup. If he hasn't made a solid desk job before that, if his job description is still Street Operational, he could be out of the service on a medical."

Christ.

"Why'd he go on that run with me last night?"

"You're Luke Zitto, for chrissake. How could he *not*?"

Luke struggled to take this all in.

"Walt, it's not just about me."

"You mean Aurora Powys?"

"Yeah."

"So *make* this good news for her, Luke. Do what Rico says. Tell her the guy's dead. Tell her he got blown out of his socks by another female officer. That'll help. Buy her a box of Black Talons, and send her out to the range. I always sleep better after a couple of hundred rounds."

"What if it isn't true?"

"True?" said Walt. "Truth is the thing with scales."

Luke looked at him. "You're quoting that New York broad at me?"

"Dorothy Parker?"

"Yeah. Her."

"Hey, Luke, I'm not just a pretty face. And it's Brontë, I think. Or somebody else. Anyway, not Parker."

There was a prolonged silence while Luke seemed to shut down from the inside out. Walt recognized the process. Finally, Luke sighed and stepped out of the van, Walt following behind him. They locked it and headed back up the street toward Paddy Riley's.

Halfway up, Luke said, "Feathers."

"What?"

"Truth. She said, 'Truth is the thing with *feathers.*' Not scales."

"Actually, Luke, the line goes, '*Hope* is the thing with feathers.' "

"So what's 'truth' again?"

"The thing with scales."

"I see. Why not hope?"

"Not in D.C., Luke."

C row had passed the rest of the afternoon on the roof-
top of Cheong Sammy's Chinese restaurant, across
the street from Quality Industrial Cleaners, watching
the green van and the office window, waiting for the cops
to arrive and go through the place. The van was thoroughly wiped clean, as was the little office space where he
had spent the last few days, the bathroom where he had
shaved and bathed, and the tiny cooking area where he
had brewed his tea and fried his tortillas.

The brutal heat of the afternoon had climbed like a
lake of lava, crested, approached a furnacelike blast of
heat, and then gradually subsided, declined during the
evening. Now, at ten o'clock, it was merely fetid, stale, and
damp, and shreds of improbable mist circled the streetlights. He had stayed perfectly still through all of these
hours, his little canvas bag full of cash on the tarry roof
beside him, the hatchet resting inside it on a pile of fresh
bills, wrapped in a deerskin chamois.

Someone in the restaurant was trying to grow herbs up here. There was a large green plastic tub shaped like a turtle, full of black earth. A few pale green shoots had struggled up above the soil, but birds had been at them and most of them were shredded and browning into death. Once, around six, an ancient Chinese man, bent and wrinkled as a troll, wearing a stained white apron over a pair of baggy gray pants, a filthy once-white undershirt barely covering his skeletal chest and spindly arms, had shuffled out onto the roof and stood for a while at the edge, puffing on a limp cigarette and staring out over the massed rooftops and tenements of the city.

Crow, motionless, had watched him from the shadows under the overhang. The old man had urinated as he stood there, spraying a pale golden waterfall down into the street below. Crow watched his thin shoulders shaking as if some ripple of amusement rattled his old bones.

He had turned then, to go back down the stairs, and stopped short when he saw Crow in the shadows. His face was a pinched network of wrinkles and sagging brown flesh, but his eyes were narrow and bright. He grinned at Crow, his mouth a twisted slit showing blackened teeth and wide gaps of gum line. Crow had not moved or registered his presence in any way. The old man shrugged, turned, leaned over, and spat a solid greenish wad out onto the baking tile roof. Crow could feel no fear in the man.

He realized there was nothing he could take from this man that the man would be sorry to lose. He found himself smiling back at the old man. The man cackled then and said something in a high fluid dialect, cackled again, and shuffled his way back to the open door of the fire stairs. He didn't look back and was gone like a ferret ducking back into a hole.

Crow settled back into stillness.

Joey Rag was now either dead or puking up the contents of his soul for a room filled with federal agents. It had been difficult to see exactly what had happened after Joey Rag had reached Rona. Crow had watched it happen through one of the big side mirrors on the delivery van—Rona's slender body, and the lumpy waddling form of Joey Rag closing the distance. Then a redheaded woman had begun shouting, more men came from cars and from the green lawn in front of the big white needle, one of them a white-haired man in a baggy brown suit. Joey Rag and Rona were inside the closing circle of shouting men and women, Crow's vision blocked by the backs of these people, men with guns out. Then shots, as loud as the sound of that black cop banging on the side of the green van. Crow had the van moving the moment they sounded, knowing what was happening. It was time to roll away down the treelined street, roll quietly into the traffic, lose himself in the grids and cross streets of the urban warren to the north. No one tried to stop him, no running men in well-cut suits jumped out of the doorways as he was passing. Therefore he was not part of the plan, he was not inside the trap. Which meant the men had been watching Paolo Rona, not Joey Rag. They had taken the bait when Joey showed that little gun.

That sad little empty gun.

Joey Rag was not a professional, not even a good watcher. Anyone with any craft at all would have felt the weight of that piece and known that it was empty. A brave man would have worked the slide and looked at the chamber, looked up into Crow's cold eyes, and seen what was planned.

But Joey was none of those things. To be of use in these times called for more than a willingness to stuff bits of toweling down a hooker's throat. He was only good enough for the part he had played, a part they had agreed to back in Atlanta. Crow had asked them if Joey Rag was expendable, but it had been a formality, a courtesy, because there was no one who was not expendable. Already, someone was on the way from Atlanta to take over the business.

For now, there was nothing to do but wait, watch, and see who arrived at the cleaning plant across the street. All of this had become inevitable when Joey Rag had given that black sergeant—CULLEN was the name in white carved letters on the man's black plastic name tag—when Joey had given him his *card*, like any fool citizen, like a simpering subservient clown. From that moment on, Crow had known he would kill him, or use him.

And now he knew that Rona was being watched.

Rona was a very street-smart man. That was his reputation, that was how he had been described in Atlanta, how he had been reported by Guillermo Barra's representatives. Either he had walked, like a fool, into a police trap—or he *knew*, and his plan was to lure Crow into that same trap. Crow did not think Paolo Rona was a fool.

Maybe Rona was dead too.

Maybe not.

Crow would wait. To wait, that was why he had been sent here. To wait and find out. To ask questions, yes, when the time came.

But now the waiting was all.

The waiting was enough.

When Luke finally got back to his apartment in Georgetown, there was a slip of paper shoved under his door, and the red light on his answering machine in his bedroom was blinking. The note was on monogrammed paper, and was written in black ink with a fountain pen.

Dear Mister Zitto:
We're having a small party tomorrow night and we'd be delighted if you could join us. There will be a few people from the university and one or two friends from the Justice Department. We hope you'll be able to join us for drinks around eight.

Cheers,
Charles Berg

Berg was one of the guys upstairs, the pair of professors who worked at the university. Luke had seen them around the neighborhood. He thought that Charles Berg was the hard-looking one, the marathon runner. If he was right, the other man, the one who looked like that old actor in the classic films, what was his name? Cecil Kellaway, maybe? That guy's name was . . . damn . . . it was Kellaway, you idiot. Something Kellaway.

So how'd they figure that he was with Justice? The car, probably; it had Justice written all over it. Or they were connected to the circuit somewhere. Well, well. His first actual real-live invitation to something that wasn't cop-related. Hell, it wasn't like his dance card was packed.

Ignoring, with difficulty, the red light on his answering machine, he dropped his gear on the bed and went into the bathroom. He ran cold water into the sink and went out to the kitchen to get a tray of ice cubes from the freezer. He broke the tray into the sink and let the cubes float for a minute while he rummaged around in the cupboards, locating a large bottle of Chivas Regal. He poured a couple of fingers into one of the crystal tumblers that had come with the apartment and sat down on the edge of the bathtub to pull himself together.

A weight like a slow descending avalanche of soft silken sand seemed to pour down on him, bending his back and making it hard to keep his eyes open. He'd been in the D.C. area for less than three weeks now, and already he felt as if he were drowning in hidden agendas, indecipherable motivations, and ambiguous definitions of right and wrong. Sighing, he pulled himself upright and went over to the sink.

Breathing in and holding it, Luke buried his head in the freezing water. It jolted him, raced through his skull like pale blue fire. His cheekbones ached, and his skull seemed to crack like a hot stone. His heart jumped, and he shook his head twice, scattering waves of cold water onto the marble floor of the bathroom. Pulling out, he grabbed a thick pale green bath towel and scrubbed his head dry. He looked into the mirror over the sink. What he saw was not appealing. He looked away.

The red light in the answering machine hunted him still, so he went out into the front room, poured himself a Scotch.

The whiskey warmed him all the way down, and he felt his nerves begin to settle. This is your new life, Luke. This is your chance for something other than Court Street and the Bronx, something better than chasing an endless supply of small-time vermin through the ruined streets and blasted buildings of a world that no one gives a damn about.

What'd he say to Doc? He was the cork in the bottle? Well, he was at the wrong end of that cork, because he was right down there in the bottle himself. D.C. was his invitation to the party.

Accept it.

Say thank you.

Say I'd be delighted, ma'am.

There was music coming from upstairs. Muted, soft, it was something from his memory. It was "Stardust," an old Hoagy Carmichael song. It had been his father's favorite song. "Sometimes I wonder why I spend the lonely hours . . . dreaming of a song . . ."

After a while, he was able to get up enough courage to go into the bedroom and hit the play button on the answering machine.

Luke? I hope I have the right number. This is Doug Powys. Are you there? . . . Can you pick up? Luke? . . . Okay . . . well, I just wanted to check with you. I think Aurora may have gotten a call today—at least there was one on the machine, and I—we were in Narragansett, Payne and I, and the rain was so bad we came home, but Aurora's gone and there was this message on the

machine—it was from . . . Payne, can you get me my . . .
thank you . . . It's from a Dennis Swayze at the Justice
Department. They wanted Deputy Powys to know that
Paolo Rona was . . . well, it's strange . . . that Paolo Rona
had been "taken out of the loop." I don't know if that's
one of your stupid federal code words . . . what loop?
Anyway, she's not—Aurora's not here, and I'm . . . I'm
hoping you might have heard from her. I'll be up late,
so if you could call me as soon as you come in, I . . .
well, I hope to hear from you. Maybe I'll call back later.
. . . This was Doug Powys, and I was calling about Aurora Powys.

All of Luke's carefully constructed, Scotch-assisted se-
renity blew up in a white-hot flare of literally painful rage,
a searing acid rush that scored a path through his belly
and set flames racing along his veins and arteries.

That unbelievable, meddling, self-important manipula-
tive little viper had double-faked him. He had decided not
to take a chance on Luke's next move. Reed Endicott had
called Aurora Powys himself, or sent a flunky to do it, and
laid what Luke was now absolutely convinced was an outrageous lie on the woman. "Out of the loop" was a spook
phrase, and in the spook world it did mean "killed," but
at Justice all it meant was that your fax machine had been
disconnected.

Reed Endicott—or Swayze—or *someone* was playing a
vicious game with a woman who was struggling very hard
to recover from a terrible sexual assault, a woman who was
drinking, who was taking Valium and Prozac and God
knew what else—how could a man be so chilly, so heart-
stoppingly dead to real suffering. . . . Luke was on his feet
and halfway into the bedroom to get his clothes on, to
locate Endicott's home address, wherever it was, when the

next message cycled up and began to play. Even before he heard the voice, his heart was heavy with certainty.

Luke? Are you there? This is me. . . . I got a call from somebody down there today, I don't know him. Do you know a Dennis Swayze? I think he's saying that federal agents took down Paolo Rona today . . . maybe not killed but something. . . . I don't know how I feel. . . . I wish you were there. I tried your pager, but all I got was a recording saying the—

Suddenly panicked, Luke fumbled at his belt and ripped his pager off the hook. It was still set to on. He pressed the button and looked at the LED display. The letters were nonnegotiable, stunning.

SYSTEM OFF

Had Fiertag gone that far? Had they actually shut off his pager? He checked his watch. It was eleven thirty-four. When had he last looked at his pager? He had no idea. When would this Swayze have called Aurora Powys? Probably as soon as the meeting at 600 Army Navy ended. What time was *that*? Six? Six-thirty? Christ. Five hours ago? How many miles from New York City to Washington, D.C.? Less than three hundred, anyway. Most of it on the New Jersey Turnpike. . . .

—on *Eyewitness News* now saying there had been a shooting in D.C.—a guy was dead—and federal agents had been involved. I have to see you, Luke. I hope you're not. . . . I have your address. Please don't be angry with me. Bye. . . . Luke? . . .

0600 Hours
Saturday, January 14, 1995
Court Street
Cobble Hill
Brooklyn

Wendy Ma put down the coffee cup, smacked it down, splashing hot coffee all over Luke's breakfast-nook table. Her perfect oval features were hard, her voice barely under control.

"What the hell did you *think* would happen, for God's sake?"

Luke couldn't look right at her. He fumbled for his cigarettes, failed to find them, and then turned to stare out the window of the flat, at the thin bare tree branches, at the scraps of dead leaves flying windblown and crazy down the cobblestone walk, at the cars hissing by on Court Street. A pale pink light was tinting the roofline of the apartment across the street, and ten thousand feet above the city, the rising winter sun was glinting off the shining hull of a La Guardia jet rising into the dawn. It looked like a diamond set into a pale pink crystal bowl, or like someone dragging the point of a diamond cutter across a windowpane etched in winter frost. Luke watched it awhile, wondering what would happen if God struck the bowl of rose-colored glass with a silver hatchet. Would the whole world crack open? If it did, what would they see? Suddenly dead-bone weary, Luke considered Wendy, studied her masklike face and the way the early morning light lay upon her cheek like a dusting of rose-colored powder.

"What was I supposed to do?"

"You could have stayed in touch! You could have *called* the poor woman, as soon as you *heard*! She should have heard it from you. But no. You wander off to some bar and play *dice*, for God's sake. You play dice to see if you'll tell her. You arrogant shits! Like it's *your* business. This is *her* pain, Luke, not yours. *You* don't own it. She does. Where was your brain?"

"I was trying to work it through with—"

"The *guys*, right? The goddamn *guys*!"

Wendy got up, pulled Luke's shirt closer around her, and went over to the stove to pour herself a cup of coffee. Luke found his cigarettes and lit one up, puffing the smoke against the chilly surface of the windowpane beside the table. He watched Wendy's body under his shirt, the way she moved, the tanned expanse of slender well-muscled legs. She turned with the cup, stopped short, stared at him.

"Don't tell me you were staring at my—in the middle of all this, you find the time to *ogle* me? Luke, the word is *e*-volve, we're *e*-volving, not *de*-volving. Who were your ancestors, anyway? Those guys in *Quest for Fire*?"

Luke set the cigarette in his mouth, leaned backward in the metal chair, ran his hands through his hair, and then rubbed his eyes. Sleep, that was what he needed now. A year would do nicely.

"Wendy, I made a mistake. I know that. There were other things to consider. There was Doc—this thing with the pills. When Walt told me that, man, I didn't know what to do. And I wanted to be *sure* before I called her."

Wendy sat down across from him, her blue-black hair falling down across her cheeks, framing her eyes. There was a light deep inside them, and Luke could see his own image in her eyes, a bare-chested man with a wild corona of hair, wreathed in a shroud of smoke.

"Luke, I understand what you meant to do. I know—I think I know you well enough now—"

"I hope so."

She smiled, reached out and took his right hand, began to rub his gold Marshals Service ring. "So do I . . . but you have to understand. To be assaulted, Luke, to be stripped of everything you have, all your power, your sense of control—and they go *on*, you know, the average sexual assault lasts four hours, did you know that? Think about it. And if you cooperate, you try to . . . you do what's necessary, then if you live, you have that on your soul forever, what you did, what you gave up, what you *allowed*, how you *sold* yourself. . . . That mark never ever fades, Luke."

Luke was looking at her.

Never fades. Well, that was very true. And not just for women. "I tried to . . . I called—"

"Doug Powys? I should hope so. What happened?"

"He was home."

Wendy sighed, waited. The interval grew.

Finally: "And?"

Luke stared out the window, hearing the rising thunder of trucks and cars on the Gowanus, the booming of tires on blacktop.

"And then I drove to the Jersey state line."

Luke went over the Patapsco Causeway at close to a hundred miles an hour, with the liquid scintillation of marina lights roiling and tossing on the blackened water on his right, and the lights and the traffic of Baltimore on his left, swirling all around him in arcs and coronas, a blur of blood reds and streaky yellows and hectic blue-white smears across the windshield, but the silence of the big blue Crown Victoria, and the muted steady roar of the wind rush all around him, kept him in a separate world, a dim green cocoon of regret, and recrimination, and fear.

He had the air conditioner on, but now and then he'd get a brief scent of the seas, a sharp, slightly rotten, half-sweet salt-rush of damp air that filled the car with the huge hidden presence of the vast booming water-fields of Chesapeake Bay.

Inside this swirling internal vortex, every little town and rest station he had blown through on his way up Interstate 95 had seemed to rise up out of the velvety Maryland countryside like a roadside carnival, had wheeled and flashed at him as he rolled onward, and then faded, glimmering, subsiding into a pale pink glow above the black shoulders of trees and the low hills in his rearview mirror.

The long empty spaces between the towns were like the brief but perfect silences that separate each heartbeat, each one a furtive, fleeting, sidelong glance down the shadowed hallways of eternity.

The dashboard lights were bright green, the numerals steady at ninety-five miles an hour, the tires booming and hissing on the smooth unreeling ribbon of the highway. Now and then he would rocket past a family sedan or a salesman's rented Sable, and he'd get a peripheral flash of the back of a woman's neck, a flicker of his own lights off the jewel on her ring finger, or the startled eyes of a driver as he passed him, the man trying to figure out what had come up out of nowhere in his rearview mirror less than thirty seconds ago and was now hurtling by him like a dark blue glimmer, the driver at the wheel hidden behind the heavy federal tint.

Now Baltimore was receding, sinking back into the Maryland countryside, and the interstate was spooling through Rosedale and Middle River. A green sign flashed by him on his right, with white letters on it, streaking past his left-hand windshield. Road signs came up and burned with green fires and then flicked out of existence like fireflies by the side of a country road. A timeless interlude carried him away, the road unreeling ahead.

An hour and seventeen minutes later, a few miles across the Delaware River, accelerating on the Jersey Turnpike, his high beams picked out the luminous side-strip panels of a New Jersey State Patrol unit sitting in a cross-over lane on the median strip. At one mile away and closing fast, Luke watched the trooper's car light up like a sideshow Ferris wheel as Luke cleared his radar horizon, a lunatic flutter of red and white and deep piercing blue. His high beams began to alternate right and left as the trooper put it in gear and waited for Luke to thunder past his position.

Luke leaned forward and picked up his blue Hot Shot light, set it up on his dashboard. He flicked it on, and the flashing blue light lit up the hood of the Crown Victoria and a lot of the highway ahead of him, blue spears of light arcing out, lighting up the trees and the blacktop and, in a few seconds, the shiny reflective paint on the side of the trooper car. The New Jersey patrol car stopped moving, but Luke knew he'd be trying to get a radio return out of this ambiguous blue rocket flying by.

Luke opened the glove compartment and punched the radio concealed inside it through to the New Jersey State–wide frequency, hoping the guy had his act together and was waiting for a callback on that channel. As soon as Luke punched the frequency, his speaker broke into sound.

"This is New Jersey State Patrol Unit Alpha Twelve. Identify."

"Bravo Sixteen, Federal Marshal, Alpha Twelve. Sorry to make you spill your coffee."

"Ten-four, Bravo Sixteen. I have you at one-ten in a sixty-five zone. State your business, please. Make it good."

"Roger, Alpha Twelve. Urgent federal matter."

"No shit, Bravo Sixteen. I had the impression it was urgent. Do you wish an escort?"

"I thank you, Alpha Twelve. I'll be the disappearing red lights on your forward horizon. If you're coming, let's roll."

"Ten-four, Bravo Sixteen. We'll see about that. Out."

Luke watched the car in his rearview as it faded into a tiny cycling spark of blue, white, and red flashing lights. He wasn't thrilled about this, but he had more or less expected it. It was a long run from Georgetown to the Jersey Turnpike. There had to be a trooper in the shrubbery somewhere on that stretch. He checked the rearview again and saw the trooper coming up on his tail, no less than a hundred yards back and closing fast. He could literally *hear* the high-pitched howl of the car's engine. Christ, the man must have one hell of a big mill in that thing. He'd heard about their new pursuit machines. This was definitely one of them.

The trooper car hurtled past him on his left side, a gray polished rocket with his roof-bar blazing. Luke got a brief glimpse of the driver, his hand raised, and he heard a short bleep from the siren. The car sounded like a bullfrog in a barrel, the banshee howl changing into a Doppler boom and then a low growling murmur as it slowed a bit, popped and rumbled, and took a post about a hundred feet in front of Luke's Crown Victoria.

Locked like two stars in a black emptiness, they both began to climb again toward one hundred and thirty miles an hour. That snaking yellow line, and the rock-steady stern of the trooper car, became the only fixed compass points in Luke's blackened and silent universe.

Watching the luminous letters on the rear panel of the state car—STATE PATROL—Luke knew the man would have already run Luke's Maryland plates and gotten a registered owner of a leasing company in Chevy Chase. Then he'd have called in to his duty sergeant, who would have punched the plates up on his NCIC/DMV database and seen a file notation—see MAGLOCEN/RTA/10-95—which would support Luke's statement that he was a federal agent on federal business. His radio crackled into life again.

"Alpha Twelve to Bravo Sixteen."

"Bravo Sixteen."

"So what's the story?"

"I could tell you—"

"But then you'd have to kill me. You feds are all the same. How do you like my ride?"

"Awesome, Alpha Twelve."

"Thank you, Bravo Sixteen. This is your basic five-liter ported and polished fuel-injected full-race Isky cam five-to-one ratio blacktop bullet. Caught a Porsche 911 with this thing last week, he was going so fast I was a day and a half younger by the time I caught him. I passed myself on the way back. Your machine's no Winnebago, man. What's in it?"

"Merc 454, tuned and blueprinted. I get another twenty out of the top-end by running it on JP5."

"Very funny. Exits coming up. Where do you want to go?"

"State patrol substation."

"Ten-four, Bravo Sixteen. That's my home station. I'll buy you a coffee. Just stay on my trunk-lock, and we'll be there in a heartbeat."

"Roger, Alpha Twelve."

The turnpike exits were coming up. Luke could see the lights of a large town in the distance, past the hundred-foot-tall signs that read DENNY'S and ARCO and HOLIDAY INN. The trooper was decelerating now, and his taillights lit up like returning fire. Luke closed in on the unit as it slowed for the exit ramp. They stopped at the lights, and Luke reached over to finish the rest of the coffee in his Thermos. He was going to need his wits about him in the next few minutes.

Twinned now, rolling quietly into a wide small-town street lined with darkened storefronts under overhanging shade trees, they reached a yard fenced in with chain-link.

A sprawling yellow-brick single-floored building took up most of the big yard. There were state cruisers all over the lot, as well as private Jeeps and vans and sedans, all waiting for their owners to come off-duty. A flagpole rose into the night sky, lit up by three mercury-vapor spots. The flag hung limp in the damp summer humidity, moths fluttering in the beams. Luke took the time to wonder why the flag was still flying after Taps. He never found out. Alpha Twelve parked his cruiser by the visitor spaces in front of the main entrance, and Luke slid his car in beside him.

The driver of Alpha Twelve climbed out and waited on the sidewalk while Luke tripped the remote alarms and walked up to meet the man.

Alpha Twelve turned out to be a black trooper in his late twenties with a shaved head and a body as short, solid, and impressive as a 105 artillery shell. His New Jersey uniform shirt was stretched out over his Kevlar vest, and a black-webbed leather Sam Browne at his waist carried about a half a ton of gear, including a Beretta nine-millimeter semiautomatic. He held his hand out as Luke reached him, grinning widely.

"I'm William Tighe. Nice to meet you."

"Good to meet you. I'm Luke Zitto."

Tighe's grip was dry and firm, his face square and rocky. He seemed to have no neck at all. Luke showed him his Marshal's star. Tighe looked at it as if he had never seen one before. Turned out he had. This was his career second for the shift. As they went up the walk toward the glass doors of the entrance, Tighe sounded like a man who had just stepped off the Hurricane at Asbury Park.

"That was more fun than I've had in a month, deputy. Except for that Porsche. Hell, we should have gone straight through to New York City."

Luke smiled at the man. Years ago, a simple high-speed

escort run would have left him as charged up and satisfied as it had left this trooper.

"Next time let's do that. I guess I'm not looking forward to this."

Tighe said nothing, and his face grew serious.

"Well, I think I know why you're here. Lieutenant Farrell's waiting for you."

"You checked, hah?"

Tighe's young face looked vaguely uneasy.

"Regulations, Deputy Zitto."

"I know that. Don't give it a second."

They reached the doors, and Tighe pulled them open. Luke walked through into a bright reception area with the New Jersey state crest laid down in brass and marble against a polished terrazzo floor. A long desk ran from wall to wall, and a duty sergeant, overweight, his white hair cropped, his tie loosened, looked up from his computer console as they reached his station.

"This the man, Billy?"

"Sergeant Wytold, this is Deputy Marshal Luke Zitto."

They shook hands across the countertop. Wytold's eyes were sympathetic.

"You wanna go back there right now?"

"Not yet. I think your CO wants to see me."

"Yeah. Come on back."

Wytold pressed a button, and the swing-gate popped open.

"I'll leave you here, Deputy—"

"Call me Luke."

Tighe grinned. "Okay, Luke. I'll be in the coffee room. I owe you one."

"Sure."

Wytold led Luke back through a series of glass-walled cubicles and a large muster room, where several young troopers, male and female, were sitting at long trestle tables writing up incident reports. They reached an office at the rear, walled in translucent ripple glass. Wytold knocked on the door. A woman's voice answered.

"Yeah?"

Wytold opened the door. A slender middle-aged white woman, her hair swept back into a severe temple-tightening bun, held in place with a black ribbon, and wearing a perfectly cut and razor-edged trooper's uniform with brass eagles on her epaulets, was seated behind a broad cluttered green-topped metal desk. There was a wide picture window behind her showing a stretch of parking lot and some trees in the shadows beyond, their leaves tinted yellow by the yard lights. One of the office walls was covered in training certificates, diplomas, four commendations, a family portrait, and even a sheepskin from the FBI training school at Quantico.

She stood up as soon as Luke came into the room, coming out from behind her desk, her strong Irish face a little closed, but with a good smile. Her eyes were a deep hazel, and two bright touches of blush or rouge floated delicately on her prominent cheekbones. There were sympathy and sadness in her eyes, but also a great deal of what Luke correctly interpreted as reflexive interagency defensiveness. She radiated a cool but not unkind intelligence.

"Deputy Zitto. You got here fast."

"Yes, Lieutenant. Is her family here yet?"

"Mr. Powys called a while ago. He has to get a sitter, so he says. I told him you were on your way. He didn't seem too thrilled."

"Mr. Powys is a lawyer, Lieutenant Farrell."

She grinned at that, then sat down behind her desk. Luke took the oak swivel chair in front of it. When he relaxed into it, a wave of weariness rolled over him. Farrell saw it passing. She opened a drawer and set out a bottle of Bushmill's whiskey and two small cut-crystal glasses.

"Call me Margaret. You look dead beat. I save this stuff for times like this. Would you like one?"

"A short one, thanks. Please call me Luke."

She poured two short jolts of the Irish whiskey into the glasses, handed one to Luke across her desk. They drank with a little ceremony. The liquid was smoky and light in his mouth and went down like a streak of amber fire. Luke patted his suit jacket and found his cigarettes. He held them up.

"Do you mind?"

"Not if you blow it toward me. I gave them up five months ago."

She patted her chest.

"Losing my wind. I grow old, I grow old . . . something about my trousers rolled? Go ahead."

Luke lit up a Kool and exhaled. The bitter mint rush raced through his lungs, calming him. Farrell watched him with a covetous glimmer in her hazel eyes.

"Have you seen her yet?" she asked.

"Not yet."

"You should."

"I know. I wanted to talk to you first."

Farrell's face settled into a careful reserve. "That's what you said. There's not much I can do. Not much, to be honest, that I *would* do, even if I could."

Luke let that go for the moment. "What happened, anyway?"

"You have the story. It's not real complicated."

"I know. I'd just like to hear it all at once."

Farrell sat back into her chair and sipped at her glass. Exhaling, she considered Luke's pack of Kools on the desk, seemed to shake herself, and put her hands together on her lap.

"There's a tollbooth a few miles back. A county unit had picked her up on radar back there, and a citizen had called her in on his cell phone. A 1990 dark green and wood-veneer side-paneled Buick Roadmaster, about the size of a coal barge. Speeding, lane changes, she was doing close to a hundred on the tollbooth approaches, but no units reached her. She braked hard about a hundred and fifty yards from the toll station. The attendant heard her brakes squealing. She got herself together and rolled up to his station, fumbling for change. Dropped a lot of it out the window. They got it on video, I hear. Anyway, she got his attention, and when she pulled out onto the turnpike again, he called it in to us, and we set up an intercept."

Farrell paused, sorting out her priorities. Then she simply raised her hands and shrugged.

"She blew right through it. One of my guys sprained an ankle getting out of the way. She grazed a highway unit and disappeared. We caught up with her a few miles later, and by that time she'd skimmed a bunch of tourists in a Grand Cherokee—got paint from that on her left quarter-panel. . . ."

Luke was staring at the Kool in his hand, at the red spark chewing its way down the narrow white cylinder, at the smoke curling up from it. He had a sudden reminiscence, bright red sparks circling around the Washington Monument, how long ago? A year? A decade?

"Anyway, Alpha Three and a couple of county units had her bracketed around an S-curve section."

"Lights? Sirens?"

It was a dumb question.

"Of course. The whole megillah."

"And she wouldn't stop?"

"Eventually. She went off the shoulder, plowed up a section of turf, and then slid into a crash barrier by the overpass. Two seconds later, we had four cars on her, and they were trying to get her door open. It had buckled a bit when she hit the impact barrels."

"Blood levels?"

"We're still waiting."

"Alcohol?"

"Be my guess. She had that look. The machine was wonky. Our lab doesn't open until ten."

"Where is she now?"

"In the back there."

"Can I see her?"

Farrell studied Luke for a long moment. "Nothing to say? Officially, I mean?"

Luke drew in a lungful of Kool, held it, and blew it out in a kind of low whistle. "That was a hell of a ride, I'll give her that."

"Oh yes. Gave us all a *big* thrill."

"What's possible?"

Farrell looked up at the ceiling and ran a hand back through her hair, sweeping a stray thread back into position.

"Not one whole hell of a lot, Luke. You have the citizen with the cell phone. He made her plates. It was a big adventure for him, so you can bet he'll talk about it. Sooner or later somebody from the regional press will get wind of it. As well, you have the paint from the Grand Cherokee. Nobody was hurt there, but this is a very litigious society. Fear and distress, anxiety, all that. About the pursuit, we might be able to do something. Thing is, people could have died. Not to mention what the press would do with it."

Luke picked up the glass and swirled the last of the Bushmill's around. "Have any press guys called yet?"

"Not yet. It's only four in the morning. They don't work our kind of hours, do they?"

"Do you know her story?"

"I know she's a very troubled young woman."

"Do you want to know it?"

Farrell considered Luke for another minute. Phones were ringing out in the hall. The sound of a sixteen-wheeler chugging up the interstate on-ramp made him think of his apartment next to the Gowanus Expressway. It was a lonely recollection.

"Yes," she said, finally. "I think I do."

So Luke told her.

Margaret Farrell listened quietly, placing a careful and pointed question from time to time. Luke left out a great deal of it, particularly the details surrounding the role of Treasury in the situation. When he was through, Margaret Farrell was silent for a while.

"That's quite a story. How much of it is true?"

"Almost all of it."

"It has some serious holes."

"Nothing that would change the basic facts."

"Interagency competition? Turf wars in D.C.?"

"Yes. Very much so."

"Are you sleeping with her?"

Luke rocked in his swivel chair. He should have expected that.

He looked down at his Kool pack, pulled one out, offered it to the lieutenant. She refused it.

"No," he said, meeting her eyes. "I'm not."

Farrell sighed, got up from the desk.

"You disappoint me, Luke. Let's go see her."

Luke never asked Lieutenant Margaret Farrell of the New Jersey State Highway Patrol how he had disappointed her.

But then, he didn't have to, did he?

The lock-up attendant was sound asleep in a wooden chair that he had propped back up against the breeze-block walls of the holding cell area. He jerked forward as Luke and the lieutenant pulled open the fire door. He was young, no more than twenty-two, with a trick haircut and too much muscle. He looked steroidal and dim-witted, and Luke didn't like him. He popped to his feet like a marionette when he saw Farrell behind Luke. A set of keys jangled from his webbing, and he was holding a Monadnock billy club in his hands. He saluted, blinking, and stared at Luke with the dull disinterest of a steer in a pen. Muscles in his jaw flexed and coiled as he chewed noisily on a wad of pink gum. His breath smelled of Juicy Fruit and cinnamon buns.

"Mike, this man's here to see the prisoner."

"Yes, ma'am. Are you carrying any weapons, sir?"

Luke unholstered his Taurus and handed it across to the turnkey. He put it into a locker and twisted the key.

He looked at Luke for another second, trying to figure out if he should frisk him.

"He's a Marshal, Mike. Just let him in. And wait outside." Farrell turned and patted Luke's shoulder. "I'll be in my office. Come see me before you leave."

Mike led him down a long hallway lined with beige-painted breeze-blocks. There were four green steel doors along the hall, each with tiny reinforced glass windows and a slot for food trays. Watching the back of Mike's neck, Luke got a fleeting image of the man standing at one of those windows during the long empty watches of the night shift, staring at Aurora, waiting for her to do something interesting. He resisted the temptation to club him across the back of that bovine-looking neck. Mike reached cell B and put a large steel key into the slot, turned it twice, then opened the door quickly, stepping inside in front of Luke so that he was blocking Luke's view.

"Hey, baby! Wakey-wakey!" said Mike. His body moved, and Luke heard the sound of his boot hitting a steel frame.

He heard Aurora's bleat of fear.

Luke reached over, got a good grip on the back of Mike's collar, braced himself as he felt Mike tensing, and jerked Mike off balance, throwing him backward against the wall across from the door. Mike bounced off it, his brutal young face bright pink, his dark eyes brimming with low-down mean.

Luke stepped into his advance and struck him square on the bridge of his nose with the meaty part of his fist, a short, sudden, upward blow. Blood spurted out of Mike's nose and sprinkled down the front of his tan uniform. His eyes crossed, and there was blood in his teeth as he gasped in pain. He lifted his Monadnock, and Luke wrenched it out of his hand. He put the cross-arm up against Mike's throat, kicked the man's feet out into a spread, and pinned him to the wall.

"Mike, can you hear me?"

Mike struggled a bit, then focused on Luke's face. The anger was fading, replaced by fear and humiliation. Luke waited until he had Mike's full attention.

"Can you hear me?"

Mike tried to nod, found his range limited by a billy club.

"Yes."

"I can and will make your life a waking nightmare, son. I am a federal officer. I can make *one* call and get you thrown under a train. You will not find work with Wal-Mart. You will not find work with Burger King. You will not ever, ever, put on a uniform again unless you're standing under a hotel awning hoping for tips. If I *ever* hear of you treating a prisoner like that again, I promise you that you will become a hobby of mine, something for me to do whenever I have a lot of anger to work out. Am I getting through to you, son?"

"Yes," said Mike.

"Yes what?"

"Yes, sir."

"You will leave this door unlocked?"

"Yes, sir."

"Fine. Thank you. Now go clean yourself up. You look like shit."

Luke threw the Monadnock down the hallway. It bounced and clattered, and Mike winced. Then Luke turned away and walked into the bright tiny cell.

Aurora Powys was sitting up on the edge of the steel cot, wrapped in a robin's-egg-blue blanket, her pale Welsh cheeks streaked with mascara, her wild blond hair matted and damp. She had paper slippers on her bare feet. She was wearing a pair of prisoner's overalls in Day-Glo orange. Her eyes were rimmed in red, bruised looking, but still the same bottomless blue, made even deeper by the tears in them.

"You love to make an entrance, don't you?" she said.

Luke went over to her, crouched down at her knees, and pulled her into him. She smelled of soap and cotton. Her hair was damp. She hesitated, and then Luke felt her strong arms go around his neck, and she hugged him in tight. Her chest heaved once, twice, and then she shook herself and pushed him away. She used a corner of the blanket to rub at her face and wipe her eyes. Then she tried for a smile, and Luke felt his throat tightening and a burning in his own eyes. He drove all of that down.

Aurora covered her mouth.

"God, I must smell like a dead bat."

He tried for Fernando Lamas.

"You look mah-velous, dahling."

She smiled again, a little stronger.

"It is better to look good than to feel good."

Her accent was always better than his. Luke touched her forehead. There was a large bruise near her temple, spreading out into her left eye in a pale purple and green stain. She winced but didn't move. She nodded toward the open door.

"Thanks for dealing with that asshole. I'm never again going to be a bitch with a prisoner. He really enjoys his work. It took him ten minutes to frisk me when they brought me here. This thing"—she plucked at the orange overalls—"if you have to go to the bathroom, you have to undo them all the way down. All I have *on* is this thing. They took everything else. I was trying to pee . . . I don't know . . . around—I don't have a watch. What time is it now?"

"Five in the morning. Monday morning."

"Where exactly am I, anyway?"

"You're in a holding cell. New Jersey troopers picked you up near the Delaware line."

"Christ . . . what a mess. Anyway, I'm sitting there on *that* thing—" She gestured toward the stainless-steel toilet-and-sink combination that was the only other piece of furniture in the nine-by-nine beige breeze-block cell. "Naked down to my ankles—I look up, and guess who's got his fat fucking face pressed up against that window there? Know what he did, Luke? That asshole *licked* the glass! When I get out of here, I'm going to come back and kick his genitalia into strawberry jam."

"Thatta girl."

"Oh, you prick! Don't *girl* me!"

Luke was grinning at her.

She pushed him back on his heels. "Sit down, will you."

"Where?"

"I don't care—on the toilet."

Luke straddled it and settled down carefully. Aurora ran both her hands through her hair, trying to straighten out the tangles. She leaned back against the wall and let out a long ragged breath that ended in a brief sob.

"How much do you remember, Aurora?"

She plucked at the blue blanket angrily, shuddered a bit.

"I remember getting that call. I was okay, I mean, I hadn't had anything. Doug and Payne decided to leave for Narragansett Saturday, so I had the whole house to myself. I was listening to Ry Cooder, a CD called *Talking Timbuktu*. The roof was like a waterfall, the sound of the rain? But it was . . . safe. The phone rang, I paid no attention. Then I heard this voice—very federal, you know? Like every word is fresh out of the box? I heard the name Rona. I reached it just as he was hanging up."

"What did he say?"

"You'd think I was talking to the CIA. Flat dead voice, said it was a courtesy call, that federal agents had . . . taken Paolo Rona out of the loop. Literally that's what he said. I asked him what the hell that meant, he said that if I watched the news, I'd see the story. He said his call was 'unofficial,' just a 'courtesy,' that the case was 'ongoing.' "

"Did he give you a name?"

"Oh yes. Dennis Swayze."

"Not Reed Endicott?"

Aurora frowned at him. "No. Swayze. Said he was with Justice. Sounded like every one of Doug's partners. So tightly wrapped that when they fart, you can't hear it, but blocks away all the dogs are howling? Wished me a good afternoon. Then . . . I'm not sure. I started to have . . . to see it all again? So I thought, well, if you just have one."

"One what?"

"A Valium. When I take Valium, I don't feel like drinking. I thought it would be safer."

"But you did drink?"

"Oh yes. . . . Once I had the Valium, everything just seemed . . . okay? Smooth? I mean, this was a good thing, right? So why not . . ."

"Celebrate?"

"Yeah. . . . Only once I had celebrated, I got this paranoid flash—what if he wasn't dead? What if they got the ID wrong? What if one day I'm sitting in my house and I look up and there he is? So then I thought, well, *you'll* know, so I called your pager, but the system was shut down for repairs."

"You checked that?"

"Oh yeah. I called Motorola. It was a Sunday, and they were doing a hardware update at the switching station. Why?"

"Nothing. I'll tell you later. Did you try Ops?"

"Yeah. I got a nice young kid, he told me you were

either at Paddy Riley's bar on M Street, or you were home."

"So then you called me at home?"

"Yes. Got your answering machine. After that, it's only three hundred miles from New York to D.C. Valium makes everything seem plausible. You oughta try it, Luke. Then I had a drink. Then I remembered what Swayze had said, so I turned on the TV. I flicked around with the remote. There was nothing. Then I got onto the radio, and there was this short piece about Treasury agents involved in a D.C. gun battle. A criminal had been killed. No names yet. That did it for me. I decided, to hell with it. Doug and Payne were gone. I needed to *do* something."

"So you climbed into that Roadmaster and grew yourself a parade of law enforcement officers in the process? Did you know you ran a roadblock?"

"Did I?" She shook her hair, sighed. "I think I remember that."

She looked over at Luke, reached out a hand. Luke held it.

"I think it's fair to say I have a slight problem with alcohol, right?"

Luke laughed, then buried it. His face turned a little stony.

"Oh yeah. I'd say so. Why the hell didn't you stay at AA?"

Aurora was quiet for a time. Luke watched her face and saw a kind of hybrid emotion, resignation mixed with anger, come over it.

"You know the trouble with going to AA? Pretty soon that's all you are ever going to be. An *ex*-alcoholic. It . . . consumes . . . them all. A lot of them, they just trade cigarettes for the booze, or coffee. And it's always the Twelve Steps, and your Higher Power. They make a *cult* out of guilt. I'm *sorry* for this and I'm *ashamed* about that, whine whine whine. After a while it starts to sound like bragging. Like, hey, you think *you're* humble, hah? Lady, *I'm* the most humble guy on the eastern seaboard! I'm not drinking because I'm weak. And I don't want to be *humble*! I'm drinking because I'm *mad*, because if I don't drink, I'll go out and find that fucking little . . . and now I can't even do that."

Her face reddened again, and she breathed deeply three or four times.

"Have you talked to Doug yet?" she asked.

"We spoke."

"How is he? How's Payne?"

"Payne's fine. I heard him playing in the background. He said to tell you he loves you."

Aurora teared up, brimmed over, and then pushed it all back down.

"And Doug? I guess I've embarrassed the Full Partner, haven't I?"

"Not so's you'd know it. He was real stand-up, I thought. All he wanted to know was if there was anything we could do. The service. He was a little bugged that I was coming, but he took it well."

Aurora smiled at that. "Considering . . ."

"Yeah. Considering. He's coming down with a lawyer in the morning. He had to get a sitter."

"Julia Stern will do it. Payne's got a crush on her."

"Aurora, they're all fine. Let's worry about you, okay?"

"I guess I screwed the pooch, huh, Luke?"

"I think you had a sudden attack of craniorectal inversion, sweetheart. What was in your mind, anyway?"

"I wanted to *see*. Who's Reed Endicott, anyway?"

Luke suppressed a tremor of anger.

"He's one of the double A's at Justice. Assistant U.S. Attorney. He's got a Treasury thing going. You ever meet Bolton Canaday?"

"Older Irish guy? Big head of white hair? Kind of leaves a trail?"

"Yeah. That's the guy."

Now that they were closing in on the central issue, Luke's indecision tormented him. "Canaday's the agent in charge. He was there when it all went down."

"What went down, Luke. Exactly what happened?"

Luke told her the story as it had been told to him by Endicott and Canaday, in Fiertag's office. He told it straight, neither selling it nor undermining it. As Aurora listened, her face settled and took on an aspect of professional interest. Luke reached the end of the story and waited for her to ask him the one question he had been dreading ever since they got that call from Brewer at Doc Hollenbeck's house.

"They showed you an ER report?"

"Yeah."

"Was it him?"

"They seem to think so."

She shook herself slightly.

"So you think he's dead?"

There it was. Luke watched Aurora, and for some strange reason thought of Margot, of Margot's accusations about moral lockjaw. So *speak*, then, Luke.

"No. No, I don't."

"Good," said Aurora. "Neither do I."

C row came up out of a strange half-sleep, half-dream where he was walking across a wide river on the backs of stones, a series of boulders that led out across the river toward a low barren shoreline half-hidden in mist and water spray. A huge ancient-looking building stood on the distant shore, a stone temple it looked like, with a long line of heavy stone columns holding up a Greek roof. It was massive—hundreds of meters in length—and half-covered in a tracery of brown lines. They were vines. Dead vines, looking like claws and webs and tangles, out of which this huge temple was struggling to rise.

The river he had to cross was slate gray, a rushing torrent, and the banks seemed to be a mile apart. The river roared at him like a panther in a pit. He felt blasted by the strength of that roaring. Other than this strange Greek temple, both banks of the river were bare or lined with stunted trees, the leafless branches coated with ice. The rocks of the riverbed were slippery and icy, but it seemed very important to cross this river. It was in his mind that he had no choice in the matter. Away in the distance he could see a huge cloud of what looked like steam, and he heard a low rumbling growling that came up from the earth itself. He did not want to enter that sweeping, rushing river, and he stood at the edge of it, staring across at the temple, buffeted by the force of the river; the wind howled at him, and the booming of the earth shook him. He was afraid.

The current sucked at his boots and swirled around his ankles, tugging him, trying to pull him down. Spray was flying, a mist of water and ice, but when it hit him, it seemed hot, seemed to burn him, and he struggled to clear it from his face. His eyes were stinging now, as if the water were acid, and he tasted salt in his mouth. He heard men's voices and knew they were searching for him. He struggled to take that first step into the river. The spray from the white water over the rocks was in his eyes, stinging them. His eyes opened.

He was being crushed by a terrible choking heat. Sweat was running off his forehead and streaming into his eyes. He blinked and rubbed them hard with the sleeve of his *guayabera*. The shirt was soaking wet. He sat forward, dizzy, momentarily disoriented. He was under a roof of some sort, and all around him there was a city, a horizon of low brick rooflines and chimneys and tangled TV antennae, wires crisscrossing in a spiderweb netting, black and thick as cables under a sky the color of burning sulfur. He looked down, away from the brightness, and saw a green face staring up at him, huge yellow eyes and a bright green beak. For a moment, it frightened him.

It was a turtle face. It was that green plastic pool full of dead herbs and dry soil. He was on the roof of Cheong Sammy's, across from Joey Rag's cleaning plant. He must have fallen asleep in the heat. That angered him. He was growing soft and careless.

He stood up, swayed a bit, walked to the edge, and looked across North Capitol at the Quality Industrial Cleaners office. The blinds were open now, and the sun was shining strongly into the office space. Crow had left them closed. Now Paolo Rona was sitting at the desk in the office, leaning back in Joey Rag's wooden swivel chair, talking into a telephone. He was upset, angry, waving his hands, making some kind of point for his listener. He could not have been more visible if he had set himself on fire.

Looking down into the street, Crow saw traffic, the people of the town walking, trudging through the heat, the shoppers and the gang kids and the rootless aimless unemployable trash that lived in this terrible city.

He saw also a van with all of its windows closed, parked on the opposite side of the street from the laundry, and another position taken by a cab with its roof light off and two men sitting in the cab. One of the men was skinny, and even from this angle Crow could see a shock of pure white hair, a section of brown cloth. Crow stepped back from the roof edge and withdrew into the shadows of the overhang.

Good, he thought.

It begins.

The D.C. duty sergeant showed them to an interview room on the third floor, next to the detectives' squad room. It was a bland featureless cubicle with walls covered in industrial burlap and a framed photograph of Bill Clinton. There was a coffee urn on a side table, and an old ceiling fan churned in the smoky air. Doc Hollenbeck and Luke sat down on opposite sides of the steel table. They wore nearly identical blue suits and black loafers. When Luke had picked Doc up in Adams Morgan, Doc had laughed and said they looked like a dance team.

Luke lit a Kool, and Doc watched him do it.

"You look like shit, Luke."

"Thank you, my son. I feel like shit."

"You get *any* sleep at all?"

"I got a room at the Holiday Inn. I think I got three, four hours. I had a shower. Got home and changed. I'll be okay."

"So you told her, hah?"

"Yeah. What else was I gonna do?"

"And she was okay with it?"

"She's a pro, Doc. Reed Endicott should have known that. Or Canaday, anyway. She was the toughest trainee I ever saw at Glynco. Not ball-busting tough, either. She was just cool and steady and . . . a pro."

"How do you think it will go?"

"I talked to the CO out there. She'll do what she can."

"Aurora's out, isn't she?" asked Doc.

"What? Out of the Marshals?"

"Actually, I meant out of jail. I don't know if she's out of the Marshals. There's things that can be done."

"Yeah. Well, we'll see. We'll see about that. What'd you tell Fiertag?"

Doc looked puzzled.

"About us. About why we're not beavering away in Target Acquisition this morning. Try to keep up, Doc."

"Oh. I told him we were chasing a fink. It's kind of true."

"How'd he take it?"

"Not well. Fuck him."

Luke considered the variables.

"Doc, if we can put the boot to Treasury in this, we might be able to cut her a deal of some kind. Endicott was *way* out of line, crossed all sorts of boundaries when he contacted Aurora—"

"He covered himself there, Luke. Dennis Swayze works in the Public Affairs Office at Justice. Letting an agent know about Rona could be passed off as routine. He never said it directly. They can call it a mix-up, whatever. Totally deniable. Aurora leaped to conclusions, that's all. He said it was 'a courtesy.' Endicott's nowhere near that call, in any way you could prove."

"We don't have to prove it in court. All we have to do is make Justice nervous enough to cut her some slack. She

sure as hell deserves it. If we can find Rona, we can give
Endicott a hard time. I gave Doug Powys a few suggestions too. I think the New Jersey CO will help out. Anyway, I got her released."

"Own recognizance?"

"Charges are pending, let's say. The lab work was really
late. Now they're saying she passed the test, so there's no
DUI. Careless driving. Speeding, certainly. Doug got there
around eight. The CO sent him over to the Holiday Inn."

"That's where she was?"

"Yeah."

"In her own room, I trust?"

Luke flashed him a hard look.

"Yeah. Of course she was. What kind of an idiot do you
take me for?"

Doc smiled.

"I'm still trying to work that out."

"Anyway, I got the CO to wake up the local circuit
judge. She arranged for Aurora to be arraigned right there.
I wasn't gonna leave her in that cell."

"What happened about the turnkey?"

"I told the CO about him. He's with the county. Not a
trooper. They hire them on for jail supervision, so they
don't have to tie up an operational trooper. She called the
county and said she didn't want him at the jail anymore."

"What'd the guy have to say for himself?"

"He said he tripped."

The door to the interview room popped open, and a
large squared-off black cop came into the room in a patrol
uniform. They got up as he came across.

"You Zitto and Hollenbeck? I'm Baxter Cullen."

They shook hands, made the introductions. He grinned
at them, his hard face breaking up into lines and planes,
his white teeth vivid against the blue-black skin.

"You two look like a dance team. Which one plays the white guy?"

"I do," said Doc. "It's not as much of a stretch for me."

Cullen laughed. "Okay, what can I do for you?"

"You signed an incident report yesterday?" said Doc. "That Treasury takedown on Constitution?"

"Yeah. Those numb-nuts."

Doc looked at Luke.

"Why numb-nuts?" asked Luke.

"You're Marshals, right? *Federales?*"

They nodded, waiting.

"Why is it you guys never want to let the city know what you're up to, hah? Lay out a takedown like that, what if one of our guys sees it, thinks it's some kind of gang thing. You could have had a bloodbath."

Doc hesitated. What the hell.

"I'm not trying to cover for Treasury. But your force has some . . . problems. Sometimes people get warned. Somebody calls his brother-in-law, warns him. It happens, okay?"

Cullen bristled a bit at that. Tried to hold his temper. He failed.

"Don't blame *us* for that. Blame the goddamn OEEO! Blame quotas. You feds ram hiring policies down our throats. You jack the standards around. Hire more Laplanders. Hire more albino lesbian dwarves with club-feet. You scrape the bottom of the barrel and shovel it off into the city police forces. So, yeah, now and then, one of these gangbangers in a blue suit makes a call. What the hell do you expect?"

"Jeez. I guess it's a sore spot, hah?" said Doc, grinning.

Cullen frowned, shook his head, finally grinned back. "Sorry. It's just . . . we used to be a good force. They made us all social workers. D.C.'s not a police force now, we're a science project."

"The Treasury thing?" prompted Doc.

"What? Oh yeah."

His face changed a bit, his eyes became wary.

"Why not ask Treasury?"

"Good question."

Cullen stared at them, thinking it over.

"They busting your balls, boys?"

"Yeah."

"Welcome to the club. The takedown was okay. Guy showed a tool, they popped him. So far so good. We get the usual, shots fired. I'm on duty at the monument, I scoot over. There he is on his back. Only thing was, I recognized the guy. I started to say something, this suit shows up with a couple of bodyguards, tells me I don't recognize dick. Blows me off, puts my guys on crowd control."

"What did he look like? White hair? Brown suit?"

"No. Tall, trick haircut. Real smoothie. Had Justice all over him."

"Reed Endicott," said Luke, looking at Doc.

"I don't know," said Cullen. "All I know is, I got shut down and dusted off. Be a good darkie there, run along and play crowd control. Fine, I figure, fuck them. I filed an incident report, signed off on the DOA sheet at Municipal. They don't want help, why should I sweat it."

"How'd you know the guy?"

"He was at the needle. In a big green van, with another guy. I rousted them. This guy, the one who got killed, breaks into a cold sweat and pisses all over himself."

"Who was the other guy?"

Cullen's face tightened.

"Now, I'd like to know that myself. He was scary. Yellow guy. Not chicken, I mean. His skin color. Looked Indio. Mean eyes. Smiled at me like I was an entree. Gave me a chill, if you want to know. Black hair, big heavy hands.

Face all pocked up, as if he had measles or something when he was a kid. Looked like he was made of leather. Had a scar on his lip that twisted it around. I wish now I'd rousted the guy. I'll give you eight to five he was holding a piece."

Doc and Luke exchanged looks. Cullen caught the exchange.

"That means something to you guys?"

Doc nodded. "I had a fink describe a guy yesterday, sounds like the same guy. He was grilling a cab driver about a takedown we had on Saturday night—"

"That was you two? That cluster-fuck on K Street?"

Doc's face darkened. Luke held up a hand.

"He's connected to what we're looking into."

"How?" asked Cullen.

"We don't know. We think he's looking for the same guy we're after."

Cullen's eyes narrowed. "What? He's with another agency?"

That was a new thought. A new, and depressing, thought.

"Not likely."

"I'll tell you what he is," said Cullen. "I've seen his type before. He's a chaser, just like you guys. No, no, I don't mean that. I mean, this guy, he's some kind of enforcer. Maybe for Cali, maybe for the wops, maybe for the Mexicans. I looked at him from *this* far away, boys. It was like looking into a dead man's eyes."

"Christ. He give you a name?"

"Not from him. The sweaty little guy, he called him Ernest. Ring any bells?" Doc and Luke shook their heads. Luke had his notebook out.

"What was the truck? You get the plates?"

Cullen chuckled, reached up to his shirt pocket.

"The little guy—the one who was pissing himself? Guy

gives me his *card*, for chrissake. Like I'm gonna send him my cleaning. Here it is."

Cullen handed him a business card.

QUALITY INDUSTRIAL CLEANERS
"The Best Deserve The Best"
2900 NORTH CAPITOL STREET
JORGE RAGUNDO—MANAGER

"Can I keep this?" asked Luke.

"Sure." Cullen checked his watch.

"Gotta go?" said Doc.

"Yeah." He got up, straightened his uniform. Luke could see the Kevlar under the dark blue shirt. It was brutally hot in D.C., had been since May first. He did not envy the man his work on the D.C. streets today.

Luke stood up, and they shook hands again. Cullen stopped at the door. "Do me a favor, will you?"

"If we can," said Doc.

"Let me know what happens. This is my beat. That guy with the yellow skin, he's serious trouble. If you get a line on him, I want to hear about it. And not through channels. I want to hear it from one of you guys. Nobody else. Deal?"

"Deal," said Luke.

"One other thing?"

They waited, their expressions careful but open.

"Whatever you do, no offense, you're gonna have to do it better than you did last Saturday night. This is not a guy you wanna screw around with. If you get a chance at him, don't talk. Kill him. Kill him a lot."

Luke and Doc looked at the man.

"You hear me, hah?" asked Cullen, his face stony.

"We hear you," said Doc.

0900 Hours
Saturday, January 14, 1995
Cobble Hill Diner
Court Street
Brooklyn

Wendy Ma was staring at Luke. She pushed her plate full of bacon and eggs away and began to ransack her purse, her face intent, her slender long-fingered hands flipping through the contents. Frustrated, she tugged out a little stainless-steel Smith & Wesson and dropped it on the countertop. Customers sitting on either side of her jumped a bit at that. The waitress at the far end of the counter put down a copy of *The Village Voice* and came back down toward their stools.

"Eggs that bad, Luke?"

Luke looked up at her, grinned, shook his head. "Not mine, anyway, Dianne. I don't know about Wendy's."

Wendy heard the exchange. Without looking up from her purse, she flipped a black leather case out onto the counter. It glimmered in the light from the ceiling lamps, an NYPD detective sergeant's badge. The people around them stared at it for a second, and then at Luke and Wendy, Luke back in his basic black, ready for day two of the fugitive operation, Wendy still in the navy blue jacket and skirt, the scarlet blouse she had been wearing the night before. Finally, Wendy found what she had been looking for, a piece of white paper folded in thirds. She handed it to Luke.

He unfolded it and pressed it flat on the countertop. It was an internal NYPD fax from the DOI, the Department of Investigations, dated Tuesday, January 10, 1995. There was a photograph reproduced on the fax, a blurred and distorted black and white image that Luke stared at for a time, trying to place the man in the picture. Damn, he ought to *know*!

"You make the guy?" asked Wendy.

"Not . . . something . . . there's something."

"Read the BOLO." Wendy's expression was ironic. "It might jog your memory. I know a lot has happened since yesterday. A couple of orgasms, and a guy loses twenty IQ points. I don't think you can spare them."

> DOI/NYPD/INTERNAL BOLO
> Department of Investigations and the Chief of
> Detectives One Police is asking all personnel
> to assist DOI and FAT team in identifying and
> locating the following unknown Hispanic male,
> believed to be in the New York City region.
> Name: unknown.
> DOB: unknown.
> Hair: black, shoulder length.
> Eyes: dark brown or black.
> Height: six feet two inches.
> Weight: 225 pounds.
> Marks or scars: facial acne or irregularity causes
> unknown. Black leather trench coat. Associated
> with Hispanic community. Last seen driving
> dark green Jeep Cherokee Virginia TZB 1511
> Registration Chesapeake Realty.

"God," said Luke, putting the sheet down. "I'm a serious moron."

Wendy patted his hand. "Not a moron, certainly. I'd go for idiot."

"I'd be happy with barely adequate. This is the nimrod we saw in Fiertag's Follies—"

"Fiertag's Follies?"

"Yeah. We had a Fugitive Ops meet yesterday, right up the street. Fiertag ran some video stuff, the Newark thing where the guy shoots himself, and some of the FAT guys brought a DOI surveillance video. . . ."

Luke became aware of the people around, the early morning workers at their breakfasts, reading papers, staring out the window at the cars going by on Court Street. He lowered his voice.

"You know Jo-Jo Mojica?"

"Of course."

Luke tapped the BOLO, his finger on the blurry photo.

"This is taken from a surveillance video of Mojica. We got a look at a guy, image no bigger than a fingertip, taken from a hundred yards or more, on the water, real unsteady. Terrible shot. Telephoto—"

He shook his head, a disgusted look on his face.

"Man, I'm definitely going with moron. Wendy, this guy was on that boat. Grizzly even said he looked Indian, like some Sioux war chief. Man! And the tomahawk! I never put it together. I never—"

"Yeah, well, beat yourself up on your own time. Get to the hatchet part. Soon. I'm saying that this description here matches this D.C. guy you've been talking about. What did that sergeant say—?"

"Cullen."

"Yeah. He said, what, big guy, black hair, yellow-looking, bad skin, scary. Indian-looking? This is the *same* guy, Luke. The same guy. Cullen said that the other guy called him a name. What was that name?"

"Ernest . . . man, we'd have to run this shot by Cullen. It was months ago, back in May last year."

Luke stared at the paper in his hands.

"So finish," said Wendy.

Luke looked at his congealed eggs. "I don't think I'm hungry anymore."

"I mean, in Washington. Now this is business, Luke. Get to the part about the tomahawk. I need to hear that part *real* bad."

"You think this is *your* guy? La Luna Negra?"

Wendy snorted, pulled her plate back, and went to work on her cooling breakfast. "Luke, as fascinating a guy as you no doubt are, I actually have a real life of my own, remember? I have not spent the last couple of hours listening to your deep manly voice and staring into your deep manly eyes out of *gratitude*. I work for a local police force, you may have heard of us? The NYPD? How many guys like *that* can there be in the world, Luke?"

Luke's eyes dimmed, and a muscle in his cheek sagged slightly.

"If there's a God, only one."

They'll be all over it, you know," said Doc, leaning forward to turn the air-conditioning to high. "Canaday, the rest of them."

Luke nodded, staring intently at the cars in front of him, trying, by a simple act of will, to make them all vaporize and reappear somewhere in downtown Beirut.

"Mebbe," he said, finally.

"Mebbe? Did you just say 'mebbe'?"

"I did," said Luke. "Traffic jams cause me to speak like Walter Brennan. It's a genetic defect."

They were trying to make their way up North Capitol Street and the traffic was jammed up around a construction site between M and Pierce. A concrete truck the size of Bozeman, Montana, was sitting halfway out into the traffic, and the driver, a snake-skinny white boy with a ball cap on his anencephalic skull that said DAIN BRAMAGE was lounging back in the driver's seat with a limp stogie hanging out of his twisted-up mouth, leering at all the young

girls who were being forced to go around the truck by hob-
bling across the shaky wooden boards and the dirt piles
and the broken pieces of concrete at the construction site
gates.

Other than that, he appeared to be doing absolutely
nothing and showed every sign of continuing to do that
until quitting time or Judgment Day, whichever came
first. Around this roadblock, cars and trucks and vans were
jammed up and idling in a smoky rusted bad-tempered
tangle that stretched for blocks in every direction. A
sweating and increasingly cranky D.C. traffic cop was out
in the middle of the street, trying to get a UPS van to back
up so a Checker cab could move out of the way of a snow-
white stretch limo that was trying to go around a stalled
Toyota with steam billowing up from under its hood. A
few of the drivers were out of their cars now, standing
around in shirt-sleeves, wiping the sweat off their faces,
cursing softly but continuously. Luke's hidden radio
squawked at them, and Doc picked up the handset.

"Bravo Sixteen."

"Hey, Doc."

"Slick. How do we look?"

"I've been on you all morning. You got no one."

"Where are you now?"

*"Where else. Stuck in this shit, a couple of blocks
back. Look, I gotta peel off, okay?"*

"Sure. All we wanted to know was, is Canaday tailing
us."

*"Well, if he has guys on you, they are very, very good.
I do this for a living, you know?"*

Doc laughed. Luke had the Crown Victoria backed up
now and was bulling it through a laneway between two
buildings. The car bounced over a culvert. Luke wheeled
it hard left and accelerated up a long garbage-strewn alley,
butting the horn to clear a couple of drug dealers out of

his way. One of them gave Luke a look at his middle finger as he passed.

"Look, Doc, he's showing us his Mr. Digit hand puppet."

Doc was still on the radio. "Why do you want to peel off?"

"The boss called. Target Acquisition wants to know where we are. One of us had better show up, or we're all toast. He asked me what I was doing, I told him we were chasing a fink. Rico's already there, and our absence has been duly noted, boys. You heard from Walt yet?"

"No. Okay, Slick. Tell the boss we'll be in by sixteen hundred."

"Well, turn on your cell phone. Walt's been trying to get to you. Ten-four, Bravo Sixteen. Out."

Doc put the handset down and slammed the glove compartment door closed. "Well, that's not good news."

"What'd you think, Doc?"

"Well, we better wrap this up, one way or another. I say we check out this laundry place, and then we do the rest of this on our own time. Fiertag's one thing. But when the CO calls you in, you better go. That guy scares me more than you do."

Luke nodded, hit the horn, and pulled the car out onto First Street. There was a huge Greyhound and Trailways bus terminal across the crowded intersection. Luke cut through the lot and out the far side, getting an ear-split-ting air-horn blast from a Trailways bus trying to come in the gate. Luke tapped the cell phone on the seat between them.

"See if you can get Walt, ask him how it's going."

Doc hesitated. "What if they have a Blackbird on this thing?"

Luke chuckled as he reached a clear section and accel-erated north on Eckington Place.

"A *Blackbird* trace? Sure, and an AWACS at five thousand feet. And you think I'm paranoid?"

A Blackbird trace was an NSA project developed in combination with Bell Systems and Motorola. Every individual cell phone, even identical models, had its own distinct radio-wave pattern, almost like a cell phone DNA. Since each phone that is actually turned on emits a locating burst on its own frequency every fifteen minutes, in order to identify itself to the broadcast system covering a certain area, the cellular system nationwide can be programmed to recognize that unique cell-phone wave pattern and signal the location of that phone to any interested party. Since cell system coverage areas can be as narrow as a few city blocks, a Blackbird trace can tell the searching agency almost precisely where that phone is at that moment, anywhere within the continental United States. Blackbird traces are extremely expensive and highly secret, but if the project Treasury was working on was vital enough, Doc's paranoia might not be paranoia.

"Come on, Doc. Even if you're right, we're running out of time."

Doc sighed and dialed Walt Rich's cell-phone number. It beeped a couple of times, and then Walt Rich answered. Luke could only hear Doc's end of the conversation. It was cryptic.

"Walt, it's Doc. . . . Yeah, Slick said. Where are you? Okay . . . okay . . . Where? . . . Yeah . . . yeah . . . Was it Canaday? . . . No, just get back. The boss is on a tear. We'll be in . . . okay, kiss-kiss, bye-bye."

"Where's Walt?"

"Just south of Fredericksburg, coming home fast."

"Well?" asked Luke.

Doc was grinning. "Damn, I'm good. Walt found the guy at work. He's not a happy puppy."

"Garcia?"

"Yeah. Lucio Garcia, of 1553 Jefferson Avenue, Richmond, Virginia. Guess who dropped in on him yesterday?"

"Treasury?"

"Yeah, a couple of guys from the Richmond office. Asked him about the loss of his American Express card. He flipped out, wanted to know why it was that somebody hooked his wallet, nothing happens for ten days, and now he's got T-men sitting in his living room. Absolutely blew up when Walt tinned him with his star. Called him a *federale*. Guess what Garcia does for a living?"

"No idea."

"He's with the Salvadoran consulate."

"Christ, what does *that* mean? And if Treasury's running Rona, they already *knew* about the AmEx card. Why heat up the vic like that?"

"Rona's pond scum. Treasury's not blind to the guy's character flaws. So they check out his story. See if it's true that Garcia's not involved somehow. And the Salvadoran connection, that would have freaked Canaday. Whatever, the main thing is, there's a Virginia driver's license out there somewhere—"

"Probably in Bolton Canaday's pocket."

"—and that means there's a *photo* on that driver's license."

"Okay. Of who?"

"*Whom*, Luke. Of *whom*."

"Whom."

"Well," said Doc. "Maybe it's the dead guy. Jorge Ragundo?"

"No. Canaday said the ID didn't match the face."

"Maybe the yellow man Cullen saw?"

"Maybe."

"You mean, 'mebbe.' Well, that's the big question, isn't it?"

"Yeah. And it answers your original question too. They

will be all over Quality Industrial Cleaners. And where they are, you can bet Rona will be around somewhere. He's the Judas goat. He'll be staked out in the open somewhere. Look, make another call for me?"

"Okay. Who?"

Luke flipped him a card. "Call that number."

"That's the service office in the Bronx."

"Yeah. Ask for Grizzly Dalton."

Paolo Rona was pacing the little office area. He was . . . unhappy.

"Look, I can't sit there anymore. This is bullshit."

The two other people in the room said nothing. One of them was a big black man in a gray suit, sitting on the floor, leaning against the street wall, holding an HK MP-5. The other was a broad-shouldered red-haired woman wearing a Planet Hollywood T-shirt and blue jeans. Rona was working himself up into a snit, a standard fink experience. Both Treasury agents had witnessed far too many of them to get excited about this one.

The noise of the laundry plant downstairs came up through the flooring, and the steam rising up from the cleaning vats was making the room a sauna, in spite of the chunking clatter of the inadequate air conditioner set into the window. The babble and sonorities of the Indio women talking happily over their work floated up through the miasmic atmosphere. Nobody down there seemed to miss Jorge Ragundo very much. Whoever ran the place had made a call—picked up on the wiretap—and now one of the women downstairs was running the place until a new guy arrived. Treasury was letting no calls go out other than the ones Paolo Rona had been making to his lawyer, to Reed Endicott, and even to Janet Reno's office. (He didn't get through.) The idea was, business as usual at Quality Industrial Cleaners, where "The Best Deserve The Best."

Not that the agents guarding Rona knew much more than Rona did. That was Canaday's way. And Endicott's, as they were in the process of finding out. So far, Sherry Wolokoff had gathered that the guy they were trying to catch, a man named Crow, was an ex-con out of Angola prison with a background connected to Marine Recon vets in the Philippines, that the guy was playing his own game with Rona, using a request for a phony ID as a way of keeping Paolo Rona in town while the people who owned this laundry—among other things—tried to figure out whether Rona was a federal snitch, and if so, for how long he had been one.

Quality Industrial Cleaners was officially owned by a numbered corporation in Atlanta. This Crow character was apparently some kind of security man for the people behind the corporation. It was all wheels within wheels, and neither Reed Endicott nor Bolton Canaday was talking much.

But for these street-level Treasury agents, this stake-out was just another hot noisy wet hell, and they were cranky, and listening to a snitch whine was not helping.

Rona was here to try to draw Crow in, because Crow had made a mistake; Canaday had made sure that Rona asked Crow for a recent photo, and the guy actually delivered one. A *recent* one, which your career criminals try to avoid. Old mug shots from Angola, Navy Department photo ID from 1966, none of that was much use. But a Polaroid from last week, well, he would want that photo back, as well as a chance to put some pointed questions to Paolo on behalf of his employers. Staking Rona out in the open like this was risky, especially if the guy detected the trap. That would absolutely confirm to him that Rona was snitching for the feds, and the boys in Atlanta would be cleaning house real fast. *If* the guy tumbled. That was the gamble today.

Of course, Paolo Rono missed all of this. He was too busy whining.

"Listen, one round through that glass, I'm applesauce. You can't do this. I want to talk to my lawyer. This is against my constitutional rights. I'm being endangered. So fuck *you*, that's it! I'm out of here!"

He headed for the exit door. Sherry Wolokoff caught his arm as he passed her and jerked him backward.

"Sit down, numb-nuts," she barked.

"I'm not getting back in that chair. *You* sit there for the next two hours, you bitch! I'm—"

Sherry reached out, casually, extended a hand, and slapped him hard across the side of his head. Rona yelped, staggered backward, holding his head, his face screwed up and wet.

"He's gonna *shoot* me, for chrissake!"

"No, he's not," said Wolokoff. "He wants you alive. If you're dead, he can't ask you any questions. He's here for the answers, not for you."

Rona's face was greenish-white.

"He's not even *around* here. Man, you dinks! You coulda had him yesterday! He was right *there*!"

"Maybe he was," said Wolokoff, her voice heavy with contempt. "If you hadn't been jerking *us* around, we *might* have nailed him. But you wanted your five bills, didn't you. You told Endicott four P.M. at the needle. You

got there at two-fifteen. You figured to get in there, get
your cash, and then walk him into a takedown at four. You
played everybody for a clown. You got me to kill a guy, his
gun isn't even *loaded.* I got to live with that the rest of my
life, you little shit. So shut up and sit down."

"He could be on the roof or something. Why don't you
have guys on the roofs? Snipers! Why don't—"

"Guys on roofs are easy to spot. You say this man's not
an idiot. The first thing he's gonna look for are people up
on the roofs, windows that are open but nobody's in them,
open doors—"

"He'll see the cars in the street."

"Not likely. We're not a bunch of Cub Scouts. Now
shut the fuck up!"

Rona vibrated in place for a full minute, caught between his fear of the Yellow Man, his fear of Sherry Wolokoff, and his hatred of women in general. Especially
women who thought they were the law. He turned and
tried to appeal to the silent black man sitting on the office
floor.

"Look, Sambo, tell this cu—"

Wolokoff stepped forward and shoved him *hard.* He
stumbled back into the square of light by the window,
caught himself at the desk.

"Rona, you are not running this. You've been jacking
us around since we got into this. You're *still* playing your
own game. Fine, that's Reed Endicott's problem, not
mine. Luther and I are supposed to see that you stay in
that chair. If you can't get your ass in it on your own, we
can strap you down. But either way, you put your ass in
that chair. Now."

Rona moaned softly. Both of the agents were sickened
by the fear-smell coming off this man. Rona moved suddenly, sat down with a convulsive shudder, turned his
back to the window.

And then he started to cry. Silently. Fat tears began to crawl, sluglike, down his cheeks, leaving shiny trails in the dirt and the sweat.

"Wonderful," said Sherry Wolokoff, sending the other agent a look. Luther just shook his head and smiled back at her. Sherry groaned and watched Rona sit there, coming apart noisily. The sound of his sniveling and snorting joined the thump and slush coming through the floor, curiously similar. Sherry's face closed up with a look of disgusted resignation.

"That's just wonderful."

"Peachy," said Luther, who didn't talk much.

"Yeah," said Sherry. "Peachy."

Crow watched the office window. He could see Rona now. He was back at the desk, facing into the room. His head was bent forward, and his hands were at his temples. Something in the way he was holding his body suggested sadness.

Or anger.

They are fighting, thought the yellow man.

Good.

Doc and Luke pulled up about a block away from the cleaning plant, parked the car, and sat back to consider their tactics.

Doc was staring hard at a van about a hundred yards up.

"That's a federal van. No doubt."

"Yeah. They're all around. You know this area at all, Doc?"

"Yeah."

"Any suggestions?"

"When's Grizzly gonna call?"

Luke looked at his watch. "Fifteen minutes."

Doc was quiet for a time. Luke looked over at him. Doc's face was set and blank. "Doc . . . ?"

"You ever afraid, Luke?"

That rocked him.

"Afraid . . . hey, Doc. Fear is my shadow. Ease up, okay? We're just gonna—all I want is to spook them.

They show me where they've got Rona hidden away, and I twist Reed Endicott's balls until somebody eases up on Aurora."

"We're not gonna try anything stupid?"

"What, like jerk Rona out of the custody of Treasury agents? No, all I want is clear unequivocal proof that they have him, and that they're playing Hide the Floppy with an escaped rapist and conman."

Doc rubbed his face with his hands. "Okay. I hope that's how it works out."

"You all right, Doc?"

"Yeah. I think I need something to eat. I feel a little weird."

"Hey, look, let's call this—"

"No. Look, there's a Chinese restaurant across the street from the cleaners. Cheong Sammy's. Sammy Kwong owns it. Give me five minutes, I'll take a post there."

"Why don't I do that? You stay here."

Doc shook his head.

"Tell you the truth, Luke, I'd rather be off to the side when you jump out of the woodwork and Bolton Canaday wets his pants. You let Grizzly Dalton make his call, I'll be somewhere out of the way where I can see it all go down and not get any on my shoes. That's the way I want it."

He picked up one of their two mobile radios.

"I'll be on channel two, check?"

Luke set his radio at channel two. "Where do you want me?"

"Right here," said Doc. "One of us has to be mobile. When they get a call—*if* they get a call—they'll bundle Rona into a mobile unit and take off. I'll get onto the radio, let you know which way. You can go—do whatever."

"You're pissed. Am I right?"

"A little. This started out just as kind of interesting. Now we're staking out a Treasury stake-out, we're playing games with a federal snitch, and somewhere out in the wilderness there's a guy who makes me think of wooden stakes and silver bullets. *Plus* my career is on the line if we step on our dicks—"

"The only dick that's gonna get stepped on is Reed Endicott's."

Doc settled down a bit. "Okay. . . . Well, any way it goes, I want to be out of the Ten Ring. I want some deniability when the CO straps me down on a gurney and reaches for a power tool. Give me five minutes."

"Double-click me when you're in position?"

Doc lifted his radio, nodded, and got out of the car. Heat flowed in around his big body, heavy with city fumes and the scent of rotting garbage, and the car was full of street sounds, horns, cars and trucks, tires on blacktop, the stamp and shuffle of the people going by. A traffic chopper was passing high overhead. Its blades hammered at the hot damp air, and the sound came down around them, a deep pounding thrumming syncopation, like a massive heart beating. They both listened to it for a moment.

"Saigon," said Doc, his face breaking up into crazy angles as he smiled broadly back at Luke. "Shit. I'm still only in Saigon."

"PBR Street Gang, this is Almighty."

Doc smiled again, closed the door with a wave, and walked quickly away up North Capitol Street. He didn't look back.

Luke watched him go, and then looked up toward the tops of the buildings, at the ragged lines of the roofs, and then into the lemon-yellow sky. A flock of pigeons blew up from a roof down the block, wheeled, soared skyward in a burst of feathery fluttering, like debris from an explosion.

Did Treasury have people on the rooftops?

Well, Doc was a pro.

Doc would find out.

1500 Hours
Monday, May 23, 1994
Operation Swallow Mobile Unit 23
Treasury Joint Task Force
North Capitol Street
Washington, D.C.

The agent at the wheel of the gypsy cab was a twenty-year man named Karl Wyzcsinsky—pronounced *whizz*-jinsky—inevitably nicknamed Whizzer, who had just come off a VIP/Senate protection tour that had lasted almost four years. Whizzer was used to air-conditioned limousines, first-class air travel, five-star hotels. Crystal glasses, compliant concierges, veal medallions in a piccata sauce, expensive call girls with names like Brooke, Beth, and Katherine.

Whizzer was not used to a five-hour stint sitting at the wheel of a rusted-out 1978 Ford Fairlane that smelled like a bucket of dead dogs, dripping with sweat, suffering from prickly heat and underwear migration, putting up with the fact that the only air-conditioning available on this stakeout was the occasional cross-breeze that blew a wave of hot wet air across the dashboard, in a part of D.C. that looked like an earthquake's practice zone.

Bad enough, but the *main* thing he was finding difficult

about this assignment was the dawning realization that Special Agent Bolton Canaday, who was sitting in the passenger seat beside him looking as untroubled by the heat as a corpse, had very few desirable qualities as a stakeout companion. He liked to put on a perky Irish brogue that grated like sand in your shorts and otherwise had the sparkling conversational gifts of industrial felt, but the very worst thing about him was that he had perfected what was possibly the single most *irritating* personal habit a human can develop; he sucked his teeth.

How Special Agent Bolton Canaday managed to do this was a mystery for Whizzer, since as far as he had been able to determine, Canaday didn't *have* any teeth worth sucking. But—there he goes again—but he achieved the effect somehow, a low-level but nearly continuous liquid, swishing, sucking puckering that always built slowly, inexorably, toward a kind of popping wet smack as the internal suction behind his tightly sealed lips reached a critical point and then—*pop*—his lips would break the seal, Canaday would jump, lick his lips, and look out at the passing street scene with a vaguely startled expression, as if the entire wide-screen panorama of tumbledown storefronts, crumbling dirty brick apartments, potholed streets, and near-zombified drug addicts had somehow *popped* into existence when his lip-seal reached the breaking point.

Speaking of breaking points, Whizzer had pretty much reached *his* a few minutes back and was entertaining himself right now with a careful consideration of precisely the right, the perfect, the—the *condign* method of execution he would shortly employ upon the person of Special Agent Bolton Canaday—cramming a plumber's helper down his throat was Whizzer's leading choice at the moment— when Whizzer's portable radio buzzed into life.

"Unit 23, this is Central."

"That's Endicott," said Canaday as Whizzer plucked up the handset.

"Come back, Central?"

"Twenty-three, one of our people here is telling me that we've just got a patch through from a DMV-NCIC link out of Southern District in New York. Is Bolton there?"

Whizzer handed the radio across to Canaday.

"This is Canaday. Go ahead."

"Bolton, this is Reed. I'm reading a DMV hit here—an NYPD traffic unit has a man stopped on Gun Hill Road, the driver has no ID but he's answering the description on our BOLO. What the hell does this mean?"

Whizzer watched Canaday's face. It had run through a couple of intriguing tints before it settled on the current one, a kind of pale puce with mottled bits of purple under the eyes. Further, Canaday was not, at this time, showing any inclination to suck his teeth. What he was showing was, in Whizzer's professional opinion, the classic symptoms of Total Testicular Retraction caused by a sudden onset of Operational Spin-Out.

Canaday's voice was tight as he answered, "Ah, say again, Central?"

"I think you copied that, Bolton."

"And he fits our target ID?"

"Close enough."

"Ahhh . . . may I suggest you contact the NYPD and ask them to detain this person? Immediately?"

"This has been done. Now what? What would you propose?"

Canaday hesitated, sent Whizzer a desperate red-eyed look. Whizzer smiled happily back at him and made winging-away motions with his hands. Canaday nodded, and got back on the radio, out of which a kind of invisible but white-hot noxious cloud of Extreme Disapproval—Reed Endicott version—was curling and rising in portentous silence.

"Ahhh . . . Reed, I'd say we terminate this station ASAP."

"Terminate? That's your decision, is it? We can log it as that?"

"Well—Reed—of course, this is a joint task force. I bow to your . . . you have the final call in this. As I understand our chain of command."

"Wait one, Bolton. . . . Wait one."

There was a span of dead air.

"Okay . . . okay, Bolton, we'll do that. Terminate. Roll them up."

"Ten-*four*, Reed. I'm behind you all the way in this. Out." Canaday hooked the radio back into the slot and sighed. "That's it, boyo. Roll them up, Whizzer."

"We're through?" said Whizzer, keeping his face straight.

Canaday groaned a little and sucked his teeth. Whizzer was able to control his facial muscles, although his hands twitched slightly and tightened around the steering wheel.

"Reed got an RTA bullet from New York State. Some traffic bull has a guy stopped back there, guy's ID fits our BOLO."

Whizzer couldn't help looking across the street toward the laundry.

"So, Reed thinks our guy skipped? The guy we're waiting for?"

Canaday rubbed his grizzled cheeks with dry palms, making a sandpaper sound. "That's what Reed's getting out of it. They're running the guy in, and somebody from the New York office will go see him."

"Why not just get a positive ID from the NYPD traffic bull on the scene?"

Canaday gave him a bleary red-eyed look.

"Operational security, Karl. Reed Endicott would rather have his nostril hairs set on fire than let out a particle of data to a city force. Well, actually, he'd rather have *your* nose-hairs set on fire. But you get my drift, hah?"

"So we're through here? You and me?"

"Yeah," said Canaday, shaking his head. "We're through."

"Damn," said Whizzer.

Doc was standing a few feet back from the large filthy front window of Cheong Sammy's restaurant, holding a cup of Sammy Kwong's Celestial Dragon tea in his hands, watching the front entrance of Quality Industrial Cleaners. Behind him the cooks were frying up squid and boiling vats of noodles, and about fifteen Chinese people were sitting around at various tables and along the counter, slurping up bowls of fragrant, delicately spiced *specialties de la maison Kwong*. Doc, who had seen Sammy's kitchen up close, was sticking with the tea.

Things were definitely happening outside. A couple of men in undercover clothes had come out of an alley beside the cleaners and climbed into a blue van with tinted windows. Then Bolton Canaday had arrived in a gypsy cab driven by a man who seemed inordinately happy. Then another van, this time carrying three armed men with federal mustaches, had pulled up, and the three men had taken up positions around the front doors, with their backs to the wall.

Doc got on the radio.

"Luke, you there?"

"Ten-four, Street Gang."

"Now's the hour, Almighty. I think they're bringing him out. If you want to catch them red-handed, Canaday's right on scene."

"Rolling, Street Gang. Thanks. Thanks a lot."

"Luke, when you come in, come in easy. They're jumpy as hell."

"Heard that. I'll wear my star, keep my hands in plain sight. Out."

Doc clicked the handset twice and stepped back out of the window line. Sammy Kwong was watching it all go down across the street. Sammy was a sleek man in his early thirties, with a handsome fine-boned face. He was wearing a spotless white T-shirt and a pair of Armani slacks. He came up behind Doc and stood beside him.

"They go now?" he said, in a broad Mandarin-tinged accent.

Doc turned and smiled at him. "I'd say so."

Sammy frowned. "They tip bad. Always come in, say cook more, leave bad tip."

"Those guys? They've been in?"

"Oh yeah. That one, white hair. He never pay, say we owe him for keep safe. Bad-teeth guy."

Doc was a little concerned. "Sammy, you have a place I can watch, maybe not so out front?"

"Sure," said Sammy. "Go on roof. Take stairs back there." He made a gesture with his hand, thumb pointing. "Pop has a garden up there. Nobody goes there."

Doc put his tea down on the counter. Now the front door of the plant was open, the van idling at the curb. He walked back toward the rear stairs that led to the roof. As he reached the bottom step, Sammy called out to him.

"Be careful of demon," he said, grinning.

"Demon?"

"Hey, Pop . . . Pop?"

A tiny skeletal man showed his head from behind a copy of a Cantonese newspaper with a picture of a half-naked girl on the cover. He gabbled something at Sammy. Sammy asked him a question in Mandarin, and then the old man looked at Doc.

He sent him a wide half-crazy grin that broke his leathery gnomish face into a thousand deep creases and lines. His mouth was a dentist's daydream. He began to nod vigorously, his tiny head bobbing like a shrunken head on a stick. He was grinning with delight.

"Demon," he said, pointing skyward.

Sammy rolled his eyes at Doc.

"Right," said Doc. "I'll watch out for the demon."

S herry Wolokoff and Luther Whitestone had just brought a shivering, near-hysterical Paolo Rona down the stairway of the cleaning plant, past the staring Indio women, and out the front hallway into the brutal white heat of the sun, when they heard a siren yipping down the block. Bolton Canaday, who was standing by the open doors of the van, raised his hand to stop them inside the doorway. Everyone was looking south down the street.

A big blue Crown Victoria was rolling up, a flashing blue light in the window, its siren chirping as the driver thumped the horn. Canaday stared at the face of the man, barely visible behind the tint.

"Oh shit," he said, finally.

Luke brought the Crown Victoria to a halt a few feet down from the van and opened the door. The first thing the waiting agents saw was Luke's hand coming out the window, holding a gold Marshals star. Canaday turned to Sherry and waved her out. The two agents stepped quickly out of the doorway, shielding Rona with their bodies, and practically threw him into the van. Sherry slammed the door shut. Luke's car was blocking their exit.

Luke got out of the car, his suit jacket open, his hands up, and his palms out. He walked up to Bolton Canaday and smiled at him.

"What the hell are you doing?" said Canaday.

Luke nodded toward the van.

"I just want to say hello to an old business associate."

Canaday hesitated, then gave it up. What was the point now? The stake-out was blown anyway. He nodded toward the agents guarding the car, and Luke started to move.

Canaday stopped him with a hand. "Your piece, there, boyo?"

Luke slipped his Taurus out and handed it to the Treasury agent.

"Okay," said Canaday.

Sherry Wolokoff unlocked the van door and slid it back. Paolo Rona was huddled in the back seat between two large men with humorless faces. Rona was holding a Kevlar vest up in front of him, and Luke leaned in and pulled it down a few inches. Rona's face appeared, his skin the color of wet Kleenex.

Luke smiled at him.

"Paolo, you know me?"

"Sí, La Culebra," he said, after a couple of tries.

"Yes," said Luke. "You know me." He looked at the man for a while, then stepped back and away. Sherry slammed the door shut.

Luke stood on the side of the road as the Treasury van maneuvered around his car and pulled out into the traffic. Canaday stared at him for a long time, saying nothing, handed him back his Taurus with a sad half-leer, half-benediction, then he crossed the street and climbed into

the passenger side of a rusted-out Ford Fairlane. As they
pulled away, the driver smiled broadly at Luke and gave
him a crisp military salute.

Luke had no idea why.

Within a few seconds, they were all gone.

Luke grinned and walked back toward his car.

The handset on his waist-belt popped and crackled.
Smiling broadly, he picked it off the loop.

"Street Gang. You see that, Doc?"

The voice that came back was not Doc's voice.

"Hello, hello, you come quick. Hello?"

Luke was running before the last word, his heart beating through his shirtfront, a sudden terrible fear awake in
his belly. The radio was emitting a terrified scream of panicky Chinese and pidgin-English chatter.

"Somebody come quick okay who there—

"Somebody come quick hello hello—

"Come here okay okay hello hello—"

Luke was coming.

Luke was coming as quick as Luke could come.

He slammed through the front door of Cheong Sammy's with his Taurus in his hand and saw a gaggle of people pressed around a doorway at the back of the
restaurant. A woman stepped out of the crowd and
screamed at him.

"Hurry—up the stairs."

Luke shoved his way through the crowd. He was at the
foot of a flight of stairs leading up a dark passage toward
a small square of yellow daylight fifty feet away. He put
the Taurus out front and went up the steps as quickly and
as quietly as he could. At the top of the stairs, he hesitated, then burst through the open door. He was on a roof,
a wide uneven stretch of tarry gravel-covered boards.
There was a kind of shelter at the back, jerry-rigged out of
plastic pipe and plastic, and set under an overhanging roof

that belonged to the next building. Two people were huddled in a shadowed mass under the shelter-roof.

Luke came up fast, the muzzle trained on this mass, his trigger finger inside the blade. A voice came out of the shadows.

"No shoot no shoot!"

It was a young Asian man, holding a radio.

Doc Hollenbeck was splayed out at his feet, his head resting on one of the man's shoes. Luke's heart stopped—he got a brief sidelong glance down a shadowed hallway—and then jumped again, thrumming against his rib cage like a free-wheeling engine.

He knelt down beside Doc's head, patting him, ripping his shirt up out of his pants, running his hands over Doc's body, looking for a wound. Doc's eyes opened, and he said something, a whisper.

"Hatchet," was what he said.

"Hatchet?" said Luke. Doc's eyes closed, and Luke realized that what was happening here was that Doc wasn't wounded, that there was no hole in Doc. Doc's skin was wet and cold, and he was in terrible pain.

Doc was having a heart attack.

BOOK THREE

Closure

As Luke and Wendy crested the rise of the westbound BQE off-ramp for the Triborough Bridge, they slammed into a seamless caravan of cars and trucks sitting stalled, idling, fuming, a chain-dance of chrome and metal trailing white exhaust fumes into the misty air, the tail end of a tie-up that looked like it stretched all the way up onto the Triborough Bridge.

The traffic flow was glacial. They could see a large black car parked off to the side of the road a few hundred feet up the Triborough Bridge ramp. Not far enough off, however, with two feet of tail-wing sticking out into the road. Cars and trucks and cabs were trying to work their way around this obstruction. Two short men in dark business suits were standing by the passenger door, oblivious to the stream of insults and abuse they must have been getting, looking at some kind of document or paper.

Tourists, thought Luke.

Goddamn tourists.

The thing to do about tourists visiting New York, in Luke's view, was to get the Disney people to set up a theme park called NewYorkLand, somewhere way off in the Midwest—Iowa maybe, or even closer to home—New Jersey. You could raze Newark—no one would notice— and build a huge tourist mill, reroute all the incoming flights, so the tourists could experience all your basic Manhattan thrill-rides, like Ptomaine Castle—where you could shell out the GNP of Ecuador for mildly lethal chilidogs served up by a psychopath/actor named Dwight, while one of your kids barfed his insides out in PervoRestRoomLand—abductions extra. Then all the survivors would fly off on the elevated Terror Train to MugMountain, where you'd get strapped into a spray-painted gypsy cab with one flat tire driven by an astigmatic Muslim cleric with Tourette's syndrome who shrieks at you in Farsi until you agree to buy your whole family a collection of hand-painted cartoon versions of the Koran while you rocket northward across 125th Street toward Free-Fire Land, at which point the cab driver promptly gets lost and stumbles off to find a methadone clinic, leaving your family to enjoy the many interesting NewYorkLand characters in fuzzy animal suits who begin to crawl out of SewerWorld and swarm around your car, drooling, screaming, and waving squeegees—look kids, isn't that Barney the Purple Dinosaur over there giving a—well, I think it's a piggyback ride—to those little dwarves called Buggy, Dark, and Lumpy, and here comes the Happy Carjack Bunny, with his basket full of stick-on Entrance Wounds. And then we finish off our Day in New York with a big parade—complete with EMS trucks and intravenous drips for everyone—across East River World—are those *real* mutant carp frolicking in the settlement pool?—to BrooklynTowne, where we cap off our NewYorkLand experience with an Up Close and Terminal look at all the latest breakthroughs in the exciting field of Mortuary Science. . . . Well, maybe a little extreme, but at least it would keep the goddamn tourists off the goddamn Triborough Bridge.

Anyway, it was too late to do anything now; they were committed. Luke slowed to a crawl, worked his way into the line. Away to their left they could make out the tips of the midtown skyscrapers, compressed and flattened by the misty air, the pale winter sunlight glinting off a million plate-glass windows. Behind the panorama of midtown, the distant skies over Cliffside and Palisades looked low and cold, heavy with the promise of rain. It was the middle of January, and so far a freak warm-weather pattern had spared the city one of those avalanche snowfalls that blow in off the Sound and settle down on the streets and expressways and huddled rooftops of the Five Boroughs, bringing a dense blanket of cold narcotic sleepiness to the peninsula.

Today was a Saturday. The air was damp and dismal, the mists of the previous night now lying on car roofs and dead grasses and dripping from chain-link fences. Across the skyline plumes of steam and vapor rose up from the cluttered buildings and trailed southward, drifting in the shifting breezes, fluttering like the pennants of a mythical city. Over the skyline scattered clouds swept through against a back-lit sky of paler gray and seamed with veins of blue, a marble sky full of the promise of rain. Wendy Ma watched the scene for a while in silence while Luke considered how often the modern world required you to sit in a metal cage accomplishing absolutely nothing while dissipating considerable amounts of the world's diminishing petroleum supplies.

"See that?" said Wendy. Luke blinked at her, followed her gesture, and saw through the wisps of cloud and fog the peaks and slabs and angles of midtown rising above the warehouses and neighborhoods of Astoria and Long

Island City. As he watched, a bank of rain clouds began to roll in out of Jersey, obscuring midtown and softening the angles and girders of the bridges.

"Yes. I see it. There oughta be a black trail in the sky that reads 'Surrender Dorothy.' "

The traffic began to move, and a man in a battered taxi leaned out the window to bellow something unseemly at the back of Luke's tan Caprice. Space had opened up in front of Luke's car. The fact that Luke had not instantly filled it was an affront to every decent citizen in all of the following cars. In the city any stretch of open space was a negotiable instrument. If you didn't pick it up, someone would drive over you to reach it, all the while informing you in marvelous detail of a wide range of your undeniable personal shortcomings. Luke edged the car forward and sighed deeply.

It had been a long night, and now it was Saturday morning, and he was supposed to meet Grizzly and Walt and Rico at the Bronx Borough Hall to kick off another takedown operation. Our contestant for today? Pigeye Quail and whoever had starred with him in that bungled bank job in Newark last week. Grizzly had reached Luke's pager while he was finishing his breakfast with Wendy at the Cobble Hill Diner. One of his snitches had come up with a lead. When was Luke going to get his antique carcass back into the saddle? Luke recognized the tone. Grizzly was full of himself today, a happy warrior with a thousand-yard shot in his foresights.

Luke was not a happy warrior today. He was exhausted, mentally and spiritually, from the long night of remembrance that lay behind the two of them. Now he was navigating the uncertain latitudes of the Morning After. He tried not to look at Wendy, tried to puzzle out a new reality. Where did they stand now? Where did he *want* to stand with her? Where did she? Was last night just a symptom of post-traumatic stress?

Now that they had spent the night together, Luke's lack of hard data on Wendy's private life made him acutely uneasy, as if he had wakened one morning in a hotel room with a woman asleep beside him and he was over at the dresser in his shorts, fumbling through her purse, trying to find something with her name on it, when she sat up and asked him what the hell he thought he was doing. Hey, relax, hon, I'm just trying to remember your name. Very romantic.

He knew Wendy was married, he had *heard*, but did not know for certain, that they were separated. She had the reputation of a solid, reliable, and consistent cop. Maybe she had no children. Maybe it would have been nice of Luke to *ask* her, to show some interest in something besides his own career tribulations in Washington, D.C. And what had made him talk like that? Hours and hours of low murmuring talk in the changing passages of the night, the gradual revelation of detail as the morning began to fill the room. This was not his style, this was absolutely not his style, and now he was into something, now he was—

"Luke, I promise I won't move my stuff in tonight. Okay?"

Luke jumped at that.

Wendy laughed. "What did Walt Rich say? About that woman from Treasury? I'm not going to ask you to bear my children, Luke."

"How'd you know what I was thinking?"

"Oh, that was a tough one. All night long, we talk—you talk—and now it's morning, you've had your way with me, and the inside of this car is like a crypt. Relax, Luke. Maybe I was just using you. Maybe this is my thing, find a guy in a moment of weakness, ravage him, and catch the next flight out. Try to relax, will you? You're making me nervous."

Luke had to pick his way through that statement. Wendy left him to do it. She was working something out in her mind. Luke studied her face for a time. The interior of the car was warm and silent, stained a pale violet by the effect of the weak winter light and the window-tint.

A sudden shaft of sunlight lay briefly across her cheek and neck. Her face was composed. She had a wonderful capacity for stillness, and being around her did have a calming effect on him. He wondered for a time what the incremental effect might be of a lifetime's exposure to raw adrenaline and fear. Maybe your talent for stillness was the first thing to go.

Thinking about adrenaline brought him back, inexorably, to the last time he had seen Doc Hollenbeck. Doc was sitting up in a hospital bed, a flower-print gown dropped forward off his chest, gray chest hairs matted, a doctor poking and tapping across his shoulder blades. He was the focal point for a network of tubes, sensors, IV drips, God knew what else under the sheets. A cardiac monitor sat on a rollaway cart next to his bed, beeping steadily. Doc's color was a kind of gray-purple, but he looked a hell of a lot better than he had about three hours back, on the roof of Cheong Sammy's Chinese restaurant.

Luke had called the fire department first, knowing that they usually arrived in a couple of minutes, while 911 might take fifteen or twenty. Or a week. The D.C. fire department was a hell of a lot more efficient. A crew was on the scene in four minutes, lumbering up those back stairs, hauling a crash-cart cardio-pak and various CPR gear. Sammy Kwong followed the three black firemen onto the roof, talking a nonstop, urgent mix of Mandarin and English. Luke was sitting on the tarry roof with Doc's head under his right hand, leaning over him, hoping through an act of his own will to keep Doc alive. The crew chief asked Luke if he had done CPR. Luke said no, that Doc was still breathing. He looked down at the man. Doc's face was wet, and the pain that was twisting his heart and lungs was like a visible coiling of brutal power, squeezing Doc's barrel chest. Doc's eyes were wide, and there was real fear in them, but he was trying to speak. Luke could not make him stop.

Hatchet, Luke, hatchet. The man had . . .

The firemen pushed Luke aside and surrounded Doc's body. They went at him like street kids rolling a rummy. It was odd to see how quickly a man could change from hard-core stand-up street agent to a splayed-out, played-out tangle of rumpled clothing and wet skin, ribs prominent and working hard, the face distorted and unrecognizable, dignity gone, strangers all around him.

And Luke had put him there.

The rest of the afternoon was etched—better to say carved—into Luke's memory: the pressing crowd of customers at the bottom of the staircase, all of whom had seen *someone*, none of whom could agree on a description; Sammy Kwong's aged father, literally cackling, a mask of wrinkles with two glittering black eyes filled with a generalized evil glee, answering Sammy's questions in lyrical Mandarin, saying only two words, *demon* and *yellow man*; an EMS van with red lights cycling, rear doors wide open, a couple of female paramedics ramming Doc's stretcher home, the steel legs folding and clattering; the trip to the hospital behind the EMS van, Luke's own Hot Shot light working, Luke wrapped in his silence, most of what he was thinking and feeling perfectly expressed by the sound of the siren coming from the roof of the EMS vehicle and the crazy fluttering circles of red and blue and white and yellow lights, a visual shout in the colors of stained glass.

Halfway to the hospital ER, Luke heard Jeffery's voice,

clearly and distinctly in the chilly dark-tinted silence of the car, his boy's voice high and bell-like, heard the sonorous lines of Jeffery's voice singing Tantum Ergo. He could even smell sandalwood and see the way the sunlight came through the colored glass window of the only Catholic church in Provo, and Luke found himself searching for old words, old rhythms . . . *Our Father who art in Heaven . . . hallow'ed be Thy Name.* . . . He even remembered a prayer to Saint Jude, the patron saint of cops and other lost causes.

He prayed like that all the way to the hospital, hectic, disconnected, half-unconscious litanies. Doc was swallowed up by the ER doors, and Luke was left to make his duty calls. Nineteen minutes later, Rico Groza arrived, his dark features grim, on his arm an elegant but weary-looking black woman who looked to be about forty, with shoulder-length hair, bruised-looking brown eyes, and stong intelligent features, wearing a pale green linen dress and a bracelet of heavy gold. Rico brought her to Luke like a juror delivering a verdict. He made the introductions.

The woman was Lois Hollenbeck, Doc's wife. She shook Luke's hand once, and released it, looking hard at his face. Luke tried and failed to make what happened sound plausible, and Lois Hollenbeck listened to it carefully, sifting his words for implications and intimations, braced for terrible outcomes. She smiled then, thanked him with every outward sign of sincerity for taking care of Doc, and went off down the hall toward the ER doors. The set of her shoulders, the way she was holding herself were a subtle but telling blend of resolution, dread, and controlled panic. Luke and Rico watched her as she went through the doors, saw a nurse come forward and speak to her, put a hand on her shoulder, saw lips moving in that silent world. Luke felt suddenly and totally drained.

Time passed, how much he was never able to remember. He thought up some strange random acts of displacement to cover the time. Doc's suit was in a rumpled brown nylon bag, handed to him by one of the EMS medics—his "effects," she had said, a chilling phrase—along with Doc's star and his service semiauto, his extra mag cases, his encoded entry pass, his service ID. Luke flipped it open and looked at the color photo inside, Doc with thirty pounds and ten years gone, his hair in a short Afro cut, his full name, Laurence Jefferson Hollenbeck. Lois Hollenbeck had called him Larry, she had asked Luke, "How's Larry?"

Doc was Doc.

Who the hell was Larry?

Luke found a clothes hanger and arranged the suit on it neatly. Rico said nothing, watched him do it, understanding what was going on. Then Luke remembered the dinner-and-drinks invitation from Charles Berg, the professor who lived upstairs. He used Rico's cell phone to search D.C. listings, got Berg's number, phoned, reached an answering machine, and left an absurdly long and maniacally detailed explanation of what had happened on North Capitol. Later it struck Luke what an odd message it must have been, but there was nothing he could do to erase it.

Rico was on the cell phone himself, keeping the CO and Fiertag up to date. Then it occurred to Luke that his car was parked in the ER lane, and he went out to move it, found some timed space in the doctors' lot, put his USMS parking permit in the front window, went back to see Rico, and was met by a nurse, a short blunt-faced Indian-looking woman who told him in a nearly indecipherable Mexican accent that Mr. Hollenbeck was asking for him and would he like to go in?

When he reached Doc's bedside in the cardiac ward, Doc was sitting up and being probed, tubes and wires and sensors all over him. Rico stood by the bed saying something about the CO, and Lois Hollenbeck sat on a metal chair filling out a Blue Cross form. Doc lifted his head when he heard Luke's footsteps. His eyes were stunned-looking, his color way off, his cheeks sagging. Luke realized with a jolt that Doc's lower teeth were out. It had never occurred to him that Doc had false teeth. The image shook him badly, for reasons he could not understand at the time. Later he realized that Doc's face had in a strange chaotic way reminded him of the way his father had looked a few days before he died. The line between youth and age, between life and death, was so narrow that Luke felt he must cross it without knowing several times a day. Doc grunted, pushed the medic away, and sat back, looking at Luke, while the doctor explained a number of new rules to him. When he left, portents swirling in his wake, Rico said that Doc had something to tell him. Luke braced himself. What followed was not an accusation, a fact that Luke forever afterward considered a gift from Saint Jude.

"They won't tell me. . . . Did you get to him? Was it Rona?"

"Yeah. Yes, it was. Doc, I want to say how—"

"Sammy told me," said Doc, his voice hoarse from the inhalator tube, his body limp against the pink hospital linens.

"Kwong?"

Doc nodded, closed his eyes.

"Sammy said there was a demon on the roof. I should have believed him. I thought it was some Chinese thing. I was wrong. Bigtime."

"Did you see him? Was it him?"

Doc pulled in a breath, winced, Lois tensed a little but said nothing, and then he relaxed again.

"They gave me something massive. I can feel it coming

on here. Anyway, the guy was . . . I walked out onto the roof, I didn't look behind the stair-cap housing. I went over toward the edge of the roof a little, and then I thought, I stick my face over the roofline, I'm going to get a whole bunch of federal rounds in my forehead. I turned to look for a better place. . . . He was right there. Right *there*—the sun was behind him, he was a big black shadow, long hair, I could see his face, yellow skin, bad skin—"

"It was him."

Not a question.

"Oh yeah. He had his right arm in the air, and I saw the thing against the sun, it wasn't a gun. It was long, had a little ax-blade kind of head. Everything was—you know—frozen. It was a tomahawk, Luke, one of those ugly little tomahawk things like the Green Berets used in Vietnam. I recognized it. It came down, I had my left arm up, and I got inside his arc, caught the blow on my forearm, butted him with my shoulder. I was getting my piece out and I *shoved* him back, shoved him *hard*, all I could think was—stay out of the way of that goddamn little tomahawk—you know, it's odd, hah? You think, getting shot, well, you're *used* to that idea—but getting chopped up by that ugly little thing—it was all I could think of, just get out from under it . . . and then *kill* the guy. Like Baxter Cullen said—kill him a *lot*."

Doc stopped there, breathing deeply, remembering. Luke, Rico, and Lois Hollenbeck watched him the way people watch the heat gauge on a long drive through a desert. He closed his eyes and spoke so softly now, it was hard to understand him. Whatever they had given him was kicking in hard.

"Then something—*big*—reached into my chest and . . . squeezed . . . so strong! It crushed me. I mean that. Literally squeezed my heart flat, like you'd crush the water out of a sponge. I think that's what they mean when they say 'the hand of God' . . . and I went down. Straight down. No discussions . . . no *negotiations* with it at all. . . . Funny thing was . . . he could have killed me then. . . ."

"But he didn't," said Lois, and they looked at her. It wasn't clear whether they were speaking about God or the Yellow Man. Tears were on her face. Rico walked over to her and placed a hand on her shoulder.

"Then . . . ?" said Luke.

Doc's eyes were closed, his face slack, and Luke's own heart leaped and stuttered inside his chest. But the monitor screen was unchanged, only the little metallic beep slowing perceptibly.

Doc was asleep.

Luke's next clear recollection from that week was of the twenty-seventh, a Friday. Luke had been suspended for the rest of the week, pending an internal departmental review of his actions and the events that led to Deputy Hollenbeck's mercifully mild incident of myocardial infarct at 1510 hours the twenty-third day of May 1994 at Cheong Sammy's Chinese restaurant on North Capitol Street.

He passed the week in his Georgetown flat, listening to a collection of songs by Tony Bennett, Bobby Darin, Matt Monro. . . . Once he answered the door and found Charles Berg standing there, holding a tray with chicken noodle soup and brownies. They had noticed his long solitary confinement in the suite downstairs and assumed that he was sick. It was a homey feeling, and Luke was grateful for the transitory sense of community. But he knew it was transitory. It had to be.

Walt Rich and Slick Stevens dropped by and dragged him out for a dinner at Houston's on Wisconsin. He went to Paddy Riley's and drank a few beers, filled Janet in on what had happened—she had seen a story in the papers—

reassured her, and said his good-byes. Doc called him every day. He heard nothing at all from Rico Groza. With Rico his silences were eloquent, his withdrawal clear. Luke had no problem with it. Rico was right.

On Friday the CO of Fugitive Operations called him personally.

Then Luke got into the blue Ford and drove away from Georgetown with a sense of imminent change, rolled down into the parking garage under the Arlington HQ, where he sat in his car for a while, feeling for the last time that he was at that moment deep inside the vast beating heart of federal law, of Washington, D.C., at what would probably be the peak moment of his career. Norm Brewer pulled into his space while Luke was sitting there, noticed him inside the car, smiled, and sent him a thumbs-up sign through the glass. Luke waited awhile longer, unwilling to expose himself to Norm Brewer's sympathy, aware of a feeling of shame.

Then he went upstairs to the CO's huge bare office. Rothgar Fiertag was there, silvery and smug in a well-cut suit of navy blue. The atmosphere in the room was dead calm, but the air was heavy with accusations. This was the miasma of disgrace. Luke found it suffocating, as he was meant to.

The CO, every inch a street cop, was a large bulky black man with heavy hands and a face like an anvil. He nodded curtly to Luke, pointed to a chair, and then looked down at a sheaf of papers on his desk. Fiertag sat at the right of the desk and managed to be silent. Luke tried to concentrate on the view of the Pentagon and Arlington National Cemetery beyond it. He was reasonably certain that this was the last time he was going to be looking at the Federal Mall and Foggy Bottom as a true Beltway insider. He was right. Finally the CO sat back and tossed a sheet of paper forward onto his desk. He asked Luke to read it.

INTERAGENCY FUGITIVE NOTICE 5/27/94
NEW YORK STATE POLICE AND NYPD DETECTIVES
REQUEST MARSHALS SERVICE ASSISTANCE IN THE
PURSUIT OF ESCAPED PRISONERS HERBERT
ARNOLD AND JOHN CASABLANCA FROM THE
MID-HUDSON PSYCHIATRIC CENTER / ORANGE
COUNTY / PRISONERS USED HANDGUN TO FORCE
TRANSPORT / DESCRIPTORS FOLLOW / BOTH
ESCAPEES DIAGNOSED CRIMINALLY INSANE /
BOTH MEN CONVICTED KILLERS / ARMED AND
DANGEROUS / CONTACT LT VITO SPANO NYPD
OR NEW YORK STATE POLICE AT ALBANY SUB-
STATION / DESCRIPTORS FOLLOW

Luke glanced at the bottom of the sheet. After a lengthy listing of aliases and known associates, the alert concluded with a handwritten addendum from a New York state cop named Holloway. Luke knew the man. In it, Holloway asked for the CO to send "one of his best people."

Luke folded the sheet in thirds and stuck it in his suit coat pocket. He sat in the stiff-backed chair and waited for the CO to say whatever he had to say. Luke kept his face stony and blank. Fiertag's face was full of a kind of gleeful animosity. Obviously, his blades were already well driven and firmly in place. Otherwise, he'd be talking, hammering at those hilts. It struck Luke then that Fiertag ought to meet Sammy Kwong's daddy. Fiertag still had a lot to learn about free-floating malice.

"You wanna catch this one, Luke?" was all the CO said.

Luke experienced a wave of blessed relief. At least his suspension was over. Thank you again, Saint Jude. He still had a job. And he wasn't going to the training center at Glynco, Georgia, and lie to roadhouse waitresses about how, once upon a time, he coulda been a contender.

"Certainly, sir. I'll leave now. I can be on the road in an hour."

He got up, paused while the CO stood up as well. The CO leaned across the desk and shook Luke's hand hard. He grinned at him, a fleeting semi-ironic twist, and then let go.

At the door, Luke said something about his apartment in Georgetown. His possessions. Fiertag snorted once and said, "You can send for them."

Luke ignored him and kept his eyes on the CO's face. "I won't be back, is that it, sir?"

The CO shook his head. "Not anytime soon, Luke."

"I'll have someone wrap up my place this weekend. About Doc—"

The CO cut him off. "He'll be fine. Sorry you don't have time to say good-bye in person, Luke. I'll tell him you asked after him."

"Sir . . . his job. He needs—"

"Doc'll be transferred to light duties as soon as he gets a medical clearance. After that I'll work him into a spot in Intelligence. His finks are too good to lose."

"So's he," said Luke.

"Yes," said the CO. "Yes, he is."

Luke pulled his nerves together and said, "Deputy Powys—"

The CO shook his head, showed Luke his rock face.

"Deputy Powys is in a world of self-inflicted shit, Luke. Only friend she has out there is somebody named Margaret Farrell, the CO of the Jersey patrol substation. But she's one of us, understand me? She always was. I have Reed Endicott's balls in my hand. I am twisting right now. We'll see what comes out of him when he gets his voice back. But you . . . you do yourself a favor, hah?"

"Sir?"

"Stop trying to help out other Marshals, okay? I know

what you're trying to do, but from where I'm sitting, it looks like you're not having the outcomes you were aiming at. You've rolled around in this situation like a gun dog in cougar scat. You're a damn good chaser, Luke. One of the very best. I know a few years back, the service jacked you around bigtime in Provo. I know that whole story. That's part of the reason you're getting some slack on this. Treasury wants your liver on a stick. This bullshit here, it went all the way up to the Mother Superior. I am flat out of markers to call in. You go back to New York City. There's a sweep coming up in January. Rico Groza will take over your post here, but he'll still be assisting on some of your ops. Walt Rich is going back to New York in September. Grizzly Dalton's already been told. We'll keep your unit together as much as we can. But from now on, and by that I mean until your retirement, let me handle our personnel problems. Do we have a deal?"

"Deal, sir."

Then Luke opened the door and went out into the hall, took the elevator, drove back to Georgetown, gathered a few things into a light nylon suitcase, packed his gear, emptied out his strongbox, and took along what was left of his Chivas Regal. While he was cleaning out his fridge, he looked across the living room toward the window where he had seen the young woman brushing her hair. How long ago? A month?

No. Six days ago.

It had taken Luke a total of twenty-six days to fry his D.C. posting. That had to be some sort of record. An hour later he was northbound on Interstate 95 with Baltimore a thin yellow line of smog on his forward horizon. Halfway to Baltimore, his cell phone rang.

"Yeah?"

"Deputy Zitto?"

"Yep."

"This is Baxter Cullen. I got your message just now."

"Hey, Sergeant Cullen! Thanks."

"I heard, you know, about the thing on North Capitol."

"Yeah. That's why I called."

"I figured. Was it him? The yellow guy?"

"Yeah. No doubt about it. I wanted to tell you that Treasury wants him, so you're not going to get a straight story on it. But you need to know, it was him. It was definitely him. The only way I can help you, Treasury's using a snitch named Paolo Rona to tiger-pit the guy. If you query Rona on any system, you'll send up a flare. The RTA is cloaked. So be careful."

"I will. We got a few moves. Maybe we rent D.C. to the feds, but it's our town. Sorry about your buddy. I hear he's gonna be okay, hah?"

"Yeah."

"You're fading. You in a car?"

"Yes. I guess I'm losing you."

"Sounds like we losing you, man. Thanks for the call."

"Cullen . . . you have this cell number. If you get a line on him, will you let me know?"

"You got it . . . soon—and—in New York—"

"I'm losing you, Cullen, I'm . . ."

The line was dead.

Wendy was speaking to him. Luke came back out of the memory and looked over at her. She had a hand on his shoulder and looked troubled.

"Where were *you?*"

"Washington. Sorry."

Wendy's face softened.

"I was thinking about Doc Hollenbeck."

"So was I," she said. "So what happened to Whizzer?"

"In the stakeout car? The guy with Canaday? Why?"

"He must have told you the story. How'd you know about Canaday's habits? The teeth-sucking thing? You weren't there. He get in trouble for talking to you?"

"Not me. Whizzer drinks with Slick. They're on the same football team."

"Oh . . . okay. Look, Doc said a hatchet, right? Is that the word?"

"Hatchet, tomahawk. A Special Forces thing, anyway."

"Cullen said that the little guy in the van called this guy . . . what?"

"Ernest? Ernie?"

"No, it would be Ernesto. He's Hispanic, right? This whole thing is Hispanic. Garcia, Rona, Ernesto. . . ."

She pulled out the DOI BOLO and opened it up.

"You know this interagency crap really gets me down. Look at this. DOB unknown. Name unknown. That's obviously crap. You think Treasury would set up a tiger pit for a guy like this and not even know who he *is*?"

"Then why not put it on the BOLO?"

"Okay . . . okay. . . . The only plausible explanation for keeping this guy's name off an internal BOLO is that the DOI and Treasury think that somebody inside the department is—or might be—passing information off to somebody on the—"

"*Inside* the NYPD? Come on—"

"What? You missed the stuff at the Seven-Three? I don't trust half the guys in my own house. Tell you the truth, we—the detectives, I mean—don't often *get* interdepartmental faxes like this. You'll get a citywide notice when you muster, or the lieutenant will pass the word around, but it's very rare to send out a fax on a guy like this. It's a real flare. I think, what they're trying to do, is to convince this Indian guy—or somebody he works for—"

"Like Jo-Jo Mojica?"

"Like Mojica—that they don't have his name yet. That they're still trying for an ID on the guy."

Luke gave it some thought. Based on his experiences in D.C. last May, it would be a typical Treasury bank-shot. His experiences in D.C. last May were times Luke had, until last night, been trying to forget. Still, it was always there, way in the back of his skull, that skinny pink T-shirt fluttering away down K Street, the look in Rona's face as he stuck that Glock in Luke's nose. He was still out there, still running his double game. Somehow, inside all of this tangle, there was a line that ran straight to Paolo Rona. The trick was, which one to pull, and who should pull it. He glanced over at Wendy, seeing the pale winter light on her skin, her eyes hidden as she looked down at her hands, her face solemn and intense.

Mojica.

The Yellow Man.

Somebody was running an op here.

Was it the *same* op that he and Doc got tangled up in last year? It could be, although about a month after he bailed out of D.C.—June 27, if he remembered correctly—a Justice task force had rolled up around sixty cartel members who were laundering drug money out of Atlanta and Central America. Was this a continuation, or something new? There were a lot of problems in Wendy's theory, but there was something there.

Starting with a good ID on this Yellow Man.

"You said Brian Crewes didn't get a look at the guy, right?"

Wendy shook her head. "Last time I talked to Jerry Boynton, Crewes was still under sedation and being treated for subdural hematoma and cranial pressure. But he got a glancing blow. I don't think he saw the guy. I'll tell you one thing."

"Yeah?"

"I'd say this guy's not a cop-killer, anyway. If it's the same guy."

Luke was watching the traffic up ahead, cars trying to struggle around a parked luxury car half-out in the cruising lane, a couple of figures beside it.

"I don't think this guy would hesitate to kill a cop if he thought he had to. Doc was pretty convincing about that. What you need, Wendy, you need to get a description. My advice? Go squeeze Doctor Dred."

"Yeah," said Wendy. "I will. And I'll check out that other homicide, had a similar weapon trace. In the Ninth."

Wendy was quiet now. Remembering La Luna Negra. Luke saw the effect in her face. Up ahead, they could see the large black BMW with its fat butt sticking out into the traffic. One of the two businessmen beside the car had a cell phone stuck in his ear. As they rolled closer, they could see the two men were Japanese. Well dressed, in nearly identical blue suits, they were being treated to a variety of Manhattan-region colloquialisms by drivers passing them. As Luke's car rolled up beside them, one of the two men noticed the car itself, a tan Chevy that looked very official. He folded up his map and came up to the window. Wendy rolled hers down. The man was in his fifties or sixties, with a strong lined face and thick folds of skin at the outer edge of very intense black eyes.

"You police?" he asked in a strong Japanese accent. His manner was, if anything, more than a little autocratic.

Tourists, thought Luke. A two-mile tie-up on the Triborough because this bonehead couldn't read a highway sign or tell east from west.

"Yes," said Wendy, a great deal of distance in her tone. Wendy's people were from Korea. Koreans never forget.

"La Guardia," said the man, slapping the map. "Map

terrible. City terrible. People terrible. Where is La Guardia?"

He was pronouncing it La *Gard*-ia. Evidently, something in his tone upset Wendy Ma. She regarded the man's face for a while, her features impassive. The man felt her look. Finally, she said a few words, slowly and clearly, so the man would miss none of them.

What she said was this.

"Hey, you found Pearl Harbor, you can find La Guardia."

When Luke came into the crowded deputy marshals'
squad room, a number of things happened at once.
First of all, he got a big round of applause from about
thirty men and women who were milling around at the
coffee-lounge end of the big room, some of whom Luke recognized as parole and probation officers assigned to Fugitive
Liaison operations, some of whom were NYPD Fugitive Apprehension Team cops seconded to this sweep from Sergeant
Mike Rizzo's office.

Luke smiled and raised a hand, carrying his gear over his
shoulder, walked through the people who were shaking his
hand or slapping his back, faces bright with the contagion of
proxy violence. He guessed, correctly, that this was a general
salute from the local law enforcement community for the
removal last night of Elijah Olney's name from their list of
possible hits, and the success of the first in a couple hundred
low-profile combined-unit takedowns planned for the next
two weeks, from the South Bronx to Buffalo.

Other teams from the joint task force were out now, using

a variety of scams and devices to locate, isolate, and arrest a variety of felons wanted on regional, state, and federal warrants. One of the teams was already back at the station, dragging in a large wart-hog-shaped white male with most of his visible skin completely tattooed. One of the agents manhandling him was dressed as a letter carrier.

Luke grinned. He'd pulled off a couple of arrests himself in that uniform. You walked up to a house that looked like a tomb, windows shuttered, no life inside. But the thing was, government checks always come by mail. Nobody turns away a postman. The door opened, and seconds later the guy was on his face with a knee on his neck, whining about fair play. The letter-carrier trick was just one out of a bagful. Luke had the rare distinction of being one of the only deputy marshals in the United States who had taken down a serial rapist while dressed as a priest, a story that had turned up in a Burt Reynolds movie later that year.

Once, in a famous takedown operation, the Marshals service had sent out word to a wide range of wanted felons that they had won tickets to meet the Yankees. Hundreds of guys showed up—the Marshals even had an agent dressed up in a chicken suit—and showed the ticket-takers real ID to prove who they were. Then they all sat down in the auditorium and waited for the Yankees to show up. One of the senior deputies went up to the podium, grinned at everyone hugely, and said, "Okay, we have some good news and some bad news. Which do you want first?"

The scam was later passed off as an NYPD stunt in the movie *Sea of Love*, something the Marshals still resented. Getting good PR was hard enough, without having it ripped off by Hollywood and handed to the NYPD.

Luke's all-time favorite takedown stunt was Grizzly Dalton's now-famous sweep of a Hell's Angels biker bar in upstate New York. Grizzly was the obvious guy to play the Biker on the Run, and he had even gone to the trouble of chasing

down a Hell's Angel wanted for interstate flight, solely because the guy was about his size and had a set of real Hell's
Angels colors that Grizzly needed for the operation.

The biker bar was called Annie's, on the outskirts of Elm-
ira, New York. The place was a kind of biker bunker, constructed out of breeze-block and concrete, with all manner of
surveillance cameras, a reinforced steel door, gun caches,
even a motion-detector security system.

Target Acquisition had good snitch information that a lot
of serious outlaw bikers were in and around the place, most
of them wanted men with charges ranging from rape and
extortion to weapons smuggling, murder, and drug plant operations. The bikers were also extremely paranoid. There was
no way the Marshals could get anywhere near Annie's without blowing the operation, and getting *inside* it would take a
mechanized assault platoon.

Grizzly had a plan, however.

Grizzly dressed himself up in this captured biker's Hell's
Angels colors and drove the man's Harley right up to the
gates of Annie's bar, where he simply banged on the steel
door until they let him in. After a few hours, once they'd
accepted him—and what Grizzly had done to get himself
accepted in that crowd was a subject he refused to discuss
until the statute of limitations kicked in—Grizzly would select a victim from the forty or fifty bikers in the place and ask
him to come out and see what was wrong with his ride.

Now, there isn't an outlaw biker in the universe who
doesn't think he is God's Chosen Authority on the subject of
Harley-Davidson cycles. They'd walk out into the dark parking lot with Grizzly, Grizzly would send the waiting Marshals
a signal—this time it was running his hand through his
hair—the team would come up in absolute silence, then a
little quick work with a sap, and the guy would be dragged
off into the shrubbery.

Grizzly went back inside and brought out another one.

Sometimes two. By midnight, Annie's had thinned out considerably, and the customers were wondering where everybody had gone. Grizzly wondered too, and even pointed out that—*saaay*—their *trikes* are still out there! Whatever could be happening, guys?

Why, you know what?

What? they asked.

Why, we oughta go out there and *look* for those guys.

Four minutes later, Grizzly Dalton waltzed every last one of the remaining bikers outside in a gaggle, like Snow White with the Seven Dwarfs. The woods were suddenly filled with coppers and agents, and bikers were being rolled up like . . . *hogs* was the only word for it.

Luke's favorite part was where the last guy, running, with eight Marshals on his heels, pelted past the front porch of Annie's, where Grizzly was leaning back on a chair draining a quart can of what he called Alzheimer's beer, and the guy sees Grizzly, and yells out, "Run for it, man, it's the cops!"

An intriguing postscript to the operation, which Luke called Pigs on Hogs, developed when Grizzly Dalton, fully aware of how important a biker's colors are to a member, had the man's colors dry-cleaned and pressed and presented to him in the visiting room of Ossining, complete with a thank-you note from the U.S. Marshals Service. Aside from the fact that biker colors are *never* washed—the grubbier they are, the higher your status—the thank-you note resulted in the man's expulsion from his chapter of the Hell's Angels, which requires the ex-member to hand over every last emblem and insignia of the Hell's Angels Motorcycle Club—including any and all tattoos.

Complete with surrounding skin.

Luke had a lot of affection for those years, partly because takedown procedures were a lot less structured then, before the onset of SWAT teams and Special Ops. Luke just hoped that a lot of the crews out today were going to have as good a time, although, looking at another part of the room, he developed some serious doubts. There was a group of eight young athletic-looking men sitting in a circle of chairs over by one of the Probation holding pens. Bags of gear were piled up around them, almost like a bunker, and they were engaged in some sort of intense discussion in lowered voices, one or the other of them tapping a map or writing something down in a notepad. They all had black SWAT-style uniforms on, heavy Kevlar vests, and a couple of them were carrying Heckler & Koch MP-5s on slings around their backs.

As he passed their station, he heard some in-group slang like "double-action transition" and "control-point shooting" and "aimed fire." Not one of these flat-faced and chilly-eyed young men looked at Luke or acknowledged him in any way. They seemed to be breathing different air, excluding all of the regular street bulls in the room. They all leaned closer together as Luke went by, an insular cadre of self-contained young males.

Jesuits with guns, thought Luke.

Stacked up next to a crate of Stingball grenades, Luke made out the black ridged tube of an ARWN 37-millimeter projectile launcher and a pack of rubber bullets. The ARWN gun was also capable of firing a spray of rubber pellets or a single sandbag knock-down device. Well, if they had *that*, they'd have it *all*.

Somewhere in the parking garage there'd be a large unmarked black van full of flash-bang stun grenades, HK MP-5s and 53s, LMGs fitted with sound suppressors, laser engagement scopes, infrared night scopes, body-heat sniffers, invisible-beam laser designators for painting a target without giving away your location, Glock pistols, Benelli Super 90 shotguns with barrel-mounted BEAM lights, Remington match-grade heavy-barrel sniper rifles in .308 or Magnum Express .470s, Starlite scopes, GPS gear—a rolling arsenal of the very best killing gear that a taxpayer's dollar could buy.

Everything about this crew said Special Operations Group in large black-edged letters, the "elite" Marshals Service unit of young hard-chargers who practiced MOUT-style assaults with state-of-the-art weaponry, the kind of full-bore military-assault tactics that had, in Luke's opinion, gone a long way to creating the disasters of Ruby Ridge and Waco. They were necessary, they were highly skilled, and they made Luke very, very nervous.

And the last thing Luke spotted on his way over to where Grizzly Dalton was standing at the side of the coffee-room door, talking to Walt Rich, turned out to be almost as alarming as the unexpected arrival of the SOG unit. Luke saw a man standing apart from all of it, writing something down in a police notebook. The man was close to six feet tall, blond, with a red mustache, wearing a long gray loose-fitting trench coat, a black T-shirt, and black jeans tucked into a pair of shiny combat boots. It looked like he had some kind of military web-gear on under the trench coat. Luke gave him a hard look as he reached Grizzly's side.

"Okay, who's the guy in the cowboy duster?"

Walt Rich rolled his eyes, made a vulgar hand gesture. "Press."

Luke shook his head sadly. "Who's next? Paula Zahn on a kick-in with the SOG kiddies?"

Grizzly, his face unshaven and weary-looking, a cup of soup almost hidden inside his hand, was in raid gear today. So was Walt Rich. Rico Groza was nowhere around. Grizzly nodded his head toward the group of men in SOG gear across the room and spoke in a soft voice.

"Special Ops got in this morning. Drove in from Quantico, I'm told."

"JTF-6?"

Grizzly's smile was remarkable for the complete absence of humor in it. Joint Task Force Six was a sticky subject inside the federal law enforcement community. CQB was the acronym the joint units used to describe themselves to each other. It meant close quarter battle.

This was delicate ground for Grizzly and Luke and Walt—the fact that federal law enforcement units were getting combat assault training on army bases such as Fort Hood and Fort Bragg was not an official secret—JTF-6 was out in the open, right there on the Pentagon's asset list—but it was a subject the Mother Superior wanted to keep below the horizon line of the national media. So far, coverage of the issue had been relegated to fringe publications such as *Soldier of Fortune* and a number of freakazoid web sites on the Internet.

The growing intimacy between the Marshals Service SOG unit and the U.S. Army was a development that made a lot of the old street soldiers like Grizzly and Slick Stevens and Luke Zitto more than a little uneasy. They had heard that, now and then, military officers had taken part in civilian SWAT-style operations just to get some hands-on combat experience.

Grizzly sipped at his CuppaSwill, and when he finally spoke, he kept his voice low and his face blank.

"I don't know why they're here. I guess we're not in the loop anymore."

"I think I do," said Walt. "Imad Mughniyeh. The Shiite rag-head who did in that CIA station chief in Beirut in 1984."

Even Luke was impressed. "He's supposed to be *here*? In New York?"

Walt shrugged. "Trying to get those zombies to talk is like trying to get a bottle of Thunderbird away from a wino, but that's what I'm gathering. They're here for some terrorist op, anyway."

Grizzly was nodding. "I saw an FBI BOLO a while back, said Ahmed Jibril was supposed to be somewhere in the U.S. as well." He crumpled up the cup and launched it across the room toward a large drum full of paper scraps. He missed. "Skroom-all, boys. We have business of our own."

"Where's Rico?"

Walt was gathering up his gear. Grizzly strapped on his sidearm and shoved a package of doughnuts into his kit bag. Luke went over to his station and plucked up his own equipment, and they all headed out toward the elevators. As they were leaving, one of the SOG members, a black kid with a shaved head, said something audible above the general noise and confusion of the squad room. Walt stopped and looked at Luke.

"I think that guy's talking to you, Luke."

The black kid was on his feet now and coming toward them. He was very heavy in the upper body, almost robotic-looking inside his Kevlar, and carrying a full Sam Browne of raid gear. All three of them stopped in the doorway and watched him as he came up.

"Excuse me, are you Deputy Luke Zitto? The DIC of Bravo Unit?"

"Yeah, who're you?"

The man offered his hand, and Luke shook it, watching his eyes.

"I'm Deputy Mark Shealey. The CO said you were looking for a sniper. For a Bravo Unit op today? That's my area of operations. I pulled the job."

"What CO?" asked Walt Rich.

"Marshal Fiertag?" He pronounced it *Fire*-tag.

Luke stared at the man.

"Rothgar Fiertag's not a U.S. Marshal, and he's definitely not our CO, deputy. He's just one of our liaison guys with Justice. Rico Groza's the senior man for this sector."

Grizzly made some kind of low-level growl.

Shealey glanced at him, confused and slightly uneasy. "But you did want a sniper?"

Grizzly smacked his hand on the doorjamb. It shook, and

people nearby stared at them. So did Luke and Walt and Deputy Shealey.

"*I* asked for the sniper, not Luke here. How the hell did Fiertag find out? How did you?"

Shealey raised his palms, his young unlined face slightly flushed.

"I just got the duty note, sir."

Grizzly said, "Look, deputy, can you give me and my guys a second?" He moved away from the man, taking Luke and Walt with him.

"Damn," he said, his voice lowered. "This is about Pigeye Quail, Luke. I know I'm out of line here, this is your unit, but while you were . . . busy . . . last night, I was having a drink with Marv Schreck—the DT who was working with Wendy Ma last night?"

"Yeah?"

"Okay, so, I figure, from what we saw on that tape, Pigeye had to have blown himself a pretty big hole somewhere down there in his nuptial vicinities, and I don't know about you boys, but if that were me, I'd be putting a real high priority on getting myself *un*-Bobbittized just as fast as I could. Well, thinks I, Pigeye knows he's got every fed in the Northeast looking for him, he knows we'll be watching all the ERs, and anyway, a guy comes in with a major bullet hole in Captain Happy, somebody's gonna notice that, even in Newark. Plus, he's not going very far, is he? What's left for the guy?"

Luke thought it over.

"I don't figure he's getting much help from his partner on the job. Blackbeard? Guy rips him off for the cash, leaves Pigeye bleeding on the floor. Pigeye stumbled out, if I recall, and carjacked a vehicle, didn't he?"

Luke fumbled in his raid jacket pocket, tugged out his notebook, flipped through the pages. "Yeah, here it is. Dark brown Honda, female driver, nobody got the plates. Newark PD was getting the DMV to check all imports, cross-reference for Missing Persons. That was Tuesday, and I've heard nothing since."

"I have," said Grizzly. "So far, Missing Persons has no calls on it. None of the money has been spent, although it wasn't all marked. I don't think Pigeye has any of it anyway. Guys like that never do. About the car, DMV got a list of 42,671 brown or tan Hondas in Jersey, and none of the ones reported stolen fit the profile. I asked Marv to check with City-Wide Auto Squad, you know, figuring that if Pigeye had to go somewhere, he'd try for upstate New York, because New Jersey, that's Outlaws, Satan's Choice, those guys, and he's Hell's Angels, he'd want to stay out of their territory, especially since he lit up a bank in hostile country. So, if he wants to go upstate, he's not gonna take I-87—"

"Because of cameras at the tolls," agreed Luke. "Although there are lots of tollbooths on the roads and bridges between here and Jersey."

"Yeah," said Walt, "but nobody's *awake* in any of those."

"Right, so that leaves the Taconic. Don't the Angels have a chapter in some little town up there?"

"Gallatinville, that's right. And the Taconic you get to through the Bronx. So I asked Marv to ask City-Wide Auto Squad to get an alert out on brown Hondas, and while he was doing that, I got onto NCIC for B and E's on private clinics, drugstores—"

"Nice," said Walt.

"And guess what? A vet shop at 120 City Island Avenue got cleaned out on Thursday night. Objects taken, sutures, ampicillin, bandages, some kind of animal morphine. Also cleaned out a small employees' refrigerator, took fruit, some bread, and a coffee machine. Here's the good part. The vet was getting his car trashed a lot, so he installed a videocamera, covers the parking lot. There was frost on the lens, so the image sucked, but the car that showed up was a small dark-colored Honda. Marv thought the color was purple or dark blue, but I got him to check out the streetlights in the parking lot. He comes back, tells me the lights are sodium arc. So—"

Luke got that. "So a dark brown car would look purple or dark blue. A blue car would look black. Very cute. But it doesn't tell you where he is now. That was two days ago."

"If that was Pigeye, then he's in bad shape," said Walt. "He won't be too far away from that vet shop."

"How about this?" said Grizzly. "Marv got the duty sergeant at the Four-Five to run him a list of ten-elevens that were cranked out as ten-90's or ten-90U's in the City Island sector from Thursday midnight to last night."

Luke and Walt were intrigued. The Four-Five is the precinct house covering City Island and Pelham Bay. Ten-elevens were alarm calls, and ten-90's and ten-90U's were NYPD radio designations for unfounded and unable to gain entrance.

"So we looked for repeats and got a bunch, most of which were bullshit—kids triggering alarms, cats walking across in front of motion sensors, that sort of thing. But one place had two ten-elevens and three ten-90's last night alone. A Five Charlie car ran the calls, tried the doors, got nothing. He figured, screw it, it's a wiring problem. Told the owners, they said they'd do something. Never did. Off season, anyway, so the place is locked up tight. Nobody lives near it, nobody goes there in January. Guess where it was?"

They looked at him for a while.

Then Luke got it.

Perfect.

1400 Hours
Saturday, January 14, 1995
Split Rock Golf Course
Pelham Bay Park
North Bronx

A bitter wind off Long Island Sound was slicing through the sere brown grasslands of Pelham Bay Park. Low pale gray clouds were flying into the west, trailing shadows across the fields and low rolling hills of the Split Rock Golf Course. On the far side of the lagoon, the parking lot and the curved park land of Orchard Beach was deserted, silent, empty. The clubhouse for the golf course was often open during the fall and spring, for parties or gallery displays, but the cold damp winds of winter usually kept people in their homes and out of the open unprotected stretch of the park. The building itself was a large wooden structure with wide porches and a broad balcony overlooking the lagoon and the view of the Sound beyond it. It commanded the approaches very well, and getting up close to it without being seen was a tactical problem that Rico Groza had been working on ever since Grizzly had asked him to stake the place out that morning.

Rico had taken a position about a hundred yards from

the building, on a small wooded rise. His Marshals van was parked down the leeward slope, out of the line of sight. Although he was wearing a black ski jacket and warm clothing, the steady currents of the wind had gradually chilled him over the hours, making the mild day in the city a distant memory. He had been watching the clubhouse through a pair of Zeiss binoculars and sipping coffee from a Thermos, now empty.

There had been no sign, no movement at all in any window or doorway or anywhere around the building. He hadn't bothered to call patrol units from the Four-Five for close-up support. They'd be too visible, and anyway, if Pigeye Quail was there, he was a Marshals target. This was what they did for a living. He figured Luke would put some city units on the park perimeter.

He turned when he heard the sound of engines coming along the Hutchinson River Parkway behind him. He saw Luke's tan Caprice, moving slowly. He raised a hand, and the car turned off the parkway and rolled down onto the rough cropped grass. Luke, Walt, Grizzly, and a young black man got out. Walt came up the low slope toward Rico's position, carrying a brown paper bag. His Irish features were rubbed bright red by the sea wind, and his lips looked a little blue as he tried to smile. He covered the last few feet in a crouch and handed the bag to Rico. The smell of chicken soup and hot coffee rose up out of the bag.

Rico watched the young black Marshal as he opened the car trunk and lifted out a long black nylon case. Rico picked up a cup of black coffee, popped the lid, and sipped at it carefully.

"Who's the shooter?" he said in a hoarse whisper. His body was shaking slightly.

"Kid named Mark Shealey."

Rico nodded. "Special Ops. I know him."

"Yeah," said Walt. "He had great numbers on the MOUT site. This is for real. Where do you want him?"

"He'll figure that out for himself. Have we got people on the exits?"

"Luke called the Four-Five. They have units at the north end of Pelham Bridge, on Park, and on City Island. We've got the Hutchinson covered. If he's in there, he's not getting out by car. If he's as bad hurt as we think he is, he's not going to walk out."

"And if he has a hostage?"

Walt glanced over to the tan Caprice, where Luke and Grizzly were standing, talking to the shooter.

"That's where he comes in," said Walt. "I hope he's good."

"So do I," said Rico.

Luke had left the car and was coming across the field to Rico's observation post. Grizzly and the Special Operations sniper were making their way to a high point where a small copse of spindly trees gave them a view of the clubhouse and the surrounding grasslands. The trees would break up their silhouette. The range from the trees to the clubhouse was close to five hundred yards.

Luke reached them in a crouch, settled down beside them. The men watched as Grizzly and the sniper disappeared into the trees. In three minutes Luke got a short double-click transmission on his radio. He clicked back once.

"Okay, they're in position. Rico, you want to do this?"

Rico nodded. Sharing command was always tricky. Given their history, and the fact that Rico had been given Luke's post in D.C., Rico was careful to observe every courtesy with Luke.

"Okay, if that's all right with you. I've been watching this place. Not a rustle. Not a blind out of place. I'm operating on the assumption that he has a hostage in there."

Walt rubbed his hands together, trying to warm them. The wind carried the smell of salt water, seaweed, dead fish. He was looking at the clubhouse as if he could stare through the walls.

"*If* he's in there. You figure the woman? The Honda driver?"

"Who else? I'd say she was single, maybe a traveler. Whoever she is, she can disappear for five days and nobody gets too excited about it. Missing Persons has nothing. But if she was free, we'd sure as hell have heard about it. She'd be onto the Newark cops, somebody. So he's holding her."

"Or she's dead," said Luke.

"Yeah, or she's dead." Rico's skin was mottled from the cold, and his breath was a short white plume. "But we can't assume that. Even in New York, somebody'd find her body. If she was in the river, she'd have turned up at the South Street Seaport or she'd have caught a snag somewhere. Floaters float. We have to operate on the assumption that she's in there, and she's alive."

"Shealey thinks we ought to call in his team. Let them do it. Hostage ops are their specialty."

"Right," said Walt. "And when does Deputy Shealey think his boys can spare us the time? Next Tuesday? Let's get this done, okay? I'm shaking so hard, I think I just snapped a vasectomy clip here."

"Well, button yourself back up," said Rico, "because we're here for a while."

Walt groaned.

Luke smiled at Rico. "I was afraid of that," he said.

"But you know I'm right?"

"Oh yes," said Luke. "No other way."

· · · ·

At four-fifty that afternoon, the sun set behind the low clustered rooftops of Baychester and Wakefield, and the monuments and crypts of Woodlawn Cemetery. The lights were coming on all around them, low distant yellow sparks in the homes and city streets. Now and then, they'd get a transmission from one of the Four-Five patrol units—breaking off for shift, or going ten-six to leave the car for coffee or to signal a replacement unit. But for the men watching the clubhouse there had been no break at all, and now the cold was working its way deep into their bodies. Coffee and soup helped, but not much.

Each hour seemed a slow progression of frozen time, each second a shard of ice cracking. By seven o'clock, it was full dark, and the clubhouse loomed in the distance like a piece of black rock. All around them the huge city hummed and boomed in the darkness, an ocean of light and noise and people. Far out in the Sound, the sea rolled in silence. At seven forty-two by the illuminated dial of Luke's Indiglo, a tiny red spark showed in the lower left-hand window of the clubhouse. At the same moment they got a triple-click on the radio. Luke had to try three times to finger the speak button.

"Six actual."

Grizzly's voice came back, low, chilled to the bone. *"Bravo Six. Shealey's got movement there. Can you see it?"*

"Ten-four. What is it?"

A pause.

"He says it's a cigarette."

"What scope has he got fitted?"

Another pause.

"He says he has a Starlite, Six actual. He can fit his infrared."

"How's his image?"

A muttered exchange sounded over the little handset.

"He has a figure at the window. Smoking. Can't tell if it's male or female."

"Does he have a shot?"

"Yeah. But who is it?"

"Ten-four, Grizzly. Tell him to fit his IR if he thinks it will help. Right now, we wait for it."

"Ten-four. Out."

The handset went dead. The men watched the clubhouse now, suddenly very awake, the chill not forgotten but somehow less intense. Four minutes passed. Then the handset again, Grizzly's hoarse whisper.

"Mark's got heat."

The sniper must have fitted his infrared scope. Now he was picking up body heat or some heat source in the frozen nightscape encompassed by the telephoto image. The view would be shades of intense black and tiny blobs of pale violet, bright red.

A sound came across the grassy waste. A muted wheezing cough that settled into a low muttering rumble. A car engine. Grizzly's voice came up again.

"More heat. Big signature. Looks like it's in that subbasement there, where the roll-up doors are. Looks like some kind of combustion."

That was enough for them all.

"Ten-four, Grizzly. We're going in. Hold your position."

"Mark says he's not gonna know who's who, Luke."

"Will he know if he uses the Starlite?"

Silence.

"He says maybe. The light's real bad, and he's getting a lot of back-scatter from City Island over there. He'd rather use the IR, but then his resolution isn't as good."

"Fine," said Luke. "Just tell him not to shoot anybody who isn't a bad guy. We have to move *now*."

They were already moving, fanning out across the golf

course. The brittle dead grass made a rustling crackle as they crossed it, and their gear jingled softly. Luke had his Taurus out. Walt was carrying a small MP-5 and Rico had a Beretta with a laser sight mounted under the barrel. In a few seconds, they closed the distance to the clubhouse. The cloud cover was hiding the stars. It was cold and dark in the low fairways. A line of trees marked the edge of the car lot. They ran lightly, Luke's right knee aching as it usually did, but they covered the ground well. As they neared the main building, the sound of a car engine grew. It was turning over quietly. Now they were within fifty feet of the subbasement doors. The sound was definitely coming from there. It was very dark and almost impossible to distinguish a bush from a man, or a man from a hostage.

Luke stopped at a low rise and picked up his radio again.

"Grizzly?" His voice was barely a breath. The wind was building now, and it rumbled across the handset mike. It cut like a knife where it curled and slid around open skin.

"We have you, Luke. You're all bunched up by the edge of the parking lot. Raise your hand."

Luke did.

"Okay, that's you by the end of the treeline. I think we can work this. I have the Starlite. Mark's got the IR fitted. What now?"

"He'll be coming out. That's a car engine. What's the heat signature now?"

"Big," said Grizzly. *"Door size."*

They heard a grating in the darkness, metal on metal. Luke knew the sound. He heard it every night on Court Street, when the bar downstairs pulled its shutters closed at two A.M.

Now radio talk was impossible. The cold air would carry the sound of a voice as if it were underwater. Luke double-clicked out. Got a single answering click. The three men moved forward toward the door, fanned out, each very aware of the position of the other two. Luke's heart was pounding a bit, as it usually did, and he pulled in a couple of slow deep breaths, trying to suppress his adrenaline flow. The main building was less than twenty feet now, and there was a faint glow showing by a line of brush near the basement door. If this was Pigeye Quail, he must have hidden the Honda in the basement. If he had, he was moving better than they thought he could. Maybe his wound wasn't as bad as it had looked on the video.

Or someone had moved the car for him.

The woman.

The woman was the key.

Rico was only assuming she was a hostage. There was another explanation: She was an accomplice. Luke put it at fifty-fifty. Whatever it was, they had to be careful around the woman. They heard a car door slam, a muffled thunk, and then another door. The soft glow they had seen was gone. The roof light inside the car. It would shut off when they closed the doors.

They.

Two people.

The noise of the engine rose, coughed, settled into a steady rumble. Then a metallic clunk as it kicked into gear.

No voices.

No threats.

No arguments.

Lights off, the little car was moving up the basement ramp. They heard its wheels as they reached the gravel road. They heard the tires grinding through the stones. Luke's radio clicked three times.

Mark Shealey had acquired a target. If Luke raised his right arm, Shealey would fire at the driver of the car.

Luke kept his arm down. They needed a positive ID. The only way to do that was to get right in there and put a light on the two people in the car. And the time to do that was now. It was making him nervous to set out here in the dark knowing that a man was looking down a sniper scope at him from five hundred yards. Luke had never met a sniper he liked.

Luke touched Rico's shoulder. Rico touched Walt.

The car was approaching their position. It would have to go past them to reach the entrance to Pelham Bridge Road. If the driver turned on the car lights, they'd be caught in the beams.

Luke's handset clicked twice. Call me, Grizzly was saying.

It clicked again. Luke ignored it.

Rico leaned forward, whispered to Luke.

"I'll take the driver," he said.

"Okay," said Luke.

Walt would hold back and cover.

The car was a black bug creeping in the velvet dark. They could see it as a kind of bulky shadow against the city-glow shining on the cloud cover. A faint glow from the dashboard light was shining on two faces, one pale and white, the driver, and the other one in the passenger seat, larger, man-shaped . . . something about the face . . .

The neurons buzzed and the synapse flared—zapped across the gap.

Pigeye Quail.

Rico gave a little grunt of effort as he pushed off the ground. Luke was right behind him. Their boots hit the gravel now, stones skittering. The driver heard them, punched the pedal, the little car jumped forward—Rico had his laser sight on, and the tiny red dot was dancing around on the driver's forehead. She screamed—Walt lit the scene up with his Maglite—they were bellowing now—"*Freeze! Federal officers!*"—the woman's voice still ringing—the car's engine snarling now—closing. Luke was turning to avoid the leading fender when the car head-lights flared on—he was blinded, had a glimpse of Rico's black form caught in the glare of the lights—Rico saying "Freeze now!" in a clear hard voice—all business—his Beretta centered, the tiny red dot a Hindu ruby in the middle of the woman's forehead—the car racing for-ward—the heat of the engine in Luke's face—the grinding of the tires rushing—the bumper went by his ribs like a bull grazing a matador's vest. He had the Taurus up now and saw Pigeye Quail—saw his ponytail hanging down, his unshaven face in the light from Walt Rich's flash—less than a second—Pigeye was staring into the muzzle of Luke's Taurus as he came closer—and he jumped—jerked—the car wheels locked up solid—plowing up the gravel—Pigeye's hands were in the air—the woman was still screaming—"*No!*" she was saying, "*No!*"—and Pigeye's ragged baritone bleat—"*Don't shoot! Don't shoot*—I'm *hurt*, man, I'm hurt!"

The car was stopped now. Rico held his Beretta steady, that little red laser dot unmoving, painted on the woman's forehead. She sat there like a dead woman, her hands locked onto the steering wheel, eyes wide, mouth open. Luke wrenched the passenger door open and pulled Pigeye Quail out onto the gravel. He hit hard and bellowed in pain, holding his crotch.

Rico was dragging the woman out from behind the wheel. Walt Rich stood back and covered both takedowns. Luke jerked Pigeye onto his face, reaching for his cuffs, wrenching the man's muscular arms backward and up. Pigeye was facedown in the gravel, a soft whimpering noise coming from his closed mouth, his lips thin and white. He had tears on his face.

The woman was thin, pale, and hunted-looking, her hair lank and unwashed, her eyes ringed and red-rimmed. She was wearing a heavy knitted sweater and jeans. Luke knew her.

"You're Fay Koenig."

She shook her head. Luke lifted Pigeye up by the cuffs and the ponytail, and he screamed out loud, an animal squeal. Luke held him up that way and stared at her.

She stared back.

Finally she said, "Put him down. Please."

"You're Fay Koenig, yes?"

"Yes," she said, while Rico was cuffing her and patting her down. Fay Koenig was on their hit list too, as a known associate of a biker enforcer named Urjo Stodt. Urjo Stodt, also on their hit list, was a very large, very bad-tempered PCP user with a NYSIIS sheet as long as the Mets' losing streak. His specialties included crystal meth labs, extortion, rape, murder, and armed robbery.

Especially suburban banks.

Urjo's nickname in the Hell's Angels was Teach. Not short for "teacher," but short for Edward Teach, a famous pirate who was also well known for something else.

His large black beard.

"Where's Teach?"

She shook her head.

Luke tugged at Pigeye's ponytail, and Pigeye howled.

"You prick."

"Where's Teach?" asked Luke, his voice steady and flat.

She paused. Luke tightened his hand inside Pigeye's ponytail again. Before he could pull it, she said, "Don't! Okay?"

"Why'd he leave Pigeye in the bank?"

"That was the deal. If either guy got cut off, the other guy was to grab the cash and split. I was supposed to hang back, see if I could help. It was supposed to look like a carjack thing."

"Where's the cash?"

"Teach has it."

"And where's Teach?"

She paused again. Pigeye's throat was working, his mouth opened up by the pressure on his neck. His breathing was coming in short sharp sobs, his breath puffing white in the harsh beams.

"Gallatinville," she said, after a long minute.

Luke smiled at her and let Pigeye drop face-first back onto the stones. His breath huffed out of him, and he twisted into a kind of fetal position, his knees tightly locked, his face bone white. He was the very incarnation of the concept of pain. Grizzly and Mark Shealey came up at a slow trot. Rico stood in silence, watching Pigeye suffer on the ground.

Luke, who knew what Pigeye's habits were, felt very little of anything. He could feel the pain coming off the man, smell it on the cold wind from the sea, a copper-scented reek. He took a deep breath and held it until his heart pounded, then let it go, a plume of white mist in the cone of light from Walt Rich's flash. He looked down at his right hand, saw the familiar, barely detectable tremor. Mark Shealey was looking at Luke's face, his eyes careful. Luke felt his look and wondered what the young man was thinking, what this scene seemed to be from his point of view. Well, he was a sniper, wasn't he?

He could afford to keep his distance.

On the Monday, three days ago now, the snows had come down out of the Tampais Mountains, out of a low winter sky of battleship gray as unvarying and absolute as a prison wall. The wet-wool clouds rolled down onto the mountains and the tops of the trees, leaching the color out of every root and branch, turning the forested slopes into a pinto-painted confusion of dead-brown wood, the wet black of leaves coating the forest floor, and the stark white of the heavy snow lying on the barren branches of the forest. Snow drifted silently down through the cold damp air like plump white feathers, snow sifted gently into cracks and gullies and spread across stony ridges, until the stillness and the heavy white silence covered the central part of the state from Middletown to Syracuse.

The train of three federal cars sped northward into the winter night, the men inside them either silent behind the wheel, or half-asleep, dreaming, calmed by the steady murmur of the engine, the rumble and pop as they changed lanes and the tires hit the little rubber knobs of the lane markers, the half-heard chatter of a late-night radio show, the low humming of the heater fan, while outside the great blankness of the northern winter night pressed against the glass. Up ahead the twin cones of their high beams seemed to conjure, out of an infinite well of blackness, the swirling galaxies of luminous snowflakes falling toward the windshield, the silvery-gray tangle of overarching branches, the angled slabs of a bare rock cliff-side, or the shining ribbons of the highway.

Only the little towns shouted at them as they passed through, a pinwheel tumble of bright neon signs—ARCO and DENNY'S and BEST WESTERN—a cluster of huddled roofs coated in melting snow, plumes of chimney-smoke spreading out flat under the clouds, the visual blare of plastic megamalls and outlet stores, the town names metronomic, syncopated, strange—Goshen and Liberty and Chenango Forks, Whitney Point, Killawog and Cortland. The mists of the previous afternoon were now glazed by the chilly mountain night, coating Luke's side windows in crystalline intricacies of molecular math, starburst radiations of ice, universes of frozen light that caught the rays of the passing town-lights and sent thunderbolts of blue fire racing up lancing web works, scattered it like shards of breaking mirror-glass over snowfields of etched glass, lakes of pale fire, fleeting rainbows of blue and violet—and then the town-lights would be gone, the silence would come rushing in again as if someone had just turned off a game show, and all that remained was the black satin surface of Interstate 81, slick, sinuous, the tires hissing on it with a steam-on-hot-iron sound, the muted distant rumble of the car engine, the sudden flash of vivid green in the road signs, or in the profound dead-eyed blindness of the night, the fleeting yellow glimmer of a farmhouse window seen through the spindly black stick-figure trees, or the pinpoint red spark of a campfire far up the hillside, strobing between the tree trunks as they passed it.

Luke was alone in his tan Caprice, listening to but not hearing a babble of talk-radio at two in the morning, watching the taillights of the two lead cars a mile ahead, his mind reeling off a seamless succession of images.

The dying ruby-red glitter in Elijah Olney's left eye as the life in him flew away, Olney's eye fixed on him the way the tiny red-lit eye of a moth had held him once, caught it in the palm of his hand on a summer night in Columbus a thousand years ago.

Fay Koenig's shopworn face, white with hatred for him, shining in the beam of Walt Rich's flash like a piece of new bone at the bottom of an open grave; Mark Shealey's cold disapproval as he watched Luke holding Pigeye by the hair; a video image of Urjo "Teach" Stodt being transferred, in leg-irons and a waist-chain, to a federal keep in Albany; Teach's sudden sideways glare into the camera, his beard a matted root-tangle, his cheeks scored and pitted, his eyes as flat as Chinese lacquer.

Aurora Powys's bottomless blue eyes in the hard white light of the New Jersey jail, and the bright-red blood drops spattering the turnkey's crisp new uniform shirt; Margaret Farrell's cynical mouth.

The fear in the face of fugitive Kali Figueroa last Sunday as he ran toward Luke's position in the parking lot behind the Wal-Mart in White Plains, Rico Groza on his heels, Kali's lithe body working beautifully as he pelted across the blacktop in the rain, running quite literally into their arms.

The slack-faced resignation on the face of thirty-six-year-old Joel Mark O'Keefe, wanted for child molestation and interstate flight, caught in the living room of his mother's house in Chenango, New York, yesterday, and shipped off to the local state police substation in his underwear and slippers.

The bright purple cheeks and wide white eyes of James Bennett, serial rapist and carjacker, when he was fighting all four of them on the floor of the Denny's restaurant on the interstate, where he had been working as a cook for weeks, the travelers screaming, the waitresses watching grimly, the manager choleric with outrage, Bennett's terrible *strength* as he lifted himself up off the floor, with Grizzly Dalton on top of him and Walt Rich struggling with one arm, the way his breath *huffed* out of him when Luke's boot connected with his crotch, the shock and disapproval of the customers watching all of this happen.

Grizzly laughing as he told a story in the stale-beer-scented dimness of a roadhouse bar last night, Walt Rich over by the exit sign, on the telephone to his wife and kids in Jersey, and Rico . . . always the face of Rico Groza . . . hard and shadowed in the half-light, those black eyes buried in bone, the sardonic twist in the mouth, the sense of calculation and judgment he radiated . . . Wendy Ma's satin skin, dusty in a shaft of moonlight . . . the wet gray hairs on Doc Hollenbeck's chest, Doc's toothless, brutally forgiving smile . . . and a yellow man Luke had only seen in dreams, with shiny blue-black hair flying like a crow's wing, and a little steel hatchet black against the sun—the car was suddenly full of a loud drumming rumble, and Luke's head snapped upward.

He was nearly off the road, his left wheels pounding over the rumble strips on the median boundary. Christ! Heart blipping, he corrected, slowed, and pressed the button to roll down the window. Cold wet air sliced his cheek, and flakes of fat white snow flew into the car. Luke picked up his handset.

"Grizzly, you awake?"

"I better be. I'm driving. Walt's having a little nappy. You know the guy snores?"

"Yeah. What you find out about a guy if you sleep with him, hah?"

"Yep. You okay back there, man? I saw your lights take a little dip there. You wandering?"

"I fell asleep. You wanna take a break?"

"I'm okay. I'm a little peaked. Hey, Rico, you there?"

Rico's voice came on, breaking up a little in the passes. He sounded as tired as Luke felt.

Luke glanced at the green numbers of the dashboard clock. Man, it was after two in the morning. They'd been on the road since Saturday night, making hits and misses all the way from Pelham Bay to Chenango Forks, scooping six people, if you included Urjo Stodt. Now they were pushing it to Tully, where they had a trooper surveilling an apartment above a muffler shop. If the trooper's ID was right, they were about to take down a very difficult target.

"Ten-four, Grizzly. Tully's only ten miles up."

"I think there's a truck stop there by the off-ramp. Can you make that, Luke?"

"No problem. I'll keep the window open. Don't want to disappoint our next contestant."

"Copy that, Luke. See you guys there."

Luke put the little radio down on the seat beside him and rubbed his face with his free hand. This was a time of night most cops called the hour of the wolf, that timeless zoned-out stretch of your shift where nothing has happened for long enough that you start to drift, to get sleepy, to get careless. So far on this sweep, they'd been lucky or smart—only the criminals had been careless, and either way they'd caught a bunch of bad people and were looking at a few more up the road, all the way to Buffalo. But the man holed up over the muffler shop in Tully was a special item.

The man in the apartment—the man they *hoped* was in the apartment—was a member of the Ghost Shadows, a New York City gang. Wu Xsin Gi, twenty-eight, wanted for escape, torture, a couple of murders. He was also a martial arts expert, according to FBI and New York State profiles.

Wendy Ma had seen his name on their top-ten hit list and tapped it with a delicate finger. They were leaning on the hood of Luke's car, looking at his route maps. It was last Saturday night, and Wendy had driven around to the Four-Five station house to watch them bring in Pigeye Quail and Fay Koenig. The takedown had been broadcast over the Four-Five detective channel. Wendy, expecting some news about Luke, had been monitoring that channel. She'd driven around to say good-bye to him and the others.

She looked at Wu Xsin Gi's photo, a black-and-white of a sullen-faced, blunt-boned Asian male with a trick haircut. His black eyes were insolent, furious, defiant. His mouth was a parable of brutal arrogance.

"Chaotic," she had said. "These people—the Ghost Shadows, they think all you white people are devils. Inferior. I mean that literally. They do not think you are human at all. Killing you is like getting a trophy head. Be careful of this one."

"I will," said Luke, kissing her good-bye. "You be careful too. If you get into anything, get backup. If you need to talk to me, you have my pager, and you have Grizzly's cell phone. Don't do anything weird, okay?"

"I won't," she said, smiling at him. "At least, not without you. I'll call you, okay?"

"Yeah, you'll call me," he said, grinning at her. "Well, you all say that, don't you?"

Luke had thought about her, on and off, all the way upstate. He had called her squad room a couple of times while they were on the road. She was always out, or in a meeting. Jerry Boynton had answered once, the Four-One detective who had answered Brian Crewes's backup request, the cop who had found Crewes on the warehouse floor of La Luna Negra.

Luke had reached him from a pay-phone booth at an interstate rest stop west of Middletown. Boynton had been cagey with Luke—more interagency tension—but because Wendy Ma had put in a good word about him, Boynton had some news he was willing to share.

It seemed that the good Doctor Dred, a.k.a. Clayton Garr, had undergone a miraculous change of heart and now found himself cured of his plea-bargain-related amnesia. The young Doctor had given them a very fine description of the guy who had rattled his patrol-car cage so impressively in the lane behind La Luna Negra.

Boynton read it out to Luke.

It was the Yellow Man, no doubt at all.

Concerning the Yellow Man, Wendy Ma had tried to run a search on the Catch and Holmes systems, looking for any ex-con with the first name of Ernesto or Ernest or anything similar. According to Boynton, there were thousands, largely because about a third of the people in American prisons were Central American drug mules, a lot of whom were known as Ernesto. Luke asked him if Wendy's NCIC search had caused any "ripples."

Boynton's voice cooled a little.

"Yeah, now that you mention it. A day later, the lieutenant hears from a suit in D.C., wants to know who, what, why—says it affects a federal operation."

"Your LT get a name?"

"Endicott. Reed Endicott. Real stiff. The LT told him to insert and twist, and the guy goes all huffy, rings off.

Nothing from him since. Do I get to hear what all this means, Luke?"

"Soon as I do. Anything else you can tell me?"

Boynton paused long enough to let Luke know he was pushing his credit line. Wendy Ma had checked out the Ninth Precinct, but the killing down there had turned out to be unrelated, a domestic thing, and the husband had used a meat cleaver, not a little tomahawk. Sergeant Brian Crewes was okay, a little memory loss, especially regarding the details around the alleged beating of his prisoner—the circumstances of which seemed to have escaped his recall entirely—but basically he was going to be fine. And one more thing. They had found Don Florida, the owner of the storage and delivery company.

"Where?" said Luke, expecting something ugly.

"Jamaica Bay. A fisherman in Big Fishkill Channel saw a couple of people pushing a sealed fifty-gallon oil drum off the Mill Basin Bridge, out by Floyd Bennett Field—"

"Who told you that?"

"The DOI passed it on. Why?"

"Just asking. What was in the drum?"

"The usual," said Boynton, his city bull's voice dry and ironic. "Garbage. Fish guts. Bait. A few spare parts. Hands, a right forearm, a couple of legs. Part of the torso. Not enough to make a whole guy, not even with directions. The hands still had rings on, and the forearm had a watch. Big gold Rolex, with an inscription on the back, *Para Mi Vida*, something like that. Guy's wife ID'd him from the wedding ring. *That* was a scene."

"You sure it was him?"

"Oh yeah. Once we got the rest of him. The city morgue guys kind of pieced it together for us on one of their gurneys. Weapon used fit the mutilations on the kids, Tito La Gaviota and the girl. Little tomahawk. Wild, hah?

Guess who the guy has connections to? Manny Obregon. Ring a bell with you guys?"

"I know who he is. He's a *jefe* in the Bronx. How'd *his* name come up?"

"The vic's sister, broad named Angela, called Obregon from a pay phone at the precinct house. We don't tape them, but we get a printout of all the calls originating. She called his unlisted number too. Interesting, right? Right now, the only thing we got going is, Florida had a helper, and that guy is still missing. Florida's sister says he was supposed to be there around that time. So either he's lying around in bite-sized chunks in some oil drum by the seashore, or he's part of the thing. Maybe an accomplice."

"What's the name?"

"Gardena. Roderigo Gardena."

"Gardena . . . ?"

"Yeah? Ring a bell?"

Luke hesitated. Yes, or no?

"Not immediately . . . something."

Boynton chuckled. "Sounds like you got the usual case of Big Al, man. I got it too."

"Big Al?"

"Alzheimer's, man. Hey, there's this old guy, sitting on a bench, he's crying, sobbing. Cop comes along, says, what's the matter, sir? Old man says, I have a sexy young wife, she's waiting for me in bed right now, I have all kinds of money, I'm popular, I have my health. Cop says, so why're you crying? Old guy says, I can't remember where I live."

Luke had heard it, but what the hell.

"Anyway," said Boynton, still laughing, "I asked the DOI guys about it, but they got all snakey-eyed and pucker-lipped, the way those mopes do, and I figured, who needs 'em, this is *my* case."

"Wheels within wheels. Where was the rest of Don Florida?"

"Well, I'll tell you, somebody out there has a sense of humor. DOI guys say they found his head stuck on an umbrella stand, down by the seashore. Wanna guess where?"

"No idea."

Boynton was laughing.

"Oriental Beach? At the pier. I loved it. Only in New York, I tell you. You get it, hah?"

"I get it," said Luke, seeing the image.

Oriental Beach lay on a flat section of recovered land, a few miles east of Brighton Beach. It projected out into a weedy stretch of ocean and inlets bounded in the south by the long barrier islands of the Rockaways.

The name of that inland sea was Sheepshead Bay.

Tully's main street was very much like the main street of every little town in rural America, a broad treeless avenue filled with fast-food places, motels, shopping malls, until you reached the older part of town, where the trees were higher and the houses larger, rambling red-brick Victorian constructions on placid side streets, some old shops in the central square, a post office, a county cop shop, and a theater. Tonight's feature, on the darkened marquee of the Lux, shrouded by falling snow, was *Four Weddings and a Funeral.*

The Apex Muffler Shop had been built into the side of a former Woolworth's, at the intersection of Miller and Main. The building was a two-story pile of red clay bricks, slightly swaybacked. The muffler shop was closed, darkened, and the streets of the town were deserted.

The snow that had been falling nonstop since Monday had covered all the lawns and trees, but a plow had been through earlier that day, so dirty wet snow was heaped up along the walkways and blocked a few of the alleys. The streetlamps were old-fashioned and gave off the warm yellow light of incandescent bulbs, so that the snow swirling around inside their halo looked like bright yellow moths fluttering around candles.

The New York state trooper car was right where he said he'd be, a slate-gray unmarked Caprice parked off on a side street, with a view of the back stairs of the Apex Muffler building. His lights were off, and the car was black and silent as Luke parked his car a hundred feet back, locked it, zipped up his black raid jacket, and put a long gray duster coat on over it. He stretched his bones and adjusted his belt and walked quietly up through the snowfall toward the state car.

He got a double-click on his handset as he reached the car. Grizzly, Walt, and Rico were in position a few hundred yards back. Once Luke got a read from the trooper, they'd decide just how this thing was going to happen. He clicked back once and tapped on the dripping side window of the car.

The window slid down with a muted mechanical whir. The trooper was an older man, with gray hair in a military cut, a large gray mustache, and wrinkled weary-looking eyes. He smelled of mint and aftershave.

"You the feds? I'm Pete Gruwchyk. Hop in."

Luke went around to the passenger door and got in, closing the door softly. The interior light did not come on when he opened the door, which reassured him. The trooper knew his trade. The cop's heavy winter jacket rustled as the man fumbled around in his pockets, extracted a pack of cigarettes, and offered one to Luke. Luke took it after a moment, Gruwchyk lit them both up and blew out a puff of smoke. Luke thanked him, asked how long he'd been on station.

He checked his watch, grinned.

"Six hours. I relieved the day man at 2200 hours."

"You sure it's him?"

"Let's see the shot again." Luke had the photo in his raid jacket pocket. He flipped it onto the radio console between the seats. The cop used a Mini-Maglite to study it again.

"Damnedest thing. You know, my wife's been buying groceries from this guy for a couple of weeks. There's a produce store, Lucky Garden, out by the arena. Chinese family runs it, been in town for years. Good people. This guy here, he starts working there a while back, my wife doesn't like him. Says the whole atmosphere in the store went sour."

"It would, if they'd been told to hide this guy, if they had no choice."

Gruwchyk nodded. "Ghost Shadows, hah? Sounds nasty."

"It is. Got any suggestions?"

Gruwchyk looked a little surprised. "You want *my* advice? You sure you're really a fed? Lemme see some tin."

Luke laughed outright. "Hey, you know the town."

Gruwchyk looked pleased.

"Well, I have been giving the matter some thought, and I thank you for asking me. Most of the time, guys like you roll into town, we do the perimeter, you run the show. It gets a little old, okay? Anyway, this place where he's staying, I've been in it lots of times. The whole upstairs over the muffler shop is a series of railroad flats—they run in a straight line from the doorway to the living room, to a kitchen, and then into a bedroom. Bedroom has one window. No windows in any other walls, because there's five apartments up there, all the same, share the side walls, see? So if you go in the door at the top of the stairs there, that door leads to the main hallway. The apartments run sideways off that hall, like the sidebars on the letter E? Only there's *five* bars, okay?"

Luke was writing this down in a notebook.

"Okay, five. Which one's *he* in?"

"According to the folks, he's in the A apartment, which does have an outside wall, so it has an extra window. In the living room. That's it right up there."

"He can see us from that window?"

"I know. But there's no other way to keep an eye on the place. I don't think we spooked him, because we always have a car sitting around on a side street these days. The kids, you know, spray-painters? Can't jail 'em, and they won't let us shoot them. So we baby-sit. There's nothing unusual about us having a car here like this. We do it all the time."

"Okay. How many other people up there?"

"That's the thing. There's the Pruitts in C, some guy works for the muffler shop in D, and Father Mike in E."

"A priest?"

"Retired. He was a Basilian. He's working on a book. His family used to live around here. He's a decent old guy. Got a weakness for single malt."

"That's a weakness?"

Gruwchyk smiled. "Not by me. But if you have to get him out of there at this hour, he may fuss a little. Trouble is, only the outside walls of that place—it used to be a Woolworth's—only the outside walls are brick. The rest is wood. Thin wallboard between the apartments too, and the floorboards are real creaky. Walking around inside there is like walking around inside a packing crate. Lousy place for a gunfight."

Luke was looking at the building. A set of wooden stairs led up to a main door—the hallway door, according to Gruwchyk, and the outside wall of apartment A had a window overlooking the main street, a window looking out onto the cluttered back lot of the muffler shop, and a single sash-window along the side wall, which gave a view of the side street, where they were parked. Tricky.

"Who's in B?"

"Nobody. Empty now. But still, there's no through-door into A."

"Damn," said Luke.

Gruwchyk was watching him, his face expectant.

"Well . . . ?"

"Pete."

"Well, Pete, you said you had an idea. What was it?"

Gruwchyk was beaming at him. He pulled on his cigarette, leaned forward, and stubbed it out on the ashtray. He looked at Luke sideways as he did this, a glimmer in his eye, his cheek scored with age lines.

"I thought you'd never ask."

0500 Hours
Thursday, January 19, 1995
Apex Muffler Shop
Miller and Main Street
Tully, New York

he first fire engine, a brand new GMC ladder truck, growled down the main street of Tully at five in the morning, coming slowly through a thickening vortex of snowflakes, its air brakes huffing, the big diesel engine snarling in a low gear. It was followed closely by a station wagon, bright red, with its roof lights whirling, sending red and white flickers flying around on the old brick buildings, scattering broken-glass glitters of light into the midst of the falling snow, so that the whole street took on the feel of a nightclub painted with stars, a glitter ball twirling insanely in the center of a cloud of white sparks. The ladder truck came to a wheezing chuffing stop outside Apex Muffler. The static and crackle of radios sounded in the stillness of the snow-filled night. Lights began to come on in the set of railroad flats over the muffler shop.

A county cop car pulled up in front of the big ladder truck, and two cops got out. They walked over to the fire truck and had a short muted conversation with the fire captain. Their breath plumed out into the headlight glow. Steam began to rise off the slick shiny metal hood of the big engine.

After they had their talk, the county cops sighed and began to walk around the side of the building, shining their Mag-Lite into the windows of the darkened garage, then upward through the blowing snowflakes toward the upper windows, most of which were now lit, with the silhouettes of tenants showing black against the soft amber glow from inside the apartments.

One of the tenants, an old man with a thick head of frowzy white hair, leaned out the front window of apartment E, overlooking the idling fire trucks, and asked what the devil was going on. Smoke alarm, said one of the men standing on the ladder truck. Got to check it out.

Damn, said the old man, pulling a faded blue housecoat around his bony shoulders.

At the rear of the building the two county cops were trudging up the staircase toward the hallway door. A young couple was waiting for them at the top of the stairs, the woman holding a baby. The cops spoke to them, their radios crackling with cross-talk. Finally, the couple began to come down the staircase. The cops went on into the hallway and began to knock on various doors. The front door to apartment A jerked open, and a young Chinese male was standing there, fully clothed, his short muscular frame blocking the doorway, a belligerent look on his face.

The county cops made their explanations, said they were sorry, but he'd have to leave the building until they could find the reason for the alarm. It was an old building, all wood inside, a firetrap. It didn't even have a sprinkler system, said one cop, looking up at the stained tile ceiling.

The Chinese man said something vulgar in an unfamiliar language and slammed the door shut. The cops walked away, continued knocking on doors. One of them laughed.

A few minutes later, the county cops knocked again at his door. He had been sitting at this chair overlooking the side street, watching a state police car. He'd been watching that car for hours. Now and then another cop would drop by, have a cigarette with the man at the wheel. It was simply routine, he felt, but it had nagged at him, and he had not been able to sleep. Now he was irritable, uneasy, and his temper was not good at the best of times. That was why he was in this dull little town, working at a peasant's job with those Hakka morons—because of his temper.

Now this stupid alarm. There was no fire. These old buildings had bad wires, bad plumbing, bad bones. They were like old people, always creaking around at night, always going to the bathroom, always with some bad trouble keeping them up in the middle of the night. It was never anything important. When the knocking at the door got more insistent, he slammed his hand on the tabletop and told the people outside the door to go away.

"Can't do that, sir," said the voice through the thin door. "Got to check all the rooms."

"No, all fine in here!" said the man, his voice thin with anger.

"Sir, I have a key here. I'm sorry to bother you and all. But it's the law. I gotta do a walk-through. I'll be in and out, sir. You'll never notice."

The Chinese man looked over at the bedroom, where he had a weapon hidden. He considered going over there and stuffing it into his pants. Decided against it. Down in the street he heard the voices of the other tenants, half-asleep, half-excited at the break in the monotony, there was a party feel in the street. If he did not go down there, he realized, he would have people wondering about him. Not to go would be to attract attention.

He got up, pulled on a jacket, and walked over to the

door. He jerked it open, saw the man in the big gray cowboy duster standing there, his dark Italian face bright and happy, his eyes wrinkled from his grin—everybody thought this was a party—then he was saying something—still a huge grin—he was yelling something in a cheerful voice—he was saying—*"It's a happy Fizzies party!"*—stupid idiot Howli peasant—and Wu Xsin Gi began to say something cutting and nasty, when the man raised his left hand—still a *big* smile—was the man a fool?—and Wu Xsin Gi stepped back reflexively, torn between two sensations, two instincts, between contempt and caution—thinking *gun?*—the man smiling still, the smile confusing him—and then Wu Xsin Gi looked at what was in the man's hand—it was a spray can? What did—

Luke gave him a five-second blast of the Mace foam—it hit Wu Xsin Gi square in the face and stuck there. The man staggered back, screaming through the bright purple foam covering his mouth and eyes and his nose like shaving cream. He rubbed at it frantically—still bellowing—his lungs were searing his ribs—a thousand hornets were stinging him—rubbed it *into* his eyes—now the pain was *huge*—he scraped some of it away—was turning—fumbling—heading for that bedroom—*gun gun gun*—when something very heavy bounced off the back of his skull—lights blew up in his eyes—his knees went wobbly, and the floor rushed up at him. He hit it square with his face, breaking his nose, bounced once—flattened again—and a black wave drove him down.

Luke stood over him, smiling down at the back of the man's head. He had a big black steel Mag-Lite in his left hand. His finger bones were still a little buzzy and numb from the impact of the blow he had given the man. Head blows were against departmental policy. Too dangerous. You might kill a guy. There were rules about it. If you were going to kill a man, you had to do it according to the rulebook. Well, thought Luke, you only go around once in this life. If you can't have some fun in life, why bother?

He nudged Wu Xsin Gi with his boot. The man groaned and bubbled a bit, coughing into the mound of purple foam covering his face.

"It's a happy Fizzies party," he said again, chuckling softly. "And *you're* invited!"

0600 Hours
Thursday, January 19, 1995
Apex Muffler Shop
Tully, New York

After they thanked the local guys—and Pete Gruwchyk in particular—they bundled a very subdued and highly purple-ized Wu Xsin Gi into the back of Rico Groza's vehicle—Rico's was fitted with a prisoner cage and was intended for transport like this—cuffed and strapped him to the floor hook, exchanged jokes and business cards, shook hands all around, and then the three cars rolled slowly away up the main street of Tully.

A few people had come out of their homes or apartments, attracted by the lights and sounds of the radios. Now at least thirty people were lined up on the sidewalk as the three cars formed a kind of procession.

In the lead car Grizzly Dalton put a tape into the tape player installed in his service vehicle. Grizzly had wired in a pair of huge speakers in the back seat, and now he turned the volume up to stun and rolled down all his windows.

The tape began. It was the theme song to the television

show *Cops,* called "Bad Boy," by Inner Circle. The rap-reggae rhythms boomed out into the streets, echoing off the walls, soaring into the black velvet and snowflake night. People began to applaud. Grizzly beamed hugely, and Walt Rich stuck his head out the side window and waved to all the women.

They kept the music on all the way into the darkness beyond the edge of town. It was a good moment.

It was fun.

Well, man does not live by the gun alone.

Luke, in the trailing car, enjoyed the theatrics a great deal. Walt Rich was now blowing kisses to the people, and Grizzly was doing that slack-wristed wave the Queen of England always used, and Luke was smiling broadly himself. He was prepared to bet that even Rico Groza—who he was beginning to think of as a kind of cold-blooded Hispanic monk—was having a good time. He was *certain* that the prisoner, who was headed for a state police lockup to await a Marshals van for transport to a federal lockup, was not sharing in the general amusement.

He managed to stay in a very good mood for about three miles, at which point they were passing a florist's shop, and although the storefront was darkened, Luke could still read the signs stuck in the front window, hand-painted ads for various kinds of bouquets, roses at ten bucks a bunch, lilies, cut flowers, and it hit him extremely hard—a Mag-Lite blow to the back of his memory—that he knew the name Roderigo Gardena very well.

Very damn well.

He picked up the handset and switched it on.

"Grizzly, got a minute?"

"Certainly, my son. Damn, that was fine, hah?"

"Yeah . . . can you turn down the music?"

"Sure. . . . There. . . . Walt says hello."

"Hello Walt. Grizzly, you remember last May, I called you, asked you to send out a flare on NCIC?"

"Yeah, I remember. What about it?"

"How'd you do it? I never asked."

"I know you didn't. Leave it that way, okay? Why the sudden interest?"

"You remember a guy named Roderigo Gardena?"

"No—wait . . . What? Yeah? . . . Walt does. He says Roderigo Gardena was one of the a.k.a.'s listed for Paola Rona. . . . He says you guys . . . you guys looked it up on Walt's NCIC set, the evening before Doc had his heart attack. Is that right?"

"Tell Walt thanks. Ten-four, out."

"Ten-four, Luke. Out."

Luke put the handset down but did not turn it off. He waited for a good fifteen minutes, but nothing came back. Whatever he was thinking, Rico Groza had clearly made a decision to *say* nothing.

Fine, said Luke, watching the red taillights weave and fade into the velvety blackness, the snowflakes spiraling crazily around his car, making him feel like a man falling through a universe of stars toward a strange conclusion.

Let Rico have his game.

Baxter Cullen was sitting on a long wooden bench in between a row of battered metal lockers, talking to a couple of patrol guys coming off duty, strapping on his Kevlar and remarking on the miserable failures who made up the backfield of the Washington Redskins when he got a call to the telephone from the attendant out in the hall.

He went out and picked up the desk phone. "Cullen."

"Sergeant Cullen, this is Luke Zitto—with the Marshals? You remember me?"

"Hell yes! How's your buddy, what's his name, Hollenbeck? How're *you*? And what's all the noise there?"

"I'm at a rest station outside Syracuse. Sixteen-wheelers all over."

"On an op?"

"Yeah. That's why I'm calling."

"Sure. What's up?"

"You remember that guy we talked about? The Yellow Man?"

"Ernesto, yeah, I remember him. What about him?"

"You said you had a line on identifying him. Did you ever run it?"

"Yeah. I'd rather not say how, if that's okay?"

"No problem. And we never talked, okay?"

"You got trouble, still?"

"I think it's the same trouble. Anyway, you *did* get it?"

"Yeah—you'll have to wait a minute. I don't have my 1994 notebook with me. I keep them in my locker. Can you hold on?"

"Sure." Baxter Cullen set the phone down.

Luke heard the background talk of various cops around the hall, metal doors banging. Behind him a huge Steiger Freightways truck was powering out onto I-90. Luke's tan car was parked at the curb. Rico, Walt, and Grizzly were still off dealing with the paperwork elements of the transfer of Wu Xsin Gi to the temporary custody of the New York State Thruway Authority police. Luke had gone ahead to make some phone calls. He figured he had about an hour here before the other two units joined him. The handset clattered, and then Cullen was back on the line.

"Yeah . . . okay . . ." Luke heard pages being flipped.

"Here we go. This guy was born—you better write this down, because I'm not sure how to pronounce it. Q, U, I, J, U, N, Q, U, E—that's Quijunque—pronounced kwee-*hunk*-way, I guess. First name of Ernesto. Date of birth July 27, 1947, in the village of Barranca, in Guyana, Central America. He's a Miskito—not mosquito—*Miskito* Indian. Let's see . . . worked as a civilian for a couple of American mining firms in Guyana . . . listed as an adviser for native relations—I like that—went with one of these firms to Indonesia in 1964—next thing you know, the guy's got a U.S. visa and he's—my notes say *attached*—to a Marine Recon division training in the Philippines—"

"Any Vietnam service?"

"None at all, according to what I got."

"But definitely military? U.S. military?"

"He was never in the corps, I can tell you. But he got some juice, I'd say. Enough to get a visa, anyway. Next thing we hear of him, he's busted for trafficking in Florida, 1968—does a hitch in Angola—very ugly rep—prison rapist, block chief, shankmeister, prison name of Crow because of his shiny black hair . . . then—*nada*. That's all she wrote. His ID fits. Nothing about the weapon—the tomahawk. But that's a Recon tool, I can tell you that myself."

"You were in?"

"Oh yeah. A Company, First Battalion, Ninth Marines. You ever hear of a place called Khe Sanh?"

"Christ." Now he knew how Cullen had discovered Ernesto's real name. The United States Marine Corps, tighter than any feds.

"You know it?"

"Yeah. Who doesn't? Bad time."

"Very bad. I was at the Rock Quarry. And Hill 64. February 8, 1968, we lost twenty-one dead, twenty wounded. Mortars. Overrun. One guy got nothing. I wasn't him. Later, Colonel Lownds told Congress our losses were light. Gotta love it, hah? You were in?"

"No . . . knees."

Baxter laughed. "Well, sounds like you got your war anyway. Does this stuff help?"

"Absolutely. Did you ever get a shot at him?"

"Nope—dropped out of sight. Every time I ask NCIC, I get a free seance with my CO. So I stopped asking. If he's out of D.C., he's not my problem."

Luke was silent, writing in his notebook.

"Luke—you think you're close?"

"Yeah. I do now."

"Well . . . remember what I told you, hah? Because so far, it's Ernesto two, feds zero. Third time lucky?"

"I hope so. Hey, Baxter—thanks."

"Long as I get—what was your buddy's favorite word?"

"Closure?"

"Yeah. See I get closure, okay. And I like happy endings."

"Yeah," said Luke. "So do I."

The line went dead.

Detective Sergeant Wendy Ma was leaning against the doorway of the detectives' coffee room on the second floor of the yellow-brick precinct house, watching Jerry Boynton struggle with a bag of coffee and a filter pack. The machine was flat-out refusing to brew a pot of coffee for him, and he resented it, took it personally. His round face was slightly shiny, and his forehead was wrinkled in concentration. Now and then a whispered curse would hiss out from between his tightened lips.

Outside, the weather was grim, gray, and chilly. They had the overhead fluorescents on, and they'd stay on until May or June. A cold rain was falling over the South Bronx, and the coffee in Wendy's hands was about the only warm spot in the world right now. One of the PWs assigned to prisoner searches stepped up and tapped her on the shoulder.

"Phone, Detective Ma."

Wendy smiled at Boynton, watched the big black man

in the dark blue suit, the intensity with which he attacked every mechanical problem. As she walked away, she said, over her shoulder, "Jerry. . . . Jerry?"

He turned, sent her a hard look, his surprising hazel eyes narrowed.

"Yeah?"

"Jorge was in last night, for the cleaning?"

"Yeah, so?"

"So Jorge always unplugs the machine to clean it."

Jerry Boynton stared at her for another second, then looked back at the machine. "Fart," was all he said.

Wendy went back to her desk and picked up the phone. "Ma, Detectives."

"Ma, Zitto. I can't believe I finally got you."

Wendy's sudden delighted smile caught the attention of a couple of her colleagues, who grinned at each other across their desks.

"Great to hear from you too. How's it going on the road?"

"Good, good—hook 'em and book 'em. Look, Wendy—hey, I *miss* you, you know that?"

"Thanks," said Wendy. "Me too."

She was extremely aware of the other cops in the room, the curious silence in the noisy squad room. She heard a wild roaring hissing sound, and the chuff of air brakes.

"Where are you?"

"I-90 rest stop west of Syracuse. Look, Wendy, can I ask you a favor?"

"Name it."

"Okay. How you fixed with the DOI?"

"Average. We don't bowl together or anything, Luke. Why?"

"You remember that DOI BOLO? The Yellow Man? No name? No DOB? You figured it was a honey trap?"

"Jeez, totally slipped my mind. Of course I do. Possible

first name of Ernesto. I tried that on every system. I need
more than just the first name and a description. You know,
they have like twenty-one thousand non-U.S. prisoners,
half of them are from Mexico or Colombia. A *lot* of guys
named Ernesto, Luke. A lot of bad skin and Indian features."

"Well, I worked that out."

"How? How in the hell—?"

"Guy I knew in D.C., he had a way. I didn't ask him
what. Got a pen?"

Wendy reached for her notebook, tucking the phone
under her chin. Luke read her out the full name and DOB
of Ernesto Quijunque, a.k.a. Crow. Told her a little bit of
his story. Wendy listened in silence.

"Okay," she said. "Got that. Now what do you want
me to do?"

"You can talk?"

"Yeah, a little."

"You're looking for Roderigo Gardena, right? The guy
who was missing from La Luna Negra?"

"Oh yeah. Very."

"So's Quijunque. So what comes next, it's gonna put
you in the same territory. You gotta be careful, right?"

"Thank you for stating the blindingly obvious. If Quijunque is the guy who did that—did what I saw at La
Luna Negra, then I'd say he's a bad guy. But this makes
him *my* guy, Luke. Not yours."

"If you can get him, that's fine. I don't think you will.
Now, Jerry Boynton there, he knows Manny Obregon,
right? Okay, I want you to ask Jerry to call Manny's lawyer.
You know who that is?"

"Yeah. Lucinda Miijas. Everybody up here knows her."

"Get him to make the call from a pay phone, because
she'll have call display. Ask him to say his name is Roder-

igo Gardena, and have him ask for Ernesto Quijunque. By name."

"What's *that* gonna do?"

"No idea. None at all. But it'll rock them. If Reed Endicott is connected to this thing at all, he'll freak when he hears those names. I know the guy. If Rona's anywhere in the mix, Endicott will try to get him moved. Just watch them all, watch them close. Somebody will break for cover. I can feel it. Can you work it? Will you work it?"

Wendy said nothing.

Luke looked over his shoulder, saw two tan cars rolling up the entrance ramp to the rest station.

"Luke . . . this is flaky. I'm not—"

"Then *you* call, call from the station there, give it a half-hour, tell her who you are, the whole official number, and *you* ask for information on a Jeep Cherokee, dark green, Virginia marker Tango Zulu Bravo one five one one, registered to one of Mojica's companies, called Chesapeake Realty. Say the Jeep was seen in the vicinity of the King's Plaza Shopping Center down by Sheepshead Bay, and the driver matched a description of a guy you're looking for in connection with a killing in the Four-One. *Don't* name him."

Wendy was looking across the squad room at Jerry Boynton. Boynton was leaning against the coffee lounge door and watching her carefully. She raised a hand, held up two fingers. He nodded and sipped at his cup, his eyes still on her.

"Okay so far. Now what?"

"Then get down to the King's Plaza Marina. Take Boynton, park yourself somewhere, and watch. Something will happen. The DOI will be all over the place, so be cool. But make sure they *see* you. That's vital."

"How will I explain being there?"

"The DOI sent a BOLO, the last time the guy was seen

was around that marina, and now the guy's ID matches a guy wanted for a triple hit at the Four-One. I absolutely *guarantee* you that they have Roderigo Gardena—I mean Paolo Rona—in some hotel. Bluff the bastards, Wendy. If you can't get them to tell you *where*, you're not the cop I know you are. Then call me at . . . 351-9399 . . . that's Grizzly Dalton's cell phone. He's on roam, so it'll ring wherever we are. Will you do all that? Especially the marina?"

Luke heard car doors slamming, heard Grizzly's big voice booming across the tarmac, calling him. Wendy heard it too.

"Okay . . . but I'm gonna cover myself, Luke. If I step into a tar pit, yours will be the first ankle I reach for. You better go."

"Wendy, I thank you."

"Bye-bye, Luke . . . love you."

Luke's belly leaped.

Fear or joy, he could not say.

"Wendy, I love you back. 'Bye."

1300 Hours
Monday, January 23, 1995
United States Marshals Office
Buffalo, New York

The inland blizzards had been blown away when they reached the coastline of the lake. Now a knife-blade wind was slicing in off Lake Erie, shredding the clouds and smearing them across a pallid blue-gray sky. Luke was standing in the window of the U.S. Marshals office in the federal building, watching the snow clouds being torn apart. To his right and left, the stone and red-brick towers and blocks of downtown Buffalo, the venerable Statler, and the concrete municipal buildings, rose above the flat, ragtag, slightly scruffy woodframe neighborhoods to the south and west. Beyond them he could see the broad white-capped sweep of Lake Erie. Far to the west, across the Niagara River and the clunky gunmetal shabbiness of the Peace Bridge, he could make out the gray masses of Fort Erie, Ontario. Across the river lay Canada.

The end of the trail.

This afternoon, the surface of Lake Erie was mud brown with white peaks of waves showing, and winds were sweeping over it, shadowing it, ruffling the water surface, changing the tints. Here and there over the peninsula of western New York State, shafts of sunlight pierced through the clouds, some of them reaching the lake, creating vivid blue-green bruises on the brown back of the lake, with streaks of yellow and green showing where the currents began to tug the lake water down into the narrow gates of the Niagara River.

This was a kind of Hell's Gate, the southern entrance to a long twisting river channel at times a mile wide, the beginning of a gathering headlong torrent of wind-whipped blue-brown water that boiled and fumed and churned between the banks, that flowed and foamed over rocks and outcrops, gathering force and speed, sweeping in two huge bends around the low grassy delta of Grand Island, joining again beyond Navy Island, where they became a mile-wide force of nature, a millrace rushing northward toward the three-hundred-foot ledge of Niagara Falls.

If he could lean way out, he would have been able to see a column of white steam rising above the gorge, more than twenty miles away. Over the twin falls, Horseshoe and Niagara, the water ran glassy green at the crest, and then lacy and white, roaring and booming, falling into a maelstrom of fumes and white foaming water, a cauldron over a fire.

Luke had been told that the falls were slowly working their way southward toward the city of Buffalo, part of a fifteen-million-year grinding destruction. Beyond the falls the Niagara Gorge, with granite walls a hundred feet on each side, channeled the river into a boiling white-water race that ran all the way to Lewiston and beyond, spilling finally out into the flat shallow expanse of Lake Ontario. Toronto was far up that flat featureless coastline. There were towers and observation decks all around the canyon of Niagara Falls where, if the weather was clear, you could see all the way from Buffalo to the distant yellow-brown smudge of Toronto, see the single spear-point of the CN Tower like a pin in a moth's spine.

"Hell of a view," said Rico, leaning back in his chair, puffing on a cheroot. The smell of it was strong and sweet, a little like burning wood and a little like sandalwood incense. He was at ease, alert, but untroubled.

Luke stepped away from the window and sat down at the long wooden table. They were in a kind of meeting room at the Western District headquarters of the Marshals Service. Walt Rich was down the hall in the computer room, talking to the Canadian Customs and Immigration guardpost at Cornwall, Ontario.

Grizzly Dalton was holding down a large leather wingback at the head of the boardroom table, his boots up on the polished wood, his beefy arms folded across his shirt. Everyone was in somber business suits today. As soon as Walt Rich came back into the room, they would begin.

Until then, there wasn't much to say.

The chase part of the operation had ended the night before, with the capture of Reo Dysart in a tiny little speakeasy called Busters Bar 'N Grill. Busters was built into what had once been a small woodframed family bungalow in a scrubby low-rent part of South Buffalo, a neglected neighborhood of ragged brown lawns and sagging porches, dead trees, rotting timbers, and peeling paint, rusted cars sitting out front, and deserted warehouse buildings, abandoned schools and pitted playgrounds overgrown with weeds, bound up like toxic waste dumps inside rusted chain-link fencing. Newt Gingrich should have been there, because this was the part of the nation where whatever it was that was supposed to trickle down during the eighties had finally pooled up and spread itself out.

The area had a Dirty Thirties look to it, although it had once, in the fifties, been a happy, prosperous region. Then the steel trade died, and Buffalo sank a long way, taking most of the people with it. Now the area was a rathole maze of gangbangers, drunks, welfare cheats, and a few struggling families trying to get by on food stamps, pick-up work, and some low-level drug dealing.

Reo Dysart, wanted for murder and gang-related gun charges, had been snitched out by a local dealer in exchange for some slack from the local DA. He was supposed to be living somewhere nearby, with a young woman and her four kids.

But according to the snitch, he drank every night at Busters.

When they had walked into Busters last night at seven, the little bar had been jumping with young black men playing video games or sitting around at rickety kitchen tables drinking Miller and Schlitz and Genesee beer. When four white men in long gray dusters walked into the place, the bar took on a very Old West atmosphere.

Naturally, Grizzly *loved* this.

He dropped into his Wyatt Earp number, swaggered across the creaking wooden floor of the bar, slapped his hand down on the sticky countertop, fixed the sullen gray-bearded black man behind the bar with a bright-eyed glare.

"Red Eye, my good man," he said, "And a sarsaparilla for my boys. Three straws."

The bartender didn't smile.

"You the Man, hah?"

Grizzly looked disappointed at the man's unwillingness to play along. This was, in his opinion, the major drawback with your criminal elements. They had no sense of humor.

He let the weight of his disappointment slowly drag his face down into a stony flat stare. He opened the duster and let the man see his black U.S. Marshals T-shirt. And his sidearm. Then he pulled his gold U.S. Marshals Service star out of his coat pocket and clipped it onto the webbing of his raid-gear belt. It was a very old routine, but Grizzly had the physical presence to make it work. Even without the Stetson.

Nobody was laughing.

Luke and Rico took up a position by the front and rear doors. Walt Rich strolled over to study the banks of video games. The customers sat quietly, staring at their hands. The dim little room smelled of flat beer, and fried food, and sweat. A Genesee beer sign blinked at them from behind the bar, cycling through reds and yellows and greens, changing the tint in the heavy smoke-filled air every twenty-three seconds.

Grizzly nodded.

"Yes, I am. We are the law in these parts. I'm Marshal Dalton, these here are my boys, Luke, Walt, and Mexican Bill."

He pulled out a picture of Reo Dysart, laid it carefully down on the bar top, spreading it out like a poker hand. The old man didn't even look at it. He never took his eyes off Grizzly's face.

"Never seen him."

Grizzly shook his head sadly.

"Well, that's a poser, you know? Because one of your sepia-hued brethren here telegraphed us a while back, said Mr. Dysart was known to frequent your establishment, was known to partake of the fellowship, and whatnot, in these here parts. It would . . . *grieve* me, sir, it would trouble me deeply, were I to discover that a fine upstanding citizen such as yourself might be misleading the forces of goodness and truth hereabouts—"

Walt Rich called out to Grizzly.

"Ahh, Marshal, got a minute?"

Grizzly turned and looked at Walt. He went to stand next to him in front of a large blinking video game called Mortal Kombat. The screen was shifting through a series of come-on images, urging the customer to drop his quarters and play a few rounds. Walt and Grizzly waited until the screen blinked a few more times. Luke and Rico watched everything and everyone in the room, saying nothing. Finally, the video game reached the screen that showed a list of the Top Ten Fighters of the Day. Each player was supposed to identify himself with three initials. The top ten screen for that day showed a column of white letters down the bright blue screen.

REO

REO

REO

REO

GRG

REO

REO

GRG

REO

REO

Grizzly stared at it for a second. He smiled at Walt, who was beaming back at him. Then he turned around and walked heavily back to the bartender, sorrow and regret in every line of his big body.

"Sir," he said, reaching for the man's shirt, gathering it in, "I believe—"

The man's eyes flicked left. A brown flash burst out of a door marked Ladies, a large young black man in baggy black hip-hop jeans, bare-chested, a Knicks cap backward on his head. He went straight at the front door.

Luke, Grizzly, Rico, and Walt all moved at once. The customers were on their feet, chairs flying. Luke pulled out his Taurus, covered the room, Rico was on the man's heels, and then Walt stepped into the running man, swinging his black Mag-Lite.

It caught Reo Dysart on the right cheekbone, a full-armed swing, as if the Mag had been a bat and Reo's head a spitball slider. Luke saw Reo's head snap back, saw him run literally out from under himself, saw the top of his head as the Knicks cap flew off, saw the bare back connect with the dirty wooden floor, bounce once.

A large butterfly knife flipped out of his slack fist and flew across the room to stop by one of Grizzly Dalton's boots. Grizzly bent over and picked it up. He turned, jammed it four inches deep into the bar top, in between the bartender's spread hands. The man jumped back.

Grizzly shook his head.

"You disappoint me, sir."

That had been it, roughly, for the preplanned section of their fugitive operations for January. They finished up the paperwork over the Sunday evening, sitting together at a Buffalo taproom called the Boar's Head, a long saloon-style room with glass lanterns and wooden booths, just around the corner from the service HQ. Out in the street a few flakes of snow blew by the stained-glass windows, and the rare pedestrian stumbled past, wrapped tight against the cold winds off the lake.

When they finished, Rico had said, "Now what?"

He was looking at Luke.

"I think you know," said Luke.

Grizzly held up a big paw, glared them into silence.

"Not tonight. Tomorrow, boys. Right now, I would like to propose a toast. Charge your goblets, my friends."

They all did, the golden ale foaming up in large frosted-glass mugs. Grizzly lifted his glass, the yellow light shining down on his lined leathery face, his large mustache wet with foam, his cheeks glowing.

"Absent friends," was all he said.

"Absent friends," they repeated, each man remembering a different name. Luke was remembering a New Jersey jail cell. They settled down to work their way through a few other toasts—Bill Degan, Hillary Clinton, most of the Earps, Matt Dillon.

Grizzly Dalton's cell phone rang around midnight that evening.

It was Wendy Ma, and she wanted to talk to Luke Zitto.

"Now?" Grizzly asked.

"Yes," she said. "Right now."

Nothing had been said for thirty minutes. Luke was leaning against the windowframe, looking out at the horizon line, watching the play of wind across the surface of the lake. Grizzly was puffing on a cheroot he had borrowed from Rico Groza. Rico was reading a copy of *The Pentacle* and sipping a mug of coffee. The door at the far end of the long room opened up, and Walt Rich came in, carrying a sheaf of fax papers and a fax copy of a color photograph. He dropped the papers in front of Rico, and Luke came over to look at it over his shoulder. There was a crest on the header of each fax paper, a circle of laurels under a crown.

ONTARIO PROVINCIAL POLICE

IN RESPONSE TO YOUR QUERY, KINGSTON DETACHMENT
CONFIRMS SUBJECT CROSSED INTO CANADA AT THE
CORNWALL BORDER STATION 2113 HOURS SUNDAY JANUARY

22 SUBJECT ID VIRGINIA DRIVER'S LICENSE IN THE NAME
OF LUCIO GARCIA 1553 JEFFERSON AVE RICHMOND
VIRGINIA / SUBJECT VEHICLE ALAMO RENTAL 1995 WHITE
MERCURY SABLE NEW YORK MARKER DRM 575. NO WANTS
NO WARRANTS ON CPIC OR PIRS CANADA-WIDE. AS PER
INSTRUCTIONS WE CONFIRM SUBJECT HEADED WESTBOUND
ON HIGHWAY 401 OPP DETACHMENTS AT KINGSTON
BELLEVILLE OSHAWA CONFIRM SUBJECT CAR PASSED UNITS
OPP MILTON AND CAMBRIDGE DO NOT REPORT SUBJECT CAR.
METRO TORONTO POLICE AND NIAGARA REGIONAL POLICE
REPORT SUBJECT VEHICLE SOUTHBOUND QUEEN ELIZABETH
HIGHWAY LAST KNOWN 10-20 BURLINGTON BAY SKYWAY
EASTBOUND 1114 HOURS 01/23/95 PLEASE ADVISE IF
FURTHER ACTION REQUIRED / DETACHMENT CO EASTERN
ONTARIO REGION / 1320 HOURS

The next fax was a short incident report from the Royal
Canadian Mounted Police detachment assigned to the
federal duty of border security in the Niagara Falls region.

RCMP BORDER SECURITY NIAGARA
UNITED STATES MARSHAL SERVICE

OPP AND NIAGARA REGION FORCES CONFIRM WHITE
MERCURY SABLE NEW YORK DRM 575 FOUND IN EATON
CENTRE PARKING LOT ST CATHARINES ONTARIO UNIT ALPHA
NINETEEN NIAGARA REGIONAL POLICE TIME MARKER 1232
HOURS 01/23/95 CONFIRM NO SIGHTING OF SUBJECT
GARCIA, LUCIO VEHICLE FOUND EMPTY KEYS IN IGNITION NO
SIGN OF FOUL PLAY / ACCOMPANYING PHOTO ID RELAYED
CORNWALL IMMIGRATION INSPECTION STATION 2113 HOURS
01/22/95 ADVISE IF FURTHER ACTION OUR SIDE? OIC INSP O
DIV TORONTO / SPECIAL I

Underneath this fax was a high-resolution color-photo
fax showing a Hispanic-looking male with a long ponytail,

wearing an expensive-looking linen jacket and a T-shirt, his ponytail contained by a black unmarked ball cap. The man was standing at the counter of a Customs and Immigration checkpoint, talking to a man wearing a dark blue sweater and a peaked cap. A Canadian flag was visible in the background, and the shot carried a time-marker in the lower right-hand corner—21:13:48 / 1/22/95.

The man was big, easily over six feet, barrel chested, and broad shouldered. His hands were spread out on the counter, and he was leaning forward slightly, his head cocked to the left, as if he had a hearing problem and was trying to understand what the immigration officer was saying to him. As a consequence, his face was slightly obscured by the angle of the shot and by the bill of his ball cap, which cast a shadow over his features. A section of his right cheek was highlighted. The high-resolution image showed a pocked surface and a distinct yellowish tint. Luke studied the image for a while.

"That's him," he said.

Walt Rich was shaking his head. "You can't be sure. But if you are, why not get the Canadians to scoop him for you? They've been tracking him all the way from Kingston."

Luke snorted. "Screw them! Those numb-nuts hung on to Charles Ng for five years, all in a tizzy because California had the death penalty and they might *execute* the slimeball. The Canadians don't have a justice system, they have a rehab farm for overworked criminals. I want Quijunque *here*, in America!"

Walt nodded. "Okay, well, I called the immigration guy in Kingston. They remembered him because he was deaf. Guy was friendly, talked very little, knew a lot about Richmond, though, because the Canadian guy had just come back from there, so they spoke a little about it, about that hotel in the Fan District, where they have that big staircase they used in *Gone With the Wind*."

Grizzly sighed and leaned forward onto the table, reaching for the sheets. "Luke, you really think this is him? Because if you do, he was within thirty miles of the border less than an hour ago. If you're gonna put a marker on him for the border guys, now's the time."

"I've already done that," said Walt. "Now what?"

Luke was looking at Rico.

"Your party," said Rico, his features unreadable.

"No," said Luke, sitting down and leaning back in one of the boardroom chairs. "It's been your party for quite a while."

Someone knocked at the door.

Walt went over, opened it, and said something to the person outside. Then he closed the door and locked it. He came back and sat down beside Rico. Grizzly and Luke were on the far side of the table. Rico lit a cheroot and leaned over to light Luke's Kool.

"Yeah," Rico said, after a long pull, the smoke clouding his features momentarily. He waved it away. "I guess you're right."

Grizzly sat back again, folded his arms. Rico looked at each of them in turn, showed them a slightly chilly, humorless grin, and puffed on his cigar. They waited.

"Fiertag," he said, finally.

Luke nodded.

"He's sick of Liaison. Sick of 600 Army Navy. The CO's been trying to get him bounced out of there for over a year. Not out, but off to some other agency. Fiertag wants to move up to Justice HQ full time. Be seen in the halls. Get all snuggly with Janet Reno. Reed Endicott told Fiertag if he could help out with a very big Treasury thing, then Endicott could mention his name in all the right offices. Endicott had a brief from the Treasury people—

they really *were* looking for that Syrian shit, those counterfeit hundreds out of the Bekaa Valley. Story ran, the money was being cycled and laundered through the help of the cartels. That's a cash-intensive business too—"

"Like running a fink?" said Luke, smiling a little.

Rico nodded. "And Treasury—Secret Service—had a big lead on a related operation working out of Atlanta. You ever heard of Guillermo Barra?"

They all nodded. Guillermo Barra was an extremely wealthy Central American entrepreneur. His businesses ranged from bauxite and copper mines in Guyana and Salvador to real estate and land development operations in Costa Rica, Panama, Brazil, Argentina. Through some Miami-based subsidiaries, he was funding a lot of Hispanic-related developments in south Florida, even parts of Georgia. Billions of dollars were involved.

"Barra went partners—silent partners—with another Hispanic, a U.S. citizen, named—"

"Dio Mojica, Jo-Jo's kid," said Luke. "That's what that DOI surveillance tape was all about, Jo-Jo talking about his kid not being embarrassed, right?"

Rico smiled.

"Yeah. Dio had a lot of Daddy's money in a company called Chesapeake Realty. They were also working legitimate operations in D.C., Baltimore, Richmond—a bunch of places. What the RICO people in Justice suspected, what they wanted to know, was how much Syrian money was . . . infecting . . . these legitimate Hispanic businesses. But they had to be cool. You go around saying there's cartel money in all sorts of Hispanic businesses, you're going to hear from civil liberties, civic groups—"

"Henry Cisneros," said Walt, getting a general laugh.

Rico wasn't smiling.

"Not funny, Walt. That's exactly what we're talking about. These are high-profile people, and they swing a lot of votes. Look at south Florida, Texas, parts of California. The cartels know this too. They also know that the fat years for the cocaine trade are over, that the U.S. can screw up all sorts of foreign investment opportunities, legitimate opportunities, *safe* ones, for South American businessmen. South American businesses are some of the most powerful in the world now, that's why Free Trade was so critical—it was one of the best ways to put pressure on the South American governments, get *them* to help wipe out the cartels. Now the floodgates are open, and a lot of South American investment money can flow north, into Mexico and the U.S. and Canada. Trouble is, a lot of that money is dirty, coke money. Reed Endicott and Bolton Canaday are part of the answer."

"Why Paolo Rona?" asked Luke.

Rico shrugged. "One of many, Luke. Plus he had a lot of motivation. He knew that you—"

"*We*," said Grizzly.

"We . . . were on his case. He's bright, he's tricky, and best of all, he grew up in the South Bronx. One of his boyhood buddies is now real tight with Manny Obregon. Manny Obregon works for Jo-Jo Mojica. The thing was, Rona had been stuffed in Ossining for a long time, and now he was out. Mojica and Obregon were suspicious about him."

"Whose idea was the escape?" asked Walt. His pale Irish features were stony.

Rico shook his head. "His own. He saw daylight and went for it. What he did to Aurora Powys, that was his style. He's a very bad guy. Hates women, especially women in uniforms. What he did, that was his alone. Once he was on the run, he knew he was toast with the Marshals. He went to Treasury on the run. He had already made contact with Manny Obregon in the Bronx. He took that connection to Treasury, made a deal. He'd fink out

Obregon in return for a stay on the assault thing. Canaday swears he was never going to let him walk on that, that he was going to hand him over as soon as their operation was finished. But they needed him. So they panicked. You scared them all. It's a trade-off, it always is, Luke."

"Trade-offs, hah? Which one was I?"

"Chasing him the way you were, that makes a big impression. The right people hear that Luke Zitto is after Paolo Rona, then they think, okay, he's no snitch, he's got a good reason to be running. Now he looks legitimate."

"So you and Fiertag decided to make me *part* of this schmuck's cover story. That makes me feel a little crummy, Rico. Just a little crummy. How's it make *you* feel?"

Rico puffed his cigar, and then shrugged. "It's just business, Luke. Nothing personal."

"It's all *personal*, Rico. I was being *run*, like some kind of snitch. Fiertag used me like a kitchen match. When I got difficult, the service *burned* me."

Rico was looking down at the smoke rising from his cigar. Without looking up, he spoke through the cloud.

"First of all, nobody *burned* you, Luke. The CO wasn't in the loop, as I hear it. The CO stepped in after the fact, pried Fiertag off your butt, and backed Justice down. He *stood* for you, Luke. He saved your ass. Anyway, national interests were involved, man. No one wanted you to get hurt. We all work for the same thing. . . . Sometimes you have to do things you don't—that you have to carry with you. That's all."

"The national interest. Sure. Okay, then what?"

"Like I said, you scared everybody. You got onto him. Nobody could figure out *how*. They knew you had an RTA on his name. Fiertag knew your personal reasons, as well. Treasury wasn't all that worried, though, because they figured you'd never actually reach him. And Fiertag was watching all of Doc's registered informants. They figured, if you got close, they'd just tip him, or pull him. Then you and Doc come blowing into the picture, and everybody wets his pants. Apparently not all of Doc's finks are on the books?"

Luke said nothing.

Rico smiled at that, puffed on his cigar. "Well, you shook the hell out of them, and they panicked. You have a big rep. Especially in the Hispanic community. In the Bronx they call you the Snake, you know that? For the Sarpente thing?"

Luke's face remained blank. He said nothing.

"Stonehenge, hah? Okay. I don't know all the details. I think it's likely that Rona spent the night pissing himself in some rathole, then he called in the cavalry. Fiertag's not telling me anything, but I'd say that bonehead stunt about Rona being dead, that was Reed Endicott's idea. Certainly Bolton Canaday has more respect for you than that, but he's a cop."

Walt Rich shrugged. "He's an Irish cop. They don't have a lot of respect for anyone who isn't Irish. Trust me, I've been one."

"How'd Rona get to New York?"

"Treasury wanted to run their own op here in New York, but the DOI already had a file open on Mojica, so they told Treasury that the only way Treasury was gonna run a snitch against Mojica was if the DOI had personal custody of him. The DOI guys have had a bellyful of federal ops running on their turf, and when the roll-up comes, the city gets left with dick. It was that way or no way. So the DOI got Rona away from Endicott, in return for some wiretap help and a promise to share whatever they got against Mojica with Treasury."

Luke lit another Kool, checked his watch.

"We don't have a lot of time, Rico. This Ernesto Quijunque, what's the story there?"

Rico shrugged, tapped his cigar ash, leaned back. "I think you can figure that out. I think you already have."

"From what Mojica was saying on the boat, I'd say Obregon never trusted Rona, right? When Rona called him, he figured he had two choices. Tell him to bugger off, in which case he'd never know where Rona was or what he was doing—"

Grizzly was puzzled. "I see that, Luke. Or say, yeah, he'd take him in, just so's he'd know where the guy was. But why not just whack him right there? Solve his problem the old-fashioned way, with a machete?"

Rico shrugged again. "No idea. He *was* one of their guys, from the old days. Those Latinos, they're a sentimental crowd."

Luke stood up, reached for his suit jacket, slipped it on. He came back to Rico's side and stood looking down at him.

"I don't think you believe that. I think Mojica got orders from somebody farther up the food chain, told him, *momentito*, pal, we're sending one of our best guys. See that he gets a chance to talk to Rona personally, so we can find out how much this fink knows. Damage control. That's why Canaday and Endicott had Rona tied up in that tiger trap on North Capitol Street. They figured, if they could bag Ernesto, they could use him to . . . or did they actually think they could trade up?"

Rico had stopped puffing on his cheroot, and his face was closed, rocky. Luke laughed, once, and shook his head.

"Was *that* it? If they get a man like Ernesto— everything *he* knows, he's their *inquisitor*, for God's sake, the man who gets the answers—why would Treasury need a little shit like Rona? Christ—Wendy's right, I *am* a moron—Rona was just a lure! It was all about Ernesto Quijunque! I'm right, hah, Rico?"

Rico was grinning, that same wolfish revelation of bad teeth, the glitter of a hard man's humorless smile.

"You're like slow glass, Luke. Sooner or later the light comes through. Yeah, it was all about Quijunque. Chess games. Finks are like pieces, you sacrifice to win."

Grizzly was pushing the chairs back into order and cleaning up the ashtrays. He glanced up, suddenly. "Rico?"

"Yeah?"

"How the hell did this Ernesto guy get a hold of that phony driver's license? I thought Rona had that. Or maybe the Treasury guys. How did *he* get it?"

"In New York. Manny Obregon told Rona to come up with it, hand it over, as a good-faith thing. Canaday went along, let him do it. I guess Luke here worked that out on his own, right, Luke?"

"It wasn't hard. If he wants to run, he needs good ID. This way, Treasury knows what ID he's likely to use. They'd go to some trouble to convince the guy it was still good."

"I have one last question," said Walt. "Luke, maybe you can answer it for me?"

"I'll try," said Luke.

"Why La Luna Negra? If Florida was only giving Rona a place to work because Manny Obregon told him to, then why did the guy go in there, bust up his whole family? Makes no sense."

Grizzly laughed outright, a bitter bark. "Sense, Walt?" he said. "These guys are animals. They don't *think*."

"Wrong," said Luke. "Everything this guy has done, he's *careful*, he's a pro. There was a reason for that butchery."

Rico stood up too.

"You're right. Rona's obsessed with his own dick. He thinks with it. That's his entertainment. I think he was coming on to somebody in Florida's family, and Florida was getting ready to snitch him out. That's bigtime disobedience."

"That's exactly what it was," said Luke. "Wendy Ma and Jerry Boynton went through all of Florida's phone calls, at his house as well as at the office. He made three calls to the New York Port Authority and two to the Immigration and Naturalization Service in the ten days before he died."

"That'd do it," said Grizzly.

Rico had his suit jacket on now, getting ready to leave. He leaned over the table and stubbed his cigar out in an ashtray. "Speaking of Wendy Ma, Luke?"

"Yeah?"

"I got a call from Fiertag in my hotel room the other night?"

"Yeah? Well, that must have been a new experience, hah? And what did Fiertag have to say . . . Rico?"

"Some guy phoned Lucinda Miijas, that's Manny Obregon's lawyer, calls from a pay phone on Webster, says he's Roderigo Gardena, and he asks for Ernesto Quijunque, right?"

"I'm following."

"Of course, Treasury has a tap on all of Obregon's people. Naturally, these two names send up a big flare. Reed Endicott popped an artery and got on to the DOI guys, demanded to know who the hell was letting Rona wander around making goddamn phone calls. DOI says, what the fuck are you talking about, Rona's right where he's supposed to be, sitting in a room at some fancy hotel on the East Side with a couple of keepers from Emergency Services. A few minutes later, a Four-Eight detective named Wendy Ma reaches the same number, and now she wants to know the whereabouts of a dark green Jeep with a Virginia plate that's linked to a Mojica company down there. Says the driver—a large Indian male—fits the description of a guy wanted for three homicides in the South Bronx. Lucinda Miijas goes all pale and shaky, of course. Now, Luke, here's the cute bit."

Luke waited, but a certain stillness seemed to have come over him.

"About six hours later, guess who shows up at the hotel? Gold Shield Detective Jerome Boynton and Detective Sergeant Wendy Ma, of the 48th Detective Area Task Force. Know what they do? They take Paolo Rona into custody—I mean, they *scoop* him—on charges of being an accessory in a homicide investigation up in the South Bronx, specifically the murders of three people at La Luna Negra Delivery and Storage, Timpson Place at 144th Street. The DOI guys bleat and fart, but they have no comeback, and now Paolo Rona is sitting in a secure lockup, and the Bronx DA is telling the DOI and Treasury that he doesn't give a rat's kidney what kind of clever stunt they were trying to pull, that he isn't going to let an escaped rapist and felon wander around in *his* town, and he doesn't care if Janet Reno shows up *personally* to go bail for the little shit. Fiertag says it's gonna take a month to sort out the jurisdictions."

"And your question would be . . . ?"

"My question would be, who the hell tipped Wendy Ma off about Rona and the DOI?"

Luke pursed his lips, pretended to consider it.

"I'd say she has good connections with the DOI, Rico. Somebody talked somewhere. Loose lips sink snitches, I guess. I mean, you never know *who* is talking to *who*, do you, Rico?"

There was a prolonged and difficult silence.

Finally, Walt Rich spoke up.

"*Whom,*" he said. "Not who. If we're gonna have a gun-fight here, at least let's respect the English language. *Are* we gonna have a gunfight—guys?"

Rico and Luke looked at each other, and then Rico turned away and walked to the door. Reaching it, he turned and looked at the other men.

"Luke, I'm sorry about D.C. I had nothing to do with that. I hope you know that. About keeping an eye on you for Fiertag, I had orders, Luke. Orders. And to tell you the truth, I think you're a guy who needs a watcher. You chase real well, but you play your own game. You did all this just to make life easier for—"

Luke came on point but did not move. He waited.

"Okay . . . for a friend. You blew a whole federal operation away just to get at an enemy. I know we'll never prove it. I'm certainly not going to say anything to Fiertag or the CO. Fiertag's gonna be history as far as we're concerned. Gone from 600 Army Navy. Probably not getting callbacks from Endicott either. So forget him. But I'd like to hear why you think *your* blood feuds are more important than the national interest. Got an answer . . . Luke?"

"No," he said. "I have a question, though. Why is it that 'the national interest' always seems to work out to be whatever is good for a bunch of suits in D.C.? How come 'the national interest' doesn't include one raped woman and two dead kids in the South Bronx? Who's looking out for them? Who's looking out for all the victims of all the snitches and finks we run, the snitches we pay off, the snitches who get to order room service at a hotel while their victims get to drink themselves into a blue ruin down in the rec room? Or rot in a shallow grave? Got an answer for that?"

Rico looked at him for a long time. Finally he shook his head.

"No," he said. "I don't. But I will share something with you. Rona? Now get this—his throat's been bugging him for months. Guess what? The little fuck has throat cancer. Inoperable. Wild, hah?"

Then he was gone.

1500 Hours
Monday, January 23, 1995
Pedestrian Walkway
The Rainbow Bridge
The U.S.–Canadian Border
Niagara Falls, New York

The Yellow Man was walking southward toward the little cluster of American flags and the United States border inspection station at the far end of the broad concrete arch. On his right, the great circle of the Horseshoe and the Niagara Falls roared at him like lions. The noise was massive, overpowering, a sound to crack the earth. The wind was racing across him, carrying the reek of ancient stones and the bite of the flying water. A huge pillar of white fumes boiled upward into the clear blue sky. The clouds of the morning had all blown away, and now a pale winter sun was shining down on the slick limestone and granite walls of the gorge beneath him. Little tugboats full of tourists in shiny yellow raincoats rode into and out of the spreading mists far underneath him, looking like water bugs against the deep roiling green of the river, and the white lace of the foam curling everywhere, as if the river were a green marble floor. The river itself rolled like a living thing, so much power and force, it shook the bridge as he crossed it.

The low gray concrete barriers of the U.S. border station were just ahead now, and he felt his heart thudding under his plaid shirt. His braids lashed at his face as he covered the final twenty feet. If they were ready, he had made his decision. He would go over the side and let the river free him.

But they would not be ready.

They never were.

Rona was beyond reach now, taken by the New York City police. They were not as stupid as the federal agents. They did not care about things beyond the city borders. Rona would go back to a prison, and someday Rona would look up and see a message in the eyes of one of the other prisoners, see his death in those eyes.

The Yellow Man would see to it. It would have been good to do it himself, but there are other forces at work in the world. No one man can see the entire face of God. You would have to step off the world to do that.

He was dressed very differently now. He had thrown away everything to do with Lucio Garcia, the clothes, even that license. The license he burned. It had been good for one use only and now it was a danger. Now he was dressed in tight black jeans and a stained white T-shirt, under a big baggy red plaid lumberjack shirt. His black hair was tied into two braids, and he was wearing a blue baseball cap with the logo of the Blue Jays. Obregon had given him a car and told him to go north. Cross into Canada—he even had the status card for him, taken from a Mohawk who had tried to cheat one of Manny Obregon's people over a trailerload of cigarettes bound for Canada. Now the Mohawk was inside an oil drum in the Big Fishkill, along with some other people. Ernesto had practiced saying his new name, George Joe Cardinal, born in Quebec. No one knew the real George Joe Cardinal was dead, least of all the Canadian government, who were too afraid of their

Indian tribes to bother them very much. The Indians who lived along the border with Canada came and went as they pleased. They had good guns, real automatic weapons. The Canadian air force would not fly over their lands, because the Indians would shoot them down. A few years ago, they had even blocked a highway leading to Canada and killed a Quebec policeman, and the Canadian Army had done very little. The Indians here had real power.

Ernesto knew how to be an Indian, so it was a good plan. Cross at the Cornwall border, where there were always Indians crossing, trust in the incompetence of governments who'd bungle the records, then drive to Niagara and come back as a Canadian—he would have to lose the New York rental car—and walk back into the United States as a thousand other people do every day. Ernesto Quijunque would no longer exist. He would be a Mohawk named George Joe Cardinal. Then he could go where he liked, go back to Guyana for a while, if he could get to Florida. He had a lot of money, and no one knew where he was now. Only Manny Obregon, and Manny Obregon would tell no one. Manny knew what would happen if he betrayed Ernesto and Ernesto was still alive.

Now the station was here. He opened the glass door and walked through into the warmth of the entrance hall. Other tourists were showing ID to a couple of bored immigration guards. The falls were always a big tourist place, and the city of Niagara Falls had told the INS and the Border Patrol not to make it hard for people to come over from the Canadian side. They needed the money badly. Ernesto had been told all of this by Obregon as they drove up the Taconic looking for the right car rental place. Ernesto was not afraid. He still had his little tomahawk.

It was funny, to have a real tomahawk. He had stopped in a gift shop on the Canadian side to buy some stupid little trinkets. One of the things he had bought was a little

Indian doll in a suede cover. It was made in China, and the little tomahawk was plastic. It amused Ernesto to carry it, and it would help with the U.S. guards. He reached the guard post. The man hardly looked at his ID.

"Place of birth?"

"Kahnawake—that's in Quebec, eh?"

He used the stiff-jawed voice and the bad French, as he had heard it spoken by the other Indians at Cornwall.

"Reason for crossing . . . Mr. Cardinal?"

Ernesto showed him the little doll, made a stupid face.

"Get some more toys. For the kids, eh? Kind of a joke?"

The guard, a youngster of around twenty, grinned back, handed him his status card. "Have a nice day, Mr. Cardinal."

"Yeah, I will, eh? You too."

He walked out through the other doors and on into the roadway. He was back inside the United States, and now he was free. He never felt free anywhere but in the United States. In many ways he loved the country, had done so ever since those Marines in the Philippines had taken him on, had helped him come to the United States. He breathed in the air and walked out in the middle of a crowd of tourists, the tourists scattering toward the overlook on the United States side or wandering into the town toward the big outlet mall. Ernesto decided to walk toward the river and then go down the road until he could get a taxi in town. He'd take a taxi to Buffalo, and then maybe a bus, or . . .

A man was walking toward him, a big man with a cowboy mustache and wearing a brown suit. The man had his hand inside his jacket . . . Crow turned. . . . Two more men, one dark and Italian looking, with a hunter's face, the other shorter, with red hair—*federales*. . . . He pulled the little hatchet and stopped. The big man with the mustache had a gun out—Ernesto ran at him—the man fired—missed—and Ernesto ran him down, cut at him with the hatchet—the man was inside the strike and caught it on his forearm—but Ernesto butted him—felt him go back—he saw the trees far off—and beyond that the broad muddy-green and white-capped plain of the river—he ran—ran *hard*—feeling the men at his back—feeling the gun-sights on him—people were all around him and he ran *into* them—they could not risk a shot—the treeline bobbed and pounded in his vision as he ran—his breath rasping in his throat—anger in him now—Obregon—Obregon had sold him—there was no other answer—he smacked into a woman and spun with her—her screams scalded his cheek—and saw the men coming up—no more than forty or fifty feet—the dark-eyed man in the lead, the big cowboy-looking one far back, limping, and—where was the little red-haired man—*there*—off to the side—trying to cut his path—the man's suit jacket flying open—Ernesto could see the man's gold star on his belt—and the black holster—these were Marshals—he had seen the star before—the treeline was here, and suddenly he was onto soft dead grasses, and the trees were flying past him, and the river edge was yards away—feet away—he saw the broad river like a field of grain waving in a wind, or like a marble highway—and across the river there was a big temple-looking building—a hundred feet wide—with brown vines crawling up the pillars—the Falls was an abyss full of terrible thunder at his right shoulder—the crest of the river was as smooth as green glass—the rocks at the edges were slippery, and he saw white water foaming and curling around them—he heard men's voices—*"Freeze! Federal officers! Freeze!"*—their bellowing voices whipped away on the cold wind and the rushing wind and the roaring wind—ten feet left, and the temple far across the water—the water so wide and the river rushing—if he could reach the temple—his *dream!* the one he'd had at Cheong Sammy's, his temple dream—the temple was a lie—he heard the pounding of heavy feet at his back—heard the impact of the man's boots—he could spin now and cut him down—the man was *close*—too close to stop—Ernesto looked back at the temple and set himself—like a bull in a corrida—he would turn *now* and gore this man—he set his right boot—began to turn—the hatchet coming up—he could feel the bite—knew where he would strike—to gut this man—out of the corner of his eye he saw a bright steel gun descending—he threw himself sideways—the bar caught his shoulder—*pain*—huge, shattering—his left arm limp—he went down on one knee—lifted his right hand—saw the black-haired man right *there*—arm raised—something shining—struck him *hard* on the side of his head—on his left ear—and he went down—went backward—the sky wheeled—on his back now—he turned—saw that distant stone temple, and the vines crawling up the pillars—and then a red wave washed it all away—his ears were filled with the buffeting roar of the water . . . he had a vision . . . he was floating . . . below him the cauldron was boiling and the water was all around him . . . white water foaming . . . and the roar . . . the sound of the wild lions roaring . . .

Luke stood over him, holding his right hand, the fingers buzzing with numbness, with pain. There was blood and black hair on the barrel of his Taurus. He watched as Grizzly and Walt cuffed the big man, as they wrapped him up in chains. His left hand was trembling a little, but his right was steady. He bent down and picked up the hatchet, raised it, and turned it in the light of the pale winter sun. The blade edge shimmered. The bar was heavy and cold in his hand. Beside him the great river rolled and rushed, and the crest of the Falls shimmered with the same light that was in the blade. He lowered it and looked out across the water. There was a kind of power plant on the Canadian side, built in the manner of a huge Greek temple, with massive stone columns carrying a vaulted classical roof.

He wondered, for a time, what there had been in that vision of the temple across the water that had seemed to hold the Yellow Man.

For just long enough.

Well, he thought.

He would never know. But right now he felt at the perfect center of his world.

Yes, he said. Fine.

Bring on our next contestant.

Message Begins
United States Marshals Service

PERSONNEL DIVISION
DEPUTY MARSHAL AURORA POWYS / IN RE
After consultation with Medical Services and counsellors Graumann and Warr, this office has completed the requested psychological and professional assessment of Deputy Powys, including full psychometrical analysis—MMP and DDSM / 94—and related tests. Results indicate that Deputy Powys has recovered fully and completely from the diagnosed PTSD and shows no current signs of this syndrome. Further, in view of the fact that the State of New Jersey has found insufficient causes to press charges of DUI against Deputy Powys—see reference attached—and that several individual members of the United States Marshals Service as well as a justice official have written lengthy letters of reference in support of her good

character and professionalism, and that letters have been received from Lieutenant M Farrell of the New Jersey State Police and from senior officials of the Justice Department—see attached—this office is pleased to recommend that Deputy Powys be reinstated as Operational and that she be allowed to resume any and all duties that she may be assigned.

Concerning the issues raised by Deputy Powys herself, regarding possible irregularities and jurisdictional transgressions committed against her by members of other Justice branches—see attached report Deputy Marshal Zitto—Deputy Powys has, upon consultation with family members, decided that no further action is required, a decision which this office feels is a clear indication of her complete emotional recovery and her very healthy desire for closure in what has been a very trying period in her professional career.

Bart Fielding, D Psych
Office of Personnel
United States Marshals Service

Message Ends

Notes on the Material

In order to understand the tensions and territorial jealousies that form a large part of this narrative, you need to consider that, in the aftermath of the Randy Weaver takedown at Ruby Ridge, the Branch Davidian debacle at Waco, and other slightly less infamous law enforcement disasters, Attorney General Janet Reno has undertaken an historic reorganization of all federal law enforcement agencies. One immediate consequence of this process has been a corrosive flood of institutional paranoia throughout the federal justice establishment.

For example, in the DEA, most—I repeat most—of the street-level agents I interviewed are convinced that their new director, Thomas Constantine, has been placed in the job with a hidden mandate to dismember the DEA and bring all of its operations under the control of Louis Freeh and the FBI. In the ATF, field agents I spoke with expressed similar fears concerning the fate of their agency and ferocious skepticism regarding Janet Reno and the

Clinton administration's true agenda. The hidden legacy of the J. Edgar Hoover era has been profound, widespread, barely submerged fear and mistrust of the FBI, a sensibility shared—with some reason—by the Clinton administration, as well as the House and Senate. When Janet Reno "relieved" the DEA of its Fugitive Pursuit functions and had them reassigned to the United States Marshals Service, the FBI acted at once to limit the role of the USMS in FBI-connected fugitive operations. In its turn, the Marshals Service has good cause to be wary of the FBI for its internal culture of secrecy and arrogance, a perception shared, in my view, by most other state and local police agencies.

Perhaps as a consequence of this erosion of law enforcement cohesion, the Justice Department's reliance on paid informants has reached terminal velocity, growing from $25 million nationally in 1985 to $100 million in 1994. Currently, field agents find themselves delivering sums of money to quasi-criminal or actively criminal informants in amounts that are four to five times the size of an agent's yearly salary. In the World Trade Center investigation, Janet Reno authorized the payment of $1 million in cash to a single informant, Emad Salem.

Many street-level agents I interviewed contend that this growing reliance on paid snitches undermines classic investigative techniques, distorts the accuracy of information developed, and rewards habitual career criminals— some of whom are as bad or far worse than the suspect being investigated—for information that is either blatantly false or skewed to satisfy the evidentiary requirements of ambitious prosecuting attorneys.

There is now a major turf war going on among the DEA, the FBI, the ATF, the Marshals Service, and related enforcement operations. Many street-level agents suspect that this war is, at best, an inadvertent side effect of Janet

Reno's heavy-handed managerial style. This strikes me as partly true and partly sexist paranoia. Whatever the root causes of this turf war, a large majority of field agents I have talked to in all four services agree that this destructive competition for diminishing federal funds, coupled with Reno's rather Draconian revisions of operational systems, has gravely eroded the effectiveness of serious street-level law enforcement, has left far too many state and local police agencies feeling isolated and ignored, and works to the advantage of only two elements in society: career criminals and defense attorneys.

Deadly Force concerns itself with only *one* aspect of these disruptive dynamics, the tensions placed upon the United States Marshals Service and its fugitive operations, the pursuit and capture of the nation's most violent and dangerous felons. The United States Marshals Service, founded in 1789, is the oldest law enforcement agency in America. Current membership in the USMS runs around 3,500 deputy marshals operating under the control of U.S. Marshals and U.S. Attorneys in 94 judicial districts nationwide. Readers looking for the definitive portrait of the Marshals Service are encouraged to read *The Lawmen* by F.S. Calhoun (Smithsonian 1989).

Carsten Stroud
Thunder Beach, 1996

ABOUT THE AUTHOR

CARSTEN STROUD is the author of the *New York Times* bestseller *Close Pursuit: A Week in the Life of an NYPD Homicide Cop*, two award-winning crime novels, *Lizard-skin* and *Sniper's Moon*, and *Iron Bravo*, which was a Military Book Club Main Selection.